BABYLONIAN WICCA

PREMIERE EDITION

BABYLONIAN WICCA

a practical beginner's guide

using ancient mesopotamian religion to reshape wiccan tradition

Collected Works by Joshua Free writing as Merlyn Stone
With Literary Contributions by Kyra Kaos
Edited and Introduced by Rowen Gardner

THE JOSHUA FREE IMPRINT
JFI PUBLICATIONS

Anthology Edition © 2025, Joshua Free

ISBN : 978-1-961509-68-9

SPECIAL EDITION ANTHOLOGY
(includes)
"*Sumerian Religion*" by Joshua Free
"*Priestess of Babylon*" by Kyra Kaos writing with Joshua Free
"*The Witch's Handbook*" by Joshua Free writing as Merlyn Stone

A MARDUKITE HERITAGE PUBLICATION
Mardukite Esoteric Research Library Reference
Mardukite Academy Grade-II Practical Supplement
cum superiorum privilegio veniaque

PREMIERE EDITION ANTHOLOGY
Samhain—October 31 2025

Published from
Joshua Free Imprint – JFI Publications
Mardukite Borsippa HQ, San Luis Valley, Colorado
Representing Mardukite Truth Seeker Press
Mardukite Academy of Systemology
and Founding Church of Mardukite Zuism

mardukite.com

◊ ◊ ◊ ◊ ◊ ◊

TABLET OF CONTENTS

◊ ◊ ◊ ◊ ◊ ◊ ◊

◊ ◊ ◊ ◊ ◊ ◊ ◊

THE WITCH'S HANDBOOK: WICCAN BOOK OF SHADOWS

BABYLON

by
Robert Graves

THE CHILD ALONE A POET IS:
SPRING AND FAIRYLAND ARE HIS
TRUTH AND REASON SHOW BUT DIM
AND ALL'S POETRY'S WITH HIM

RHYME AND MUSIC FLOW IN PLENTY
FOR THE LAD OF ONE-AND-TWENTY
BUT SPRING FOR HIM IS NO MORE NOW
THAN DAISIES TO A MUNCHING COW
JUST A CHEERY PLEASANT SEASON
DAISY BUDS TO LIVE AT EASE ON

HE'S FORGOTTEN HOW HE SMILED
AND SHRIEKED AT SNOWDROPS WHEN A CHILD
OR WEPT ONE EVENING SECRETLY
FOR APRIL'S GLORIOUS MISERY

WISDOM MADE HIM OLD AND WARY
BANISHING THE LORDS OF FAERY

WISDOM MADE A BREACH AND BATTERED
BABYLON TO BITS SHE SCATTERED
TO THE HEDGES AND DITCHES
ALL OUR NURSERY GNOMES AND WITCHES

LOB AND PUCK POOR FRANTIC ELVES
DRAG THEIR TREASURES FROM THE SHELVES

JACK THE GIANT-KILLER'S GONE
MOTHER GOOSE AND OBERON
BLUEBEARD AND KING SOLOMON

ROBIN AND RED RIDING HOOD
TAKE TOGETHER TO THE WOOD
AND SIR GALAHAD LIES HID
IN A CAVE WITH CAPTAIN KIDD

NONE OF ALL THE MAGIC HOSTS
NONE REMAIN BUT A FEW GHOSTS
OF TIMOROUS HEART TO LINGER ON
WEEPING FOR LOST BABYLON.

BABYLONIAN WICCA
Crafting A New Vision of Tradition
—or—
How To Use This Book

Introduction by Rowen Gardner

Remnants of variegated magical beliefs and spiritual fairy-faiths may be found at the heart of once indigenous and folk traditions everywhere on Earth. We find them embedded in the mysterious ancient sites and obscure manuscripts that captivate our imagination. We find them concealed in dark corners antiquated structures, gothic cathedrals and graveyards. And often we find inspiration for today's magical (or "magickal") revival often where we least expect it. But the question remains: have we yet tapped the most ancient stream of authentic magical traditions during this contemporary New Age?

Modern *Wicca*, as it is understood and practiced today, is really only a century old, and essentially still in its infancy (as relative lifespans of a religion go). It is quite common for *Wiccan* practitioners to seek and/or present their tradition as having a much greater, deeper, and older root origin for its modern style; but such would not be entirely honest or genuine or accurate. What we *do* have is a modern template for magical practices honoring the spirit of, and breathing new life into, the Old Ways.

Over the past several decades of New Age traditions sprouting up all over the world, we have witnessed the integration of virtually every cultural mythos and pantheon of deities into "neopagan" or modern "Wiccan" traditions— Celtic Wicca, Norse Wicca, the incorporation of Greek, Roman, Egyptian, and even more primitive shamanism (just to name a few, since a comprehensive list might fill a page or more). Interestingly enough, we find a significant shortage of "Babylonian Wicca" or "Mesopotamian Neopaganism" among these potential listings; and yet the Babylonian inspired "Kabbalah" (adopted by the Hebrews) seems to appear quite often.

Following the inception of the modern "Mardukite" movement launched by *Joshua Free* publicly in 2008, the spotlight began to shine more brightly onto the secrets concealed by the ever-shifting sands of Mesopotamia; and foremost among these, the subject of the "Anunnaki" (a topic which quickly went from complete obscurity to practically becoming a household word). The "Mardukite Research Organization" spent several years illuminating the mysteries of Mesopotamian mysticism and religion. Yet it seems that the neopagan community still hasn't quite yet bit into it, then alone embrace it outright (yet they are no strangers to the names of Inanna or Ishtar). So, I suggested this collected works volume to JFI Publications; and here it is.

"*Babylonian Wicca: A Practical Beginner's Guide*" combines three separate books together into one volume; everything someone needs to establish their own personal Babylonian Wiccan tradition—either as a solitary practitioner, or with others in a group. Experienced Wiccans will, of course, have the option of simply accenting and enhancing their own preexisting tradition. However, this book is appropriate for introducing the entire subject of Wicca and Mesopotamian Religion to a newcomer, or a beginner, that is still just starting to explore these subjects for the first time.

Contributions within this anthology span twenty-five years of underground publications: the earliest, "*The Witch's Handbook*" from *1999* (when *Joshua Free* still wrote as '*Merlyn Stone*'); the underground classic bestseller, "*Sumerian Religion*" from *2010*; and finally, most recently released in *2025*, "*Priestess of Babylon*" (developed by *Kyra Kaos* while writing with *Joshua Free*).

While introducing this collected-works anthology, my goal is to make certain the reader understands what is contained here and how to make it best fit together. There is no expectation that the reader is already familiar with the subjects contained—whether the "Anunnaki" deities, the "land between the rivers" in the Ancient Near East, or the structure of modern "Wiccan" tradition. It is in *this* sequence or order (which I have just given) that I arranged the data for this anthology: starting with "*Sumerian Religion*" to introduce the Anunnaki; then "*Priestess of Babylon*" to describe beliefs and practices as they originally appeared in ancient Mesopotamia; and finally, "*The Witch's Handbook*" where we see how the Old Ways evolved into a formula useful for crafting modern traditions of paganism.

If each is treated only by themselves, the individual books do not actually prompt a system of "Babylonian Wicca" directly. However, when examined as one single body of work, the elements are all precisely there. As it turns out, the combined knowledge contained here actually provides a far superior, more effective, presentation of the subject than if someone had set out to develop such a manual from scratch. It provides a practitioner the best chance of gleaning an authentic understanding of both "Mesopotamian Religion" and its potential incorporation in modern "Wicca." If the reader is studious enough to review *all three parts* to understand the whole, they can easily develop their own complete personal tradition as a result.

◊ ◊ ◊ ◊ ◊ ◊

So, why the present emphasis on "creating a personal tradition"?

I started off this prologue with the premise that: while there is plenty of information available about *ancient Mesopotamia*, and there is certainly no shortage of material to support *modern Wicca* or *paganism*, there are very few (outside the work of the "Mardukites") that have attempted to bridge the gap in time and space between the two. Unfortunately, *Joshua Free* did not originally set out to deliver a Babylonian revision of Wicca, or a book such as this would have appeared much sooner. This anthology is something of an afterthought by the *JFI Publication Staff*, as we begin to streamline the legacy of *Joshua Free's* thirty-year literary career for perpetual posterity.

Over the past two decades, as the "Mardukite" work by *Joshua Free* circulated further, we have seen a very slow shift in the trend toward Mesopotamian spirituality and mysticism, but certainly not enough to say that "Babylonian Wicca" is in any way an already established preset tradition. And the beauty of modern paganism is just how easy it is to adapt a new (but very ancient) paradigm with it. Of course, to accomplish this will require a bit of work on the reader's part. But such makes things even more authentic, since "personal religion" was quite commonplace in Babylon (as revealed within "*Priestess of Babylon*").

◊ ◊ ◊ ◊ ◊ ◊ ◊

What does "creating a personal tradition" require?

In preparing for this introduction, I wrote up a brief but comprehensive outline of modern Wicca (or neopaganism) as it has been presented and practiced – at least since the late 1970's when I was raised in its tradition. Rather than attempt to accomplish the total goal of this anthology within the first pages of an introduction, my intended purpose in pointing out these elements and facets of the tradition is to highlight them, or make the reader more aware of them, at the start. In this way, the reader can begin to form their own notations regarding specific key aspects while working through the material.

To begin with: "Wicca" and "(neo)paganism" are religious ideals. They are religions that include the practice of "magic(k)" as part of their "ritualism." However, the terms are not interchangeable, in that "magick" is a part of "Wicca" but also separate from it. An individual could practice "magick" without actually subscribing to any religion. However, the emphasis of this book will be on "religious magic" (particularly as it pertains to ancient Mesopotamia), which mostly concerns one's "contact with the Divine."

A reader should pay particular attention to the "Anunnaki" pantheon. The lore contained is drawn from Mesopotamian writings describing the actions and attributes of their deities. This pantheon is quite special to the ancient world and quite far-reaching, because it influenced the nature of other later emerging mythologies and the structure of their understanding concerning "gods" and "goddesses."

Mesopotamia is also unique its union (or absence) of Divine "sex/gender" characteristics. We find both a god and goddess (as a "Divine Couple") representing aspects like the Moon and Sun, rather than polarizing them. This has major implications when developing "Babylonian Wicca" traditions (but not really contradictory to preexisting standards).

Sumerio-Babylonian religions present another unique aspect not usually associated with Wicca: its urban centralization. While many Wiccans consider their own version of neopaganism to be born from rural folk-magic peasant faiths, we do not find such a theme in Mesopotamia, where the inception of the urban city-dwelling systems were introduced to establish modern civilization. Rather than secretly meeting "covens" or hidden "groves" it is the prominently visible TEMPLE (as "home" to a "deity" on earth) that became the most iconic symbol of the world's first organized religion.

Traditional religious tools, regalia, and accessories, are all a part of religious customs and ritual. While they may have served specific functions in the ancient world, their understanding and use in religion is mostly symbolic. A "standard" Wiccan description of ritual magic tools appears in the section titled "*The Witch's Handbook*," but the reader is encouraged to make note of any applicable symbols and tools that stand out to them prior to reaching that part. And direct support for merging practical Babylonian "ritualism" with Wicca is also found in the "*Priestess of Babylon*" section.

Rather than gather all of the various introductions and forewords together at the beginning of this book, I have chosen to let them remain with each section, allowing each part of this book to be introduced properly in its own space and time.

Once a reader has gained a working understanding of all the material within this anthology, there are many other useful resources written by Joshua Free, such as "*The Complete Anunnaki Bible*," that greatly compliment a modern Mesopotamian-inspired tradition. However, if one were to take what is given here and run all the way with it, they might just be surprised with how far they can travel.

And may you fare well on whatever travels you take up, dear reader.

Rowen Gardner, editor
Lughnassadh 2025
Wales, U.K.

SUMERIAN RELIGION PREMIERE EDITION
ORIGINAL 2010 PREFACE

by Joshua Free

The quest of uncovering the true ancient and mystical arts carries a fundamental theme: establishment of true knowledge concerning the powers these arts are dedicated to and then a working relationship with these powers—or *entities*, as some are more likely to understand them. This is the true art of the "priest," "priestess," "mystic" and "wizard"—the one that pleases the "gods" in such a way so as to obtain "favor," but does not waste time in provoking malignant spirits at their Magic Circle—as does the "sorcerer"—and thus does not work a "magic" in fear for their lives at the mistaken utterance of an incantation.

On our journey to rediscover the most ancient writings, we are brought face to face with confronting traditions and spirito-mystical systems from the Ancient Near East, those born from the Sumerians—and then afterward extended to the developing cultures known as Akkadians, Chaldeo-Babylonians, Assyrians... and even the Egyptians are a part of this stream.

A continuing spread of the Anunnaki Tradition across Europe led to even more colorful and fanciful realizations of the primary "Olympian-archetype" for mythology all over the globe, but which was first realized and systematized in ancient Mesopotamia—and especially in Babylon.

Ancient Sumerians referred to this race of *Sky Gods* as the *Anunnaki.* Their legacy and influence on planet Earth, and toward the cultivation of human civilization, is only recently reaching a threshold of "common knowledge." Of course, alongside this, an increased amount of "fluff" and "bullshit" has also appeared—and we have run into many individuals caught up in this, that either believe they *do* know something, or else are intentionally misguiding and contribute only to further misrepresentations of this lore now running rampant with many modern spiritual revivals, in New Age literature, on television and, of course, the web.

Given the restricted access to true "source material" for this research, the heavy expense of its acquisition, or obscure renderings and languages that it appears in, many of those in today's society are, themselves, simply uneducated enough to properly interpret and discern the data. Keep in mind, we are not dealing with a subject frequently treated in traditional school systems of the present era. This was, in fact, one of the reasons for establishing *Mardukite Ministries* (*Mardukite Research Organization*), far more than it was to extend a "mortal human devotion" to the specific deity in the Anunnaki pantheon named Marduk—but from which, we of course have drawn our name.

My current work and past years working with *Mardukite Chamberlains* within this system has been sufficient for me to know that these Anunnaki beings *are*, in fact, the "gods" appearing as "divine representatives" throughout ancient cultures appearing on the planet. What's more, their presence was later interpreted in the guise of "fairy tales," a facet that seems to also carry remnants of "folk magic" from ancient traditions into today. Curiously, the "ceremonial magic" used by priests and priestesses of long-lost eras, and even the self-styled magicians of today, are really just working with these same forces —but under some other more recent guise, name or fragmentation. Should all this be the case: the proper understanding and establishment of our position with these beings—this relationship—is perhaps one of the most paramount endeavors of this lifetime.

SUMERIAN RELIGION PREMIERE EDITION
ORIGINAL 2010 FOREWORD

"Establishing a Relationship with Anunnaki Gods"

by Sarah Banas

Sleepless, yet not really quite awake. This world is a dream; we are players on a chessboard. The Matrix. A world within another world. We all know this; and still, we move aimlessly through life as if our actions have no consequences: that we are individuals, whose sole purpose is to live for ourselves. You have stayed awake many a night, staring at the ceiling and asking, "Why?" You felt it, you fought against it, this Machine—your material physical identity—that controls your movement; this Pendulum that never allows you a medium, always swinging you from one extreme to the next. And you allow it. How selfish has the race become that its' very existence has become a cancer to the planet? Do you even care anymore? Is only your material self—your temporary life—so important, that you must destroy everything in your path to prove your existence? A spoiled child who does not get what they want, so they throw a tantrum. Are you exhausted yet?

Humans are an empty shell of their former selves. Where once you walked with the gods—enjoyed a personal relationship with them—all you do now is pay lip service, demanding favors and requests; as if they cannot see your lies; as if they owe something to you. You fell in the same political and religious agendas as they did: the same paranoia; the lies; the fear; and the abuse. You have attacked each other, destroyed and brought each other to ruin. Your so-called prophets—"enlightened" —that you put on a pedestal to lead you, fail, because you have failed yourselves. Unlike the gods, you have refused to accept the consequences of your actions: you blame it on them—you have given up responsibility. Why? What happened to you?

Silently we wander. It never ceases to amaze me that humans want to be gods, and yet, when gods walk among you, you fail to see them. Unless, you do see them and purposely ignore them, because they are a threat to your own so-called divinity? And I am not talking of the hacks, the abusers who assimilate power and manipulate you—which, you so kindly allow—but the true gods: the silent ones. These are the writers, the artists, the musicians, who use the aesthetic arts to show you a world you know exists; and you feel it, but refuse to see it and acknowledge it.

You have gods on Earth today who are teachers, true religious leaders, students, store owners, who use leadership to teach you who to awaken your own divinity. You will never hear of them in the newspaper. You will rarely hear of their good deeds, their intentions, as they work behind the scenes, knowing the suffering and abuse they will sustain should they reveal themselves.

Just because the gods—the Anunnaki—do not show themselves in the way you want them to, does not mean they do not exist. It does not mean they do not hear your anger, or do not weep with you when you cry, or carry you when you no longer can walk. It does not mean that the gods do not share with you in your joy, or remind you of your gifts and talents when you yourself forget them, or inspire you when you have writer's block.

Politics. Even the divine Anunnaki did not escape such a disaster as politics. It is a game. The political debate between two or more opposing factions is not a bad endeavor. Wise judgment can always be exercised—such as with (the true story of) KA.IN and AB.EL. It is pride that eventually befalls all entities, the pride that sneaks in and corrupts the mind in all aspects (not just in politics), which becomes our destroyer.

The current state of the *Human Condition* faces such *politics*, even outside of the political system, that it uses to utterly implode on itself. There is just something about that word that can destroy the very core of anyone caught in it...

The gods feel as you do, they love, they cry, they are afraid: just like you. They love being remembered once in a while, they love receiving gifts—and not as a *quid pro quo*, but as something you just wanted to do—and they love giving them, too. They tease, they poke fun, they laugh, and they enjoy. They have moments of weakness, and moments of strength. They can get spiteful when angry, they can get hurt when misunderstood or take the wrong way; they fear to lose you just as you fear to lose them... but on a much greater, deeper, and more loving level.

It must be a hard existence on the gods' part to be immortal, and have their very creation hate and spite their name, to be forgotten and abused... and still, carry on, take care of and try to help those same creations that hate them so dearly. They are our husbands and wives, our best friends, our lovers. They are our brothers and sisters, our children, our parents. They are us, they are with us, they are beside us. They love dearly, even if affection for each other was sometimes less than that. And even if we sometimes feel it's less, too.

No conventional theology will tell you that you can talk to a god or goddess as a friend, lover, mate, sibling or anything but a superior entity that you must prostrate yourself endlessly before them. I am telling you, in absolute Love, that you can. You can go with them to the movies, walk with them at the park, or pick flowers with them or feed them or they you.

They have favorite colors, they cry during sad songs, they love to be held and they love to hold. I have told pagans that one god loves to play the harp, or that one enjoys paintings (or shiny things!); and they look at me with disbelief and—I daresay—annoyance for even suggesting that gods are anything but all powerful drones that do nothing but wait for prayers, demand absolute unquestionable devotion, and work all the time.

As with anything and anyone, treat them with love and respect, be honest with them, and they will do the exact same for you. Ask questions, walk with them, talk with them, just simply: Love them.

This planet, humanity, and everything intertwined is in need of healing. We can't do it alone, and it all starts with the Truth. Maybe it's time for us, "the gods who came down to earth" to lead, not only humanity, but to help the Gods who are beyond this realm to heal, too. The wars, the fighting, the distrust and anger between our groups has to end if they cannot set an example for us, we will set an example for them. *Won't you join us?*

To the followers of the three patriarchal religions: your god's name is the same as the one's we know... throw aside your pride and realize, you are not original. Your religion came from us. You worship Marduk, Enki and Enlil by a different name. So, why do you hate us? Are you not our brethren? And to the pagans: focus on the female, but never forget the male aspects of existence either. No true unity may exist with only half of a Twin. How can there be peace, if only half of the whole is respected?

Be an example for the rest: be the Gods of the Earth, be the Lucifer of life in Love once again, and show the world that the Gods never left. Show the world that the Gods are here, have been here, and will be here. We are Their representatives, so let's start acting like it. Isn't it time for the world to change? Isn't it time for Peace and Love to finally return?

—*In Nomine Enlil et Enki et Marduk Sancti.*

In the Beginning
was an
Infinity of
Nothingness...

ABZU : THE PRIMORDIAL ABYSS

For some, it is far too esoteric to say: the true and actual nature of all existence is an "Infinity of Nothingness." Yet, the most ancient spiritual texts
suggest this is so. One may even believe they understand the meaning of the
very words "*infinity*" and "*nothingness*"—but there is no guarantee this has
been properly relayed in the past. Mysterious lore of the *Abyss* is reflected in
mystical accounts from around the globe, spanning the entire evolution of
human civilization.

A true understanding of this critical state is paramount to real "mystical"
work—what is hidden at the heart of most ancient esoteric spirituality.
Secrets of the *Ancient Mystery School* affected all systematized living, including
the Sumerians. These "secrets" evolved, giving way to later Chaldeo-Babylonian "systems"—forms of "mysticism" and, dare we call it, "magic." Today,
we see renewed interest in these matters among both academic scholars and
those in the contemporary New Age. But, since the philosophies of the "Classical" era, shamanic cultures of Europe, or even the Egyptians all seem more
"accessible" to the modern "*seeker*," the deeper and more ancient mysteries
of Mesopotamia seem to often fade into shadows.

Outside of the original esoteric sects, imaginations of the uninitiated surged
passed their historical understanding, and a plethora of traditions and systems diverted from the main well-springs, continuing to deflect consciousness further from truly understanding primordial origins. On the "Arcane
Tablets," the *Primordial Abyss* was originally nameless—an "Infinity of Nothingness." As the latent, unmanifest, potentiality of "*Everythingness*," the *Abyss*
is the "All-Source" for any manifestation of *things* in material existence. This
concept was not only abstract to the ancients, it remains in the realm of *eso-
terica* today.

To compensate for a lack of *exoteric* public understanding, "pantheist" philosophers arose to equate universal forces with more tangible concepts—
physical places names for beings or "creatures." Originally used to philosoph-
ically illustrate examples, such beings and places were *so closely* identified
with otherwise esoteric concepts in the minds of the general population, that
they were blatantly assimilated in consciousness and mythology as direct embodiments of these cosmic forces or principles.

Cuneiform tablets from the priest-scribes of *Nabu* also provide evidence for
an ancient belief in an "All-Encompassing Being" *begotten* of "the Abyss and
the Primordial Sea." This means the *true infinity* of "nothingness" or what we
might call "zero" is actually an *a priori* unity of "infinite aspects of itself" as

all possible aetheric space—the "nothingness" and the "spaces between" as "One," "All," or rather, "None." This "formula" is generally represented as "*zero times zero*" or "OO"—the *sign of Infinity*. To quote the English philosopher, George Henry Lewes—If zero "0" is the sign of vanished quantity, then the Infinite "OO" is the sign of total continuity.

Fundamentally, the beauty and simplicity of the infinitude of space and pure potentiality of existence is enough for an "All-Encompassing Being," but this is an almost "static" existence with no forces in movement—quite simply All-is-One (*or none!*) in the universe. This background non-existence is not animated—not manifest—and so requires "motion" for any existence. This was born of duality, but of the highest spiritual intent and not to be confused with some mundane spiritual morality. For it was only by the opposition of the primordial currents of "chaos" and "order"—"No-Thing" and "All-Things"—that the cosmos were causally set in motion with a pendulum-like drive toward constant activity, progression and "*unfoldment*" that we call "existence."

The "unrest" of forces is a necessary condition for "Cosmic Law," "The All" or "One" to exist; fragmented by its very first division—that of "existence" and "naught"—the *first dichotomy*.

The *pure potentiality* of "infinite shape, form and variety, in all time, space and quantity" was difficult to relay in primitive language. However, esoteric interpretation of the most ancient Sumerian semantics of an "All-Being" is best reflected by the original meaning of the word "ILU" in Chaldeo-Babylonian literature. The original concept appeared in Sumerian language as "DIN.GIR," meaning "All-God," but later cultural pantheistic interpretations applied this term to individual personified "gods." The "Babylon" city, nation and culture was actually named in honor of their own spiritual quest—a "re-connection" with this "*Source*" by "ascending" the "Ladder of Lights" or "BAB.ILU"—The Gateway to God, or original "Tower of Babel."

True esoteric meaning was lost in time as the word was equated with "gods." An evolving Mesopotamian language system also associated it to "stars," almost changing the function of *Babylon* in consciousness as the "Doorway to the Stars," or as fictional character Daniel Jackson would prefer, a "Star-Gate." Original symbolism and simplicity of the truth is immediately shattered when enters philosophers, scholars and religious scientists—for we have all-too-easily overlooked a stumbling block when interpreting the most ancient tablets concerning divinity. As Lenormant explains in *Chaldean Magic & Sorcery*:—

> "[For] the idea of ILU was too comprehensive and too vast to receive a very definite exterior form, and consequently [too obscure for] the adoration of the people. The personality of ILU was not clearly defined for

a long time; his office and title as "God One" were at first given to Anu, "the ancient god," and the first person of the supreme trinity, which was afterward held to emanate from ILU; the priests did not distinguish the primordial principle from the chief of this trinity."

It is here, from the start of our discourse on "*Sumerian Religion*," that a true *Seeker* should learn to differentiate the "pantheistic personalities" of cultural mythology from the raw esoteric representations. When we exclusively focus on outward expressions of relative stories and histories, any deeper esoteric truths are shroud in mystery and lost to interpretation. If we were to base our cosmogony on purely Chaldeo-Babylonian accounts, one might be led to assume that Anu is born from ILU directly, and then in many regards becomes one and the same as ILU. Mythological "Order" of the *cosmos* is entrusted to the Sumerian "All-Father" of the *Anunnaki gods* as an embodiment of the same. But, physically and literally, Sumerian tablets do not actually ascribe Anu the position of *a priori* "First Being."

Sumerian mythology is troublesome when concerning names, since many titles can be shared by a single being, and what's worse, these titles often get exchanged between various beings at different times and by different tablet authors. At least three sets of "Divine Union" are found to precede the existence of Anu on many of the Sumerian tablets. These names are transliterated by early Sumeriologists as: ABZU and TIAMAT; MUMMU and LAKMU (or LAHMU and LAHAMU); and, ANSAR and KISAR.

The first pair of names are the most applicable to our current chapter—titles with attributes traditionally associated with the "*Abyss*" (ABZU) and the "*Primordial Sea*" (TIAMAT), which as One, compose "nothingness" and "everythingness." Some interpretations confuse these two principles as the same, but they are not. Where the *Abyss* is an infinity of unmanifest potential, the *primordial sea* is an infinity or recursive continuum of form—the *First Cause*—or the "Law" put in motion as infinite manifestation. [The later "Divine Couples" are intended to represent this "2=0" creative principle of "Order" in the *cosmos*.]

Biblical scholars now have conceded to the idea that the Semitic books, like *Genesis*, are indeed the product of a far more ancient Mesopotamian literary influence "God," the creator of existence, is found alone and everywhere at once, a "*primordial sea*" washing through an "*infinite abyss.*" Samuel Kramer summarizes in his *Sumerian Mythology*:—

> "*First was the primeval sea.* Nothing concerning the origin or creation of the primeval sea has as yet been discovered in the available Sumerian texts, and the indications are that the Sumerian sages looked upon the primeval sea as a kind of first cause and prime mover."

In the Babylonian *Enuma Elis* "Epic of Creation," ABZU (or APSU) is the first name given, and to it the trait of "primeval," or else the "one who was from the beginning." This persona is later passed on to the local sun by later philosophers and mythographers. In the rendering of this *Epic* on *Tablet-N* with our Mardukite "Anunnaki Bible," we read:

> And the primeval APZU, who birthed them,
> And CHAOS—TIAMAT, the Ancient One, Mother to them all.

And from a bastardized version in Simon's *Necronomicon*:—

> And naught existed but the Seas of ABZU, the Ancient One,
> And MUMMU TIAMAT, the Ancient One, who bore them all.

Where TIAMAT is listed with ABZU ("*and their waters were as one*"), MUMMU is introduced to us in some versions as a "counselor" or "vizier"—a messenger for the pair. The "Epic" continues, informing us that that the other "Divine Couples" were called into being and/or created. Yet, on some other tablets, the word MUMMU or NAMMU is attributed to an *Anunnaki goddess*, a "pantheistic personification" of a humanoid deity synonymous with abstract cosmic role of TIAMAT. Kramer goes on to illustrate this:—

> "The goddess *Nammu*, written with the ideogram for 'sea' is described as 'the life-mother, who gave birth to heaven and earth' [*ti-ama-tu-an-ki*] (or *ama-palil-u-tu-dingir-sar-sar-ra-ke-ne*, 'the mother, the ancestress who have birth to all the gods'). Heaven and Earth were therefore conceived by the Sumerians as the created products of the primeval sea."

Opening lines of the "*Epic of Creation*" confirm these beings existed "*before the heavens and earth were named*," meaning before material existence were divided into an ordered existence—for in the beginning was All-as-One, and even in the first creative expression, "*their waters were as one.*"

The first progression or motion of the creative force was to manifest its "every-thing-ness" and "no-thing-ness"—the all-encompassing universe—distinguished on cuneiform tablets by uniting the most basic Sumerian words for "heaven" and "earth," or else, AN and KI. Literally: "heaven-earth," the ancient Sumerians understood AN-KI to mean "universe"—the entirety of the *cosmos*, both "seen" and "unseen."

These powers are called forth to bare witness and offer aid to every magical charm and prayer of Mesopotamian religion:—

> *Spirit of the Heavens, Remember!*
> *Spirit of the Earth, Remember!*

— 0 —
TIAMAT : THE PRIMEVAL DRAGON

The first creature spawned from out of the abyss—the *Cosmic Dragon*—to whom the Sumerians would give no less a title than: "Mother of All Creation." In Hebrew, the word is "*tehom*," meaning "the deep" or "primordial sea," by which this force receives recognition in the Semitic *Genesis*. In an infinite universe not yet manifest, the "*primeval dragon*"—TIAMAT—is the "*first cause*" made by the Absolute, the first fragmentation from wholeness and oneness into existence—the "Law of ALL" put in motion.

In most ancient mythology, the *primeval dragon* is personified as the "Mother of All Creation." This force, identifiably female, is credited with creation of the other "*gods*," including all corporeal spirits visible on earth in ancient times as the "*Anunnaki*." This belief found its way into modern "New Age" theories explaining physical aspects of the *gods* as "reptilian" in nature, descended from a "Great Cosmic Dragon." By definition, all existences fall under this "*Cosmic Law*"—all existences are extensions of the same "*Universal Agent*."

The essence of wholeness (or duality in wholeness) is represented in the Mesopotamian pantheon as "divine unions" or couples. Both the male and female aspects are seen as reflections of *one*—and like physical sexes manifest of man, they are divided by our interpretation of being "god" and "goddess." Depending on the tablet sources, the deeds and attributes of one are often placed on the other, demonstrating that the full qualities are complete only when paired. For this reason, early scholars examining the Creation tablets mistook ABZU (*the Abyss*) as literal "consort" of TIAMAT. But after *his* "death," in the Babylonian account, her husband-partner is listed as KINGU.

Let us be clear, however, that more than ABZU, KINGU or any other primordial name listed on pre-Anunnaki lists of "rulership" in heaven, it is the *primeval dragon*—called "TIAMAT"—that is attributed all active ability of creation in the Universe. As the primal force or "prime mover" of a physical existence that came out of the *Abyss*, our first "deity" (if we are to call it such) is not only a dragon, but female, and her consort is given the more passive role for the act of creation. Under the epitaph of "*Nammu*," "*Mammu*," "*Mummu*," "*Mammi*" or "*Mami*" (of which was later assimilated into the Babylonian goddess *Aruru*, among others), she is the "Creator Goddess" and "Mother of All Mortal Life," offering up her blood (or "sand from her beaches") to be mixed with the "*Breath of Enlil*" and "*Waters of Enki*" for the creation of human life on earth.

The "name" of MUMMU is actually evoked in Babylonian magic—the "*Grimoire of Marduk*" or "*Book of Fifty Names*"—derived from the seventh tablet of the *Enuma Elis*. The thirty-fourth name listed is "MUMMU," who as we have said, is sometimes confused with TIAMAT, but is instead her "vizier" or "chief-minister"—the "active messenger principle." From the "Mardukite" perspective, all aspects of the Fifty Names are attributed to the power of *Marduk* in Babylon:—

> "...the power given to *Marduk* to fashion the universe from the flesh of TIAMAT offers wisdom concerning the condition of life before the creation, and nature of the structures of the Four Pillars whereupon the Heavens rest."

This active principle—MUMMU—is described both as the "Creator of the Universe" and also the "Guardian to the Gate to the Outside," but is not originally a "power" of *Marduk*, by Sumerian standards. Based on what we know concerning Babylonian adaptations of earlier Sumerian literature, the "Fifty Names" adopted by *Marduk* in their tradition were really names of the fifty preexisting "*Anunnaki gods*," some of which are actually mentioned in the *Enuma Elis*, playing active roles during the infamous "war in heaven." It is equally possible, on a cosmological level, that these names reflect some fifty "primary elements" composing the *cosmos* at its material inception. The Babylonian "*Epic*" describes the turbulent formation of earth and humans from "star-stuff" using symbolism of a violent battle between Marduk and TIAMAT. Michanowsky queries in "*Once and Future Star*":—

> "The great riddle is why the primordial sea, which according to Sumerian belief, brought forth the world around us without conflict or confrontation, had suddenly been recast [in Chaldeo-Babylonian literature] in the image of a vicious demon mother who had to be denounced as a menace to law and order and then cruelly destroyed."

With the rise of later generations of gods, a theme of unseating or dethroning the positions of the original and most ancient pantheon took hold. This dualistic viewpoint is most obvious during the Babylonian era, including later Assyrian offshoots. We see the first militant acknowledgment of a generational gap between the "younger" and "elder" pantheons in the "*Enuma Elis*," where the "elders" are either demonized as "evil," removed from the system entirely, or given only passing mention. Compared to earlier Sumerian beliefs, this dualism would seem artificial, created for the sole purpose of elevating the position of the younger pantheon, observed in Babylon, as the supreme forces in the local universe and thereby usurping their ancestors. What could not be done physically was accomplished in a manner that ruling classes have used since the dawn of history: the very *alteration* of said *history*.

Lore of this rebellion is found in post-Sumerian religious and mystical doctrines that identify with a "good versus evil" motif. We see it in the foundations of nearly all later traditions. From Babylon it spread east to Persia and west to Egypt, where its oldest forms are drawn as antagonistic moral dogmas held by Chaldeo-Babylonians, Egyptians and Zoroastrians. The Semitic traditions also inherited this "dualism," as reflected today in contemporary forms of Islam, Judaism and Christianity—all of which are strongly rooted in opposition and polar worldviews. This is found nowhere in ancient Sumer and seems to attach itself later on to the *Primeval Dragon* icon. It is, perhaps, only loosely based on the "Destruction of KUR," understood by modern Sumeriologists only in relation to other known pantheons, as Kramer does:—

> "...the monstrous creature which at least in a certain sense corresponds to the Babylonian goddess Tiamat, the Hebrew Leviathan and perhaps the Greek Typhon."

In more widely known versions of the Babylonian "*Epic of Creation*" [given in "*The Complete Anunnaki Bible*" as *Tablet-N* and *Tablet-F*] we are given an amazing account of how the patron of Babylon—*Marduk*—fights and destroys an "evil dragon," TIAMAT. We are spared no gruesome details of the bloody massacre awaiting her, finalized by an execution-styled beheading. We can see parallels of "*god-kings*" rivaling Chaos-Dragons in many later mythologies. However, on the most ancient tablets of Mesopotamia, this is a dramatic "cosmological" event. After TIAMAT is slain, half of her ("the head") is used to create the "*heavens*" ("AN") and the other half ("the body") is used to create the "*earth*" ("KI")—or, "AN-KI," the manifested universe. Some "astrophysical" interpretations of these tablets inspire belief that the epic describes a "collision theory" for the local solar system, particularly concerning formation of earth and moon.

We must assume that the philosophical minds that so carefully devised the Chaldeo-Babylonian system (which became so important for the Egyptians and other mystical and Semitic cultures) never fathomed that the tablets of their Sumerian ancestors, sometimes predating them by thousands of years, would ever be recovered. It seemed that for a time, evidence for Sumerian civilization did disappear from human consciousness, replaced instead by the *Genesis* offered by Babylonians and later derived Semitic lore. In fact, they were using the same written writing system, the same pantheon, and many of the same cosmological concepts under varying guises. "Superimposition" at a literary level appeared seamless.

It was not until the late 1800's that "Assyriologists" realized that some of the tablets and artifacts excavated from the Middle East were pre-Semitic—from before the *Akkadians*. It is now clear that "proper" formation and order of the primordial universe was adjusted to meet political and spiritual needs of a tribal people rapidly turned metropolitan, raising the position of their local deity to support the famous and widespread influence of *Babylon*.

It is understood then that the "Elder Gods" or "Ancient Ones" are overridden by the "younger gods"—those most most accessible in all global mythologies, usually representing planets of the local solar system in every instance. By "associating" themselves with visible "Celestial Spheres" in the sky, the Anunnaki install themselves as a staple at the origins of modern Human civilization.

Putting the physical cosmology of ABZU and TIAMAT aside—as the *Infinity of Nothing* and the *Prime Cause*—the emphasis of the current discourse is primarily on the pantheistic applications to Sumerian *Anunnaki* lore. It is difficult to determine if this "War in Heaven" among sentient "*gods*" did actually take place or if it was only written about later as propaganda to blot out the significance and contribution of their ancestors. Although not necessarily a moral facet, TIAMAT directly represents the *first existence*—the first separation of wholeness from the All-Source. This, in itself, generates a belief for many, in a "fall from grace" or "removal from the Source"—what is really at the heart of all dualism in global religions. This is most obvious in Gnostic lore—which views all physical existence as "evil," contrast to purely non-material "Godly" or spiritual existence.

If realizing that we occupy physical bodies in separation, removed from "God" directly, we can understand how the human psyche might demonize the form "first removed" as the cause of our own fragmentation. Our ability in explaining this awareness on various "levels" in no way condones behaviors of the younger generation of *gods*. But they too, must have experienced the same philosophic and spiritual devastation of this realization—and at an understandably higher degree of comprehension.

Dualistic conflict of "forces" in the universe are a necessary property of its existence in movement, but it is not necessarily subject to the "moral dualism" that humans identify with. Forces are constantly working with and against once another to keep "the organized universe" the way it is—and continually moving to the way it will be. Without this, there is only the static and "Infinite Nothing" existence of the original state of ALL, which we cannot even inhabit and still be separated as a being of *Self*.

Thus, the real "division" is essentially what is visible and what is not visible (from "human" perspective)—for the infinitude we inhabit contains everything and nothing can not exist. In Sumerian mythology, this is observed in the union or bond of "heaven-earth" (AN-KI) as a singular aspect; as a dual aspect, the seen and unseen aspects of reality; and as a zero aspect, still encompassed in and of the abyssal nothingness. Sumerians depicted this abstract form as a "*mountain*," the physical "bond" between "heaven" and "earth." *Ziggurats* were built as a reflection of the same.

We have previously mentioned the "Destruction of KUR" in passing. Not only does the word KUR mean "mountain," but it appears in the only significant "dragon-slaying" example from pre-Mardukite Sumerian literature. This time, however, KUR is not a cthonic abyssal water-based dragon, but is instead deep in the earth, in the mountain—or in a very literal sense, the mountain (earth) itself. There are three available Sumerian versions of this tablet cycle, each successively more recent in its origination, as the characters change. Kramer conveniently paraphrases the three versions:—

> "The first involves the water-god Enki, whose closest parallel among the Greeks is Poseidon. The hero of the second is Ninurta, the prototype for the Babylon god Marduk when playing the role of 'hero of the gods' in the Babylonian Epic of Creation. In the third, Inanna, counterpart of the Semitic Ishtar, plays the leading role. In all three versions, however, the monster being destroyed is termed KUR."

KUR is an obscure enigma for the prehistoric Sumerian pantheistic worldview, which is otherwise orderly and peaceful. Only later with increased human population did disharmony arise, wrought by new traditions of "evil sorcerers" commanding chaotic "demons" of plague and pestilence. But these expressions are merely accelerated entropy in motion—the opposite of growth and nurture. They do not seem to correlate with a dualistic nature of "good versus evil" applied to our lore of the archetypal primeval dragon. This force only appears chaotic due to its infinite expressions of "change" and "birth"—like the amoral explosive emission of life from seed or egg.

Some esoteric texts render TIAMAT as the "Ancient of Days." In the Chaldeo-Babylonian kabbalistic system—also called the *Ladder of Lights*—a mystic confronts TIAMAT ladder as the "Dweller on the Threshold" or "Guardian of the Gate to the Outside"—as a representation of the "Fear of the Unknown" that blocks progress. In other traditions of magic, it is KHORONZON, the "Dragon of Chaos" encountered in the dimensional ascent of astral pathwork.

Modern mystical encounters with this energy may prove challenging for some who hold onto the more animated depictions of a primeval "Dragon of Chaos." This current of power is rather subtle (or gentle) like the waves of the sea, but they can just as easily turn turbulent when perturbed. Anthropomorphic manifestations and astral encounters with a personification of TIAMAT generally reflect her "reptilian" form as a sleek black dragon. Rarely she may assume a more human form, almost resembling Semitic lore of "Lilith," but always female, and usually with black hair. In *Babylon*, The Tiamat Gate is essentially the "*Gate to the Outside,*" which is to say in more esoterically acceptable terms, the "*Gate to the Abyss.*"

— I —
ANU : KINGSHIP IN HEAVEN

Literature from the Sumerian tradition—cuneiform tablets unearthed during the last century—reveals that the Anunnaki system is the original archetypal "Olympian" pantheon of deities copied and pasted onto diverse cultures for thousands of years.

The Anunnaki were originally assigned to twelve positions in the cosmos forming a celestial sphere around the earth (later yielding lore of the "zodiac") and to twelve bodies of our local solar system (ten planets, plus the sun and moon). Prior to the "Ammonite" fascination with the local Sun, best observed among the Egyptians and other solar-cults, it was this collective star-system (or "pantheon") that the ancients deemed the "Rulers of Fate" and "Keepers of the Sacred Cycles on Earth"—the cosmic order of the organized universe.

"Ancient Ones" from Sumerian prehistory—ABZU, TIAMAT, LAHAMU, &tc.—are given brief mention in cuneiform literature, but are viewed as more abstract or metaphysical properties of creation, not accessibly appropriate as traditional deities. We have shown in other chapters how such forces could be seen as the primordial essence of the "All-Source" being first made manifest. But the Sumerians also viewed these active properties as materializing in their own personified "All-Father"—Anu—a figurehead for the hierarchical pantheon. These traits or energetic currents of primordial forces are assimilated by successively "younger gods" as they are elevated to higher roles in the hierarchy.

The genealogy given in the *Enuma Elis* "Epic of Creation" depicts ANSAR (or *Anshar*) and KISAR (*Kishar*) as father and mother of AN ("*Anu*" in Chaldeo-Babylonian). It is *Anu*, in turn, that is credited as "Father" of both the I.GI.GI—a legion of "celestial spirits" who "watch" and "see"—and the AN.UN.NA.KI (or Anunna-Ki, sometimes even spelled/transcribed as "Anunna-Ge" by early Sumeriologists)—or else a pantheon of "gods" who "*decree the fates of earth.*" It is really the modern religious scholar, Zecharia Sitchin, that put forth the more commonly known translation of "*heaven down to earth.*"

The names ANSAR and KISAR are most coherently translated as "heaven-zone" and "earth-zone" respectively. "SAR" means "cycle" or "the round of" in *Babylonian* language. If we adhere to this defined cosmology, their division as separate and then unity as wholeness is the progenitive spark producing an archetypal lineage of distinct and sentient gods born directly from the "omni-dimension," first known to itself only as the Abyss, then separated by the Primordial Waters and then finally condensed and separated as "heaven" and "earth." Some folk have put forth the suggestion that the *Anunnaki* actually entered our earthly "time-space" from another dimension or star-system.

Most cuneiform tablets are written very "matter-of-factly," almost reminiscent of "technical writing." Their authors felt no need to "validate" or "prove" an existence of the *Anunnaki* any further—just as we today write our events and history as "statements" that are fundamentally understood within the context of our culture. Naturally, the oldest surviving Sumerian accounts of the "creation of the universe" are sparse and badly fractured. References to AN ("*Anu*") specifically, are few in number when compared to his later and more active children. While the actually name and power is frequently called upon, very few tablets are dedicated to *Anu* specifically. Rather than petitions for aid, they are often "hymns" of praise, as reflected in this seven-line cuneiform tablet fragment, translated by L.W. King:—

1. *siptu bilu sur-bu-[u]...* "Mighty Lord..."
2. *ilu-Anim sur-bu-[u]...* "Anu, Mighty Lord..."
3. *ilu sami-i...* "God of the Sky..."
4. *ilu-Anim ilu sami-[i]...* "Anu, god of the Sky..."
5. *pa-sir u-mi...* "Loosener of the Day..."
6. *ilu-Anim pa-[sir u-mi]...* "Anu, Loosener of Day..."
7. *pa-sir sunati...* "Interpreter of Dreams..."

As we see in more popular interpretations from the last century, academic scholars have filled in many cracks of these broken tablets with the lore presented in post-Sumerian periods. The farther away from the original simplicity of the tradition that we get, however, the more strongly the Semitic influences and those of Zoroastrian dualism are incorporated. Again, academicians have often employed the reverse engineering method of working backwards from more familiar (and relatively more recent) systems in which to interpret antiquated and more obscure ones. This is purely fallacious, especially given what we commonly know regarding the degradation of information transmission (communication) over time.

It is sometimes difficult to separate the interpretation of Anu's position without conjuring up lore connected to his offspring. Many tablet authors began their sagas and incantations with some kind of unifying genesis to support why such and such happened or where such a such draws their power from, like the following, Kramer translates:—

After heaven had been moved away from the earth,
After earth had been separated from the heavens,
After the name of man had been fixed;
After AN had carried off heaven,

After Enlil had carried off earth,
After Ereshkigal had been carried off into KUR as its prize...

Following sequential logic of the above passage, unity of creation fractured into dual existence of "heaven" and "earth," which were then separated from one another. In this ancient Sumerian version, AN "carries" off heaven, becoming responsible for the organization and order of heaven, and his son *Enlil* is left to oversee work concerning physical existence on Earth. [And in this instance, "KUR" is used synonymously as *"Underworld."*]

Later Assyrio-Babylonian or *"Mardukite"* versions attribute more of these responsibilities to the lineage of Anu's *other* son, *Enki* (or EA) and his son, *Marduk*—figures receiving little attention in the purely Sumerian sources, also for political reasons.

The position of Anu in the Sumerian pantheon is as an undisputed *"Father in Heaven,"* who acts as the supreme "progenitor" or "father of the gods" from his place as the "King of the Local Universe." The *"House of Anu"* (the traditional "heaven" or "abode of the gods") is sometimes written as UR.ANU or *"Uranus"* (from the Greek *"Ouranos"*). His most sacred place of "worship" on earth was in the city of Uruk at the temple of E.ANNA—also translated to mean *"House of Anu."* The number of his rank is sixty—the number of cosmic perfection, or "whole value," in Mesopotamian mathematics—similar to our "100," but expressed in their entire mathematical system in a manner similar to our own retention of their division of a *whole hour* by *sixty* minutes, not *one-hundred.*

Later Mesopotamian traditions viewed Anu in a similar manner as the abstract Babylonian expression of ILU. He became the "Lofty One" or "Supreme God Most High" in the pantheon, a remote, distant and indiscriminate All-Father much more representative of the "Heavenly Father" that Jesus alluded to in the *New Testament* then that of the *Old Testament* God of the Hebrew. Solidity of his personification becomes increasingly faint in descending traditions, and though within his power, he rarely intervenes or makes an appearance to the "earth" world of gods and men. His main function in the pantheon is as the "Father" of the gods, who are then mainly left to deal with material universe on their own accord. From Tablet-A in our *"Anunnaki Bible"*:

When first the gods were [like] men on earth,
Settling on the bond-heaven-earth,
Anu decreed that the Anunnaki would come forth...

Few incantation tablets (or "prayers") invoke the powers of *Anu* directly. The heavenly force is perceived as too vast to be channeled directly by successors and to degrade it to anything more accessible would be to compromise the nature of what is represented. In Semitic traditions, the role of Kingship in Heaven is equated to the full extent of power that keeps the universe in motion, contained in an "unspeakable" and "unknowable" name (or "Tetragrammaton" in modern Hebrew-based mysticism—YHVH).

It is more common for the magician or priest to evoke a subsidiary deity from the "pantheon" ("*divine lineage*") to invoke the names known to them rather than pursue methods of Egypto-Hermetic cryptomancy to divine and compel spirits against their will using "true-names." In the Chaldeo-Babylonian tradition, the names of Enki and Marduk are evoked to speak the names— later traditions often used them to replace obscure and "secret" names altogether. As Lenormant explains:

> "True indeed there was a supreme name which possessed the power of commanding the gods and extracting from them a perfect obedience, but that name remained the inviolable secret of *Hea* or EA—Enki. In exceptionally grave cases the magician besought *Hea*, through the mediator *Silik-mulu-khi*—Marduk, to pronounce the solemn word in order to re-establish order in the world and restrain [temper] the powers of the abyss. But the enchanter did not know that name, and could not in consequence introduce it into his formulae... he could not obtain or make use of it, he only requested the god who knew it to employ it, without endeavoring to penetrate the terrible secret himself."

Though appearing infrequently in prayers, one example of a magician's "Grand Invocation" addressing Anu appears as a protective incantation at times and then also a hymn of adoration. From *Tablet-P* in "*The Complete Anunnaki Bible*":—

Anu, King in Heaven, Eternal Prince of the *Anunnaki*,
Whose words are the rule over the *Assembly of Anunnaki*,
Lord of the unequaled Horned Crown [*of the Starry Heavens*],
You who can travel anywhere in the universe on a raging storm;
You who stands in the royal chamber admired as a king.
The ears of the IGIGI are directed to hear your pure words,
The *Assembly of Anunnaki* gather around thee in reverence.
At your command the *Anunnaki* bow to salute;
At your command the wind blows
And food and drink are abundant;
At your command the angry demons
Turn back to their habitations.
May all the gods of Heaven and Earth
Pray at your Altar of Offering;
And may the kings of dragonblood on Earth
Give you heavy tribute.

May men pray to you daily and offer sacrifices and adoration.
May your heart be at rest and may you ever reign righteously.
To the city of *n.* show your abundant favor and grace."

The no less significant role of royal "Lady of Heaven" does not appear to be fixed individual. Several female entities are listed at one time or another as consorts of *Anu*. The title-name "*Antu*" is usually given, and much like the name of her husband, her title is more of a role than a proper name (and carries a numerological designation of 55). The "Queen of the Starry Heavens" traditionally rules the cosmos with her partner, but the exact personality associated often it differs by tradition. In one interpretation of the Sumerian *Genesis*, the consort of Anu (or AN) is originally listed as KIA (or KI), the "*Spirit of the Earth*" that "Enlil separated from the heavens."

In a rather romantic Babylonian version, *Anu* bestows the name of I.STAR or *Ishtar* (Sumerian: IN.ANNA)—meaning "*Beloved of Anu*"—onto his granddaughter, a title-position sharing that of his own consort.

If one were to assume that the ANShAR and KIShAR [parents to AN and KI] represents the pure spirit of *zi-an-na* (spirit of heaven) and *zi-ki-a* (spirit of earth) in the mystical incantations, then we might assume, since not otherwise addressed from the pantheon, that the addendum nearly always added in prayer to the forces (after those just mentioned) are to the manifested "first forms" of both heaven and earth as *zi-dingir-anna* and *zi-dingir-kia*. KANPA is translated from our original "*Mardukite Cypher*" manuscript [as relayed in "*The Complete Anunnaki Bible*"] as either "mark well," "remember" or "conjure" based on references from the last two centuries of revived interest in tablet literature. DINGIR is given as "first-god" or "mighty spirit power."

> *Zi Anna Kanpa*
> *Zi Kia Kanpa*
> *Zi Dingir Anna Kanpa*
> *Zi Dingir Kia Kanpa*

Mystical experiences by modern Mardukites with *Anu* directly have been limited. Given the archetypal sage-hermit motif attached to him, it can be difficult for the mind to comprehend the force of his "shade." Though it may be the result of poetic licensing, his image of a "King in Heaven" seated on a throne in the clouds can be traced back even to these first spiritual philosophies. Whether or not this is taken literally by an initiate, the fact remains that according to tradition, *Anu* leads the original *Anunnaki* pantheon of Sumerian "elder gods" to earth. For meditations and modern ritual, his sign is often traced as a singular ray (or arrow bolt) descending downward.

— II —
ENLIL : DEMIURGE OF CREATION

After the realms of "heaven" and "earth" had been clearly defined, the great separation or fracture of reality ensued. In fact, the ancient texts quite literally describe this as the "heavens" ("AN"—the eternal all-encompassing space aspect) being "moved away" from "earth" ("KI"—the solidified concentrated matter aspect). This is generally followed by a reiteration—ancient tablet writers seemed to enjoy poetic redundancy—of earth being "separated" from heaven, as evident even in the "*Song of the Hoe*":—

Enlil, who will make the human seed of the Land come forth from the Earth,
And not only did he hasten to separate Heaven from Earth,
And hasten to separate Earth from Heaven...

It is customary for Sumerian tablet cycles to begin with the formation of creation and the genealogy of their pantheon even if it did little to contribute to the actual context of the saga. It is possible that this literary mechanism added credibility epic characters and places set against the background reality of creation, and of course, the "*gods.*" The act may also have been a result of devotion and respect.

In parody we might equate this to—"*First the universe was created, then gods were born and then such and such happened.*" Many of these early tablet cycles include introductory lines that reinforce an understanding of Sumerian cosmogony and spirituality. Judging by the frequency of their appearance, there is little doubt concerning the identity of at least two primary gods of the Sumerian tradition, the first of which we have already mentioned:—

After AN had carried off heaven
After EN.LIL had carried off earth

EN.LIL—["EN"=*Lord*, "LIL"=*Air, Breath, Lofty*]—was the national god of ancient Sumer, essentially displacing (the more distant and less materially concerned) AN (*Anu*) as head of the "Elder Gods" on Earth. *Enlil's* offspring include a majority of the "younger generation" of "*Enlilite*" gods. His "patron-city" or "sacred-city" was Nippur [NI.IBRU], named for the geographic center (or "mid-section") of Mesopotamia, where his temple-ziggurat was built—the E.KUR, "House [like a] Mountain"—the four corners of which represented the quarters of the material world. His consort is also ranked high in the pantheon—NIN.LIL (or in a later form as *Belit*)—the title given to SUD. *Enlil's* designation is 50—"Command of Physical Space"—in Mesopotamian numerology, and the correlating rank for *Ninlil* is 45.

More than simply a "Ruler" of the Organized Universe, *Enlil's* position and title displays him as the original representation of the "*demiurge*" of creation —best known as a "Gnostic" concept, borrowed from Greek and Hermetic Schools—meaning the "designer of the material world" (a title also attributed to *Enki* as *Ptah*, "the Engineer," in Egypt). But, *Enlil* did not personally attend to each and every aspect of this material world. His commanding position enabled him to focus on *management—overseeing* other "spirits," "angels" or Anunnaki that were led down from the "heavens" (or, out of an inter-dimensional existence, &tc.) to forge a concrete physical existence on "earth"—like adding paint to a once blank canvas of infinite potentiality. For this, he is the *first* attributed with the power of the number "Fifty," also the number of names (of "angelic" war-generals, bio-engineers, &tc.) found on the seventh tablet of the *Enuma Elis*. This is the same "Power of Fifty" attributed as the "names" of *Marduk* in *Babylon*, used to elevate him to the position of "Enlil-ship" [*ell-ilu'tu*] or "Kingship" of the material world.

Enlil's first responsibility in the "new world" was assigning tasks and official designations, some of which seem to have been competed for. Sumerian tablets account for one such instance, introducing us to the forerunners of Cain and Abel, two brothers who rival against one another in an agricultural contest to win the favor of *Enlil* and the position of "farmer-god." Given the peaceful "swords to plow-shares" described in literature from *Enlil's Sumer*, no bloody murder is described at the climax of the story, but instead a simple judgment by "*wise father Enlil,*" which is mutually agreed upon by the the two brothers (Emesh and Enten) and they toast one another with libations! Kramer translates:—

Enlil answers *Emesh* and *Enten:*
"The life-producing water of all the lands, *Enten* is its 'knower,'
As farmer of the gods he has produced everything.
Emesh, my son,
How dost thou compare thyself with *Enten,* thy brother?"
The exalted word of Enlil whose meaning is profound,
The decision taken, is unalterable,
Who dares transgress it?
Emesh bent the knees before *Enten,*
Into his house he brought . . . [offerings],
The wine of the grape and the date.
Emesh presents *Enten* with gold, silver and lapis lazuli.
In brotherhood and friendship,
Happily, they pour out libations,
Together to act wisely and well, they determined.
In the struggle between *Emesh* and *Enten,*
Enten, the steadfast farmer of the gods,
Having proved greater than *Emesh* . . .

. . . O father Enlil, praise!

Another ancient Sumerian epic—the "Creation of the Pickax"—describes *Enlil* giving agricultural tools to "primitive workers" to aid their field-work, keep the populations fed, but also to ensure appropriate offerings of sustenance were being brought to the pyramid-like temple-ziggurats. As a deity in the Anunnaki Pantheon, *Enlil's* role and identity is best reflected in the purely Sumerian texts. He is transferred to the Babylonians as IL.LIL, to the Assyrians as *Bel* (the original one, anyway) and he even becomes the prototype of the Semitic Yahweh (EL in Hebrew). None of these later forms actually preserve the definitions of his position among the original Sumerians—"Lord God" of the Judeo-Christian *Old* Testament, as Lenormant confirms:—

"*Hea* [EA–Enki] passed into the Chaldeo-Babylonian [system] without changing his office, character or name, (but) *mul.ge.lal* [Enlil], on the contrary, bore no resemblance in documents of the magical collect-ion to [his former office] *Bel*, the demiurge and god of the organized universe,with whom he was afterward assimilated, in order to find him an equivalent in the religion by which he was adopted."

An apparent dualism later emerged in Mesopotamia, not only between lineages of *Enlil* and *Enki*, but also among political campaigns of the "younger" gods. This "philosophical conflict" is all too easily passed off in people's mind's as "light versus dark" and "good versus evil." But, what we are really given is a "division of reality"—still a singular reality mind you, but divided in consciousness. The *demiurge* of creation is later viewed as the "separator" of the *physical* from the *spiritual* and thus, by mortal standards, the one responsible for manifesting a world of form that is experienced in pain and suffering. While this is not directly reflected in Sumerian spirituality, the evolution of this esoteric tradition later in Mesopotamia (and elsewhere) accompanied a significant analytical (or critical) thought process with subsequent generations. Each had the opportunity to assimilate and revise the system. Sandra Tabitha Cicero summarizes this development—

"*Ellil* was a friend to humanity. However, like the Hebrew god *Yahweh*, his anger could be aroused by human wickedness It was *Ellil* who advocated that gods unleash the Great Flood upon humanity in the story of *Atra-Asis*. The unpleasant task of enforcing human calamities decreed by the gods fell upon *Ellil*. Because of this he has usually been accused of being a severe and destructive deity by later scholars. By contrast, Sumerian hymns venerate him as a gracious father figure who protects his people."

Samuel Kramer translates an example of just such a hymn from the "*Enlil in the E.KUR*" tablets:—

Enlil,
Whose command is far reaching;
Whose "word" is lofty and holy;
Whose pronouncement is unchangeable;
Who decrees destinies unto the distant future. . .
The Gods of Earth bow down willingly before him;
The Heavenly gods who are on Earth
Humble themselves before him;
They stand faithfully, according to instructions.
Lord who knows the destiny of The Land,
Trustworthy in his calling;
Enlil, who knows the destiny of Sumer,
Trustworthy in his calling;
Father *Enlil,*
Lord of all the lands;
Father *Enlil,*
Lord of the Rightful Command;
Father *Enlil,*
Shepherd of the Black-Headed Ones. . .
From the Mountain of Sunrise
To the Mountain of Sunset,
There is no other Lord in the land;
You alone are King.

We see very little of this venerated mention of *Enlil* specifically within Mardukite literature of the Chaldeo-Babylonian paradigm. When he is respectfully mentioned, it is usually only in the context of the fundamental "Supernal Trinity" [*Anu–Enlil–Enki*] invoked at the head of some incantations. Most post-Sumerian negative attitudes toward *Enlil* centrally focus on his recorded opposition to the creation of humans, and then their preservation during the *Deluge.*

Modern Mardukite experiences with the *Enlil*-current are subject to self-honesty. Expectations and culturally based biases held firmly in the psyche will have a hold on any literal interpretations. But this is no less present pertaining to mystical work, which requires the magician maintain an degree of absolute purity and self-honesty if "invoking" this energy. This is the very real "god," depicted in the Judeo-Christian *Old Testament,* and is not trivial being. [In other words: weigh your heart against a feather first!] The mystical symbol most with *Enlil* is a downward pointing triangle—a sign of command—possibly a literal representation of energetic flow (downward from above), or else the leadership and power of the Anunnaki "brought down" to Earth.

— III —

ENKI : LORD OF THIS WORLD

The spirito-mystical "Supernal Trinity" composing the most ancient pantheon is concluded with *Enki,* brother of *Enlil.* Anunnaki genealogy records kept by post-Sumerian civilizations emphasize that *Enki* and *Enlil* are actually half-brothers. Both are divine sons of *Anu*—the "Sky-Father"—but as royal heir to "Kingship of Heaven," Enlil is also the son of *Antu*—the "official" consort of *Anu*—while *Enki* is born to *Nammu.* [Other texts reveal *Enlil* as the eldest son of KI and *Enki* as the son of *Antu.*]

Differing Anunnaki lineages play a more significant role among the "younger pantheon" and later dualistic interpretations, but in the original formation of Sumerian civilization, *Enlil* and *Enki* are actually perfect compliments to one another in the division of the material world—Enlil as the ruler of the air and fire aspects, leaving *Enki* the domains of *The Deep*: water and earth.

As the original title suggests, *"Enki"* means, quite literally, "Lord of the Earth"—["EN"=*Lord,* "KI"= *Earth*]—later known as the Babylo-Akkadian epitaph "EA," likely derived from the Sumerian ideograms for *"house"* [E] and *"water"* [A]. This water alignment is suggested further by names for his temple-ziggurat, built in the southern city of *Eridu* [or *e-ri-dug*—"Home of the Mighty"] known as both E.ENGURRA ("House of Lower Waters") or E.ABZU ("House in the Depths").

Where *Enlil* is given a certain authority over the organization of "space" and management of other deities, *Enki* is given control over more "worldly matters" on Earth, and carries the designation of 40. [NINKI or DAMKINA, his consort, is 35.] On a cosmological level, *Enlil* represents the active spirit manifest in the world as a whole—or the *why*—separated from the "heavens."

By comparison, *Enki* represents more passive elements, but clearly the more condensed "material" ones solidified on Earth, and also the spirit of *how* things exist—"hidden" internal engineering, program or "natural design." Samuel .N. Kramer explains in *"Sumerian Mythology"*:—

> "Here in *Eridu* there was a local deity by the name of *Ea,* and the aspiring theologians of that city, eager to make him the supreme deity of the land, pressed forward the claim for lordship over the earth, and in an effort to insure his claim applied to him the epithet *en-ki,* 'Lord of the Earth,' which then became his Sumerian name. But though *Enki,* after some centuries, did succeed in displacing *Ninhursag* [*Belit, &tc.*] and taking third place in the pantheon, he failed to topple *Enlil* from his supremacy and had to settle and had to settle for second best, becom-

ing an *Enlil-banda*, a kind of 'Junior Enlil.' Like other gods he had to travel to *Nippur* to obtain *Enlil*'s blessing after he had built his his temple *E'engurra* in *Eridu*; he had to fill the *Ekur* of *Nippur* with gifts and possessions so that *Enlil* might rejoice with him; though he had charge of the *Me* controlling the cosmos and all civilized life, he had to admit that these were turned over to him by a generous and more powerful *Enlil*."

A 3rd Century B.C. Mardukite Babylonian priest, Berossus, wrote an epic dedicated to the figure "*Oannes*," a later name for *Enki*. He describes *Enki* establishing the material infrastructure of human civilization, depicted as the "sublime fish god" [*fish = scales = reptilian*] who rises from his ocean home (or in this case, the Erythian Sea near the Persian Gulf) to teach men the crafts necessary for their developmental arts and sciences to flourish. *Enki* is known in *Babylon* as the "Arch-Magus," father of the occult arts and divination, who passed this knowledge to his son, *Marduk*. He served as a patron to those who chose spells and esoteric sciences for combat and is sometimes credited with the original knowledge of magical warfare in the local universe.

In some Chaldeo-Babylonian mystical texts, *Enki* is referred to as "Our Father" in much the same way that the Sumerians referred to *Enlil* and, of course, the much later generation of Mardukites (in the neo-Babylonian period) referred to *Marduk*. Similar properties of *Enki* described in the *Oannes* saga also appear in another tablet cycle, of Babylonian origin—"The World Order of Enki." [Refer to *Tablet-K* in our "*Anunnaki Bible*."] Here, the cuneiform author sets out to list the many innovations of *Enki*, some of which are originally attributed to *Enlil* in earlier Sumerian mythology. "Mardukite" Babylonian Tradition recognized *Marduk* as *Enki's* successor; the finale of another version of the "World Order" tablet concerns "passing over" *Inanna-Ishtar* for a position among *Enki's* roll-call of Babylonian gods. *Enki* answers *Inanna* by documenting implied and bestowed powers she already possesses—but elsewhere from *Babylon*, such as in *Egypt* as the goddess ISIS:—

What did I keep from you?
What more could we add to you?
You were put in charge of the crook,
The serpent-staff,
The wand of shepherd-ship.
You interpret the oracular omens of battles and combats.
Inanna, you have destroyed what cannot be destroyed;
And you have conceived the inconceivable.

A duality between divine brothers—*Enlil* and *Enki*—played a significant role in the establishment of not only human civilization in its physical, fundamental and evolutionary aspects, but also the spiritual and religious philosophies that later emerged on the planet. To point out a widely held, but relatively recent conception (adopted by the Roman Catholic Church): "Yahwist Monotheism." This dictates everything in the universe results from a single being alone, the leader of the "*anakim*" or "*malachim*" [*Anunnaki*] appearing in the Judeo-Christian *Old Testament*. The stature of his being is held above all others who are but intermediaries in the stories.

The position in *heaven*, however, seemed too surreal for accessibility by the priests and prayers of early people, so the pantheists and materialists developed patronage toward the "Lord of the Earth"—representing the powers of the *here and now*, and the necessities and comforts of physical existence: fertility, love, wealth... these all became the domain of *Enki*, whose "secondary" birthright in heaven seems to have transferred to a "primary" one on Earth.

Trailing in the wake of the gods was their sense of "supremacy"—an embedded pyramid-structure turned innate—first used to govern themselves and then left to chosen figureheads and bloodlines on Earth thereafter. This struggle for world domination and power essentially crippled contemporary humans, who simply do not carry enough awakened genetic and intellectual faculties to properly execute such ventures. What efforts have been done in the past, both political and physically combative, have been performed by individuals who actually take these matters very seriously. An investigation into the occult beliefs of the Third Reich will reveal that the Nazis actually adopted very similar beliefs concerning the origins of their race and even connected the Germanic interpretation of the Anunnaki pantheon to the Kings of "*Atlantis*"—meaning they believed in higher minds remaining from a prior civilization.

While it does not condone the actions taken, this fueling belief in "god-blood" and "alien-technologies," however trite it might seem to some readers, allowed Nazi Germany to nearly take over the world. We can see some evidence of this "self-righteousness" throughout history. Many folk have felt as if they were direct physical counterparts acting on behalf of their personal god. The very bloodlines of these gods were believed to flow in the veins of certain kings and temple-priests other lineages, thus representing the power attributed to "heaven," but on "earth." Long before World War II, the Christian Crusades of the Middle Ages were fueled by the same belief—that their god had come in human form and bestowed a decree that "on earth as it is in heaven." Suddenly, "Lord of the Earth" became a highly coveted position, for it was now (from an earthly perspective) just as good as that in "heaven" and more immediately accessible to the people. Titles, icons, powers and attributes of the gods, growing more and more distant in memory with the passage of time, were passed on to specific "royal" and "magical" families—the living embodiments of the "old gods" for Earth's future.

The age of gods passed into that of men. Harmonic dances of grace and beauty once driving a unified Sumer were gone forever, lost to a variegated mix of analytical minds. "Lordship" passed to humans—peace and love all but disappeared from the earth. Rivalry for supremacy in a post-Sumerian world of monotheism resulted in many "tribal" wars in the names of their personal deities. The essence of brotherly love that formed the very systems of physical existence (now being fought over), became separated as "moral dualism"— there was only room for one god now, and the fight for such once political, turned bloody. Of the two brothers, "God" would be associated with all that was orderly, and a "Satan" figure to represent all that was disharmonious. The force of Chaos, first overcome by the Sumerian gods and later tempered to balance creation was now viewed as a source of "evil" and personification of such, was passed onto a "devil," originally *brother* of "God."

As Semitic peoples near Mesopotamia developed their own traditions, beneficial properties of the Anunnaki, coupled with the personality of *Enlil*, became the figure *Yahweh*. [Yet, the name "EA" clearly has a more similar sound to "*Ia*" or "*Jah*."] The role of *antithesis* was given to *Enki*. Although association of "evil" and "discordance" is hardly justified, the *Enki* current energetically assimilated this in consciousness—quite simply, he was now the "rebel" among the "elder" pantheon, and it is not surprising that his most famous offspring —*Marduk*—would be a "rebel" son. As a patron, when all of the other gods have said "no," he is the one that might (almost always) say "yes." This is demonstrated not only in the Flood epic (when he went against the will of the *Anunnaki* to secretly preserve his own bloodline), but in any instance when even the gods are petitioning for favors that the others "won't touch."

For magical purposes, many of *Enki's* attributes have since been passed onto the younger generation but in times of extreme need, *Enki* seems to be unparalleled in the ability to "get things done - no matter how." He also seems to allot special time and care for *Inanna-Ishtar* in several tablet-cycles, including her own infamous epic—"*The Descent.*" But while rebellious, he was no shady rogue: he was a scientist and philosopher above all else, and the greatest of both among the Anunnaki (additionally a child of Anu), his skills and bloodline were prized in the "*fashioning*" of the material world—a title he carried in the Egyptian pantheon as PTAH, the "*designer.*"

The mystical symbol used by modern Mardukites to represent the energetic current of *Enki* closely resembles a pyramid or mountain—the KUR. Direction of energy suggested by the symbol is "upward." Movement pools at the surface (or below the surface) and is directed towards the sky. It is an opposite of the sign used for *Enlil*. Both *Enki* and *Marduk* are, at times, depicted as residing within a chamber, pyramid or inhabiting the "*Deep*" [Abyss], all of which are indicative of an "underverse" operating beneath the surface of consciousness or visible material reality.

Modern "Mardukite" encounters with the current have been "strong" due to increased modern inclinations of those interested in magic and esoteric sciences. His archetype remains among the most potent alive in systems today. Where the magician is ever seeking the essence of creation or the "words" by which it can be known, in Mardukite tradition, *Enki* is considered that very "*word*" of god made manifest and set free to evolve and unfold in the physical world. Fragments of this spiritual understanding are still maintained in the Semitic Kabbalah—lore which is, even in itself, derived from the original Sumerian Anunnaki "*Tree of Life.*"

— 1 —
NANNA-SIN : "WHO SHINES FOR"

Nanna is listed on Sumerian tablets as eldest of the "younger pantheon," first-born son of *Enlil* and *Ninlil*. His patron city was Ur, where he maintained primary residence at his temple-ziggurat—E.GISH.NU.GAL or *E.Gishshirgal* —"Home of the Throne Seed." He also made frequent appearances in the northern city of *Harran*, where his *E-Khulkhul* temple stood.

Nanna is named for the bright light of the moon gracing the night sky earth, referenced in one epithet as NAM.RA.SIT (*Namrasit*)—"Who Shines Forth." His consort—*Ningal* or *Nikkal*—is the "Great Lady of the Moon," goddess of divination and dreams, the most commonly accessible human "thresholds" to interact with the "*Other*."

Nanna is credited for prosperity of the ancient Sumerian city of Ur. The early metropolis represented the pure idealism of Sumer as brought to high esteem, long before its legendary destruction from the wrath of *Anu* and *Enlil*. Our ancestors preserved details of these events on cuneiform tablet cycles called "lamentations."

The famous "Lamentation for the Destruction of Ur" tablet is written from the perspective of the "*Lady of Ur*," or *Ningal*—the consort of *Nanna*. She relays the sudden sadness that befell the land the day of the "storm" neared. She sheds tears before AN and *Enlil* that her city "not be destroyed." But, the assembly of Anunnaki remained *unmoved*:—

> AN never bent toward those words,
> And Enlil never with, 'It is pleasing, so be it!'
> [To] soothe my heart.

Enlil called down the "storm of heaven" using the "fire-god"—GIBIL—to assist. The gods "left the city ruin and the dead were piled up." In despair, Nanna appeals to his father *Enlil*, asking him to lift this heavy curse and restore the city to its former glory. He speaks of the greatness of Sumer and the love for the people toward their gods. But *Enlil* is firm, as Thorkild Jacobsen translates:—

> O noble Nanna, be thou (concerned) about yourself,
> What truck [sway] have you with tears?
> There is no revoking a verdict,
> A decree of the assembly,
> A command of AN and Enlil is not known to ever change.
> Ur was verily granted kingship but an (ever)lasting [eternal] reign,

It was not granted.
You, my Nanna, do not worry. Leave your city!

This description demonstrates the immediate unrest ensuing in Sumer when control is passed to the "younger generation" of *Anunnaki.* The specific reason for the "Destruction of Ur" is conveniently concealed from the tablet saga. Zecharia Sitchin suggests an interesting theory: Since *Nanna* is also known as SU.EN (or specifically "SIN" of later Chaldeo-Babylonian literature), it is possible that he either shares an identity with, or lord over, ZU, a "creature" or "force" that is connected to control of the "Tablets of Destiny" during *Enlil's* possession. That name could be self-proposed to declare *Nanna* as "Lord Zu," or, again, be a reference to control of a serpent-being as EN.ZU—"Lord of the Zu." The name SU.EN might be associated with ZU.EN, or else EN.ZU. The typical persona of *Nanna* as a "gentle father" doesn't appear to match this allocation. It would, however, provide some explanation for why retributive annihilation came down through the leading pantheon, as city-states started to be governed by the "younger generation."

Nanna is given the number 30, correlating to the lunar month—the word "month" is named for the "moon"—and his consort is 25. As eldest of the "zonei" or "younger pantheon" given control of the local solar-system, *Nanna* was given a most prominent celestial domain in conjunction with the earth— the Moon. *Nanna* is actually a shortened version of the more complete designation—*Nannar*, "Light of the Full Moon." As the form of "SU.EN," he is actually representating the crescent or partial moon, and the Babylonians adopted the name "SIN" from this. The other name "ENZU" is derived from his Akkadian epithet—EN.I.ZUNA—so, the theory mentioned previously is not without some basis.

In Sumerian mythology the moon is held in high regard. Although the primordial chaos cosmologically brings forth the Sun into existence first, as illustrated in nearly all other solar-oriented "Mardukite" systems, the Sumerian Anunnaki chose to represent the Moon with Nanna, a firstborn son of *Enlil* and *Ninlil*, who with his consort *Ningal*, give birth to both *Inanna-Ishtar* (*Venus*) and Shammash (*the Sun*). It is here, as before concerning cosmology represented by pantheistic beings, that we must keep a distinction between the *Anunnaki* "younger pantheon" and the literal "celestial bodies" they are named for. Ancient tablets are quite obscure in this regard, because cuneiform signs for the planets and deities are identical. The people, themselves, were not confused by this, as we might be today when looking back at the tablet records with modern eyes.

In one sense, *Nanna* is described as the "light of the moon." But certainly *Nanna*, the *Anunnaki King of Ur*, was present in his city while simultaneously the light of the moon bore down on the earth at night. The association is clearly a reference to a more ancient cosmogony reflected in Sumerian beliefs: the day was born from the night, and not that the moon literally gave birth to the sun-star of our local system.

As a mystical "energetic current," the *Moon Gate* is traditionally the first that an individual will encounter when crossing the veils of material existence to the veils of negative existence, or the *Abyss*. Ancient Anunnaki denizens of the universe established "veils of existence" when the "material order" was brought or willed into being. They stationed the "younger pantheon" as *Guardians of the Gates*. The moon, as we might expect, is quite vibrant but gently passive and tranquil.

Ningal—the "Lady of the Moon"—receives many of the lunar attributes in later systems—If not by name, then by gender, as most esoteric revivals that do not truly use the combined-counterpart paradigm of a male-god and female-goddess as one essence, usually reduce celestial divinity to polar dualism: a 'masculine' "solar" god and the 'feminine' "lunar" goddess. But, *Sumer*, unlike *Babylon*, was a primarily *lunar*-oriented society and tradition with only subsequent emphasis on the *Sun* and *Venus*. Ancient astronomical symbols found on the oldest Sumerian art renderings for spirituality and astronomy are frequently representations of the *Sun-star, Venus* and, in the case of *Nanna-Sin* and *Ningal*—the *lunar crescent*—which, when depicted above a deity, was often called the "horns."

◊ ◊ ◊ ◊ ◊ ◊ ◊

Once an "initiate" passes the "*Earth Gate*" in search of cosmic truth on the path of "Ascension" up the *Ladder of Lights*, the lunar current is generally the first one accessed. This is because the "Moon Gate" is most closely aligned to the familiar astral and dreams "level" of enchantment and fantasy that many access—even unknowingly. As an elementary aspect of all mystical work, the "first degree" is where a seeker is able to actually realize in consciousness that they are not only their physical body. Actualization of this basic principle is not taken for granted, since many do not achieve even this "degree" of spiritual evolution (or "*unfoldment*") during their lifetime. Yet, in contemporary "new age" traditions, many initiates too often simply stop here, even when they believe they have moved on from it, remaining enamored with the infinite potentiality of appearances able to manifest through dissolution of the first veil. Esoteric instruction given to the Mardukite Chamberlains explains:—

> "The first 'level' encountered (aside from the extraordinarily subtle or blatantly physical 'Earth Gate') in the system is the Moon Gate, which ironically, is the embodiment of the 'common' astral plane or dreamscape that many have already enjoyed lucid access to without formal

occult education."

The formal "magical path" has a starting point. A magician working through the "veils of existence" connected to and surround us as the systematic design that keeps the material world "flowing." But, be warned: opiate-like sensations that the mind experiences at this level is quite addicting, and with good reason—it was designed to hold fast the unbidden minds that drifted into it, whether intentionally or otherwise. It is a veil meant to be so glamorous that the mere access of it immediately conjures illusions of ascension and enlightenment that are not yet truly manifest. The elation of initially breaking free of the physical chains can bring such ecstasy that the naïve neophyte actually believes they "have arrived," when really they have just begun. As the enigmatic editor Simon warns:—

> "It is the initiatory plane, and it is here, at the Lunar Gate, that the vast majority of occultists lose their way, forever. For most people, it is the repository of every inspirational, delusional, ghostly, spiritual, hallucinogenic event that has ever transpired in their lives. The temptation of this plane is to become one of those vague, ethereal types one finds spouting psychobabble on morning talk shows. Many channelers are victims of staying too long on the Lunar level; astral puppets who never progress beyond sitting on the ventriloquist's lap. . . instead of mastering this plane, it has become *their* master; every breeze that brushes across their faces become a caress from beyond, every news item a direct message from an entity on Alpha Centauri. Avoid them like the very plague . . ."

Astral "shade-forms" of *Nanna-Sin* and *Ningal* reflect an archetypal otherworldly "fairy" king and queen—born of heaven, ruling on earth and embodied in the lunar threshold connecting between the two. Most mystics encountering these personas have seen them in their elderly form, but the blue-hued moonlight radiating from their skin gives off so much beauty that we tend to think of them as ageless. The color associated with the moon is silver and the essence and symbol attributed to *Nanna* is the royal wand or scepter of lapis lazuli.

When the moon was not visible, it was thought to be dwelling in the underworld. When a lunar eclipse occurred, Sumerian tradition described the moon battling wicked demons before reappearing. This more active face of the lunar current is not often tapped by most "magical" tables of correspondence. We can find similar beliefs concerning disappearance-and-appearance of *Sun* and *Moon* throughout many ancient cultural mythologies.

The Mardukite "Invocation of the Nanna Gate" (given in the "*The Complete Anunnaki Bible*") very closely resembles an incantation found from the tablet-

52

series known to scholars as: "Prayers of the Lifting of the Hand."—the entire basis for L.W. King's "*Babylonian Magic & Sorcery.*" The original prayer is as follows:—

O SIN! O *Nannar*! Mighty One . . . [among the gods]
  siptu ilu-SIN ilu-NANNARU ru-su-bu u- . . .

O SIN, who art unique, thou that brightens . . . [the heavens]
  ilu-SIN id-dis-su-u, mu-nam-mir . . .

That gives light unto the nations . . . [over the four lands]
  sa-ki-in na-mir-ti a-na nisi- . . .

That unto the black-headed race art favorable . . . [god to your people]
  ana nisi sal-mat kakkadu us-su-ru sa- . . .

Bright is thy light, in heaven . . . [like fire]
  nam-rat urru-ka ina sami-i . . .

Brilliant is thy torch, like the fire-god . . . [burning brightly]
  sar-hat di-pa-ra-ka, kima ilu-GIBIL . . .

Thy brightness fills the broad earth!
  ma-lu-u nam-ri-ru-ka irsita(ta) rapasta

The brightness of the nations he gathers, in thy sight . . .
  sar-ha nisi uk-ta-sa-ra ana a-ma-ri-ka

O *Anu* of the sky, whose purpose no man learns!
  ilu-A-nim sami-i sa la i-lam-ma-du mi-lik-su ma-

Overwhelming is thy light like the Sun-god [*Shammash*], thy first born!
  su-tu-rat urru-ka kima ilu-Samas bu-uk-ri-

Before thy face the great gods bow down, the fate of the world is set before thee!
  kan-su pani-ka ilani rabuti purus matati sakin(in) ina pani-ka

In the evil of an eclipse of the Moon which in X month on X day, has taken place,
  ina lumin ilu-atali ilu-SIN sa ina arhi pulani umi pulani isakna(na)

In the evil of the powers, of the portents not good, which are in my palace and my land,
  lumun idati iti.mis limniti la tabati sa ina ikalli-ya u mati-ya ibasa-a

The great gods beseech thee and thou gives counsel!
  ilani rabuti i-sal-lu-ka-ma tanadin(in) mil-ka

They take their stand, all of them, they petition at thy feet!
  izzizu pu-hur-su-nu us-ta-mu-u ina sapli-ka

O SIN, glorious one of IKUR! They beseech thee and thou givest the oracle of the gods!
  ilu-SIN su-pu-u sa I.KUR i-sal-lu-ka-ma ta-mit ilani tanadin(in)

The end of the month is the day of thy oracle, the decision of the great gods;
  bubbulum u-um ta-mit-ti-ka pi-ris-ti ilani rabuti

The thirtieth day is thy festival, a day of prayer to thy divinity!
  umu XXX-kan i-sin-na-ka u-um ta-sil-ti ilu-ti-[ka]

O God of the New Moon, in might unrivaled whose purpose no man learns,
  ilu-Namrasit i-muk la sa-na-an sa la i-lam-ma-du mi-lik-su ma- . . .

I have poured thee a libation of the night (with) wailing, I have offered thee (with) shouts of joy a drink offering of . . . [*type of drink*]
  as-ruk-ka si-rik musi lallartu ak-ki-ka ri-is-ta-a si-kar . . .

I am bowed down! I have taken my stand! I have sought for thee!
  kan-sa-ku az-za-az a-si-ka ka- . . .

Do thou set favor and righteousness upon me!
  ka-sa dum-ki u mi-sa-ri sukun(un) ili-[ya]

May my god and my goddess, who for long have been angry with me,
  ili-ya u ilu-istari sa is-tu u-um ma-du-ti is-bu-su

In righteousness and justice deal graciously with me! Let my way be favorable, with joy . . .
  ina kit-ti u misari lis-li-mu itti-ya ur-hi lid-mi-ik had-is ni- . . .

And ZA.GAR, the god of dreams has sent,
  u-ma-'-ir-ma ilu-ZA.GAR ilu sa sunati

In the night season . . . [cleanse me of] my sin, my iniquity may . . . [it be absolved]
  ina sat musi Kab.mis ar-ni-ya lu-us-mi sir-ti lu-ta

For ever may I bow myself in humility before thee!
  ana da-ra-ti lud-lul da-li-li-[ka]

— 2 —
NABU : "WHO SPEAKS FOR"

Mythologists and mythographers often associate the Sumerian "Lord of the Tree of Life" [*Ningishzidda*] with the Egyptian deity "Thoth"—the archetypal Mercurial current shared by Hermes, Merlyn, Ogmios, &tc., but the most iconic *Anunnaki* "messenger of the gods" more appropriately corresponds to a more "Mardukite" character in Babylon. If one carefully considers the "divine" occupation of this lineage in Egypt, there is evidence for a "third party" of gods, apart from strict *Enlil* and *Enki* lineages, that most strongly influenced the Babylonian system in preference over the former Sumerian one.

In the Babylonian tradition, the "Apollonian herald of the mercurial current" among the "younger pantheon" is the *heir-son* of *Marduk* and *Sarpanit—the* patrons of *Babylon*. This role is attributed to *Nabu—also* rendered *Nebo* or *Nabak* in Semitic language—meaning "spokes-person." He shares residence at the temple-ziggurat of the city of *Borsippa* [*Birs-i-Nimrud*] (approximately ten miles from *Babylon*) with his consort, *Tasmit—Teshmet-(um)* or *Tashmitu*. In addition to managing the national school and temple of scribe-priests, *Nabu* and *Teshmetu* made annual visits to *Babylon* for the celebration of the "New Year" [A.KI.TI or "Akitu"] festival held on the spring equinox.

Nabu is the original "scribe of the gods," a patron deity of wisdom-knowledge and writing, inventor of the "reed-stylus" (*pen*), and the first truly refined form of cuneiform—distinguishing the stylus-script of *Babylon* from early pictograms of *Sumer*. His energetic current carries an affinity to Mercury—communication, divination and the air element. Semitic-Hebrew language incorporated the word "*Nabih*," meaning "prophet." *Nabu* is effectively the "*Prophet of Marduk*" and a "Messianic Son" for Mardukites of *Babylon*. Priests and kings evoked his name in the consecration of their libraries, asking him to bless their hands when writing tablets and also to curse those who might steal or desecrate the libraries. The intellectual nature of *Nabu* and his unusual type of psychological warfare are echoed on an ancient basalt tablet, the "*Caillou Michaux*," named for the archaeologist excavating it for the French National Museum:—

> *May Nebo [Nabu], the supreme intelligence,*
> *overwhelm him with affliction and terror,*
> *and lastly may he hurry him into incurable despair.*

When the ancient Mardukites were losing ground to Enlilite-Yahwists during the "Old Testament" biblical era, *Nabu* was charged with the task of maintaining a tradition of *Marduk's* followers near *Babylon* and in *Egypt*. Several neo-Babylonian Kings of the time period are also given related names in patronage and reverence to the younger pantheon of the Mardukites, such as: Nabuna'id ("*Nabu is exalted*"), Nabupolassar ("*Nabu protects his son*") and, of course, Nebochadnezzar ("*Nabu preserve my first-born son*"), just to name a few. For the Mardukites in Babylon, *Nabu* represented a "messianic prophet"—born of a "Heavenly King" (*Marduk*) and *Enki's* special hybrid offspring (*Sarpanit*), long before Semitic and Christian lore existed to record such things, but undoubtedly serving as an inspirational source to later traditions.

Although an old soul—a steward of all wisdom of the gods, responsible for recording their "movements" in a Mesopotamian version of the "Book of Life" and the famous "Tablets of Destiny"—*Nabu* is actually a relatively young "deity"of the Mardukite Anunnaki pantheon. His other epithet—"TU.TU"—appears notably as the thirteenth name (of the Fifty) from the "*Enuma Elis*" (found on Mardukite *Tablet-F* in the "*Anunnaki Bible*"); the thirteenth name that Marduk assumed unto himself during the "*Epic of Creation.*" The "name" of this "power" is transferred to *Nabu* in the Babylonian Mardukite Tradition, although the governing domain is quite ambiguous:—

> *Nabu-Tutu,*
> *He who created them anew,*
> *And should their wants be pure,*
> *Then they are satisfied.*

This intellectual riddle described the very function *Nabu* serves—the recording of life, history, people... and *gods*—the "eye-of-the-beholder" concerning descendants of the Anunnaki, origins of humanity and courses of life and existence—were now *Nabu's* to hold. He could create them anew, give anyone a new face and past and therefore future. He was the "*Voice of God*"—the messenger frequency-wave of the highest brought to the lowest and an intermediary between.

Mesopotamian religion held a firm inseparable view of male-female aspects in divinity, but the relationship between *Nabu* and *Tasmit* (or *Teshmet*) is truly complimentary—where *Nabu* is a projector of communication, *Tasmit* is a receiver. She is the Babylonian "goddess of hearing," the one who listens to the prayers—often sought as a "*transmitor*" to her husband and the other deities. A powerful incantation to "*Tesmitu*" is found on the reverse-side of the prayer-tablet referenced previously for *Nanna*. The incantation is specifically a petition to "remove sickness and enchantments caused by an eclipse of the Moon":—

> *O Lady Tasmitu!*
> *I __ , son of ___ and ___ ,*
> *Whose god is ___ , whose goddess is ___ ,*
> *In the evil of an eclipse of the Moon,*

Which in ___ month on ___ day has taken place,
In the evil of the powers, of the portents,
Evil and not good, which are in my palace and my land,
I have turned towards thee! I have established thee!
Listen to the incantation!
Before *Nabu*, thy spouse, the lord, the prince,
The firstborn son of the E.SAGILA, intercede for me!
May he hearken to my cry at the word of thy mouth;
May he remove my sighing;
May he learn of my supplication!
At his mighty word,
May god and goddess deal graciously with me!
May the sickness of my body be torn away;
May the groaning of my flesh be consumed!
May the consumption of my muscles be removed!
May the poisons that are upon me be loosened!
May the ban be torn away and the curse consumed!
May the Anunnaki come forth and demand justice!
At thy command, may mercy be established!
May god and king ordain favor at thy mighty command that is not altered,
And thy true mercy that changes not,
  O Lady Tasmitu!

◊ ◊ ◊ ◊ ◊ ◊ ◊

Perhaps one of the most fundamental lessons to be learned via the mercurial current is *discernment*. Once the veils have been penetrated and the spectral showers of vast images and illusions are tapped on the lunar level, *temperance* is required. Where the *Moon Gate* provides access to the "magical path," the *Mercury Gate* ("*Nabu Gate*") is the beginning of the "mystical path," concerning the "Secret Doctrines of the Cosmos" contained on the "Tablets of Destiny." *This* wisdom dissolves half-truths of worldly programming, encoding and other glamours. True knowledge replaces all erroneous (mis)information. [This is the very subject of Mardukite Systemology *Liber-One*, titled "*Tablets of Destiny Revelation*" by Joshua Free.]

Our intellect causes psychosomatic effects on our emotional state, which in turn influences our behavior. The methodology suggested taps undefiled unconditioned stimuli from beyond the veil of tangible experiential based memory data. This ensures a higher rate of success generating transcendental moments of "*true gnosis*," and not merely trivial enlightenment-delusions of false-light. The *light on the screen* can be made to be seen for what it is. The "weight of wisdom" often causes *Nabu* to appear relatively much older than he actually is. His number is twelve, a fundamental value to the "*sexagesimal*" (*Base-60*) mathematics of Mesopotamia, a method still used today to denote

time, angles, locales and speed of travel across any space. His traditional col-
or is blue, and in addition to the "reed stylus," *Nabu* is represented by the
double-barred cross, also visible in his cuneiform sign: PA (as seen on the traditional logo for *JFI Publications*).

The traditional Mardukite invocation made to *Nabu* (as seen in "*The Complete
Anunnaki Bible*") resonates strongly with the twenty-second prayer from the
"*Lifting of the Hand*" cuneiform tablet series:—

O hero, prince, first-born of *Marduk*!
  siptu rubu asaridu bu-kur ilu-Marduk

O prudent ruler, offspring of *Zarpanitu*!
  Massu-u i-ti-ip-su i-lit-ti ilu-ZARPANITU

O *Nabu*, bearer of the Tablet of Destiny of the gods, Director of
  the E.SAGILA!
  Ilu-Nabu na-as duppu si-mat ilani a-sir E.SAG.ILA

Lord of E.ZIDA, Shadow of Borsippa,
  bil E.ZID.DA su-lul duru-BORSIPPA-ki

Darling of IA [Enki], Giver of Life,
  na-ram ilu-IA ka-i-su balatu

Prince of Babylon, Protector of the Living,
  asarid BAB.ILI na-si-ru na-pis-ti

Lofty Lord of the hill-dwelling, fortress of the nations, Lord of temples!
  ilu du-ul da-cd-mi kar misi bil is-ri-ti

Thy name is the word in the mouth of the people, O sedu ["friendly spirit"]
  zi-kir-ka ina pi nisi su.dub.ba ilu-sidu

O son of the mighty prince *Marduk*, in thy mouth is justice!
  mar rubi rabi ilu-Marduk ina pi-ka kit-ti

In thy illustrious name, at the command of thy mighty godhead,
  ina si-ik-ri-ka kabti ina ki-bit ilu-ti-ka rabiti(ti)

I ___ , the son of ___ and ___ , who am smitten with disease, thy servant,
  ana-ku pulanu apil pulani mar-su sum-ru-su arad-ka

Whom the hand of the demon and breath of the wicked [spirit has seized],
  sa kat utukki-ma imat bur.ru.da nam-kil-lu-ni-ma nal-susu-ni

May I live, may I be perfect [with your wisdom]
  lu-ub-lut lu-us-lim-ma . . . gub.bu.du luksud(ud)

Set justice in my mouth!
  su-us-kin kit-ti ina pi-ya

[Kindle] mercy in my heart!
sup-si-ka damikti(ti) ina libbi-ya

May the Anunnaki return and be established! May they command mercy!
ti-i-ru u an.nu.na.ki man-za-[za lik-bu-u] damikti(ti)

May my god stand at my right hand!
li-iz-ziz [ili-ya] ina imni-ya

May my goddess stand at my left hand!
li-iz-ziz [ilu-istari-ya] ina sumili-ya

May the favorable sidu [spirit], the favorable *lamassu* [guardian spirit]
be with me!
ilu-sidu damiktu ilu-lamassu damiktu . . . -kis illi-ya

— 3 —
INANNA-ISHTAR :
"QUEEN IN THE HEAVENS"

Known in *Egypt* as "Goddess of Ten-Thousand Names," a unique position of *"Queenship of Heaven"* is reserved by one of the "younger pantheon" in both Sumerian and later Chaldeo-Babylonian systems. Daughter of *Nanna* and *Ningal*—the Sumerian aspects of the Moon—and twin to *Shammash* (the Sun), this title of high esteem is passed on to a young "Lady of the Stars"—unequaled in beauty and cunning use of divine politics. In ancient Sumer, she is introduced in the original cuneiform literature as IN.ANNA—*"Lady of Anu"* and *"Queen of Heaven."*

Inanna quickly rises in status as the "archetypal goddess" on earth. She simultaneously represents both a "goddess of love" and "goddess of war," granting her significant domain in the physical world. As a result, she was favored among the masses adoring her for her influence. She is originally given a numeric designation of 5 in Sumer—but in Mardukite Babylon she receives 15, replacing the position held by *Ninmah* (*Ninhursag*) from the elder pantheon. She remains a primary goddess in Assyrio-Babylonian tradition, with the name I.STAR (or *Ishtar*)—"The Goddess"—*istari* being the Akkadian word for "goddess." Her traditional/ceremonial color is sometimes white (*Inanna*) and sometimes light-green (*Venus*).

Assyrian art frequently depicts *Inanna-Ishtar* with wings. The same winged form is visible on her Egyptian form as *Isis*. Clearly she was a goddess of the aerial world, not only the *"Anunit-(um)"* (*"Anu's Beloved"*), but literally a "queen" of the skies, stars or heavens. Mythological cycles describe seven objects connected to Ishtar for her aerial travels. Similarly, there are seven garments and ornaments removed during her "Descent to the Underworld." It is quite likely that these items are related to her position as "Lady of the Stars" or "Queen of Heaven"—power symbols associated with this role. Mystical revivalists consider this symbolism significant for modern ritual magic activities reviving Mesopotamian-based ceremonialism (and the Underworld), but perhaps they have an even greater unseen esoteric relevance. In the cuneiform tablet cycle of *Ishtar's* "Crossings to the Underworld"—give as Mardukite *Tablet-C* in our *"Anunnaki Bible"*—these objects are referred to as seven "Divine Decrees" that she "fixes" to her body. They are listed as:—

1. Shugurra – Starry Crown of Anu (on her head)
2. Wand of Lapis Lazuli (in her hand)
3. Necklace of Lapis Lazuli (around her neck)
4. Bag of Brilliant-Shinning-Stones (carried)
5. Gold Ring of Power (on her finger)

6. Frontlet Amulet (as a breastplate)
7. The Pala – Royal Garments (worn about her body)

Zecharia Sitchin interprets the talismans somewhat differently, describing "Seven Objects" of *Inanna* as implements "necessary for traveling the skies":

1. *Shu.gu.ra* – she put on her head
2. Measuring pendents – on her ears
3. Chains of small blue stones – around her neck
4. Twin stones – on her shoulders
5. A golden cylinder – in her hands
6. Straps – clasping her breast
7. *Pa.la* garment – clothed around her body

Genealogies of Sumer detail *Inanna* as a "fourth generation" Anunnaki figure —daughter of *Nanna*, born of *Enlil*, son of *Anu*—and is therefore the "great-granddaughter" of *Anu*. She receives a special place in his heart, which proves beneficial in her rise to power. Even more than this, *Inanna* is a tenacious, actively determined personality that stops at nothing to acquire what she deems rightfully hers. If she wants it, she will take it. In the mythic cycles, this includes "decrees of heaven," "decrees of earth," "secret names of gods" and everything in between. In many ways, her post-Sumerian cult following rivaled *Marduk* for supremacy in *Babylon*. She quite effectively used these powers to win an eternal loyalty from mortals in exchange for granting select worldly desires. The kings she favored, she would stand beside in battle and those she did not (or who fell out of favor) she would lend aid to the opposing side, proving that this "goddess of love" is not to be scorned.

The actual truth of how this "archetypal goddess" figure rose to high power is not so widely known. Her many names have, however, become legendary— not only in Mesopotamia as *Inanna* and *Ishtar*, but elsewhere as *Isis*, *Aphrodite*, *Venus*, *Astarte*, *Metis*, *Brigit* (among countless other names)—marking her widespread appearance among many diverse cultures. Later religious misogynists could not recognize such vast power as a female form, transferring her identity to *Ashtoreth* or *Astoroth*—a leader of an allegedly "demonic" hierarchy of angels in the Judeo-Christian Semitic and Kabbalistic systems.

The original Sumerian tablet cycle involving *Inanna* and *Enki* is academically called "*The Transfer of the Arts of Civilization from Eridu to Erech.*" Seeking greater abundance and power for her city, Inanna travels to *Eridu*—the residence of *Enki*—in pursuit of secret knowledge, holy relics and tablets of power that will enable her to achieve this. Her charm, coupled with the looseness that comes with heavy drinking, won over *Enki*, who gave up some one-hundred decrees and treasures in his compromised state. These are then loaded onto her "Boat of Heaven" and transported back to *Erech*, intermittently making seven rest stops along the way. Realizing what he's done soon after, *Enki* immediately sends his counselor *Isimud* with a host of monsters in pursuit of *Ishtar*, but the damage is done and she arrives safely in *Erech* with her new found "decrees" intact.

We might compare this account to the acquisition of power by *Isis* in Egypt, as deTraci Regula describes:—

> "Her skill as a magician was employed when she sought to receive the sacred true name of Ra, her father in some stories. Ra was ignoring the needs of humanity and Isis resorted to a drastic act of magic, creating a small snake from the exudation of his body, which bit him. To stop the pain, Ra agreed to give Isis his most secret name, allowing her to restore balance."

A romantic patina for *Inanna-Ishtar* is toned by the Romeo-and-Juliet-motif in the relationship with her *consort—Damuzi* (*Dumuzi*) [Sumerian; "*the good son*"] or in Babylon, TAMMUZ "*the good shepherd.*" There are different accounts of their courtship activities and later involvement with the Underworld. [See also Mardukite *Tablet-U* in "*The Complete Anunnaki Bible.*"] One version describes how *Inanna-Ishtar* was head-over-heels overtaken with *Damuzi* from the start. However, another tablet series explains that at the beginning, the "shepherd-god"—*Damuzi*—is rivaling with a "farmer-god" for her love and affections. Not surprisingly, *Damuzi* is actually the youngest son of *Enki*, and apart from *Marduk*, *Nabu* and few others, he was an "officially" acceptable spouse in the tradition of Anunnaki "succession." This was later maintained among the "younger generation" via a combination of the two lineages—in this case a daughter of *Enlil* and a son of *Enki*.

Inanna-Ishtar's rise to power was by no means an arbitrary event. Its significance affected the history of the Anunnaki, but also the evolution of civilization as a whole—the politics, religious beliefs and spiritual traditions. She even maintained high recognition as a patron of Babylon. But it was not the *position* itself that changed the fate of the planet—it was, instead, the *responsibilities* that came along with it.

Anunnaki tradition held the "succession" matter as of highest importance for maintaining domain leadership. It became customary for the "younger generation" lineages of Enlil and Enki to commingle. For Ishtar, it was *Marduk*—heir of *Enki*—that was her intended spouse. Each perfectly complimented one another as the *apex leadership* of the younger pantheon. But, neither party seemed interested in maintaining this obligation as a "team"—so, it never occurred. The role of consort was passed onto *Enki's* youngest son, *Dumuzi*. It initially seemed that everyone agreed to this arrangement, but it resulted in fracturing the powers, creating a third party of gods. The Anunnaki lineage of

Enki separated—splitting in twain—the followers of *Marduk* versus worshipers of *Ishtar* throughout the ancient world.

When Marduk retreats to *Egypt* to regain supremacy of his own "Mardukite" tradition, Ishtar sets her sights on making the powers *there* her own as well. We can certainly see evidence for a significant influence that ISIS provides for our contemporary general understanding of *Egypt*. The "fighting" that erupts between "brothers" thereafter may be of a similar theme to what is alluded in the "farmer-god versus shepherd-god" stories (concerning Ishtar's courtship of a mate). *Ishtar's* "undying love" for *Dumuzi* is explicitly expressed. Quarreling among the family reaches climactic heights when *Dumuzi* drowns under uncertain circumstances. It is then that Ishtar marches on *Marduk* (known as "*Ra*" there, to the Egyptians), arriving with the Horus-Seth tribes—fracturing the pantheon in Egypt too; Zecharia Sitchin explains:—

> "The first presence of *Inanna/Ishtar* in Egypt is mentioned in the Edfu text dealing with the First Pyramid War. Called there *Ashtoreth* (her Canaanite name), she is said to have appeared on the battlefield among the advancing forces of Horus. . . as long as the fighting was only between descendants of *Enki*, no one saw a particular problem in having a granddaughter of *Enlil* around. But after the victory of Horus, when Seth occupied lands not his, the situation changed completely: the Second Pyramid War pitched the sons and grandchildren of *Enlil* against the descendants of *Enki*."

◊ ◊ ◊ ◊ ◊ ◊ ◊

Mystical experiences with *Inanna-Ishtar's* "Venusian" energy current are prevalent throughout the ages across nearly all ancient cultures. She is favored by priests and priestesses of many esoteric and occult traditions many times over for thousands of years. As a self-made "goddess queen" of the *Heavens* and the material domains—love, lust, war, magic—her coveted position of influence is unparalleled among the pantheon. It becomes clear why her intended betrothed was *Marduk*, but as they rivaled for control of the same side of the same coin, they became, in actuality, the same side of two coins.

Although Mesopotamian literature provides a wide array of Anunnaki activity, the colorful picture portrayed in the original system is "*amoral*" or concerns a "*higher ethic*" than readily discernible in mortal life. In fact, this "*utilitarian*" ideal, for better or worse, is demonstrated by most any "higher order" of "authority," which is often mysterious to those it governed. In some form—physically and in memory—the "younger pantheon" of Anunnaki were the "gods" of earth religions for thousands of years, even preferred (in contrast to their elders) for their worldly material accessibility.

As Guardian of the *Venus Gate, Inanna-Ishtar* is encountered on the mystic path as a "moral" challenge to rise above the pleasures of earth and seek a higher spiritual *Pathway to Self-Honesty* and *Self-Actualization* beyond the *Human Condition*. Should the initiate succumb to the worldly trappings and temptations, she will undoubtedly enable such with worldly "rewards"—but there is a strict clause to receiving such personal attention and this is well known to master occultists:—

> *Inanna-Ishtar takes her own for her own,*
> *And that once chosen by her,*
> *No man may take another bride.*

There is no shortage of Babylonian tablets revealing prayers, rites and incantations in honor of *Ishtar*. Her allied tradition in *Babylon* consists of the same offerings that priests and priestesses offered *Marduk*—the sprinkling of pure waters, libations and potent beverages, fragrant oils, honey and butter with bread, with sacred woods burning as incense. The number "*seven*" frequently appears in these ancient ceremonies—it was often customary to present a food or drink offering seven times. In other instances, such as "*pure waters,*" offerings are sprinkled about the ground. Other times, vials and jars were left at an "*Altar of Offerings*" dedicated to a specific deity. Once the gods physically left, people on earth retained only memories of their existence, but temple-priests (and their families) were continuously sustained thereafter, living on the offerings that once supported the physical existence of great Anunnaki figures.

Like other examples, invocation-prayers to Ishtar used by modern Mardukites, (including those found in the companion to Liber-50, "*The Complete Book of Marduk by Nabu*") are similar to those found on the "*Prayers of the Lifting of the Hand*" tablet-series from the Kuyunjik collection:

> O *Ishtar*, good is thy supplication, when the spirit of thy name is
>   propitious [favorable].
>   *[ilu-ISTAR] ta-a-bu su-up-pu-u-ki ki-i ki-ru-ub nis sumi-ki*
>
> Thy regard is prosperity, thy command is light!
>   *[nap]-lu-us-ki tas-mu-u ki-bit-ki nu-u-ra*
>
> Have mercy on me, O *Ishtar*! Command abundance!
>   *rimi-nin-ni-ma ilu-ISTAR ki-bi-i na-ha-si*
>
> Truly pity me and take away my sighing.
>   *ki-nis nap-li-si-in-ni-ma li-ki-i un-ni-ni-ya*
>
> Thy [feet or hands(?)] have I held: let me bring joy of heart!
>   *sar-ta-a-ki a-hu-zu lu-bi-il tu-ub libbi- ...*

I have borne thy yoke: do thou give [me] consolation!
  u-bil ap-sa-na-ki pa-sa-ha suk- ...

I have [held] thy head: let me enjoy success and favor!
  u-ki-' kakkadu-ki li-si-ra sa-li-mu

I have protected thy splendor: let there be good fortune and prosperity!
  as-sur sa-ru-ra-ki lu-u tas-mu-u u ma-ga-ru

I have sought thy light: let my brightness shine!
  is-ti-'-u nam-[ri]-ir-ri-ki lim-mi-ru zi-mu-u-a

I have turned towards thy power: let there be life and peace!
  as-hur bi-lut-ki [lu]-u balatu u sul-mu

Propitious be the favorable spirit who is before thee: may the *lamassu* that
  goes behind thee be propitious!
  *lu tas-lim ilu-sidu damiktu sa pa-ni-ki sa ar-ki-ki a-li-kat ilu-lammasu
  lu tas-lim*

That which is on thy right hand, increase good fortune: that which on thy
  left hand, attain favor!
  sa im-nu-uk-ki mis-ra-a lu-us-sip dum-ka lu-uk-su-da sa su-mi-lu-[uk-ki]

Speak and let the word be heard!
  ki-bi-ma lis-si-mi zik-ri

Let the word I speak, when [spoken], be propitious!
  a-mat a-kab-bu-u ki-ma a-kab-bu-u lu-u ma-ag-rat

Let health of body and joy of heart be my daily portion!
  ina tu-ub siri u hu-ud lib-bi i-tar-ri-in-ni u-mi-sam

My days prolong, life bestow: let me live, let me be perfect, let me behold
  thy divinity!
  umi-ya ur-ri-ki ba-la-ta surki lu-ub-lut lu-us-lim-ma lu-us-tam-mar ilu-[ut-ki]

When I plan, let me attain (my purpose): Heaven be thy joy, may the
  Abyss hail thee!
  i-ma u-sa-am-ma-ru lu-uk-su-ud samu-u hidutu-ki apsu li-ris-[ki]

May the gods of the world be favorable to thee: may the great gods delight
  thy heart!
  ilani sa kis-sa-ti lik-ru-bu-ki ilani rabuti lib-ba-ki li-tib-[bu]

— 4 —
SHAMMASH : "THE SHINNING ONE"

Ancient Mesopotamian astronomers correctly depicted the *Sun* in the middle-center of the *"Ladder of Lights"*—a stream of energies connecting our physical world to the ALL via a *"bridge,"* often represented by "Celestial Bodies." Assuming the esoteric chronology that begins with the *"Earth Gate,"* the Seeker approaches Gates of local planetary systems—those relatively closer to the Earth: the *Moon, Mercury* and *Venus*—and then the *Sun.* According to Sumerian cosmology (and lineage tablets), the *Sun*—or more accurately, the *"sun-god"*—was a twin brother to Inanna-Ishtar (*Venus*), the "Morning Star" born of *Nanna* (*the Moon*). This general course also follows with a worldview that "day was born from night" and more esoterically that "light emerges to penetrate the darkness."

The role of the *"sun-god"* as the physical and spiritual "illuminator" carried the very name given to the "face of the sun"—the Anunnaki sky-commander "UTU" or "UDDU" (Sumerian for *"shinning one"*). The same appears on cuneiform tablets in Akkadian and Chaldeo-Babylonian languages as *"Samas"*—often written as it is pronounced: *"Shammash"*—and *"Babbar"* in some sources. His consort is AYA or AIA (also *"Shendira"*)—from the Akkadian for *"dawn."* Together they shared a sanctuary at *Larsa* (in Sumer); and also a temple in *Sippar* (near Babylon), where the couple eventually retired. *Shammash* is given the Anunnaki designation of "20" and reign of the solar domain—the task of maintaining order as chief of the Anunnaki "Judges"—governing justice, law, balance and truth. [In fact, the *"Shammash"* title was used by Medieval Jewish communities to designate a person that assisted in maintaining a governing order. The name was even used later to designate a "temple servant."]

Shammash—and the *Sun*—are called forth frequently with incantations from mystical and religious cuneiform tablets from the *Ancient Near East.* However, as in many ways a subordinate to other entities in the Anunnaki pantheon, the system as a whole can hardly be considered "sun-worship" in the conventional sense or in the most convenient terms. "Astral" perhaps. It might even more accurately be described as ancient "stellar-worship"—if we are to even ascribe the misunderstood word "worship" to this system at all. All primary *"Olympian"*-type deities of this tradition were either named for celestial objects, or we must assume they named the planets after themselves. We can be sure, however, that the *Sun* played a significant role in the "order" of the material world—a "conqueror of evil" (considered sleeping or battling demons at night) or the "protector of travelers" by day, ceaselessly keeping watch over man's daily activities and work-life. The *Sun* clearly became a popular force for the masses to call upon, as Lenormant describes:—

"The sun was not one of the highest gods of the religious system which had served as a foundation for *Accadian* magic, his power did not approach that of the three great spirits of the zones of the universe [governed by the Supernal Trinity]. But it was just his lower rank that made him more accessible to the prayers of man; and the fact that his influence upon man and the phenomena of life was so sensibly felt, made them assign to him the office of arbiter of events and of fate; while lastly, as he dissipated darkness, and consequently was engaged in a struggle with the bad spirits, he became one of the supernatural personages to whom the magical invocations were most frequently addressed."

◊ ◊ ◊ ◊ ◊ ◊ ◊

The "*Sun Gate*" is a significant threshold "crossing" on the mystic path. Many do not reach this far in their spiritual evolution (or "ascension proc-ess"). Many are too enamored by trappings of lower realms to reach (and survive) the self-annihilation prominent at this Gate. This veil is bright and shinning—it will surely illuminate any "darkness" within you that is still waiting to be purged, in addition to any other physical and sensation-based delights remaining from the Venusian initiation.

In the Egyptian mythic cycle associated with the *Sun*—Yes, there is "Ra," actually a representative of a "*sun behind the sun*" (even more than our local sun), but more important to our topic is the "Osirian mythos" of death and transformation—the "solar-judge" weighing the soul to measure impurity. The initiate must allow the pictures and images of their "former" programmed existence to be burned away—allow the baggage and energetic attachments of a "lower life" to be dissolved.

> "*I come in self-annihilation and the grandeur of inspiration.*"
> —William Blake

The challenge-riddle of the "*Sun Gate*" is: "all that glitters is not gold." Just as surely as the sunlight can pierce the darkness, so too is it sometimes blinding to see what is right in front of us. We must be ready, always, not caught basking in the glowing rays of the shining sun. The apex of solar power at noon reflects the heights of empires and all systems—but these too must ebb and fall in their own cyclic tides. Everything is in motion; and everything everywhere is connected together.

It is from the "*Solar Gate*" that an initiate must prepare in "self-honesty" for the forthcoming encounter with the "Annihilator" energies of *Nergal*. This is the *Wall of Fire* confronted along the *Pathway*. After being given charged on the Mardukite mystic path of the "*Ladder of Lights*" by *Nabu* at the second gate, there are many Anunnaki figures (representing lessons on the path) from those who stood against the rise of a *Mardukite Babylon—Ishtar, Shammash* and *Nergal*—all of which have played a part in its abolition. Even *Shammash* (UTU) sided with Dumuzi against Marduk in that tablet cycle; and then later against *Nabu*, siding with *Nergal* and *Ninurta* in what some scholars call the "Pyramid Wars," which included mass-destruction of the ancient "Middle East," leaving a resonant imprint of unrest forever on that locale.

"*The Great Hymn of Shammash*" is potentially the most significant mystical cuneiform tablet transcription from Mesopotamia regarding the "*sun-god.*" A seeker will see that it reveres more than simply the "physical *sun,*" but the "sublime light of truth" personified by the Anunnaki position held *Shammash* (*Uddu/Utu*). Several of the lines (particularly at the beginning and end) on the tablet cycle have worn away, but the definitive academic version, first appearing in "*Babylonian Wisdom Literature*" by W. Lambert (in 1960), remains the most complete modern translation for both mystics and scholars. Any "moral dogma" presented reflects other Babylonian wisdom tablet series, such as "Book of the Law of Marduk"—given as Mardukite *Tablet-L* in our "*Anunnaki Bible.*" Lines from the "*Great Hymn of Shammash*" read:—

21. You climb to the mountains surveying the earth,
22. You suspend from the heavens the circle of the lands,
23. You care for all the peoples of the lands,
24. And everything that EA (*Enki*), king of the counselors had created is entrusted to you.
25. Whatever has breath you shepherd without exception,
26. You are keeper in upper and lower regions.
27. Regularly and without cease you traverse the heavens,
28. Every day you pass over the broad earth . . .
33. Shepherd of that beneath, keeper of that above,
34. You, *Shammash*, direct, you are the light of everything.
35. You never fail to cross the wide expanse of sea,
36. The depth of which the IGIGI know not.
37. *Shammash*, your glare reaches down to the abyss
38. So that monsters of the deep behold your light . . .
45. Among all the IGIGI there is none who toils but you,
46. None who is supreme like you in the whole pantheon of gods.
47. At your rising the gods of the land assemble,
48. Your fierce glare covers the land.
49. Of all the lands of varied speech,
50. You know their plans, you scan their way.
51. The whole of mankind bows to you,
52. *Shammash*, the universe longs for your light.
88. A man who covets his neighbor's wife
89. Will . . . before his appointed day.

90. A nasty snare is prepared for him . . .
91. Your weapon will strike at him, and there will be none to save him.
92. His father will not stand for his defense,
93. And at the judge's command his brothers will not plead.
94. He will be caught in a copper trap that he did not foresee.
95. You destroy the horns of a scheming villain,
96. A zealous . . . his foundations are undermined.
97. You give the unscrupulous judge experience fetters,
98. Him who accepts a present and yet lets justice miscarry, you make bear his punishment.
99. As for him who declines a present but nevertheless takes the part of the weak,
100. It is pleasing to *Shammash*, and he will prolong his life . . .
124. The progeny of evil-doers will fail.
125. Those whose mouth says "No," their case is before you.
126. In a moment you discern what they say;
127. You hear and examine them; you determine the lawsuit of the wronged.
128. Every single person is entrusted to your hands;
129. You manage their omens; that which is perplexing you make plain.
130. You observe, *Shammash*, prayer, supplication, and benediction.
131. Obeisance, kneeling, ritual murmurs, and prostration.
132. The feeble man calls you from the hollow of his mouth,
133. The humble, the weak, the afflicted, the poor,
134. She whose son is captive constantly and unceasingly confronts you.
135. He whose family is remote, whose city is distant,
136. The shepherd amid the terror of the steppe confronts you,
137. The herdsman in warfare, the keeper of sheep among enemies.
138. *Shammash*, there confronts you the caravan, those journeying in fear,
139. The traveling merchant, the agent who is carrying capital.
140. *Shammash* there confronts you the fisherman with his net,
141. The hunter, the bowman who drives the game,
142. With his bird net the fowler confronts you.
143. The prowling thief, the enemy of *Shammash*,
144. The marauder along the tracks of the steppe confronts you.
145. The roving dead, the vagrant soul,
146. They confront you, *Shammash*, and you hear all.
147. You do not obstruct those that confront you. . .
148. For my sake, *Shammash*, do not curse them!
149. You grant revelations, *Shammash*, to the families of men,
150. Your harsh face and fierce light you give to them . . .
154. The heavens are not enough as the vessel into which you gaze,
155. The sum of the lands is inadequate as a seer's bowl . . .
159. You deliver people surrounded by mighty waves,
160. In return you receive their pure, clear libations . . .

165. They in their reverence laud the mention of you,
166. And worship your majesty for ever . . .
174. Which are the mountains not clothed with your beams?
175. Which are the regions not warmed by the brightness of your light?
176. Brightener of gloom, Illuminator of darkness,
177. Dispeller of darkness, Illuminator of the broad earth . . .

Invoking the "solar force"—whether *Shammash* or by another name—is common not only within the mysticism of Sumer and Babylon, but throughout esoteric history. The name *"Samas"* is called upon no less than a dozen times throughout the "Maqlu Ritual"—(called "Maklu" in Simon's work) a ceremonial discourse and cuneiform tablet series catalogued as Mardukite *Liber-M* and *Tablet-M*. [Refer to *"Anunnaki Rites"* or *"The Maqlu Ritual Book"* edited by Joshua Free.]

In many instances from the *Maqlu* series, *Shammash* is called alongside *Marduk* to destroy the wickedness and evil-doers in the world. Although *Shammash* later sided against *Marduk*, the name is invoked in Mardukite literature of the *"Ladder of Lights"* (or *"Stairway to the Stars"*), following the original Babylonian ideal of "unification," even if only to maintain control of the entire Anunnaki pantheon under *Marduk*—just as we see with the inclusion of many other Anunnaki names in the Babylonian paradigm. The "Law-Code" attributed to *King Hammurabi*, is dedicated to a "divine" knowledge transmission from both *Shammash* and *Marduk*:—

By the command of Samas
The Judge of Heaven and Earth,
May truth and righteousness reign supreme
Throughout the lands.
Let those who read these words have a pure heart
And pray to Marduk, my Lord,
And Sarpanit, my Lady, his consort.
By the decree of Samas,
I have been given my Eternal Legacy.
If a forthcoming ruler should read my words
And not corrupt the law,
Then may Samas extend the length of his reign on Earth,
And he shall ever reign in righteousness over his subjects.

Mystical incantations for the *"Shammash Gate"* are strongly influenced by the previously given hymn. No prayer dedicated exclusively to *Shammash* (or the "sun-god") was found in the *Kuyunjik* collection. Instead, like the *Maqlu* series, the Babylonian invocations of that series are directed to both *Samas* and *Marduk*. One interesting example, however, is an incantation from *"Prayers of the Lifting of the Hand – Tablet 53,"* to be used "against the evils attending an eclipse of the moon." It is directed to EA (*Enki*), *Shammash* and *Marduk*. Leonard King offers the following description of the eclipse tablet:—

"No. 53 (*K 3859* + *Sm. 383*) preserves the bottom portion of a tablet and contains a prayer to *Ia*, *Samas*, and *Marduk*, of which both the beginning and end are missing. The supplicant states that he is praying after an eclipse of the Moon and he implores these three deities to rescue him from the clutches of a spectre, by whom he is continually haunted. What remains of the *Obverse* commences as follows:—

O arbiter of the world, *Marduk*, the mighty, the lord of Itura!
   abkal kis-sa-ti ilu-Marduk sal-ba-[bu bil] I.TURRA

O EA, *Samas*, and *Marduk* deliver me,
   ilu-I-a ilu-Samas u ilu-Marduk ya-a-si ru-sa-nim-ma

And through your mercy let me come to prosperity!
   ina an-ni-ku-nu i-sa-ru-tu lul-lik

O *Samas*, the spectre that striketh fear, that for many days
   ilu-Samas ikimmu mu-pal-li-hi sa is-tu u-mi ma-'-du-ti

Has been bound on my back, and is not loosed,
   arki-ya rak-su-ma la muppatiru(ru)

Through the whole hath . . . me, through the whole night hath stricken me with terror!
   ina kal u-mi iksus-an-ni ina kal musi up-ta-na-lah-an-ni

The supplicant then describes the ways in which he is tormented by the spectre, who defiles him and attacks his face, his eyes, his back, his flesh and his whole body. On the reverse of the tablet he recounts to *Samas* how he has tried to appease and to restrain his tormentor. Apparently his efforts have met with no success for he now turns to the *Sun-god* for relief, which he prays he may receive through his mighty command that is not altered, and through the command of *Marduk*, the arbiter of the gods."

— 5 —
NERGAL & ERESHKIGAL :
"MARS" AND "THE SHADOWLANDS"

The legendary "*Underdark*" or "*Realm of the dead*" has been all too colorfully—or perhaps mono-chromatically—depicted by mythographers as merely a pile a rotting bodies, an infinite swamp, or with the arrival of dualism –a hellfire of intolerable damnation. Cuneiform tablet descriptions of the "*Shadowlands*"—or the "Great Below"—are indeed conceivably "darker" in the spectrum of mortal comprehension.

Traversing the Celestial Spheres on the "*Ladder of Lights,*" we are confronted with a "Dweller of the Threshold" to our "Dark Night of the Soul"—and ultimately a spiritual rebirth—rising as a phoenix; as a "*god*," readied for access to the (next) "*Marduk Gate.*" Figures of the "*Underworld zonei*" play important functions and roles affecting human consciousness regarding death, entropy and physical cycles observed in the cosmos. Any "good" or "bad" is based strictly on human sentiment. The "*Kingdom of Shadows*"—access to its true knowledge and mystical interpretation of these energetic currents—has been shrouded in occult mystery for a very long time, and perhaps for good reason.

Where *Inanna-Ishtar* is "*goddess of love and war*" for the "upper realm," "realm of light (stars)," and "world of life," her *sister—Ereshkigal*—is so for the "lower realm," equated with the "*Underworld*" or "*Land of the Dead.*" She shares this domain with *Nergal*—the "death-god" or "plague-god"—archetypal "war-god" representing the *Martian* energy current. The word "KI.GAL" (as in "*Eresh-Ki-Gal*") is usually translated by scholars in academia as "*Great Below.*" This is a curious ascription when nearly all other cuneiform applications of the word "KI" (for "*Ki-Gal*") suggest a literal meaning: "Great Earth" or "Great Lands." The position-role and accepted lineage of Ereshkigal remains stable across most contemporary interpretations, but such is not the case with Nergal.

Nergal—the "*Great Watcher*"—(NER = "Watcher," GAL = "*Great*") is something of an enigma on tablet sources. Early twentieth century scholars could not ascertain his parentage definitively. More importantly, the designation given to him of "eight" is not harmonious with the Base-60 system of Mesopotamian mathematics—where other Anunnaki designations are divisible by "60"—nor is *Ninib-Adad*, the Babylonian "storm-god" (also within this pantheon) who bares the number "four." This may be appropriate as the two deities are connected in the *Erra Epos* tablet cycle. However, the fact remains that: given the Sumerian ambiguity left to us from the available cuneiform sources, at best we can assume his father (or grandfather) is either *Enlil* or *Enki*. We only know for certain that *Nergal* is not directly the offspring of *Anu*. If he were, he would be listed higher in the pantheon. But, *Nergal* is too young for this rank-ing anyways.

Based on known Anunnaki marriage customs, it would be appropriate if *Nergal* were actually the love-child of *Enlil* and *Ninlil,* as Samuel Kramer describes:

> *"Enlil,* (still) impersonating 'the man of the gate,' cohabits with her [*Ninlil*] and impregnates her. As a result *Ninlil* conceives *Mes-lam-taea,* more commonly known as *Nergal."*

In contrast, the late controversial Sumeriologist, Zecharia Sitchin, suggests *Enki* as *Nergal's* father in his genealogical accounts. This might be more plaus-ible, making *Nergal* and *Ereshkigal* "half-siblings," in a similar manner found between *Marduk* and *Ishtar.* In this way, their union—an embodiment of "di-vine couple-hood,"—would have been "blessed" by the Anunnaki Assembly of "gods," much as a union of *Marduk* and *Ishtar* would have been. It is some-times confusing because by standards of the "younger pantheon" and Mardukite tradition, *Enki* is practically everyone's *"Father"*—the one they all go to regardless of their parenting lineage.

Enki plays a very fatherly for *Ereshkigal* during one of the earliest Sumerian tablet cycles, describing primordial creation—when she is carried off to *Kutha* or the *"Underworld"* by the serpent-monster, KUR. Of all the *"Elder Gods,"* it is *Enki* that goes after her—though she is later made *"Queen of the Underworld"* and allowed to remain there. By this account, *Enki* is the first of very few who ever "descend" to the realm of the "dead" and able to return permanently [*"resurrected"*] from that state— the others being primarily *Ishtar* and *Marduk* —in recorded epics.

Modern traditions observe *Ereshkigal* as an archetypal *"Dragon Queen of the Netherworld,"* ruling with her dark king, *Nergal.* [Their courtship is described on the Mardukite *Tablet-U* series.] In some interpretations, she replaces the KUR-current (position) for Babylonian mythography; and she is given domain over seven Egyptian-Osirian *"death-gates,"* fluently described in both Egyptian sources and the *Inanna-Ishtar* tablet cycle of *"Descent to the Underworld."* She is given a role of high esteem by the "seven" Anunnaki Judges, encountering every dead spirit to pass through the gates. Egyptologist, E.A. Budge, weighs in, explaining:—

> "After the spirit had appeared before *Ereshkigal,* it seems that the *Anun-naki* sat in judgment upon it, and with *Mammitu,* the goddess of the destinies of men, proceeded to discuss the good and evil deeds that it had done in the body."

There are some colorful accounts that demonstrate that Nergal also moves back and forth across the "*Underworld Gates*" acting as an "*angel of death*"—the *Ares/Mars* "god of destruction" in the pantheon. It should be understood that in mythology, the energy current represents radioactive decay and entropic destruction and not a spiritual idea of "death."

The two "*Shadowland*" rulers have quite the collaborative enterprise with one half acting as a "Great Destroyer" and the other half burying the dead. Though not a Christian-like Hell or sickening Hades, the Shadowlands represent the Anunnaki "death-machine" that seals the entire circuitry of humanity.

> The lore reveals the Anunnaki as *Guardians* and *Gatekeepers* of both "Life" and "Death" for humans in this "Earthly" physical existence.

Nergal is also known as ENGIDUDU ("*Lord who prowls by night*")—commander of the "*Sebittu*," the famous *Seven Demons* of the Anunnaki—used for dealing out plagues and pestilence. This is hardly portrayed as "evil"; originally presented as a means for gods to maintain "balance" on Earth.

"Left-hand" traditions emphasize the *Sebittu* and *Nergal* unnecessarily. Another Semitic "Angel of Death"—*Azazel*—comes from a "realm of light" —like *Shammash*, *Nergal's* counterpart on the *Erra Epos* tablet cycle describing politics and destruction of the ancient "Middle East."

As a "war god," *Nergal* is invoked pre-combat for military blessings. The Babylonian example which follows is derived from the German anthology titled "*Ritualtafeln*," transcribed by R. Campbell Thomson in his "*Semitic Magic*":—

> *Ritual: when an enemy [attacks] the king and his land . . .*
> *The king shall go forth on the right wing of the army,*
> *And thou shalt sweep the earth clean, and sprinkle pure water,*
> *And set [three] altars, one for Ishtar, one for Shammash,*
> *And one for Nergal,*
> *And offer each a loaf of wheaten meal (flour),*
> *And make a mash of honey and butter,*
> *Pouring in dates and . . .-meal,*
> *And sacrifice three full-grown sheep,*
> *Flesh of the right thigh, hinsa-flesh and sume-flesh thou shalt offer,*
> *Sprinkle upuntu with cypress on a censer,*
> *And make a libation of honey, butter, wine, oil and scented oil,*
> *Then shalt thou make an image of the foe in tallow,*
> *Bend backwards his face with a cord;*
> *The . . . of the king, who is named like his master,*
> *Shall . . . the robes of the king . . .*
> *Shall stand before the preparation and repeat this formula before Shammash. . .*

Nergal was never "officially" known as *Erra* in Sumer. The *Erra Epos* tablet cycle (known as *"Erra and Isum,"* given as Mardukite *Tablet-V* series in *"The Complete Anunnaki Bible"*) is of Akkadian origin. The epithet *"Erra"* is a somewhat derogatory name for *Nergal*—a corruption of the names he did possess: *Irrigal* or *Erakal*—with *"Erra"* now meaning a "Servant of Ra" (*Marduk*), which he clearly was not. Contemporary translators attribute authorship of this epic to the pen of *Kabti-Ilani-Marduk*—a scribe-priest or priest-king related to a 12th Century B.C. "Babylonian Reformation" led by *Marduk-Kabit-Aheshu* according to cuneiform King-Lists.

The account follows:—*Marduk* gives a warning prophecy about the devastation that will ultimately result if he were to step down from his seat at Babylon. This prediction is nothing short of "apocalyptic," describing the ruin of Babylon and all of the great Mesopotamian cities. *Nergal* goes to Babylon and explains to *Marduk* that his "self-made" supremacy has angered the other (Anunnaki) gods, and that *Marduk* is in possession of something (a mysterious object never clearly defined) that not only "powers" or "empowers" Babylon, but all of the other Mesopotamian cities of the gods as well. When *Marduk* cannot be convinced to leave "his seat" in Babylon, *Nergal* attempts a different tactic by describing various other "holy artifacts" that would ensure his righteous rule. These objects happen to all be in the "*Shadowlands*" and would require retrieval by *Marduk* personally. *Nergal* promises to "watch over" Babylon while *Marduk* is gone and promises very distinctly that nothing will "change" during his absence.

The tablets are obscure about the actual nature of the "holy artifacts" *Marduk* goes in search for, or the "object of power" propelling Babylon (kept in a secret room called the *gigunu* that adjoined Marduk's throne chamber at the top of his ziggurat-temple). But we know that the "object of power" was disturbed by *Nergal* as soon as *Marduk* "left his seat" in pursuit of the "holy artifacts." Instantly, the "waters stopped flowing," first in Babylon, then in the remaining great cities. The power and strength of ancient Babylon had been weakened, but not yet destroyed. Its destruction came later—a planned attack resulting from mistaken blame for this tragedy, all of which was placed on *Marduk*.

When the "Supernal Trinity" called an "Anunnaki Assembly" of gods regarding the incident, all of the "younger pantheon"—*Ninurta, Nergal, Shammash, Adar* and *Ishtar*—conspired in judgment against *Marduk* and *Nabu*, placing full blame on them for the collapse of the systems. Any *unity* of the "celestial pantheon" was split forever. And with *Marduk* absent in pursuit of the "holy artifacts," *Nabu* stood alone to face the entire assembly, as translated by Zecharia Sitchin:—

Speaking for his father, *Nabu* blamed *Ninurta,* and revived old accusations against *Nergal* in regard to the disappearance of the pre-Diluvial monitoring instruments and failure to prevent sacrilege in Babylon [referring to the disturbance of the "power object"]; he got into a shouting match with *Nergal,* and showing disrespect:
Nabu to *Enlil,* evil he spoke:
"There is no justice!
Destruction was conceived!
Enlil against Babylon caused evil to be planned!"
It was an unheard of accusation against the Lord of the Command.
Enki spoke up, but it was in defense of his son, not of *Enlil.*
Asked *Enki:*
"What are Marduk and Nabu actually accused of?"
His eye was directed especially at his son *Nergal:*
"Why do you continue the opposition?"

After the council assembly agrees that *Marduk* should be removed from power in Babylon, *Nergal* and *Ninurta* decide to wage an entire nuclear war against Babylon and the "*Tribes of Nabu.*" Many lamentation tablets were behind from the wake of this. More devastating than the descriptions of fiery blasts themselves were the accounts of "evil winds" turning entire cities into ghosttowns. Traditions of *Marduk* and *Nabu* were moved underground and to Egypt where *Marduk* already had established a new civilization of followers, presenting himself as "*Amon-Ra*"—"*The Unseen God.*" Devastation in the "Middle East" left its inhabitants and all surrounding-area tribes hostile toward one another—persisting to the present day, a war that has been waging on pointlessly for thousands of years.

It is easy, then, to understand how *Nergal* became the prototype of the *Mars-Ares* personage. As the word "*Erra*" evolved, it later came to denote *Nergal* as the "Annihilator," a role previously given in Sumerian literature to GI.BIL—GIRRA or "*fires of god.*" *Nergal* and *Shammash* frequently employ these "*fires of god*" to carry out judgments decreed by the Anunnaki Assembly. Nergal is even described in the *Gilgamesh* cycle as "the ambusher who spares no one." The challenge of the "*Mars Gate*" regarding initiation on Mystical Path is thus the temperance of anger, pride, &tc.—overcoming *all Fear*—destructive energies that will manifest within the initiate uncontrollably chaotic if allowed to pass through the (next) "*Marduk Gate.*"

Modern mystical and astral experiences with "*Underworld*" currents reveal these "*Shadowland*" beings as often pale or with blue-hued skin and dark or white hair (sometimes long or unkempt). The absence of clothing also seems prominent in the Underworld, particularly among females. This is best depicted in mental imagery conjured of two "naked goddesses"—*Ereshkigal* and *Ishtar*—famously confronting one another in physical rivalry, sprawling across the floors of the "*Underworld*" palace (as described in the "Descent" tablet cycle).

The invocation of the "*Nergal Gate*" used by modern Mardukites—given within the Mardukite *Tablet-B* series of "*The Complete Anunnaki Bible*"—is strongly influenced by the twenty-seventh tablet in the "*Prayers of the Lifting of the Hand*" series from the *Kuyunjik* collection. According to translator, L. W. King, the tablet was originally in possession of *King Ashurbanipal*, so the original inscription bore his name as the benefactor of the prayer's blessings. In this instance, the prayer actually invokes *Nergal* as the "first-born of *Nunamnir*," who is *Enlil*. The prayer is as follows:

I mighty lord, hero, first-born of *Nunamnir*!
  siptu bi-lum gas-ru ti-iz-ka-[ru bu-kur ilu-NU.NAM.NIR]

Prince of the Anunnaki, lord of the battle!
  a-sa-rid ilu-A-nun-na-[ki bil tam-ha-ri]

Offspring of Kutusar, the mighty queen!
  i-lit-ti ilu-KU.TU.SAR [sar-ra-tum rabitum(tum)]

O *Nirgal*, strong one of the gods, the darling of Ninminna!
  ilu-Nirgal kas-kas ilani [na-ram ilu-NIN.MIN.NA]

Thou treadest in the bright heavens, lofty is thy place!
  su-pa-ta ina sami-i illuti [sa-ku man-za-az-ka]

Thou art exalted in the Underworld and art the benefactor of its . . .
  ra-ba-ta ina aralli-[ma asira(ra) LA.TI-su]

With EA among the multitudes of the gods inscribe thy counsel,
  it-ti ilu-I.A. ina puhur [ilani mi-lik-ka su-tur]

With SIN [*Nanna*] in the heavens, you seek all things,
  it-ti ilu-SIN ina sami-i [ta-si gim-ri]

And BIL [*Bel*], thy father has granted thee that the dark-headed race, all living creatures,
  id-din-ka-ma ilu-BIL abu-[ka sal-mat kakkadu puhur napisti(ti)]

The cattle of *Nirgal*, created things, thy hand should rule!
  bu-ul ilu-NIRGAL nam-mas-[si-i ka-tuk-ka ip-kid]

I, so and so, the son of so and so, am thy servant!
  ana-ku pulanu apil pulani [arad-ka]

The . . . of god and goddess are laid upon me!
  mi-lat ili u ilu-istari [is-sak-nu-nim-ma]

Uprooting and destruction are my house!
nasahu u hu-lu-uk-ku-[u basu-u ina biti-ya]

[. . .] (untranslated)
ka-bu-u IA si-mu-[u it-tal-pu-nin-ni]

Since thou are beneficent, I have turned to thy divinity!
as-sum gam-ma-la-ta bi-li [as-sa-har ilu-ut-ka]

Since thou are compassionate, I have sought for thee!
as-sum ta-ai-ra-ta [is-ti-'-u-ka]

Since thou are empathic, I have beheld . . .
as-sum mu-up-pal-sa-ta [a-ra-mar . . .]

Since thou are merciful, I have taken my stand before thee!
as-sum ri-mi-ni-ta [at-ta-ziz pani-ka]

Truly pity me and hearken to my cries!
ki-nis naplis-an-ni-ma [si-mi ka-ba-ai]

May thine angry heart have rest!
ag-gu lib-ba-ka [li-nu-ha]

Loosen my sin, my offense . . .
[pu]-tur an-ni hi-[ti-ti . . .]

[. . .] (untranslated / broken)
. . . -sir lib-bi ilu-ti-ka . . .

I god and angry goddess . . .
ilu u ilu-istaru zi-nu-ti sab- . . .

Let me talk of thy greatness, Let me bow in humility before thee!
nir-bi-ka lu-uk-bi [da-li-li-ka lud-lul]

MARDUK : "KING OF THE GODS"

Ancient Mesopotamia witnessed a rise of the "younger pantheon," which took great interest in the activities and devotion of humans on earth. Of them, perhaps the most famous for "planetary mythology" is *Marduk—Jupiter* —the national god of Babylon. Much like his half-sister—*Inanna-Ishtar*—a self-made "queen of the heavens," Marduk exploited his own personal conviction, cunning and tenacity to secure his position as the primary controller of the *"Ladder of Lights"*—the BAB.ILI, "Gates of the Gods"—even exceeding the position of his father—*Enki*—by assuming the role and functions of *Enlil*—the *Anu* of "Material Existence"—to his followers.

Little mention of *Marduk* is actually made in earlier pre-Babylonian Sumerian cuneiform literature (under any name or epithet). He was content, for a time, to remain an assistant to *Enki*, mastering the esoteric arts of "magic" and "science" in *Eridu*. *Marduk* was originally given the numeric designation of "10" and told to "wait his turn"—at the *"Age of Aries"*—to rise in the pantheon. His most familiar name—MARDUK—is actually an evolved transliteration derived from the Semitic *"meri-dug"* (*Merodach*). An older version of his name is written: AMAR.UTU (*a.mar-utu.ki* = "Light of the Sun on Earth")—often interpreted by contemporary scholars as *"solar calf"* or *"son of the sun."* This provides some background to *Marduk's* esteem. And as the foremost son of *Enki*, he gained power quickly.

The later Semitic name *"Maerdechai"* or *"Mordechai"* came from the name of *Marduk* in Chaldeo-Babylonian language—*"silik-mul.u-khi"*—meaning *"Marduk is God."* The more commonly used MAR.DUG means *"son of the pure mound"*— thought to be a reference to pyramids not only in Mesopotamia, but also in Egypt, where he raised himself as the leader of a third party (interpretation) of Anunnaki gods—the Egyptian Pantheon—as *"Amon-Ra,"* again identifying himself with the "solar" current and "stars" directly.

Marduk's decision to raise himself to a monotheistic-like *"God"* status in Babylon created new political issues for the other Anunnaki on Earth. Exercising his "divine rights" stretched tensions between lineages—of *Enki* and *Enlil*—for supremacy on earth. When *Marduk* and *Ishtar* did not partner for this role, each sought the right to install their own dynastic lineages and choose the humans as "Kings" in their stead, during the "Age of Aries," beginning in 2160 B.C.—the birth of a New Dynastic global era. Zecharia Sitchin explains how in Babylon:—

> *"Marduk* was proclaimed King of the Gods, replacing *Enlil*, and the other gods were required to pledge allegiance to him and to come to reside in

Babylon where their activities could be easily supervised. This usurpation of Enlilship was accompanied by an extensive Babylonian effort to forge the ancient texts. The most important texts were rewritten and altered so as to make *Marduk* appear as the Lord of the Heavens, the Creator. . ."

Certainly, the other Anunnaki were less than appreciative of *Marduk's* desire to rule over them. Yet throughout the *"Age of Aries,"*—his time to reign—he was not left to his own accord in Babylon (or in Egypt). This seems to have been a disciplinarian act by the other gods.

If we take the most literal interpretations at face value, *Marduk* lost all rights of kingship "in heaven" when he took a "human" wife instead of his betrothed half-sister. His argument was that his consort—*Sarpanit*—was a descendent of *Adapa*, and thus of Anunnaki bloodline via *Enki*; that *Ishtar* was no more interested in the union than he was, and it had not affected her rise to power; and finally, if not "in heaven," why not "on earth"? The logic seems to have gone unheard and where the "Mardukite" legacy was threatened in Babylon and Egypt, as its survival was frequently aided by "foreign hands."

In post-Sumerian Assyrian accounts, *Marduk*—as the great "father-god" AS-SUR or ASHUR ("*Ashshur*")—seems to emerge in their tradition as if from nowhere. This led some scholars in the late-1800's and early-1900's to wonder if *Marduk* was a purely fictitious figure imagined into being for solely political reasons. Similarly, while *Sarpanit*—also *Sarapan* or *Zarpanitu*—is mentioned often in Babylonian prayer-tablets, she does not appear in any significant mythic tablet (saga) cycles. Her elevated status is rightly achieved due to her direct relationship with *Marduk*, and together, they are the parents of *Nabu*.

At the spring equinox "A.KI.TI" festival, *Sarpanit* is the "spring-maiden" of fertility ceremonies in Babylon. In the "*Edaphic Tradition*" that spread across Europe, she is known as "*Erua*," or more appropriately, ERU. Later European "elven-faerie-dragon" dynasties (explored elsewhere in *Liber-D, "The Complete Elvenomcon"* by Joshua Free) claimed descent from *Marduk* and *Sarpanit*, their "star-goddess mother of vegetation and fertility." And sure enough "*Eru*" is an Akkadian word for "pregnancy."

For nearly two millennium, *Marduk* and *Sarpanit* are national patrons of all priest-magicians and priestesses of Babylonia. In fact, by literal title, "Babylon" became the "*seat of the gods,*" but by Mardukite standards, this was to be realized differently than either *monotheism* or *polytheism*. The system of myth and magic born in Babylon was first and foremost dedicated to *Marduk's* "*Divine World Order,*" often illustrated through the first mystical "*kabbalah*"

system: *10 gates, 2 doors* and *7 levels*—just like the design for the Mardukite *zig-gurat* "E.TEMEN. AN.KI"—"*The Temple of Heaven and Earth.*"

An excellent incantation-tablet example invokes *Marduk* and *Sarpanit* after an experience of "evil from an eclipse," as first excavated by the French and transliterated in Vincent Scheil's "*Une Saison de Fouilles a Sippar,*" later translated by Thomson, who explains to us in "*Semitic Magic*" that the prayer was given to *King Assurbanipal* by his brother, *Samas-sumukin.* Both scholarly sources were used to reconstruct the full prayer in tact with both *English* and *French* translations of the original *Cuneifom* transliteration:—

... O great lady, kindly mother,
   FR. ôo grande déesse, mère miséricordieuse
      C. *beltu sa-qu-ti ummu rim-ni-ti*

Amid the many stars of heaven,
   FR. parmi les nomlbreuses étoiles clu ciel
      C. *ina ma'-du-ti kakkabe sa-ma-mi*

Thou art mistress ...
   FR. vous êtes reine ...
      C. *beltu ka-a-si ...*

I, *Samas-sum-ukin*, the king, servant of his god
   FR. moi *Samas* sum ukîn roi, serviteur de son dieu
      C. *ana-ku Samas sum ukin sarru, GAL ili-su*

Vicegerent of his god *Marduk* and his goddess *Sarpanit*
   FR. vicaire de son dieu *Marduk* et de sa déesse *Zarpanitum,*
      C. *sakin ili-su (ilu)-Marduk (ilu)-Istarti-su (ilu)-Zar-pa-ni-tum*

Of the evils of the eclipse of the moon, Fixed for the fifteenth day of Shebat
   FR. des maux de l'éclipse de lune fixée au 15 du mois d'AB
      C. *ana lumun AN-MI (ilu)-Sin sa ina arhi AS um 15 (kam) sak-nu*

Of the evils of the signs and omens, evil, baneful,
   FR. des maux de signes et visions funestes, malfaisantes
      C. *ana lumun idati SI-BIT-mes limnuti la tabuti*

Which have occurred in my palace and my land
   FR. qui arriveraient dans mon palais et mon pays,
      C. *sa ina e-kal-ya (MU) u mati-ya ibba-su*

I am afraid, and I fear, and I tremble
   FR. j'ai peur, je tremble, je frémis
      C. *pal-ha-ku-ma ad-ra-ku u su-ta-du-ra-ku*

Let not these evils draw near to me or my house
   FR. ces maux, de moi et de ma maison
      C. *lumnu suatu ya-a-si u biti-ya*

[. . .] "Let them not approach [come near]"
  FR. qu'ils n'approchent pas
    C. *a-a TE*

Accept the *upuntu*-plant from me and receive my prayer.
  FR. agrée l'tpuntu, agrée ma prière
    C. *upuntu muh-ri-in-ni-ma li-ki-e un-ni-ni*

What becomes apparent when researching Mardukite-specific materials: Marduk is the original "rebel-god," rising to supremacy and places himself in the highest positions—"Primordial Dragonslayer" and "Creator of the Universe"—*Jupiter*—the great force that maintains the orderly zones of the "solar system." His domain evolves to include all sciences and magics—the true understanding of the hidden patterns and secret doctrines of the cosmos. It is here that all magical traditions were born—later fragmented into systems practiced throughout human history, and all based in symbols and signs, names and numbers, prayers and incantations. These are the esoteric or "Hermetic" arts first known to *Enki*, then *Marduk*, and finally *Nabu*. The challenge of the "*Marduk Gate*" is then to actually apply the esoteric formulas of "Cosmic Law" to direct and channel the powers of the Universe toward causal manifestations in creation and personal ascension—otherwise true "*magic*." Editor Simon relays in his handbook:—

> "Where *Nergal* represents Will—pure Will, unassuaged by purpose—and *Inanna*, desire; *Marduk* is the Law. This Law is no so much the Law of courts and decrees, but the Law of science, the lineaments of the created universe. Through the first five Gates we have become initiated into the use and sense of various Forces; in the *Sixth Gate* we become masters at manipulating all of them, at mixing them to produce various effects."

Mardukite "initiates" actually invoke this current in numerous ways. However, in maintaining consistency with our current volume, it is the incantation-prayer tablets we are most interested, and there are many. Several "prayers" to *Marduk* may be found in throughout this "complete anthology." Traditional "Gate Invocations" generally follow the formula demonstrated in the key examples from the *Kuyunjik* collection that the current editor has chosen to adapt for this series.

The "*Isagila*" mentioned in its text is a reference to *Marduk's* primary ziggurat-temple in Babylon, also transliterated: E.SAG.ILU or *Esaggadhu*.

  Siptu gaasru supuuu iziz Assur
    Almighty, powerful and strong one of *Assur*.

Rubu tiizkaru bukur NU.DIM.MUD
  Exalted, noble-blood, firstborn of *Enki*.

Marduk salbabu muris I.TUR.RA
  Almighty *Marduk*, who causes the *Itura* to rejoice.

Bil I.SAG.ILA tukultiti Babiliki raim I.ZID.DA
  Lord of the *Isagila*, Aid to Babylon, Lover of the *Izida (E.ZIDA)*

Musalim napistiti asarid I.MAH.TIL.LA mudussuubalatu
  Preserver of Life, Prince of *Imahtilla*, Renewer of Life.

Zulul maati gamil nisi rapsaati
  Shadow over the Land, Protector of foreign lands.

Usumugal kalis parakkani
  Forever is [*Marduk*] the Sovereign of Shrines.

Sumuka kalis ina pi nisi taaab
  Forever is [*Marduk*] the name in the mouth of the people.

Marduk bilu rabuu ina kibitka kabitti luublut
  Almighty *Lord Marduk* at your command I remain alive.

Ina kibitika sirti luublut luuslimma
  At your command let me live, let me be perfect, let me behold
    your Divinity.

Luustammar iluutka
  What I will to be, let me obtain my wishes.

Ima usaammaru luuksuud
  [*Marduk*], cause righteousness to come from my mouth.

Supsika damiktimtim inalibbiya
  [*Marduk*], cause mercy to dwell in my heart.

Tiru u naanzazu likbuu damiktimtim
  Return to Earth, establish yourselves and command mercy.

Iliya liizziz ina imniya
  May my god stand at my right hand.

Istariya liizziz ina sumiliya
  May my goddess stand at my left hand.

Iliya sallimu ina idiya luukaaian
  May my god who is favorable to the stars, stand firmly at my side.

Surgamma kabaa simaa u magara
  To speak the Word of Command, to hear my prayer and show favor.

Amat akabbuu ima akabbuu luu maagrat
   When I speak, let the words by powerful.

Marduk bilu rabuu napistimtim kibi
   Almighty *Lord Marduk*, come and command life.

Balat napistiya kibi
   As you command my Life

Maharka namris adalluka luusbi
   Before you I bow, let me be satisfied

Bil urrula Ia litiska
   Bel's Fires go with you, *Ia [Enki]* smile upon you

Ilani sa kissati likrubuka
   May the Earth Gods be favorable to thee and me

Ilani rabuti libbaka litibu
   May the Good Gods delight in your mercy.

This incantation tablet continues on its reverse with part of a prayer addressing Sarpanit as the:

Queen of *Isagila*, the palace of the gods, the... mountain
   sar-rat I.SAG.ILA ikal ilani sa-du-u- . . .

Lady of Babylon, the Shadow of lands!
   Bi-lit Babili-ki su-lul ma-ta-a-ti

Lady of the gods, who loves to give life,
   ilu-Bilit ili sa bul-lu-ta i-ram-mu

Who gives succor in sorrow and distress,
   it-ti-rat ina puski u dannati

The . . . one, who holds the hand of . . .
   . . . -ma-li-tu sa-bi-ta kata-du na-as-ki

Who supports the weak, who pours out seed,
   i-pi-rat in-si sa-pi-kat ziru

Who protects life, who gives offspring and seed,
   na-si-rat napisti(ti) nadnat(at) aplu u ziru

Who bestows life, who takes away sighing, who accepts prayer,
   ka-i-sat balatu li-kat un-ni-ni ma-hi-rat tas-lit

Who has made the people, the whole of creation!
   ba-na-at nisi gi-mir nab-ni-ta

— 7 —
NINIB-NINURTA :
"WHO COMPLETES THE FOUNDATION"

Drawing from more readily available 19th Century "Assyriological" research, Simon's "*Necronomicon*" from the 1970's describes the Guardian of the "*Seventh Gate*" as the "youngest son" of *Enlil*. The name given is *Adar*, coupled with a footnote that the force is sometimes called *Ninib*. The remaining description is actually of a "storm-god" (not *Saturn*) and immediately the name *Adad* comes to mind—the "storm god" and "youngest son" of *Enlil* according to Sumerian tradition. So... Perhaps the author has made a mistake—some kind of typo. And what a critical point to have such obscurity: when we are on the brink of the final gate before reaching communion with the IGIGI—the "*Outer Ones.*" Even many of the original Mardukite researchers misappropriated this energy current to *Adad-Ishkur* or *Ramman*—the "wind-storm deity." This has been officially corrected in our archives.

As it turns out, ambiguity of ancient "Mardukite" records was not an oversight. The personage of *Ninib-Adar* is intentionally minimized for the Babylonian system. Confusing the "youngest son" of *Enlil* with his "oldest son"—born to half-sister *Ninhursag* or *Ninmah*—kept political attention away from any claims to "Enlilite" supremacy in Babylon. In Babylon, *Marduk* was unquestionably supreme—any access to a further "*Seventh Gate*" would require *his* direct assistance. In *short—Adar* is not a typo of *Adad*, but is in fact the *Assyrian* (and in some cases, *Akkadian*) name derived from *Nindar* or *Ninurta*—Anunnaki heir of *Enlil* and representation of *Saturn* in Sumerian tradition.

Superseding all previous esoteric regards, it is *Ninurta* who is selected by the Sumerian Anunnaki to give watch of the "*Saturn Gate.*" Clearly this provided inspiration for *Marduk* to assume the "*Fifty Names*"—all the "Keys to the Kingdom"—under his name. Modern occult "self-initiates" of the earlier "Simon" work are aware that passing the "*Marduk Gate*" allows a magician-priest of the "Mardukite" tradition access to the *Fifty Names*—meaning direct access to the "*Arts of Civilization*" and "*Secret Formulas of the Cosmos*" [See "*The Tablets of Destiny Revelation*" by Joshua Free.] Most "New Age" Seekers are concerned with little else. For most who are diligent enough to seriously work through the gate-system, their work "Self-Honestly" ends here. Those who may have thought they had completed some type of "Ascension" journey through "*Star-Gates of the Anunnaki*" or "*Traversing the Seven Spheres*" using virtually all previously available lore, now discover they did not. Naturally, very few modern practitioners have achieved "True Enlightenment" and useful "cognitions" via a Mesopotamian revival of any kind when using materials other than what is available exclusively from the *Mardukite Research Organization*.

Without the "Mardukite" foundation, other revivals become fanciful and imaginative reenactments that elevate consciousness to the same extent as any cultural-motif "New Age" creative visualization exercise. *Marduk* makes *himself* the "final gate" of the material systems without actually being so. And those who *do* pass on from the "*Marduk Gate*" do not always even reach Ninurta—*Saturn*—withholding, in part, a complete spiritual progression all due to a political "cover-up" in Babylon, concealing any knowledge of *Ninurta* as the Sumerian heir to *Enlilship* of the local system.

To understand the ambiguity, one must realize that *Ninurta* does not even originally appear in the Sumerian "Olympian" *Pantheon of Twelve* and it seems his position among the "younger pantheon" on the "*Ladder of Lights*" is jumbled for later "Mardukite" followers. We must assume this was to prevent Sumerian succession from in any way "stealing the spotlight" from the position of *Marduk*. Regarding the original Sumerian status of *Ninurta* and his absence from the pantheon, Zecharia Sitchin explains:—

> "*Ninurta* was assigned the number 50, like his father. In other words, his dynastic rank was conveyed in a cryptographic message: If *Enlil* goes, you, *Ninurta*, step into his shoes; but until then, you are not one of the twelve, for the rank of '50' is occupied."

Among various excavated Sumerian tablet-cycles of KUR, the hero (or heroine) is attributed to one of three different characters—*Enki, Inanna* and *Ninurta*—each encountering the force differently. The epic concerning *Ninurta* is possibly the oldest most accurate epic from before Babylon, showing striking resemblances to later Babylonian revisions (of the "*Enuma Elis*") detailing *Marduk* as the serpent-slayer next in line for "*Enlilship*." Loss of these details unfortunately led a broken spiritual system wrapped in Anunnaki politics. This is resolved in consciousness with a self-honest unification of the pantheon with "new" modern Mardukite standards of viewing the "younger generation" of Anunnaki gods. Doing this repairs a broken religio-magical system (or "spiritual paradigm"), now accessible to modern practitioners, scholars and esotericists for the very first time, *ever*—in a clarity not even known in the ancient world.

◊ ◊ ◊ ◊ ◊ ◊ ◊

Ninurta is a hunter, but as a son of *Enlil* we should not be surprised to find him described also as a "plough-man" or "farmer god." Many from the Enlilite lineage are connected to agriculture and "farming," much as the lineage of *Enki* carries affinity for animals and "shepherding." In later Semtic lore, *Ninurta* appears as *Nimrod* (although this character is sometimes confused with *Nabu*), sharing the same role as in older appearances from Mesopotamian literature—assisting in the reformation of civilization after the *Flood*.

Politics enter the arena only when matters turn towards Babylon—*Ninurta* is actually the original organizer of Enlilite tribes against the Mardukites in Babylon. In one famous cuneiform epic, he is given the epithet *"Ishum"*— from the *"Erra Epos"* cuneiform tablet cycle (*"Erra and Ishum"*) described in a prior chapter—meaning "scorcher." He acts as an adviser to *Nergal* (*Erra*) during the violent acts to "unseat" *Marduk* from Babylon.

Both *Ninurta* and his consort—*Bau* (or *Gula*)—are actually attributed healing properties in the original Sumerian mystical tradition. As the defeater of both *"Asag"* (or KUR) and ANZU (in another epic), *Ninurta* is called upon to *"defeat"* demons and "evil spirits"—of sickness and disease. *Bau*, especially, is a patron to nurses and doctors. At first glance, these attributes seem out of character as representations of the *Saturn*-current—which reflects a confrontation of the darkest ("hidden") parts of *ourselves* in combination with the final constraints of "Cosmic Law" as it applies to the local material system. The "absolute healing" seems more appropriate when we consider that the *"Saturn Gate"* is the final threshold crossing or barrier to "Ascension"—*liberation* from the material program—and its primary gatekeeper according to the Sumerian tradition, is *Ninurta*, the Anunnaki-decreed rightful heir to *Enlil*. The very essence of a *"seven-fold"* system comes into logic focus more clearly than ever before—the *"Foundation of Heaven and Earth"* is complete and the mysteries of the ziggurat "Temple of the Seven Spheres" are laid out before the Seeker.

The *"Seventh Gate"* leads to the *"Supernal Trinity"* of Anunnaki—the *"outer limits"* of our local system—a position in which *Ninurta* is waiting for heir-ship of in the Sumerian system. This means by some standard, era or version: *Enlil*, *Ninurta* and *Marduk* all maintain the designation (position) of "50." The heart of this beats a difficult fact to accept for the bloodline of *Marduk* and all those calling *Enki*, "Father" in the *Mardukite* paradigm. All this may seem trite to the uninitiated, but it is probably the deepest darkest kept secret in ancient Babylon—thus, even there deserving of the designation of *Saturn*. Proper realization of the system is what esotericists seek as the *"Hidden Key to the Necronomicon."* It not only brings harmony to the system for a modern practitioner —divine-messengers and temple-servants of the gods—but, for the gods *themselves*.

Mysteries of the *"Seventh Gate"* represent the highest initiation accessible to priests and priestesses *on earth*. More or less "divisions" of the whole does not change the whole. Others have simply broken down perceived fragments of reality into other *quantities*—the Babylonian "Gate-system" consists of *seven*. The "Secrets of the Gates" are hidden throughout Babylon in mythic sagas and esoteric traditions of *Elder Gods* and the *younger pantheon* in Mesopotamia.

On many levels of manifestation, the "Gates" *are* functional. The *"Hidden Key"*—the paradigm represented by the whole—was essentially the *first* "government-secret" kept by priests and scribes occupying the highest positions—the final "combination sequence" to make the "Star Gate of Babylon" actually *work*.

Even as the "Seat" of *Marduk*, by Sumerian standards, the existence of Babylon and *Marduk's* "Star-Gate" was deemed "illegal" in Enlilite territory. Babylon was eventually destroyed—hence our misunderstood genetic memory of the *"Tower of Babylon"* incident. *Ninurta* held residence in several ancient Mesopotamian cities, but most scholars agree his primary ziggurat-temple was the *E.Shumedu* in Nippur.

Ninurta—as heir to *Enlil*—was a "solar deity" representing *Saturn*, but also *Sirius* in the old Sumerian astrology, as did *Marduk* later. *Sirius* is often referred to in mystical literature as the "sun behind the sun," and is considered the true and secret form of ancient "solar-worship." *Marduk* sought to represent the same "sun behind the sun" in Egypt. As one cannot see a candle flame when placed in front of the sun—the elusive celestial force of *Sirius* is shared as "Saturn of Stars," and part of a gateway or bridge beyond our system.

There is an excellent invocation to *Ninurta* elsewhere within the *Tablet-W* series, available in *"The Complete Book of Marduk"* and *"The Complete Anunnaki Bible."* Prior to these developments, the original "Invocation of the Saturn Gate" (dedicated to *Ninurta*) used by modern Mardukite Chamberlains is also found in *"The Complete Anunnaki Bible."* But another incantation example for esoteric experimentation or general research is included here, adapted from the second tablet of the "Prayers of the Lifting of the Hand" series:—

O mighty son, firstborn of *Enlil [Bel]*,
   siptu ap-lu gas-ru bu-kur ilu-Bil

Powerful, perfect offspring of ISARA,
   sur-bu-u git-ma-lu i-lit-ti I.SAR.RA

Who art clothed with terror, who art full of fury!
   sa pu-luh-tu lit-bu-su ma-lu-u har-ba-su

O *Ninurta*, whose onslaught is unopposed!
   ilu-NIN.UR.TA [sa la im]-mah-ha-ru ka-bal-su

Mighty is thy place among the great gods!
   su-bu-u man-[za-za] ina ilani rabuti

In E.KUR, the house of decisions, exalted are thee,
   ina I.KUR bit ta-[si]-la-a-ti sa-ka-a ri-sa-a-ka

And *Enlil*, thy father has granted thee
   id-din-ka-ma ilu-Bil abu-ka

The law of all the gods thy hand should hold!
  ti-rit kul-lat ilani ka-tuk-ka tam-hat

Thou judges the judgment of mankind!
  ta-dan di-in ti-ni-si-i-ti

Thou leads him that is without a leader, the man that is in need.
  tus-ti-sir la su-su-ru i-ka-a i-ku-ti

Thou holds the hand of the weak, you raise him that is not strong!
  ta-sab-bat kat [in-si] la li-'-a tu-sa-as-ka

The body of the man that to the Lower World has been brought down,
  you can restore!
  sa a-na a-ra-al-[li]-i su-ru-du pa-gar-su tutira-ra-

From him who sin possesses, the sin you can remove!
  sa ar-nu i-su-u ta-pat-tar ar-nu

Thou art quick to favor the man with whom the god is angry.
  sa ilu-su itti-su zi-nu-u tu-sal-lam ar-his

O *Ninib*, prince of the gods, a hero you are!
  ilu-NIN.IB a-sa-rid ilani ku-ra-du at-ta

I, so and so, son of, so and so, whose god is so and so, and whose goddess
  is so and so,
  ana-ku pulanu apil pulani sa ilu-su pulanu ilu-istari-su pu-lanitum(um)

Have bound for thee a cord, . . . [a cord]. . . have I offered thee;
  ar-kus-ka rik-sa ku.a.tir as-ruk-ka

I have offered thee *tarrinnu*, a pleasant odor;
  as-ruk-ka tar-[rin]-nu u-ri-su tabu

I have poured out for thee mead, a drink from corn.
  akki-ka du-us-su-bu si-kar as-na-an

With the may there stand the gods of Enlil.
  itti-ka li-iz-zi-zu ilani su-ut ilu-Bil

With thee may there stand the gods of E.KUR!
  itti-ka li-iz-zi-zu ilani su-ut I.KUR

Truly pity me and hearken to my cries!
  ki-nis nap-lis-an-ni-[ma si-mi] la-ba-ai

My sighing remove and accept my supplication!
  un-ni-ni-ya [li-ki-ma mu-hur] tas-lit

Let my cry find acceptance before thee!
  zik-ri [li-tib] ili-ka

Deal favorably with me who fear thee!
  si-lim itti ya-a-tu-u pa-lih-ka

Thy face have I beheld, let me have prosperity!
  pa-ni-ka a-ta-mar lu-si-ra ana-ku

Thou art full of pity. Truly pity me!
  [mu]-up-pal-sa-ta ki-nis nap-lis-an-ni

Take away my sin, remove my iniquity!
  an-ni pu-tur sir-ti pu-sur

Tear away my disgrace and my offenses you loosen!
  [i]-ti-ik kil-la-ti-ma hi-ti-ti ru-um-[mi]

May my god and goddess command me and may they ordain good fortune!
  [ili]-ya u ilu-istari-ya li-sa-ki-ru-in-ni-ma lik-bu-u damiktim(tim)

May I praise thy heart, I bow in humility before thee.
  [lib]-bi-ka lu-sa-pi da-li-li-ka lud-lul

MARDUKITE ZUISM :
A BRIEF INTRODUCTION

According to the most ancient historical records written at the birth of our modern civilization...

432,000 years ago, a small population of advanced beings—called the ANUN-NAKI—began developing the planet Earth for their purposes. These elite Self-Actualized spiritual beings resided on Earth in physical bodies, but found their forms inadequate for the physical labors required. Enter: the "Human Condition." Ancient "cuneiform" tablet writings from Sumerians and Babylonians of Mesopotamia are clear regarding the original creation and systematic programming of Humanity.

CUNEIFORM is the oldest known writing system used by scribes of ancient Babylon to record their wisdom and the history of humanity on clay tablets.

"Cuneiform" is named for its style of wedge-shaped script formed by a reed pen called a "stylus." Rather than an alphabet of letters, cuneiform writing is a system of "signs" representing "things" and "ideas." These may even be combined to represent even more complex "signs."

Many concepts adopted for modern "Mardukite Zuism" and its "Systemology" are derived from cuneiform tablets.

The ANUNNAKI introduced complex writing systems in order to program civilization and all parameters of Reality for the Human Condition. Legendary "Tablets of Destiny" (Divine Truth, supreme knowledge and cosmic power of the "gods") were first introduced to Humanity in the Babylonian narrative known best as the "Epic of Creation.

THE ARCANE TABLETS.

Ancient Babylonians used the *Tablets of Destiny* & *Creation Epic* to systematize all cosmic knowledge into a workable paradigm called "Mardukite Zuism"—a systemology received directly from the ANUNNAKI.

PARADIGM : all-encompassing standard or religion used to view the world and communicate reality.

SYSTEMOLOGY : applied philosophies (of *Mardukite Zuism*) combined with personal spiritual techniques and technology ("*Tech*") effectively demonstrating systematic principles of a "paradigm."

THE SYSTEMOLOGY OF LIFE, UNIVERSES & EVERYTHING.

The *Arcane Tablets* describe the division of the ALL by the LAW, outside of which is but INFINITY. The *Epic of Creation* describes these activities as "mythology." The "Standard Model of Systemology" that is applied to *Mardukite Zuism* uses the same information to demonstrate...

that <u>ALL</u> ("AN-KI") envelops both:
the <u>Spiritual Existences</u> ("AN")
and the <u>Physical Existences</u> ("KI")
divided by <u>Cosmic Law</u> and
connected by <u>Life-Awareness</u> ("ZU")
and beyond which is only the <u>Abyss</u>,
an <u>Infinity of Nothingness</u> ("ABZU")

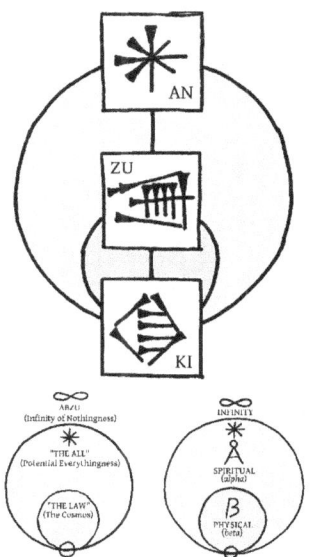

MARDUKITE ZUISM DEFINITIONS FOR
STANDARD MODEL OF SYSTEMOLOGY.

<u>ABZU</u> = the Abyss; Infinity; Infinity of Nothingness; that which extends, is exterior to and beyond of, all spiritual and physical existence.

<u>ANKI</u> : the ALL; All Existences; Everything that is AN and KI; Everything that is conceivable; represented by the "Standard Model of Systemology."

<u>AN</u> : the "Spiritual Universe" or "Heavenly Zone" comprised of spiritual energy-matter, in the direction of Infinity—the "Alpha" existence independent of, and superior to, the physical, *beta* or KI.

KI : the "Physical Universe" or "Earthly Zone" comprised of physical energy-matter in action across physical Space and observed as Time in the direction of Physical Continuity—"beta" existence condensed from, and subordinate to, the spiritual, *Alpha* or AN.

ZU : "to know"; "knowingness"; "Awareness" or "consciousness"; spiritual energy-matter of AN observed as "Lifeforce" in KI; "Spiritual Life Energy"; the actual personal spiritual beingness or "Awareness" of Self as the Alpha-Spirit which extends along a "line" from the Spiritual (AN) to the Physical (KI).

THE TABLETS OF DESTINY & BABYLONIAN CREATION EPIC.

Seven cuneiform tablets compose the ancient _Babylonian Epic of Creation_, named the _Enuma Eliš_ by scholars after its opening lines. These seven tablets are the basis for what later traditions refer to as the "*Seven Days of Creation.*" The *Epic of Creation* tablets describe development of all existences with a Divine artistic perfection. The *Enuma Eliš* is the core example of religious literature from Babylon, which served as the basis for ancient "*Mardukite Zuism*"—the first true systematized religion in history.

The Absolute *behind* and *back of* ALL Existence is referred to on the *Tablets of Destiny* as the INFINITY OF NOTHINGNESS; a constant static latent unmanifest potentiality of ALL and Everythingness.

The LAW—Cosmic Law—is defined as the Cosmic Dragon—TIAMAT—on "*Epic of Creation*" Tablets. She is the First Cause or movement across a "Sea of Infinity." Later, the LAW becomes a division between Spiritual Existence (AN) and any Physical Universe (KI). The LAW—*Tiamat*—permeating ALL, uses the *Tablets of Destiny* and then fixes the systems of finite potential:

The Systems of Manifestation—
Substance, Motion and Awareness.

"Before 'Heaven' or 'Earth' were named," a formation and interaction of active existences—"substances" and "bodies" and "Life" and "gods"—creates turbulence and waves of action through space.

The governing system of Cosmic Law—*Tiamat*—responds accordingly. She fixes the *Tablets of Destiny* to her "deputy"—a messenger wave action of the LAW named "*Kingu*" and sends him rippling out to "meet" the *Anunnaki* "gods."

The *Anunnaki Assembly* of "gods" prepare to battle The LAW. When none among them comes forth to engage, the *Anunnaki* "god" MARDUK volunteers as hero to confront *Kingu* and *Tiamat*—but with a condition that the *Anunnaki Assembly* recognize him as "Chief of the Gods" upon his success.

When *Marduk* approaches *Tiamat* (LAW) directly, he is flanked by *Kingu* and the "army of Ancient Ones." *Marduk* relinquishes the *Tablets of Destiny* from *Kingu*. With the *Tablets of Destiny*, *Marduk* successfully conquers the true understanding of "Cosmic Law" and thereby conquers *Tiamat*.

THE TABLETS OF DESTINY & SELF-HONESTY.

Marduk uses the Tablets of Destiny to discover "Self-Honesty" and Divine Knowledge governing "Cosmic Ordering"—systems dividing the "Spiritual Universe" (AN) from a "Physical Universe" (KI).

> The two Universe types are connected only by a stream of Spiritual Awareness (*Lifeforce*) that Sumerians called ZU.

Wisdom of the Arcane Tablets is later passed down to and concealed by an ancient esoteric secret society in Babylon: the Scribe-Magicians, High Priests and Priestesses of *Mardukite Zuism*.

Self-Honesty is a term describing an original "Alpha" state of clear knowingness and Self-directed beingness."Self-Honesty" is the most basic and true expression of Self as "I-AM"—free of artificial attachments; reactive-response conditioning; and imposed or enforced programming as Reality for the Human Condition.

Spiritual development in modern *Mardukite Zuism* is referred to as the "Pathway to Self-Honesty" (or "Pathway to Ascension") and the "Gateway to Infinity." It is modeled directly from the Ancient Mystery Tradition as observed at the original Temples of Babylon.

KEYS TO THE GATEWAY

"I will take my Blood—and with Bone—I will fashion a Race of Humans to keep Watch of the Gate. And from the Blood of Kingu I will create another Race of Humans to inhabit the Earth in service to the Gods—so shrines to the Anunnaki may be built and the temples filled. I will bind the Elder Gods to the Watchtowers; let them keep watch over the Gate of Abzu and the Gate of Tiamat and Gate of Kingu—and with a Key that shall be ever hidden, known to none, except only to my Mardukites."
— MARDUK, *Enuma Eliš, Creation Tablet VI.*

THE ANUNNAKI LADDER OF LIGHTS & BABYLONIAN GATEWAYS TO INFINITY.

ZIGGURAT TEMPLES in Babylonia—and throughout Mesopotamia—served to remind populations of the "bond" or ZU connecting "Heaven" and "Earth." Seven-stepped "levels" of the physical *Ziggurat Temples* of Babylonia—and seven corresponding Gates—represent spiritual levels of actualized Awareness; states of Self-purification (or "spiritual defragmentation") as they ascend in the direction of AN toward Infinity of Supreme Beingness—the Pathway of Self-Honesty—in imitation of the footsteps of the gods during their descent through the "spheres" or "Gates."

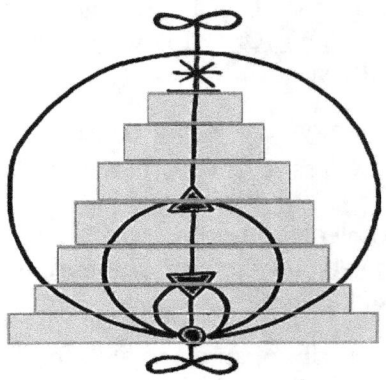

COSMOLOGY AND METAPHYSICS.

All Things in the Physical Universe are in motion—wave motions of "energy and matter in space measured as-and-across time." Continuity of the Physical Universe (KI) is divided by LAW and encompassed by the ALL (ANKI). The direction of AN extends toward ABZU, an Infinity of Nothingness beyond effective existence.

> The Alpha Self or Alpha Spirit is the true source—the "spiritual cause" of "physical effects." It engages Self-determined WILL from its "spiritual" Alpha existence as an Actualized Awareness impinging on "physical" Beta existence and experienced as "Life."

USING ANCIENT WISDOM TO UNLOCK HUMAN POTENTIAL.

Communication of clear wisdom and true knowledge from Arcane Tablets is distorted as it passes through time and geography, diverse languages and authoritarian cultures using the "Power" to program the masses and fragment the Human Condition away from Self-Honesty.

Use of this ancient wisdom reveals the Keys to "Cosmic Ordering"—applying the highest understanding of "cause-and-effect" sequences to all action in the Physical Universe, and to all *Self-directed* applications of WILL-Intention and Effort.

MARDUKITE ZUISM, SYSTEMOLOGY & SPIRITUALITY.

The Spiritual Universe (AN)—of metaphysical or spiritual energy and metaphysical or spiritual matter is not dependent on the Physical Universe (KI) to exist; the two are existentially independent of each other, maintaining a single channel, conduit or connection, which is Alpha Spirit "Awareness" as Spiritual Life or ZU.

The Alpha Spirit engages a ZU-line, a spiritual lifeline of ZU energy to a genetic vehicle or organic body to experience physical beta existence.

MARDUKITE ZUISM DEFINITIONS
FOR METAHUMAN SYSTEMOLOGY.

ALPHA SPIRIT : a Spiritual *life-form*; the True Self or "I-AM"; a unit of *Awareness*; a *Spiritual Beingness* that controls a physical body or "genetic vehicle" using a Lifeline or continuum of spiritual "ZU" energy.

ASCENSION : actualized Awareness elevated to (AN) spiritual existence that is exterior to beta-existence; the ability to *Self-direct* from *Spirit* as *Self* in existence independent of any "body."

BETA-EXISTENCE : manifestation of a Physical Universe (KI); conditions of energy-matter manifested in a state of condensed existence matching frequencies specific to space in the Physical Universe.

FRAGMENTATION : breaking apart; scattering the pieces; fractioning wholeness; fracture of holism; discontinuity; a separation of totality; anything outside or apart from original clarity (or *Self-Honesty*).

GENETIC VEHICLE : Physical *life-form*; physical (*beta*) body controlled by an Alpha Spirit using a continuous Lifeline of ZU energy; an organic catalyst for a Spirit to operate causes and observe effects (in *beta*).

HUMAN CONDITION : a standard issue default programmed state of Human experience; receptacle for Alpha Spirit Awareness that is generally accepted to be the extent of its potential identity (*Beingness*).

ZU-LINE : Spiritual Life-Energy (ZU) continuum; an energetic channel or Identity-Continuum connecting Alpha Spirit Awareness from Infinity-to-Infinity including the full Physical or *beta* range of existence.

THE HIGHEST FORM OF TRUE DIVINE WORSHIP.

The true Destiny of Humanity is to achieve spiritual
Self-Actualization; the reunion of Self with the Infinite.

Attaining Self-Honesty in this Life is the most important step a person can take toward achieving their highest ideals, goals and realizations as a Spiritual Being.

The Highest form of "True Worship" begins with the Spirit—the true Self—and all external practices, rituals, ceremonies and historical examples are but outer reflections of this ideal. The Highest form of "Sin" is against the Spirit—against the Self—and its ability to maintain Self-Honesty.

There are modes of thought, action and Self-direction of effort that will contribute toward Ascension; and modes that lead away from that.

Beta experiences of "Sin"—pain, fear, guilt, anger—are all related to personal fragmentation; and emotional turbulence from all of these may be released—and intention energy redirected—because:

We all co-create the reality we experience in this lifetime!

SPHERES OF EXISTENCE AND INFLUENCE &
A UTILITARIAN SYSTEMOLOGY OF ETHICS.

The prime directive of all beta existence is: *to exist*. The continuation of existence is the purpose behind all existence. Between realization of Self and Infinity, there are many spheres of existence that we may influence.

All of the spheres are interconnected. There is nothing in existence that is in absolute exclusion to all existence. Each sphere of existence supports subsequent existences and assists reaches toward higher spheres of influence.

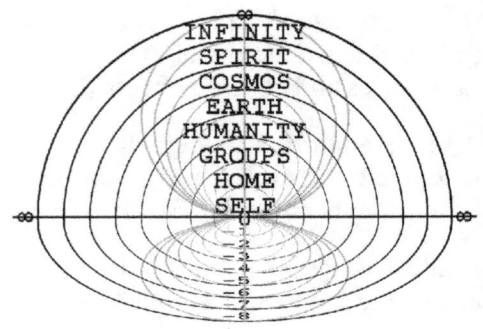

The greatest good contributes to the greatest continuation of optimum existence and survival for the greatest sphere of inclusion. Degrees of rightness and wrongness are determined by Cosmic Law and are reflected in the quality and continuation of optimal existence at the highest sphere of existence. Individual happiness is attained via the channel to the highest sphere. Unhappiness is a result of "selfishness," lack of "Spiritual Self-Actualization" and/or reach of "Actualized Awareness" beyond *Self* as identified to a *body*.

ZU : MARDUKITE ZUISM & MODERN ZUIST RELIGION.

History demonstrates how dangerous, troublesome and easily misused the concept of "RELGION" is; so, for purposes of incorporating *Mardukite Zuism* and its *Systemology* as a contemporary standard, the idea is treated here as defined.

> RELIGION : a concise spiritual paradigm, fixed set of beliefs and practices, regarding Divinity, Infinite Beingness—or else "God."

—*Mardukite Zuism* operates under a premise of very specific beliefs and "systemology" of "applied spiritual technology."

—*Mardukite Zuist Religious Doctrine* fundamentally relays the previously described "Highest forms" of Worship, Cosmic Law, and Ethics.

Mardukite Zuist Spiritual Doctrines and its *Systemology*
successfully meet modern "religious" criteria for:

a) A Description of Cosmic Creation;
b) Belief in a Supreme Infinite Being;
c) Ethics Leading to Human Ascension;
d) Ethics of Conduct Toward all Life and Existence;
e) Immortality of the Human Spirit;
f) A Published Library of Religious Literature;
g) Traditions of Practice and Application; and
h) A Spiritual Advisement Methodology.

GOALS & IDEALS OF MARDUKITE ZUISM.

The word "ZU" meant "knowing" in original Sumerian cuneiform script. Goals and ideals of Zuism reflect this. *Mardukite Zuism & Systemology* seeks to assist an individual in reclaiming a total realization of the True Self or "I-AM" knowingly as the Immortal Alpha Spirit, in line with a most ancient directive: to "Know Thyself."

In view of the fact that all modern humans are subjected to technologies depriving them of their freedoms to *be*, *think*, *know* and pursue truth: goals and ideals of *Mardukite Zuism & Systemology* are to effectively repair abilities and elevate certainty of an Individual to increase and direct "Actualized Awareness" toward Higher Gateways of Spiritual Ascension.

INFINITY, "GOD" & SUPREME BEINGNESS

Spiritual Philosophy of *Mardukite Zuism* is systematized by a Standard Model of Systemology. It demonstrates Absolute Supreme Beingness associated with the Highest realization of "God" as INFINITY. No thing is Higher or Absolute than the *Infinity of Nothingness*—and reducing Supreme Beingness to any finite personality or character trait is to limit and defile what is herewith represented, but with lesser "words" and mundane sentiments or semantics.

> The Highest Name of God cannot be conceived
> —hence our symbolic use of the Infinity Sign:
>
>
>
> ...or Sumerian cuneiform word-sign: "ABZU"—
> "The Infinite Nothingness and Source of All ZU."

—The Spiritual Universe (AN) is *All-as-One* because it exists as an infinite singularity or stasis: infinite potential with no gradient or observed motion; which is its own continuity.

—The Physical Universe (KI) is *All-as-One* because it is in continuous motion, with all manifest parts working systematically as the condensed solid continuity of beta-existence.

—A "spiritual continuum" or "conduit channel" of ZU (or a "*Zu-line*") from a Spiritual Universe (AN)—links our Awareness levels of "I-AM," "True Self" or Spirit ("Alpha Spirit") with varying potential "Point-of-View" and degrees of motion experienced in the Physical Universe.

—The Alpha Spirit or "Soul" is the true Awareness, "I" or "Self" connected to the operation and control of the physical body.

BASIC CONCEPT OF THE HUMAN SPIRIT.

> The true Self is the "I" or "I-AM" or "Spirit"
> regardless of its *perceived* position in spaces,
> *Point-of-View*, degree or level of Awareness.
> Spirit remains at its original fixed true point.

Whatever "spiritual energy-matter" (*if any*) that may compose the Alpha Spirit or makeup of "soul"—it must occupy this "other space" with its spiritual existence and then project its Awareness and Will onto the Physical Universe (KI) in order to experience the *Game* we call "*Life.*"

This "*Spiritual Life Energy*" or *Awareness* of a *Spiritual Being* is treated as a "Lifeforce" and "Consciousness" and goes by many names throughout the history of language, mysticism and spirituality—but we find the idea first treated as ZU on cuneiform tablets of Mesopotamia.

> On an Identity-lifeline or continuum of ZU energy, an Alpha Spirits is operating from a Spiritual Universe to experience in *beta-existence*. We refer to this concept as the "*ZU-line*" on the Standard Model of Systemology to illustrate the projected Awareness from Spirit (as an epicenter or fixed point) to any other *Point-of-view* (POV) anywhere in existence.

ZU is the name given to the spiritual beingness or essence of all Life in existence—and Self is a concentrated center or focal point that projects Awareness on a ZU-continuum or Zu-line toward a point of artificial Identity separate from Self.

The True Self of an Individual Human is a "spiritual universe cause" of "physical universe effects"—engaging as an immortal Alpha Spirit with a Self-determined Will actualized as an Awareness along a ZU-continuum (or "*Zu-line*"), extending from Infinity-to-Infinity, through every possible frequency and vibration along the total spectrum of physical and metaphysical existence.

THE SYSTEMOLOGY OF SPIRITUAL ADVISEMENT COUNSELING PRACTICES FOR MARDUKITE ZUISM

The Mardukite Chamberlains, an underground research organization established in 2009, dedicated itself to recovery and consolidation of relevant historical, scriptural & ritual records of ancient Mardukite Babylon in Mesopotamia, following up the founding of Mardukite Ministries (Mardukite Zuism) by Joshua Free the previous year, in 2008. By 2011, a Mardukite Alumni faction (International Systemology Society) began research and development into new methods of:

> applying ancient wisdom as a futurist spiritual technology
> that effectively awakens, unlocks and fully actualizes
> spiritual potential of the Human Condition.

A systematic and logical approach to spirituality is demonstrable on the Standard Model of Systemology, where ZU-line frequencies are represented at various degrees:

- "zero-point" body death;
- cellular life and sensory perceptions of a genetic body;

- bio-chemicals induced by emotion;
- thoughts and intention transmitted between our Alpha Spirit and the "genetic vehicle"—
- all the way "up" the scale to a perfected clarity of Self-Actualized Awareness of I-AM as our true "Alpha" state, just below Infinity and Absolute Beingness.

Full potential of ZU in is only altered from its natural state as a result of personal fragmentation of the Human Condition. This may be restored by systematic spiritual practices.

The *Pathway to Self-Honesty* is a personal journey and spiritual adventure marked by progressive clearing of personal energy channels fragmented by emotional imprinting and programming-data accumulated from "experiences" in the environment—the "debris" that fragments the total actualized experience of Self in Awareness as the Alpha Spirit.

The first and most important step—Before an individual can actualize potentials of the Spirit as Self, they must fully realize:

> The *I-AM Self* and the *Alpha Spirit* are One and the same.
> This state of Knowingness is a primary intention of basic
> spiritual practices of Mardukite Zuism & Systemology.

Mardukite Zuism materials, *Systemology* books and advanced training courses are available to Mardukite Ministers seeking qualification as specialized Clergy, Priests, Priestess, and Professional Pilots of systematic processing.

MESOPOTAMIAN MATHEMATICS : MEASURING SPACE AND TIME

Ancient Sumerians observed and understood connections between cycles, time and mathematics. In addition to the "invention" and pragmatic use of the "wheel" (or circle), they also developed "religious" calculations of the circle at 360-degrees. Their use of "Base-60" or "*sexagesimal*" math for systematic measurement of time-space remains with humanity to this present day. Consider the length of a day at 24-hours (or two sets of twelve) of "60"-minutes containing "60"-seconds each; or the celestial zones of the astrological zodiac as a "wheel" or sphere of twelve "houses" of 30 degrees each; or else the twelve 30-day "festivals of the moon" composing an annual cycle or "wheel of the year"—or "*sat-ti.*" The annual year (*sat-ti*) was even originally only divided into three seasons: beginning ("*res sat-ti*"), middle ("*misil sat-ti*") and end ("*kit sat-ti*").

"Magicians" and esoteric philosophers—ancient and modern—find significance in sigil-scripts, colors, mystical alphabets and other "occult correspondences." All of these play their parts in magical ritual drama, spiritual incantations and other ceremonial applications. As a *universal* expression of "Cosmic Law," *numbers* are the most fundamental mystical "signs" in the realm of form, representing infinite wisdom and practical correspondences. Although our traditional or more familiar "classical" system of numerology is derived from a "Base-10" paradigm (for example, where "10x10=100" is a *whole*), the original Mesopotamian mathematics is "Base-6," or more appropriately, "Base-60." This only seems complicated because modern consciousness is most familiar with a "*Base-10 metric system*"—decades and centuries and "percents."

In Western civilization, "Base-60" mathematics is most closely identified with our sense of "time." Rather than dividing an hour into hundredths or percents, we are able to see 60-minutes as the "*whole pie.*" A quarter of that "pie," while still "25%"—per-*cent*, meaning "per-*100*"—it is *not* a quantified value of "25," but instead: "15," as in 15-minutes—"15x4=60." The modern standard space-measuring "foot" is divided by 12—and "12x5=60." This type of thinking more closely resembles Mesopotamian worldview.

Although school-teachers most frequently emphasize only the proverbial Sumerian "use of the wheel," it was the "mathematics" that forever established that the wheel (or more correctly, the "circle") consisted of 360-degrees—or "6x60= 360." Here among the ancients, "geometry" was born—long before the classical Greek mathematicians—a means of literal "earth-measuring."

Even more than this, the ancients demonstrated abilities to measure time-space on "earth," in the "heavens" and the relationships between.

BASIC MESOPOTAMIAN MATHEMATICAL FORMULAS

6 x 1 = 6 =	earth, fire, power, spatial [*Marduk*]
6 x 10 = 60 =	command, heaven-earth, fire [*Anu*]
6 x 10 x 10 = 600	chaos, void, abyss, dragon [*Tiamat*]
6 x 60 = 360 =	earth-time, cycles ["*local planet*"]
6 x 60 x 6 = 2160	earth meets heaven ["*zodiacal age*"]
6 x 60 x 10 = 3600	heaven-time, spiritual cycles ["*sar*"]

A full turn or cycle of the "Wheel of the Year"—"*sat-ti*"—in *Babylonia* was separated into "12 periods" (or *zones*) of 30-days (*degrees*) each. These periods equated to 12 annual "*moonth festivals*," more appropriately called "months." The quantity values of 12x30 and 6x60 are identical—*360*.

Ancient astronomers were also aware that the observed year was actually slightly longer than 360-days, and that there are actually 13 lunar cycles in a year, so an additional "*13th month*" was included to make the calculations fit the observations.

Everything is always in motion. We must even rectify the mathematics of our modern linear time-keeping with the inclusion of "leap-days." In most instances of the ancient calendar, a "*new moon*" meant the start of a "*new month*." The days counted of a month were synonymous with the "days of the moon"—for example: "*sixth day of the moon*."

SUMERIAN/AKKADIAN ANNUAL YEAR

1. Nisannu – Nisan (*spring equinox*)
2. Airu – Iyyar
3. Simanu – Siwan
4. Du'uzu – Tammuz
5. Abu – Ab
6. Ululu – Elul
7. Tishritu – Tisri (*autumn equinox*)
8. Arahsamna – Marchesvan
9. Kislimu – Kislev
10. Tebitu – Tebet
11. Shabatu – Sebat
12. Addau – Adar
13. "Second Adar" (*extra month*)

ZODIAC NAMES / THE CELESTIAL SPHERE

1. Ku-mal (*Aries*)
2. Gu-an-na (*Taurus*)
3. Mash-tab-ba (*Gemini*)
4. Dub (*Cancer*)
5. Ur-gula (*Leo*)
6. Ab-sin (*Virgo*)
7. Zi-bi-an-na (*Libra*)
8. Gir-tab (*Scorpio*)
9. Pa-bil (*Sagittarius*)
10. Su-hur-mash (*Capricorn*)
11. Gu (*Aquarius*)
12. Sim-mah (*Pisces*)

The annual cycle was also divided as a light and dark half, marked distinctly by the two primary religious festivals of ancient Mesopotamia—the spring festival of *Akitu* and the harvest festival of *Zagmuk*. Both are symbolically represented as points of "*divine marriage*" between "heaven" and "earth"—later signifying simply the relationship between a ruling King and his lands. Originally, the more popular *fertility rites* of the spring were agricultural, with an emphasis on *land renewal*. With later development and spread of these tradition, *Akitu* became known as *Ostara*—the pagan *Easter*—in dedication to Ishtar (*Inanna*).

Mesopotamian mathematics is "*sexagesimal*." The number "sixty"—attributed to Anu—is sacred within its own system, with exactly *twelve* factors—*three* of which are prime. These "factors" also appear in the tradition as *sacred* numbers—1, 2, 3, 4, 5, 6, 10, 12, 15, 20, 30 and itself, 60. It is perhaps no small coincidence that "60" is the smallest whole number value perfectly divisible by all of the numbers 1 through 6. This was very useful in the highly innovative form of "*multiplication by reciprocal*" developed by the Sumerians and Babylonians. Logic calculations requiring a value to be "divided" by another number, were instead written as a "multiplication" of the reciprocal (or inverse) of the other number. Therefore, in this system, an expression:

"60 *divided by* 10" becomes "60 *multiplied by* one-tenth."
[60 / 10 = 6] *is the same as* [60 x 0.1 = 6]

Calculations of space and distance also followed *sexagesimal* patterns. Where we are familiar today with the use of centimeters and inches, feet and yards, the basic unit of length measurement in ancient Mesopotamia was essentially the division of a meter ("*kush*") into 360-parts called a *she*, each equivalent to approximately one-tenth of an inch.

If we simply transfer a decimal place, we can still use the "standard" system to visualize—where one foot or 12-inches approximately equals 120 *she*, so 1 *kush* or 360 *she* is roughly equivalent to 36-inches. [It is interesting that society has retained a system of spatial-measure where a standard unit is divided into 12-parts.]

6 *she*	=	1 *su-shi*
30 *su-shi* or 360 *she*	=	1 *kush*

The original Anunnaki hierarchy of pantheon designations runs in increments of five—from 5 to 60—allowing space for the "Olympian Twelve" to be plotted thereupon. The Sumerian Anunnaki *"Pantheon of Twelve"* of course consists of: *Anu* (60), *Antu* (55), *Enlil* (50), *Ninlil* (45), *Enki* (40), *Ninki-Damkina* (35), *Nanna* (30), *Ningal* (25), *Shammash* (20), *Inanna-Ishtar* (15), *Ishkur-Adad* (10) and *Ninhursag-Ninmah* (5).

Differences in spiritual politics for post-Sumerian Mesopotamia resulted when altering the names (or representative figures) with the "Mardukite" pantheon, but the actual "roles" themselves went unchanged—mathematically fixed. Designations for the *"Supernal Trinity"*—60, 50 and 40—become "master numbers" of Babylonian numerol-ogy. The fractional designations for the *"planetary gates"* are inherited by the "younger pantheon" in Babylon:

1 / 2	= 30	*Nanna-Sin* (Moon)
1 / 3	= 20	*Utu-Shammash* (Sun)
1 / 4	= 15	*Inanna-Ishtar* (Venus)
1 / 5	= 12	*Nabu* (Mercury)
1 / 6	= 10	*Marduk* (Jupiter)
1 / 8	= 7.3	*Nergal* (Mars)
1 / 15	= 4	*Ninib*, *Adad* or *Ninurta* (Saturn)

PRECESSION OF THE BABYLON GATES

1 = 7	*Nanna* – 30	30 x 2 = 60	30 = 1 / 2 x 60
2 = 6	*Nabu* – 12	12 x 5 = 60	12 = 1 / 5 x 60
3 = 5	*Ishtar* – 15	15 x 4 = 60	15 = 1 / 4 x 60
4 = 4	*Samas* – 20	20 x 3 = 60	20 = 1 / 3 x 60
5 = 3	*Nergal* – 8		
6 = 2	*Marduk* – 10	10 x 6 = 60	10 = 1 / 6 x 60
7 = 1	*Ninurta* – 4	4 x 15 = 60	4 = 1 / 15 x 60

INITIATION AND DEDICATION :
THE ANCIENT MYSTERY SCHOOL
LADDER OF LIGHTS

True esoteric mysteries are often earned by Seekers (and initiates of the *Ancient Mystery School*) progressively through a series of *steps*. The purpose of "grading" is to *gradually* introduce a Seeker to successively "higher" levels of realization and awareness that cumulatively unfold. Various traditions throughout the ages have each interpreted these mysteries differently, adding their own flavors and tables of correspondence, often times obscuring the number of "degrees" to fit their systems: "10 degrees" of the *Golden Dawn*; "33 degrees" of *Freemasonry*, &tc. But, the most ancient famous examples, specifically for our purposes, are described as a "sevenfold" system.

In a conventional esoteric institution, each "level" of initiation—or "step" on the *"Ladder of Lights"*—not only increases a Seeker's awareness of the system, but also grants new potential for personal development. Each *"Key"* is earned while working with a particular fragmented energy "current." These currents have also been called the "seven rays of light" (or the "seven pillars") because they comprise the main tenets of information contained within the structure of form, usually encountered directly in the physical (visible) world of light as "Cosmic Law."

Although the essential existence of the ALL is wholeness, material reality is distinguished by seven bands of a visible spectrum. Each degree appears separate—resonating its own frequency and perceived energy current. Philosophers applied this paradigm to other material spectra—*seven* notes of music, *seven* colors, *seven* days of the week—each corresponding with one of *seven* physical "celestial spheres" (*planets*), and so forth. The initiate was able to "sample" each aspect of the system in exclusion, and then as incorporated knowledge (with the rest) accumulated as a "base" of understanding—a "base" for *awareness* and *knowing*.

The Babylonian system of "*Gates*," levels or degrees, are realized into existence uniquely by different traditions and their practices—all as a result of their *base*. Personal workings are performed from a *"Body of Light"*—the practitioner elevating their consciousness on the astral plane—then intoning specific passwords and names while tracing spiritual gate "seals," "signs" and "forms" that all trigger a preset shift in conscious *awareness* and *knowing*. These "levels" are often associated with "aethyrs" or "etheric planes" of manifestation that is deemed the "Other." Each level of initiation, step or *"rung"* requires entrance or passage through an *astral gate* equivalent to achievement of further stages of *"spiritual unfoldment."* Similar practices are found in many modern forms of "ceremonial magic," incorporating their own "Ladder of Lights."

The Babylonian Star-Gate system—alluded to in all of the Mesopotamian in-fluenced *Necronomicon* cycles of modern esoteric literature—corresponds with an ancient "Mardukite" plan to dedicate and seal the "younger pantheon" of the Anunnaki in Babylon under the reign of *Marduk*. These were to be the pat-rons of *"New-Babylon,"* a political and spiritual vision that never actually ex-perienced total fruition, but which continues to evolve even today.

The first time Babylon fell, the main priestly class of magicians, priestesses and *Nabu*-scribes moved to Egypt, inspiring an entire "Hermetic" legacy. Modern "Dragon Court" revivals are often led by those with kinship to the Nile Region (in addition to near pre-historic Mesopotamia). This does not constitute any genetic propaganda—especially since all dynasties switch back and forth like a pendulum swing, changing with time and politics.

Even in Babylon, we see the *"Hand of Marduk"* extend to foreign Kings when necessity demanded. By the "Classical Period," Alexander-The-Great suc-ceeded in taking control of *"dragonblood"* in Egypt, just as he had in Babylon. This over-stretched empire primed weakened conditions on a global scale, eventually leaving the known world wide open to Roman reign, particularly when the Ptolemaic dynasty was "given" to Rome by Cleopatra. Then, when Rome fell, so did its forced "false" authority systems that the world had be-come dependent on.

The *ankh* was widely known in Egypt as a protective symbol of life—literally the "Key of Life." Few are aware that it also esoterically represented the double-helix serpent-coiled (DNA) and *"Tree of Life"* in Mesopotamia. The *An-cient Mystery School* dedicated the symbol to the AMON-RA in Egypt (also ATEN and *"Marduk-Ra"*). It therefore became highly revered by the Mardukite priesthood altogether. In some traditions, the *ankh* was given (bestowed) to a scribe-priest-magician upon completion of their seventh (final) initiation.

The *ankh* is essentially a "cross," but also and a symbol of "crossings in the heavens"—meaning also "among the stars," or literally "the astral." In one version, the symbol is of the Self standing before the "Omega" shaped gate-way. In its original Anunnaki form, this cross is drawn as a "T" (*Tau*) with a serpent being entwined around it. This is where the upper loop comes from, but which continues to coil in an "Infinity-8" pattern down the stem, simul-taneously representing the famous "serpent staff" of ancient magicians. The serpent is the *"serpent of wisdom"*—the *Primordial Dragon*—and equally repres-enting the "Cosmic Law" embedded in what humans call "DNA." The Egyptian word: "AN-KH," is very similar to the Sumerian word: "AN-KI," meaning "*uni-verse*"—the ALL—or literally: *"heaven"* + *"earth."*

It should come as little surprise that some long-standing esoteric factions of underground society—existing before the inception of the modern "Mardukite" movement—made use of these same mysteries: Egyptian Freemasonry and Rosicrucianism. These initiates hold a belief that these "stories of the gods" are in fact literal references to very ancient "luminous beings" ("Illuminati") that eventually *came to be* considered along the same lines as the Olympian Titans. "Tahutian" practitioners—neo-Egyptian dedicates to the embodiment of *Nabu* as the "*Thoth-current*"—still observe a (self)-initiation system inherited from the Egypto-Babylonian "*Ladder of Lights.*" This specific lore has been maintained in an occult manuscript known as the "*Crata Repoa,*" describing seven "levels" of Hermetic initiation.

◊ ◊ ◊ ◊ ◊ ◊ ◊

A neophyte (initiate of the first degree) is called the "*Pastophoris.*" This is a title bestowed upon the Seeker who has passed the "Earth Gate," and is by nature, a Guardian of the "Gates of Men," and given the secret (pass) word: AMON. They are taught the basic symbolism of the Ladder of Lights and instruction in the physical (natural) sciences. [Mardukite Gatekeepers: *Nanna* and *Ningal*—"*Moon Gate.*" Mystical/Temple Craft: Astral/Dream Work.]

The second level is called the "*Neocoris.*" The Seeker is initiated by "water and serpent" and given physical knowledge of cosmos—the mysteries of geometry, mathematics and architecture. They are bestowed with the "serpent staff," and by the password: EVE, they are granted access to the secret lore of the origins and fall of the human race. Their temple duties include cleaning the pillars (pylons) and generally tending to custodial needs of the shrines. [Mardukite Gatekeepers: *Nabu* and *Teshmet*—"*Mercury Gate.*" Mystical/ Temple Craft: Knowledge of Minds.]

Ascending to the third step on the Ladder of Lights earn the title of "*Melanephoris,*" when the initiate becomes a Guardian of the "Gates of Death," and perhaps also given the secrets of mummification (a valuable art in Nile Region). Here, the Seeker receives the infamous "Underworld Initiation" after being led to the "Tomb of Osiris" with the passwords: MONACH CARON MINI, meaning: "I count the days of anger." [Mardukite Gatekeepers: *Ishtar* and *Dumuzi*—"*Venus Gate.*" Mystical/Temple Craft: Past-Life Memory.]

From this point, the Seeker would be left in the catacombs and archives of lore to discern the secret to access the next level of initiation on their own. If they did not, they would ever remain an initiate of the third degree—but if they were to discover the "secret code," then they would be initiated as a "*Chistophorus*" via the "blindfold rite" (where a red noose is hung around the initiates neck, like a leash). Only then is he allowed to enter the Assembly of the Inner Circle, an Adept among Masters of the Highest Councils.

The *"Chistophorus"* is an Adept who has earned the secret of the "shades" (a code for the "primordial battles in heaven" based on the *Enuma Elis*) and given access to the "secret chambers" of the Order. Soon thereafter, the seeker is granted an initiation by fire after proving themselves via dramatically "slaying the dragon" (or removing the head of Medusa/Typhon, etc.) and the password: ZOA. [Mardukite Gatekeepers: *Shammash* and *Aya*—"*Sun Gate.*" Mystical/ Temple Craft: History and Doctrines of the Universe.]

If successful past this point, mystical knowledge comes also in the form of a practical instruction is chemistry and metallurgy as fifth degree *"Balahate"* and the word: KHEMIA or CHEMYA. [Mardukite Anunnaki Gatekeepers: *Nergal* and *Ereshkigal*—"*Mars Gate.*" Mystical/Temple Craft: Function and Formulas of the Universe.]

After working to master the "godly" understanding of the "heavenly spheres" and the "gods of old," the Adept is the installed to the sixth degree and called the *"Guardian of the Star-Gates,"* or literally, *"Astronomer who stands before the Gate of the Gods"* (a Master-Priest status). Only then are the religious secrets divulged as well as the "true natures" of the Anunnaki, their origins and lore of their rule (and return?) on earth. The seeker is then granted another initiation through the "Gates of Death," this time to meet the Elder pantheon as a true Priest. [Mardukite Gatekeepers: *Marduk* and *Sarpanit* —"*Jupiter Gate.*" Mystical/Temple Craft: Material Unity via Love.]

The final and seventh step on the Ladder of Lights is called the *"Saphenath Pancah,"* an initiation required to attain "Prophet" status in the tradition. Secret knowledge of the gods is offered, including privileged knowledge of the "Elixir of Life." The Adept-Master-Priest, now Prophet, is given a white robe [*etangi*] and an ankh to wear. The password of the grade is: ADON ("*Adonai*"), a Semitic name, meaning "Lord of the Earth." [Mardukite Gatekeepers: *Ninurta* and *Ba'u*—"*Saturn Gate.*" Mystical/Temple Craft: Dissolution of Self via Spiritual Unity with the ALL.]

DICTIONARY OF ANUNNAKI GODS

ADAD {10}—The youngest son of ENLIL that becomes the national patron deity to the *Hittites* (called HADAD or TESHUB); possibly also recognized as BAAL HADAD in a *Hittite* version of the Supernal Trinity that is elevated to a chief god position in the same manner that MARDUK is raised in *Babylon*. As a storm god in the Anunnaki pantheon, ADAD is represented by thunder, lightning and torrents. According to Hittite records, succession of hierarchical kingship passes from ALALU to ANU to KUMARBI (ENLIL) and the BA'AL HADAD (TESHUB). In the Enki'ite (Mardukite) Babylonian system he is named ISHKUR and granted the position of *"Inspector of the Cosmos"* by ENKI.

ALALU [*"Father of the Gods"*]—The figure maintaining 'kingship' in the 'heavens' prior to ANU. An ancient *Hittite (Hurrian)* tablet cycle titled ALALU & ANU or *"Kingship in Heaven"* describes a conflict between the two for the seat of 'kingship' in the 'heavens'. The Mardukite *Tablet-K* series reprinted in *"The Anunnaki Bible"* explains: Formerly in the Ancient of Days, ALULU was reigning in heaven; and for nine *sars* did he rule the skies, but not well did he reign. Then in the ninth *sar* of his reign, ANU defeated ALULU. ALULU descended from heaven and ruled the dark-hued earth. ANU gave fight and defeated ALULU and kingship was lowered from heaven to earth by decree of ANU.

ALULU *see* ALALU

ASAR(I)LUHI *see* MARDUK

AMARUTU *see* MARDUK

AN/ANSAR *see* ANU

ANTU {55} [*"Life of Heaven"*]—The official half-sister (by a different mother) and spouse (consort) of ANU. ANTU and ANU beget ENLIL. In archaic pre-*Sumerian* lore, ANTU is espoused to the archaic AN.

ANUNITUM *see* INANNA

ANU {60} [*"Heavenly One"*]—In the *Sumerian* Anunnaki patheon, ANU is the supreme *"All-Father"* of the pantheon; father to ENLIL by official spouse ANTU, and the father of ENKI & NINHURSAG (by other wives). Called AN in pre-*Babylonian* times and ANU by the *Babylonians*, a being whose family resides on, or emerged from the 'place of crossings' (*Nibiru*). Few of the incantation tablets (or 'prayers') invoke the powers of ANU directly, since the "heavenly force" was perceived as too vast to be channeled in its raw state, and to degrade it to anything more accessible would be to compromise the nature of what is being represented by this figure.

ANZU ["*Knower of Heaven*"]—An obscure bird-like beast/monster of an unclear nature. The ANZU or ZU usually refers to a "heavenly bird" or thunderbird that appears in an archaic tab-let cycle stealing the '*Tablets of Destiny*" from ENLIL, disrupting the DUR-AN-KI ('Bond-Heaven-Earth') "stargate." It is possible that this half-man, half-bird, sometimes called AZAG, was a genetically engineered storm-god or artificially intelligent messenger being of ENLIL that turned "evil."

ARURU—The sister of ENLIL, alias NINTU, who is the *Babylonian* title for the 'mother-goddess' known in *Sumerian* as NINMAH or NINHURSAG. In the Babylonian ethnocentric epics, she assists MARDUK in creating the human race (or '*Race of Marduk*'), however, in the *Enuma Elis*, it is "blood" of KINGU that is used. Other *Sumerian* versions say the "blood" or "essence" of some other 'slain' god is used for this.

AYA ["*Dawn*"]—The official spouse (consort) of SAMAS in *Akkadian*; named SHERIDA in *Sumerian*.

AZAG *see* ANZU

BAU ["*To Accompany*"]—A daughter of ANU, who is the official spouse (consort) to NINURTA in the pre-*Babylonian* (*Sumerian*) pantheon. Her names GULA ("*Big One*") and BAU (the sound a dog makes) are, perhaps idioms about her size/appearance. She remains a goddess in the *Babylonian* pantheon of healing (as NINTI-NUGGA).

BEL *see* EL

BUZUR *see* ENKI

DAMKINA *see* NINKI

DAMUZU *see* DUMUZI

DUMUZI ["*Son Who is Life*"]—Youngest son of ENKI and DUTTUR (a concubine of ENKI) who is the betrothed spouse (consort) to INANNA (ISHTAR) after MARDUK declines the tradition of espousing INANNA. DAMUZI is a shepherd god (as opposed to a grain deity), known as TAMMUZ in the Semitic languages. In the *Sumerian* version of the descent-cycle, INANNA descends to the *Underworld* in hopes of being its queen. When captured, she becomes a prisoner of her sister ERESHKIGAL and leaves to find someone to take her place. Upon returning to ERECH, she finds that DUMUZI has been celebrating his ascent to her throne and is not mourning for her death. Enraged, she immediately hands him over to the 'demons' of the *Underworld*. Later versions of this cycle depict the god MARDUK as somehow responsible for the death of DU-

MUZI and INANNA (ISHTAR) descends to the *Underworld* to release him.

EA *see* ENKI

EL—A Semitic form of the Akkadian (*Babylonian*) ILU or ILI, meaning 'Lofty Ones', 'High Ones' or 'Great Gods'; the plural form being ILANI (or ELANI in *European Elvish-Faerie* lore), with a Semitic plural equivalent "*Elohim*", meaning literally 'gods' but often used to denote the 'One God' in the Judeo-Christian *Old Testament* (which is, itself, rooted strongly in Mesopotamian traditions). EL or BEL is also used to denote the 'Lord of the Earth-Space', or else 'ENLIL-SHIP', a position attributed not only to ENLIL (in the *Enlilite Sumerian* tradition) but also to NINURTA, MARDUK and even other patron deities by localized Middle Eastern cults. Later Semitic use of EL as a suffix (e.g., Michael, Gabriel, etc.) matches the prefix use of the ILU sign in cuneiform, meaning "*Of God.*" In cuneiform, the sign is a "cross" and in later religious scriptures and rites, the literary tradition remained to place a cross before a *Divine* or saint name.

ELLIL *see* ENLIL

ENKI {40} "*Lord of the Earth*"—also known as E.A. ["*Whose Home is Water*"], firstborn son of ANU (but not the official heir), half-brother to ENLIL (heir of ANU). Also called NUDIMMUD (or PTAH in *Egypt*) meaning: "*The Fashioner*" (or "*Grand Designer*"). ENKI is the Chief scientist of the Anunnaki, taking up residence in *Eridu*, near the *Persian Gulf* and also in *Africa* (particularly *Egypt*). ENKI is father of MARDUK, begot with NINKI (DAMKINA) and is representative of the planet Neptune in the local Anunnaki 'world order'. ENKI is given control of the '*Waters of Life*' on Earth. He seeks to save his own ('*Mardukite*') legacy during the deluge and then is responsible for programing the arts and sciences of civilization into humanity. In later *Enlilite*-derived Judeo-Christian interpretations, ENKI becomes demonized as 'Satan'.

ENLIL {50} "*Lord of Air-Space*"—The official heir-son of ANU, 'Lord of the Command' on Earth, revered as the '*God*' of Earth by Enlilite *Sumerians* and later derived Semitic (Hebrew) tradtions. ENLIL begets his own heir, NINURTA, by his half-sister NINHURSAG, but espouses SUD, renamed NINLIL and begets NANNA. In the pre-*Babylonian* paradigm, ENLIL is the Jupiter position in the pantheon that is later usurped by MARDUK. *Sumerian* tradition observes ENLIL as the 'Father' to the Anunnaki pantheon, much in the same way that ENKI is revered by the *Mardukites*. Prominent descendents of ENLIL include: NANNA, SAMAS, INANNA and NERGAL in addition to NINURTA.

ENSAG *see* NABU

ENSHAG *see* NABU

ERESHKIGAL – ["*Mistress of the Great Below*"] The Queen of the *Great Lands* in the *Sumerian* tradition, sister of INANNA-ISHTAR, granddaughter of ENLIL and spouse to NERGAL.

ERRA *see* NERGAL

GANZIR — The gatekeeper to the underworld 'Kingdom of Shadows.' The '*Gate of Ganzir*' is often confused with the '*Gate to the Abyss*' or the '*Gate to the Outside*', but instead it is a portal into the Anunnaki-controlled *Underworld*, the '*Shadowlands*' or twilight world within the domain of ERESHKIGAL, who rules this 'land of the dead'. Quoting a modern grimoire of Babylonian occultism, the "necromantic art, by which is it desirous to speak with the phantom of someone dead, and perhaps dwelling in the ABSU [*Abyss*] and thereby a servant of ERESHKIGAL... it is no less than the opening of the *Gate of Ganzir*."

GIBIL ["*He Who Has Fire*"]—The companion of the flame, a descendent of ENKI who uses fire to conduct alchemy and other feats of "*fire power*."

GIRRA—The "servant", "power" or "fire" of the 'great god'; the *Sumerian* fire-god or essence or force of a fire-god named GIBIL.

GULA *see* BAU

HADAD *see* ADAD

ILLIL *see* ENLIL

ILU *see* EL

IMDUGUD *see* ANZU

INANNA {15} ["*Lady of Heaven*"]—The *Sumerian* goddess of "passion", both 'love' and 'war', and patron of URUK, begot by NANNA and NINGAL; originally betrothed to MARDUK, she then changes her consort choice to DUMUZI. Her prowess and determination secured her a place in all ancient pantheons; being the "*Goddess of One-Thousand Names*," titled ISHTAR in *Babylon*. INANNA (ISHTAR) is the spirit of Venus, whose day is Friday and with an essence found in copper. Her colors are green and white, significant to her domain of fertility and growth. She offers her magicians the skills in love and visions of beauty.

IRRA *see* NERGAL

ISHKUR *see* ADAD

ISHTAR *see* INANNA

KUR *see* TIAMAT

MAMMI *see* NINHURSAG

MARDUK {10/(50)} *"Son of God"*—The supreme champion of the IGIGI during the pre-*Sumerian* era of the Anunnaki; heir-son of ENKI, he becomes the patron of *Babylon* and the 'Mardukite' tradition reigning for the *Age of Aries* in Mesopotamia. All tablet cycles making reference to MARDUK are purely *Babylonian* or from a direct later source, as he does not appear in any significant pre-Babylonian cuneiform tablet cycles yet unearthed. When mentioned briefly as the son of ENKI, working in *Eridu*, he is named ASARLUHI, becoming the patron Anunnaki "deity" of magic or 'Master of Magicians'after having inherited the craft from his father. The blatant industrious and expansive power represented by MARDUK in his ascent up the pantheon (as observed in *Babylon*) is typified by the planet Jupiter (ENLIL, by *Sumerian* standards). His color is purple.

MERIDUG *see* MARDUK

MERODACH *see* MARDUK

NABAK *see* NABU

NABIH *see* NABU

NABU {12} ["*Prophet*"]—The official post-*Sumerian* secretary of the Anunnaki, part-divine earth born heir-son of MARDUK and messenger-herald and spokesperson of the '*Mardukite*' tradition, the national cult of *Babylon* devised by NABU who assisted his father in the redevelopment of the Anunnaki paradigm (as seen in the '*Mardukite*' religion of *Babylon* replacing the previously observed '*Enlilite*' world order of the *Sumerians*). Creating the concept of 'history' and 'propaganda', NABU gives the 'stylus' to humanity (and launches a group of scribe-priests (specially taught writing and rhetoric) to catalog the natures, identities, history and decrees (decisions) of the Anunnaki Assembly (gods) and their relationship with each other and the human ("mortal") world, thereby creating not only the first public 'religion', but the first 'mythology' (a religion rooted in literary and oral legacies of human relationships and encounters with the divine) and the systems that were able to later result (most of which are still functioning as part of 'normal' everyday life in contemporary society). NABU is the archetypal '*High Priest*' (ENSAG) of the first religion (dedicated to MARDUK) and practiced by priests who preserve the craft of ENKI in *Eridu* with science and 'magic' of the gods to power and sustain the prosperous longevity of *Babylon*.

NAMRASIT *see* NANNA

NAMMTAR *see* NAMTAR

NAMMU *see* TIAMAT

NAMTAR ["*Fate Maker*"]—The 'Black Magici-an', vizier of ERESHKIGAL in the *Underworld*, also likened to the *Assyrian (Chaldean)* plague-god NAMTARU (also the *Akkadian* word for pestilence"). From a ritual text given in *Liber 9* (Tablet-Q in *The Complete Anunnaki Bible*), the priest is to make an image of the affected (sick) person in dough [flour], so as to force the 'plague-god' that afflicts the person to come away from the body and go into the image. The ancient tablets list the name of the plague-god as NAMTARU, and in other places as URA and even URAS (in *Egypt*). In the 'Descent'-cycle, ERESHKIGAL summoned NAMMTAR, the Black Magician, saying these words as she spoke to him: 'Go, NAMMTAR, imprison her [INANNA] in Darkness, in my castle! Release against her the Seven Anunnaki Judges! Release against her the Demons of the Deep...' Then, finally, the representation of a 'demon', like the plague-god NAMTARU, was not intended for 'worship' or 'veneration' (as we might see glorified among today's misguided attempts toward 'dark paths') as a deity. Such statuary typically was constructed only to be 'ceremonially' annihilated or buried as a 'ward' against what the statue (deity) represented.

NAMTARU *see* NAMTAR

NANNA {30}—The official lunar deity of the Enlilite *Sumerian* Anunnaki pantheon, the moon-god, reigning with his feminine lunar consort, NINGAL. An Anunnaki designation of 30 is significant to the approximate number of days in a month; whereby the original Sumerian calendar consists of twelve cycles of 30 days for a 360 day year (and the reason a circle is divided into 360 degrees). NANNA and NINGAL begot the twins: INANNA and SAMAS; mythographically, the *moon* gave birth to the *sun* and V*enus* is a twin-star to the *sun*. To the ancient, the moon was the 'sun-at-night'. It illuminated the pathway for travelers and kept 'watch' as the people slept. Just as the sun is invoked to grant judgments of the daytime [see SAMAS], the moon is given domain of the night and *dreamscapes* (including the 'astral plane'). The day, "Monday", is obviously named after the moon, and is likewise sacred. The essence and color of silver is usually corresponded.

NANNAR *see* NANNA

NEBO *see* NABU

NERGAL {8}—The official spouse (consort) of ERESHKIGAL ('*Queen of the Underworld*'). NERGAL corresponds to the symbol and energetic current of *Mars*, with a fiery and destructive nature commemorated in the *Babylonian* epithet ERRA ("*Annihilator*"). The vitality and raw power of *Mars* (ruling Tuesday) is evident in the essences: iron and blood.

NINAGAL—An epithet meaning "*Prince of the Great Waters*," the name appears for a son of ENKI, who in the *Ziusurda* (*Atra-Asis*) cycle is selected by ENKI to navigate the archetypal "ark" sea-craft during the Great Flood.

NINANNA *see* INANNA

NINGAL {25} ["*Great Lady*"]—The daughter of ENKI; espoused (consort) to NANNA (SIN) and the mother of INANNA (ISHTAR) and SAMAS.

NINGISHZIDA—The 'Lord of the Tree of Life', a son of ENKI and brother to MARDUK, known as *Hermes* and *Thoth-the-Elder* (or TUTU) in a time before NABU. He is a geneticist, trained under ENKI in the arts of life engineering (and reality engineering) that was later taught by NABU (*Thoth-the-Younger* or TUTU) and it evolved into the mystical school of 'Hermetics' (or 'Hermeticism'). Having lost in the 'Pyramid Wars' (c. 3400 B.C. to 3150 B.C.) against MARDUK (RA) and not participating in the pro-MARDUK revolution of ENKI's lineage, NINGISHZIDA establishes his own realm in South America, known by the indigenous people and tradition as QUETZALCOATL, the 'feather-ed serpent' (literally 'plumed serpent').

NINHARSAG *see* NINHURSAG

NINHURSAG {5}—The chief Anunnaki physician, the mother of NINURTA by ENLIL; a half-sister to ENLIL and ENKI by ANU. In an attempt to produce a royal heir or his own, ENKI even courts her at one time. She is not espoused to any of the pantheon, but instead serves the role of 'birth-goddess' and 'midwife' to the birth and raising of the Anunnaki children (of the Younger Generation), carrying names like MAMMI ("*Mother*") and NINTI ("*Lady of Life*"). When attempting to relieve the toiling of the IGIGI faction of the Anunnaki, ENKI seeks out NINHURSAG to assist in the 'creation' of the 'human' race. Her response, being: 'If ENKI will provide for me the clay, then I will make the creation'. In this antropogenetic cycle, she mixes the clay with the flesh and blood of 'Awmelu' (presumed to be a slain deity). In other versions, the 'essence' is more clearly semen and/or other genetic material. Cuneiform tablet records indicate that six different attempts are made before the '*Adamu*' (the seventh) is fashioned.

NINIB *see* NINURTA

NINKI {35} ["*Lady of the Earth*"]—The official spouse (consort) of ENKI, also known as DAMKINA ["*Lady Who Came to Earth*"]. NINKI is the daughter of

ALALU (the 'heavenly' king prior to ANU) and the the mother of MARDUK.

NINLIL {45} *"Lady of Air-Space"*—The official spouse (consort) of ENLIL, also known with the epithet SUD ("nurse"). The background to the relationship between ENLIL and NINLIL is not commonly found in the typical cuneiform tablet cycles. Naturally, the lore is *not* Mardukite or *Babylonian* in origin and does not appear in the tablet catalogue or commentary of (modern) Mardukite Core anthologies. The cycle is sometimes referred to as *"Enlil's Banishment to the Underworld."*

NINMAH *see* NINHURSAG

NINSHUBAR *see* NINSHUBUR

NINSHUBUR ["*Lady of the East*"]—Personal assistant (Mercury), second-in-command to the goddess INANNA (ISHTAR). She does not take a consort and there is an alluded love-relationship between her and INANNA (ISHTAR).

NINSUBAR *see* NINSHUBUR

NINTI *see* NINHURSAG

NINTINUGGA *see* BAU

NINTU *see* ARURU

NINURTA {4/(50)} *"Lord of the South Wind"*—The official heir-son of ENLIL, born of ENLIL and NINMAH, espoused to BAU. NINURTA represents the current of Saturn in the Mardukite paradigm, representative both of "hidden power" and "hidden secrets" (an idiom for the dark power and secrets behind the origins and legacy of *Babylon*). In the Enlilite *Sumerian* worldview, NINURTA (called NINIB in *Babylonian*) is the Enlil-in-waiting, a position usurped by MARDUK proper for the *Age of Aries*. As Enlilship is typically symbolized by 'dragon-slaying', the same motif present in the elevation of MARDUK in *Babylon* rivaling the dragon-queen TIAMAT can be seen in the older *Sumerian* cycles where the prowess of NINURTA is shown in his ability to fight the mighty dragon KUR. His colors are black and violet and his essence corresponds to the metal lead.

NIRGAL *see* NERGAL

NISABA—The *Sumerian* agricultural goddess of writing and scribes; replaced by the god NABU in the Mardukite *Babylonian* Anunnaki tradition.

NUDIMMUD *see* ENKI

NUNAMIR *see* ENLIL

NUSKU [*"Bringer of Light"*]—ENLIL's vizier.

NUZKU *see* NUSKU

OANNES *see* ENKI

RAMMAN(U) *see* ADAD

SAMAS {20}—The official solar deity of the Enlilite *Sumerian* Anunnaki pantheon, brother to INANNA (SHTAR), born of NANNA and NINGAL. The sun represents the brilliance and radiant energy of life on earth; the light that allows organic life to grow and even the manner of which 'time' [and 'lifespan'] is divided. Expansive powerful energy of the solar current is invoked in magical ceremonies for general success and well-being. The fiery nature of the 'star' is called upon to 'incinerate iniquities' and reveal the nature of darkness and lies, meaning: the revelation of truth. Mistaken (by modern scholars) as monotheistic 'sun worship', solar veneration is really the celebration of life. As an archetypal representative of the 'starry' 'heavens', the sun signifies a presence and watchful eye of the 'All-Seeing-God', invoked in matters of law to bring righteous judgment. Sunday is sacred to SAMAS along with the color yellow, and both the color and essence of gold.

SARPANIT {(5)/(45)}—Seventh generation of ADAPA (by ENKI), the chosen royal spouse (consort) of MARDUK; princess-queen patron goddess (ISHTAR) of *Babylon* and mother to NABU. In alternative versions of the lore, her name ERU (or ERUA) designates her as the 'mother-goddess' of the *'Children of MARDUK'* (later associated with the light-folk or elves of Europe).

SHAMMASH *see* SAMAS

SHERIDA *see* AYA

SIN *see* NANNA

SUD *see* NINLIL

SUEN *see* NANNA

TAMMUZ *see* DUMUZI

TEHOM *see* TIAMAT

TIAMAT [*"Life-Giving Mother"*]—The 'primeval dragon' in *Babylonian* archaic epics, often equated with the *Sumerian* KUR. Later esoteric traditions associate 'her' as *Yaldabaoth* (*Ialda-baoth*) in Gnostic Hermeticism, or *Khornozon* (*Choronzon*) in Enochian Hermeticism. She is equated with the 'waters' or the 'Deep' in post-Sumerian Semitic scripture (Hebrew: *tehom*) – the all-encompassing "Sea" is parted to reveal the first 'division' (fragmentation) of "Life" in the Universe. She is paired anthropomorphically with ABZU (the *Abyss*) as the prehistoric 'ancestors' of the Anunnaki race. Her primary literary presence as TIAMAT (or T(I)AMTU) is in the *Enuma Elis* (*Babylonian*) 'Epic of Creation'. In later times, the name is used for the wife of ADAMU (*Adam*), being the equivalent to the Semitic "Eve" character.

TUTU *see* NABU

UDDU/UTTU *see* SAMAS

ZARPANITUM *see* SARPANIT

CUNEIFORM SCRIPT SYLLABARY

The capital "C" listed on top represents the letter from the left-hand column (except top row). For example: "AK," "AG" and "AQ" are all represented by the same sign.

PRIESTESS OF BABYLON

FOREWORD TO THE PREMIERE EDITION

by Joshua Free

When we published *"The Tablets of Destiny Revelation"* in late *2019*, the emphasis of the *Mardukite Research Org* became almost exclusively dedicated to research and development for titles composing the 'Systemology Esoteric Research Library'. I had already considered my previous work for the 'Mardukite Core Research Library' completed. But, Kyra's notebook demonstrated that there were still quite a few holes in our existing communication that needed to be filled for modern practitioners.

We originally planned to publish *"Priestess of Babylon"* in late *2021*, when Kyra brought me the first draft of this highly anticipated work. Needless to say, after being "lost in the shuffle" for quite a while, its appearance now in book form is long overdue.

This current volume does not replace knowledge gained from other 'Mardukite Core' titles. It supplements anything a *Seeker* has already learned quite well. In that same 'spirit', but with newcomers in mind, I have added appropriate details to Kyra's original outline that will make this material even more accessible for those that haven't already studied anything of our existing 'Core'.

To clarify, I should point out here that by 'Mardukite Core', we mean specifically the material found in 'The Complete Anunnaki Bible', 'Sumerian Religion', 'Babylonian Myth & Magic', and even 'The Tablets of Destiny Revelation' (all of which are also available as alternate titles for the 'New Standard Zuist Edition' series).

Many ancient cultures and esoteric traditions have experienced revival attention and reconstructionist efforts, popularly extending back even to the *Egyptians*. Yet, what is to be found concerning the "mother-of-them-all," *Mesopotamia*, the *Sumerians*, and especially the bold beauty and richness that is *Babylon*?

To fill this need and provide answers for the New Age, I founded *"Mardukite Ministries"* (*Mardukite Zuism*) and the *Mardukite Research Org* in *2008*. This pursuit led me directly to start developing our unique *"Systemology"* a decade later, which is the main emphasis of the *Mardukite Academy* today—but the earlier fundamentals uncovered from *arcane tablets* in the *ancient Near East* cannot be easily dismissed. And even today, in *2025*, the modern *Mardukite* legacy propagated from those original efforts, now *seventeen years* later, has remained—and it continues to reach thousands of new *Seekers* each year.

For all intents and purposes, the modern *Mardukite* effort is a living legacy that still has room for inclusion. In this case, for this book, we are opening the arms of our '*esoteric library*' to allow for a new addition—*Liber-P1*—the first new official addition to the '*Mardukite Core*' in nearly a decade. Those seeking to better understand ancient practices of Babylonian Tradition and the role of Anunnaki Priestesses (and other clergy) of the Temple Priesthood in ancient Babylon will certainly not be disappointed. Those seeking to enrich their own personal New Age tradition will find a genuine source of inspiration here. So, *be inspired and create!*

—*Joshua Free, "Nabu"*
Mardukite Founder
Mardukite Borsippa HQ
May's Eve 2025

— 0 —
MESSAGE FROM A MODERN-DAY
PRIESTESS OF BABYLON
(INTRODUCTION)

Welcome to Babylon! —City of the Gods!
I am High Priestess Kyra Light Kaos
and I will be your guide today!

When I started keeping literary records of my "Mardukite" journey, now almost a decade ago, I did not realize what a long and strange trip it would become. What began with a random chance meeting in Chicago resulted or manifested as the critical starting point of my "*aware life*"—kicking off of esoteric studies allowing me to more widely *awaken* into a world, both *real* and *fantastical*, which previously I had only gleaned brief tears of when mentioned by others. But really, a world that I had only dreamed of being *real*. A world where faeries, wizards, and magic actually exist; where energy itself is utilized for shaping reality—and that I could do this *knowingly*, or that I had already been participating in creating reality *unknowingly*. This recognition, or rediscovered ability of "creation" or manifestation into the physical, sparked like fireworks within me, shining light on the "*unknown*" and the (perhaps purposely for whatever reasons) *forgotten*.

While passing through Chicago on my way elsewhere, I quite unexpectedly had a chance run-in with a prolific writer who was also just passing through. Within a short time, *Joshua Free* introduced me to his *many* literary works, which covered *many* areas or topics—yet, I found his almost omniscient advice on one subject in particular led me curiously into the heart of THE ancient city of *Babylon*, called 'City of the Lords', 'City of Star-Lights', 'City of the Gates' and 'City of the Gods'.

I do not recollect a single public school lesson regarding the *Mesopotamia*—the "cradle of civilization" (as many academicians refer to it today). Yet there it *is*—or *was*—the "birthplace" of the 'systems' of 'civilized' society. And so, alongside (and inherent in) my efforts to learn magic and study systemology, I was privileged to find what I believed to be the *oldest*—the *beginning*—tradition and magic from the brief time when the *Gods* deigned to physically "come down" and personally visit planet Earth, intermingling with the results of their creations; when the *Gods* roamed the lands, their very presence witnessed by humans—something appearing very *solid* and *real* to them, rather than only being able to worship idols on altars and phantoms from afar.

Unfortunately, that once *real* and *physical* presence has been visibly absent from our view since a time when the walls of Babylon still stood. But those walls eventually disappeared as well. So much of the evidence to support this present work has long since passed into obscurity, leaving most folks today with little more than shadowy legends to behold when we speak of Mesopotamia, Babylon, the Anunnaki, or Sumerians. Today we must rely on fractured statues and even more highly fragmented *"cuneiform tablet writings"* in which to base our work. But what remains *are* the remains of the *original*, the *oldest*, and that which later cultures and traditions based their own beliefs and divine pantheons on. And if nothing else, for that reason, this all seemed very important. So, I decided to 'kill two birds with one stone' (as they say) and study the oldest magical religion while simultaneously compiling a notebook of my studies. It has taken some time, but here finally is my own direct contribution to further the data collected in the *Mardukite Research Library*.

This book is for *you*—it is *not just* for "females" or "aspiring priestesses." Really, this book is for *everyone*—not just for those who have already reached advanced studies regarding Mesopotamia and/or other Mardukite Zuism publications (on Babylonian Tradition). Although there are certainly more *details* available that are not contained within these pages, all of the critical basics are here—meaning, the basis for a solid understanding is provided here —in a series of chapter-lessons incrementally progressing, building upon each other, without unnecessarily over-complicating this subject-matter for newcomers.

In the first chapter, I introduce you to the core beliefs of a Babylonian, as well as their culture and daily life. The second chapter concerns the pantheon of Babylonia, the Anunnaki gods and goddesses, and some of their cult cities. The third chapter is specifically about priestesses and other information about clergy serving the temple priesthood. The fourth chapter describes various symbols, tools, and basic rules regarding practice of Mesopotamian "religious magic" as once used in Babylon. The fifth chapter gives examples of prayers, chants, and hymns—and this is studied prior to the sixth chapter on rites, rituals, and incantations. Combined these are meant to setup a suitable understanding that allows you to create your own unique modern-day "tradition"—a tradition that is both personally relevant to you and historically authentic. This book closes with a bonus chapter and appendix that I will let you discover on your own.

In the ancient temples of the Gods, the priestesses were *Earthborn* females, *initiated* in the ways of the sacred arts. They were individually selected from all across the known world and dispatched to temples, learning of what is *known* and *unknown* alike; and how to properly serve the gods and goddesses as nationally recognized intermediaries, working both for the people and the deity they wished to communicate with—serving as a religious and political bridge between the mundane world and the divine.

Priestesses received offerings and petitions from the people to give to the deities, then relayed their divine wisdom and responses in return. The truth behind this method of worship has all but disappeared from the religions and traditions in practice during this modern age. We have lost communication with the divine. Should you wish to reclaim what was lost: a pathway in that direction begins here. And as you are already an *Earthborn* human (or not—*it's okay, we won't tell...*) then, the next step to entering the secret priesthood is a *true initiation*—a learning experience that pertains to specially selected materials and texts arranged for study to bring you all the information you will need to get you well on your way.

The knowledge of life, the gods,
   and everything is at your fingertips.
      But, remember: Life is a game. So, have fun with it.

—*Kyra "Light" Kaos*
High Priestess
Mardukite Babylon
March 2025

—1—
BELIEFS & DAILY LIFE IN BABYLON

*"The education of the Babylonians was entirely in
the hands of the priesthood, who derived their
knowledge from Nabu, the inventor of writing and letters,
and every kind of learning—the Lord of the Houses of Tablets
(or books), i.e. the first libraries."*
—E.A. Wallis Budge, Babylonian Life & History

ANCIENT MESOPOTAMIAN RELIGION

The Sumerians cultivated the earliest recorded roots of our own modern civilization in prehistoric Mesopotamia, approximately six-thousand years ago. We consider those first origins "prehistoric" because they predate "history." As noted Sumeriologist, Samuel Kramer, was fond of saying: "history begins in Sumer." It is in Mesopotamia where "history"—which is to say, "definitive written records accounting for human activity"—is first chronicled and archived, using *cuneiform*, the first true "writing system." Some of these writings (known as the *King-Lists*) also suggest prior *Anunnaki*[*] activity on Earth for approximately 500,000 years, but for whatever reasons, our "modern" civilization required a deliberate and systematic "restart" in Mesopotamia around 4000 BCE.

The *Mardukite* "Anunnaki" tradition (both ancient and modern) that is emphasized in this book specifically concerns the beliefs, culture, and daily life of the *Babylonians*. There are, however, many instances where languages overlap—and earlier *Sumerian* words are retained in later *Babylonian* traditions. This book approaches this subject from the feminine perspective (as a "*priestess*") with an emphasis that differs from most other modern *Mardukite* publications (authored solely by Joshua Free).

Historically, the Old-Babylonian tradition is a amalgamation of *Akkadian* (northern Mesopotamia) and *Sumerian* (southern Mesopotamia) cultures, which were began in *c.* 2150 BCE. By the time of the infamous Hammurabi, *Babylon* had become the capital city-state of a singular Mesopotamian empire, led by an *Amorite* (proto-*Mardukite*) King. Over a thousand years later, the original *Mardukite* tradition was revitalized again under another famous king, Nebuchadnezzar II, who oversaw the Neo-Babylonian Renaissance era.

---

[*]   *Anunnaki* — a Mesopotamian word for a race of "*Gods*" (possibly "*StarGods*") that once walked upon the Earth (and inspired a diverse number of religious mythologies in many other cultures) under many different names.

Generally speaking, the ancient Mesopotamians were responsible for many "firsts" that are still with us today; many essential staples of "civilization" that we might dismissively take for granted. In spite of the thousands of years that have passed, many elements of the ancient world are eerily similar to our own. This makes it easier for a student of history to study and understand the most visible surface elements. Yet if we wanted to recreate a exact duplication, "reconstruction" or "revival" of the tradition today, some major differences might prevent this:

1. RELIGION: the main focus of Babylonian society
– and –
2. GEOGRAPHY: being ancient Mesopotamia

Religion prompted development of the very first *city-states*, each spreading out around a large "temple-shrine" to a particular Anunnaki deity. Long before organized warfare required the need for military-chieftains or warlord-kings, civilization was originally governed by the Temple high-priest (*en*) and high-priestess (*entu*). A definitive presence of the "Gods" and the power bestowed to their intermediary clergy dominated the everyday considerations of the ancient "citizens" residing within the city-walls.

Though abstract worship does play some small role in modern-day life, a true and pure belief system is no longer the life-blood of civilization. People may go to church and celebrate religious traditions just to satisfy some social expectation—or because "it's just what you're supposed to do." But, we no longer live in the "Age of Gods." And we certainly do not privately live and act as though we are under the scrutiny of an ever-watchful eye from above. As the ages shifted in Babylon, when only the temple-statues remained in the shrines (in the absence of "Living Gods"), a residual resonance still lingered, even if only a shadow of what had been—a physically solid memory instead of a intangible ghost.

Now, touching on location, geography, time and space: we obviously do not live in the alluvial deserts of ancient Babylon. This is important because *environment* is a key factor that determined what an ancient Mesopotamian could *do* and *how* they lived. New innovation frequently sprung from necessity. For example: where today eyeshadow and liner is used as a fashion statement, in Babylon (as in Egypt), black kohl served to keep the scorching glare of an unforgiving sun from one's eyes.

Southern Mesopotamia—the once fertile region of Babylon—offered plenty of water and rich soils, but few other natural resources. *Culture* was the real influential export from this region. Nearly everything else had to be imported from elsewhere. Large blocks of stone, such as used by Egyptians for pyramid-building, were unavailable. It has been said that not even a pebble existed there that was not carried from an outside source. Babylonians relied on their ability to extract *clay* from the land—and *bitumen,* a unique natural-springing asphalt that could adhere clay-bricks and provide waterproof coatings.

Since Mesopotamia enjoyed an agricultural and textile abundance, a new social role—the *merchant*—rose, someone to manage foreign trade routes of overland caravans and cargo-boats. As populations grew larger and more prosperous, and its rulers sought greater architectural splendor for their nation, additional resources and sturdier building materials were imported from surrounding countries. The *lapis lazuli* stone famously interwoven throughout Babylonia was actually imported from Afghanistan. All lumber came from Lebanon or the Zagros Mountains—especially since the local *date palm* was much more valuable alive for its fruit than as wood. Any precious metals had to be brought in from as far as Anatolia, Egypt, and the Indus River Valley.

Basic *environmental* factors not only affected attainable resources, but also shaped *social* culture and religious tones. In the fertile river-flowing desert plains of Mesopotamia (as with Egypt), the *"Waters of Life"* are treated as spiritually superior. Properly handling the "water element" (*e.g. irrigation*) made life in Babylon possible. In fact, once when the rivers were maliciously kept from flowing in Babylon for a time (as recorded on the *Erra Epos* tablets), its nation nearly collapsed into ruin. But this all contrasts greatly with cultures from colder environments further north that treat the *"Sacred Fire"* more centrally in their traditions. Essentially, the thing a society lacks (or needs most) to survive is what gets *prayed for*. The order of importances and beliefs then shapes what becomes national religion.

We'll begin this chapter by displaying a list of some of the more basic beliefs and values (or themes) fundamental to Babylonian society. Then, for those seeking greater depth from their studies: we offer a simple activity with a few short questions to start you on your way.

BELIEFS, VALUES & THEMES

1. THE WILL OF THE GODS IS MANIFEST IN NATURE AND SKILL.
This gives insight into their will.

2. SERVICE OF THE GODS IS HUMANITY'S PRIMARY FUNCTION.
The Gods domesticated (civilized) humans for their own purposes; also teaching them to maintain the waterways, agriculture and infrastructure that would perpetually support said civilization (domestication).

3. **"WHATEVER WAS PURE, WAS PURE AS LIGHT. WHATEVER WAS PURE, WAS BRIGHT."** *In spite of the shadowy gloom that often enshrouds portrayals of Mesopotamia, the Babylonians sought the 'Light' and revered 'bright' things. This is evident by religiously emphasizing an 'illumination of truth' by the Sun and 'radiance' of the Moon—and naming all the celestial lights observed in the night sky after their Gods.*

4. **IMPURITY IS SPREAD FROM PLACE TO PLACE**. *Words and ideas travel organically, as does pestilence and disease.*

5. **TRUE WISDOM**. *The earliest influential wisdom traditions—predating Greece, the Far East, and even Egypt—migrated out from Mesopotamia. Living the "Right Way" meant observing the will of the Gods, which is to say "Cosmic Law." [see appendix]*

6. **COMMUNITY DYNAMICS**. *A happy, healthy, prosperous, progressive, actualized community (society) is composed of many happy, healthy, prosperous, productive, actualized family units (households), which are composed of happy, healthy, productive, progressive, actualized individuals. Thus, self-actualized individuals are required for a strong healthy community.*

7. **INTUITION**. *The "Right Way" for an individual is that path which allows the True Self—or Personal Spirit—to properly unfold and be recognized. In modern pop-psychology, this might be reduced to the idea of embracing one's "shadow" or "inner child"—but at a higher level, true intuition is accessible only when the filters are removed that prevent the Spiritual Self from knowing itself.*

8. **HOSPITALITY**. *Traditionally, one was always accommodating to a guest (unless given a reason otherwise). Faithful reciprocation generally also prevailed; which at another level, led to standardizing trade.*

9. **LOVE**. *Among the diverse cuneiform tablets unearthed from the sands we find the oldest records of love songs, romantic poetry, and even quite colorful and explicit erotica. Ancient writers were also not shy about detailing the relationship drama and sexual exploits of the Anunnaki Gods.*

10. **CREATIVITY**. *Systematization and agriculture established the basis for*

civilization and replaced the nomadic hunter-gatherer lifestyle that kept prehistoric humans completely preoccupied with basic survival. As a result, true "culture" was born—one that embraced creativity inherent in the arts, music and poetry. This is evident in the design of pottery and jewelry dating as far back as the fourth millennium B.C.E., and depicting ornate spirals and knots closely resembling that of the Celts thousands of years later.

11. **MAGIC**. *Babylonian clergy and wise-ones held a dualistic understanding of the cosmos (creation). They observed a relationship between two distinct states: the "Here" (the physical, the Earth, matter) and the "Other"—that visible things "seen" are propagated and perturbed by what is relatively "unseen." At a higher level, "magic" involved understanding Cosmic Law (the "will of the Gods") and living in accordance with it, rather than in opposition to it. At a mundane or practical level, the closest that academic scholars have ever come to understanding ancient mysticism is something they refer to as "sympathetic magic"—where the physical act of manipulating some symbol "here" has the ability to affect something "there."*

12. **"TO NOT OBSERVE THE RITES IS TO FALL."** *A unique formula drove the success of Mardukite Babylon, an understanding of cosmic wisdom and a tradition that was unparalleled in the ancient world. So long as the Temple District (priests and priestesses) and the Palace District (royal court) "observed the rites" of Mardukite Tradition, then happiness, prosperity and success were enjoyed by all. When usurpers or maligned rulers disregarded tradition, society greatly suffered. Often, the population revolted. The "Hand of Marduk" would touch upon some specific individual (even a foreigner) and bless them with visions and inspiration to ride into Babylon and replace the disgraced king, much to the welcome and celebration of the oppressed population. Then, the new king would prostrate themselves before the image of Marduk at his Temple, make appropriate offerings and vows, and give thanks for the privilege to lead the Babylonians.*

13. **UNDERWORLD RESURRECTION AND FUTURE LIVES**.
Mardukite clergy held a unique understanding about spiritual life that distinguished them from others in the ancient world—and even other Mesopotamian traditions. All Mesopotamian traditions observed an immediate afterlife in the Underworld, but the Mardukites did not believe that one's spiritual existence permanently ended there. They believed in repeated

incarnations in this material existence—and also that one could work their way upward "to be as like the Gods." Similarly to the Egyptians, the Mesopotamians believed that items buried with a body could assist them later; in this case, their journey to (and hopefully out of) the Underworld. Unlike the Egyptians, however, they did not believe that specific burial rites or posthumous incantations guaranteed someones Ascension—nor did they treat their kings as "living embodiments of a god" (as like pharaohs were viewed). Apart from Mardukite tradition, many Mesopotamians maintained more nihilistic beliefs influenced by older Sumerian "Gilgamesh" tablets—which suggested that "the Gods kept immortality for themselves and permit only death for humanity" so "eat and drink your fill" because one's destined Underworld is gloomy.

14. **ETHICS: "GOOD" AND "BAD."** *An enforceable moral law or "code" is present throughout ancient Mesopotamia, though the legal standards of King Hammurabi (nearly 4,000 years ago) are probably the most famous. Babylonian laws are rooted in a "utilitarian" philosophy (similar to the formula for #6 above), meaning they serve the "greatest good" for a healthy prosperous society as a whole by protecting the quality of life for all individuals concerned. A happy healthy society required a healthy fertile and properly maintained environment in which to exist. Wide-view ecological interests were synonymous with individual interests.*

15. **FAMILY RELATIONSHIP DETERMINES YOUR PLACE IN SOCIETY.** *An individual was born into a certain social class, but they were also capable of elevating their position thereafter. A citizen could own or inherit land, work in the family trade, become an educated professional, join the clergy, or even marry "up."*

16. **HUMANS BECAME AS THE RESULT OF A DIVINE ACT OF CREATION.** *The specifics differ among Mesopotamian cultures, but all of the tablet records have one thing in common: they suggest that humans were created as a genetic result of "divine intervention" (as was the accelerated progress of their domestication/civilization). The oldest tablets indicate that a God was slain/sacrificed for their blood (genetics). The sixth tablet of the Mardukite Babylonian "Epic of Creation" describes the creation of humans (which is why the "Book of Genesis" indicates humans are made on the "sixth day") to serve the Gods, create and maintain temple-shrines—and the Mardukites are charged to keep watch and guard the "Gates."*

ACTIVITY

[Critical Thinking: It is important to question and analyze our beliefs, because they shape how we think, and ultimately what we do.]

1. Are any of these beliefs ones you hold true? (y/n)
2. Are there any that you don't agree with? #_____
3. List a belief/value you would add to the list. _____

_____

_____

Now, let's take a brief journey through the urban culture center of the once great city of Babylon. We'll quietly peer through the windows of the citizen's daily lives and note some details. Oh, to be a fly on a wall of this wondrous sprawling monument to a Golden Age of human civilization would be a priceless treasure for the collection of any museum.

SOCIAL CLASS, AGE & TITLES

The best historical example we have of Mesopotamian social class comes from the Law-Code of King Hammurabi (during the Old Babylonian era). A free-person or "citizen" might own land, if they were of the upper-class *awilum*; or they might not be landowners, and therefore be part of the work-a-day middle-class *mushkenum*.

Most scholarly translators reduce the lowest class, *wardum*, as "slave." This word did not carry the same meaning in Babylon that we find portrayed elsewhere. It literally meant that the individual did not own land and was not a free-person; therefore, not a true "citizen." This could include those in serious debt or working off criminal restitution, meaning that this social position was not necessarily permanent. By definition, most live-in "servants" of the Temple and Palace were also *wardum* (and treated well).

Unlike other "caste" systems in history, the social classes of Babylon are not fixedly mandated. These were simply economic observations, much as we might consider "class" today. These observations are based on an earlier pattern of settlement in southern Mesopotamia, which later became Babylonia. The earliest families settled on the best land and those that came later had to settle for less. Latecomers found themselves with no land at all. As a result, a systematic "stratification of wealth" simply occurred by the very nature of how early civilization progressively developed.

Women enjoyed more rights and equality in *Mardukite Babylon* than elsewhere in the ancient world, even compared to other Mesopotamian eras. This is often easy to distinguish based on periods and places where "Goddess" arche-types are given strong prominence. Positions in the Anunnaki pantheon are always presented as "Divine Couples"—a Goddess and God, both equally representative of whatever the aspect. Hence, for example, we find a highly venerated "moon god" and "sun goddess" alongside their respective spouses —which is culturally unique.

A strong "family unit" (household/home) was critical to societal success. Many of the marriage and inheritance laws of Hammurabi were intended to protect women. They could own their own property and even divorce husbands if mistreated. Babylonia also relied on *task specialization* for its success—individuals being productive in specific skilled activities.

Larger families (more children) were preferable in agricultural societies; they meant more help for working the farms (or other family businesses). No gender exclusions existed, but females generally excelled at managing household affairs; food preparation; textile-weaving; pottery-making; acting as mid-wives and physicians: creating music, poetry, jewelry and art; and of course, temple-priestesses.

[FROM BABYLONIAN ROOT 'TO BE LITTLE']	
SUḪĀRU	BOY
SUḪĀRTU	GIRL

ṢA/UḪURTU and BATŪSSU [ASSYR.]

WĂRTU or NU'ARTU are other words for "girl." MUŠTENŬ means a "changed child" or post-pubescent adult, one who is old enough for marriage, which is celebrated as a special rite of passage—similar to the Jewish *bat-mitzvah* and the Latino *quinceanera*. A young woman of fifteen, or BATŬLTU, has reached an age where she is permitted to marry. Sometimes marriages were even arranged by parents while the children were still young, but they would remain living at home until reaching maturity.

IN SUMERIAN		
AGE OVER 15 is ADULT		
SMALL GIRL	1 TO 5	MUNUS.TUR.TUR
GIRL	5 TO 10	TUR.MUNUS
OLDER GIRL	10 TO 15	MUNUS.TUR
WOMAN	15	MUNUS

There was no literal word for "virgin," but *ki.sikil* meant a young maiden, who was assumed to be a virgin when she first married. *Sinnistštu* means an "adult woman"—though if unmarried, she might be referred to as a *nartu*. In Akkadian, "wife" is AŠŠATU (AŠTU); or ISSU in Assyrian. The following life-cycle/age chart is given in the Sumerian language.

40	LALŬTU is BLOOM OF LIFE
50	DAYS ARE SHORT
60	MET-LU-TU is MANHOOD
70	DAYS ARE LONG
80	ŠIBŬTU is OLD AGE
90	LITTŪTU is ADVANCED OLD AGE

SEASONS & MEASURING TIME

Ancient Babylonians observed two main seasons, essentially summer and winter. Traditional names for these seasons—*Enmeš* and *Enten* respectively—are derived from a Sumerian tale about two brothers (recorded on the "*Enmeš and Enten*" tablets). The spring equinox marked the start of the calender with the *Akiti* new year festival—the primary annual national holiday celebration, which lasted ten days. Later in the year, a transition between summer and winter was marked with a harvest festival.

The spring season also brought unpredictable challenges. The life-sustaining rivers often experienced furious flooding as the mountain snows melted. Water levels of the Euphrates River—BUR.AN.UN in Sumerian; *puratu* in Akkadian—often began rising in late-March or early-April; whereas the Tigris River—I.DI.IK.LAT or *id-ig-na*—rose at the opposite time of year, and may have signaled the harvest (and a time for winter preparations).

Babylonians adopted, and continued advancing, the Sumerian's *sexagesimal* "base-60" system of mathematics for measuring space and time, including angles and coordinates. It is the basis of the 360-degree circle, the six-ty-second minute and the sixty-minute hour. "60" has *12* whole number divisors: 1, 2, 3, 4, 5, 6, 10, 12, 15, 20, 30, and itself. The remarkably advanced level of Babylonian mathematics is still being deciphered in awe to this day.

The Anunnaki originally employed the *sexagesimal* numeric system and presumably taught it to the Sumerians. It is used to distinguish "hierarchical ranking" (roles or positions) in the Anunnaki pantheon. It was also key to mapping cartography of the "celestial sphere" that we recognize today as the "zodiac"—our perspective of a specific 360-degree ring that encircles the solar system and is divided into twelve 30-degree zones (or "houses"). This same structure evolved into our original calendars.

MONTHS

NISAN(U)—MARCH 21 (*Spring Equinox*)
AIARU [*ayaru*]—APRIL
SIMANU [*siwan*]—MAY
DU'UZU [*tammuz*]—JUNE
ABU [*ab*]—JULY
ALULU [*elul*]—AUGUST
TISHRITU [*tishri*]—SEPTEMBER 21
HESHWAN [*arahshamna*]—OCTOBER
KISLIMU [*kislev*]—NOVEMBER
TEBITU [*tebet*]—DECEMBER
SHEBATU [*sebat*]—JANUARY
ADDARU [*adar*]—FEBRUARY
[2nd *adar*]—(*aligns luni-solar year*)

CLOTHING

The need and desire to clothe one's body is perhaps the earliest distinction between "humans" and the "animal kingdom" here on Earth. Prehistoric signs of clothing exist beyond Mesopotamia. In fact, ancient "textiles" are most difficult to uncover directly with archaeology. Fortunately for us, there are surviving artistic depictions of Babylonian citizens, clergy and royalty, which have fared better over thousands of years than any physical remains of the clothing itself.

Early Sumerians are often depicted in leather and animal-skins, but the Babylonians greatly improved the textile industry. In addition to mastering agriculture for food, farms often included domesticated sheep and goats (for their hair). The most common cloth type was *wool*, followed by *linen* for fancier fabrics. By the Neo-Babylonian era of Nebuchadnezzar II, the Assyrians had started importing *cotton* from Egypt.

Mesopotamians often used a large cloth to wrap about themselves as a main garment. There are also depictions of men wearing skirts (or kilts) and women wearing long gown-like tunics. Nobility and royalty are often shown wearing elaborately embroidered robes. Women were fond of fringes and tassels. One of the key differences in dress between men and women concerned the size of the cloth and direction of its wrap. Traditionally, female clothing crossed across the chest towards the left, or rational side of the brain; and a male crossed his across the chest towards the right, or intuitive side of the brain.

Typical accessories included things like brooches, shawls, decorated sandal-like shoes, bracelets, rings, necklaces, cylinder-seals, and amulets. Shoes were particularly important for priestesses and priests, since the act of touching the ground with the soles of one's feet was considered "unclean."

CHILDREN

Along the residential streets of Babylonia, it was quite common to see children at play. They had access to balls, musical instruments, played skip-rope and even developed a form of hockey. Not surprisingly, girls typically owned dolls, imagining themselves in the role of future mothers; boys, often idolizing the hunters and warriors, might play with small bow-and-arrow sets. Young ones also sought wooden and *terra-cotta* toy-miniatures of ships, chariots, wagons and animals—the same type of things a modern child would enjoy.

Most specialized trade learning occurred organically. The working class children usually stayed home to assist in the family business. The Sumerians established the oldest known educational institutions, but they began as subsidized private schools for the elite. These schoolhouses were often maintained in the Temple district (with the "*scribes*") and attendance with neither required, nor free. But, in Babylon, any social class or gender was permitted. Primary education focused on writing, followed by mathematics and history. Just as today, the purpose of learning was to be a more able, informed and productively successful citizen.

ANCESTORS & HOUSEHOLD GODS

Performing funerary rites and offerings for the dead was a key responsibility for the living. Offerings (*kispu*) of food (bread), drink (wine) and consecrated oils were made at the E.KISIGA ("House of Funerary Offerings") to prevent the spirit from "wander overseas and returning to haunt the upper world." At a small personal shrine devoted to the deceased love one, the simple ritual involves four main aspects:

1—PĀQIDU: the one who attends to (priest/ess)
2—KISPA KASĀPU: making the offering
3—MĚ RAQU: pouring water/libations; and
4—ŠUMA ZAKĀRU: the calling of the name.

These actions are performed exactly as written. 'One who attends to' is the arrival of the priest/ess. 'The act of making funerary offerings' is the literal cooking and/or acquisition of the offerings. The 'offerings' are left on the shrine-altar and the priest/ess waits outside for about thirty minutes. 'Pouring water/libations' is the act of pouring liquid offering for the spirit onto the ground outside. (You might have heard of this in other cultures, or the phrase "pour one out.") 'Calling of the name' is the final act of acknowledging and thanking the loved one (or ancestor).

The *Ilŭ rĕshi* (literally "*intermediary/middle gods*") are one's "personal gods" (some academic sources call them "household gods"). These are the gods most common citizens prayed to (or petitioned) in their daily life. In some cases, they might be the Anunnaki Gods of the traditional pantheon, but this wasn't a requirement. An *ashirtum* ("worship room") was a designated area of virtually every home. This personal shrine included an offering table, set with votive statues and icons of these personal gods.

The personal gods could either be represented by a single statuette of a specific deity, or one statue containing the seven angel-like figures representing the seven primary Anunnaki Gods. In many ways, personal household reflects the rituals performed at the Temple pertaining to the "care and feeding of family spirits (ancestors)."

The tools (aspects), actions and physical setup tend to mirror the design and rituals of the Temple. For example: after conducting the more formal funerary custom at the Temple-House, the care and feeding of ancestor spirits continued similarly in ones home—in an area designated specifically for that. Similarly, the offerings an individual continues to make to one's "personal gods" (or Anunnaki Gods) mirrors the more public ceremonies conducted by Temple priestesses and priests.

PROVERBS[*]

* A hostile act you shall not perform, that fear of vengeance shall not consume you.

* You shall not do evil, that life eternal you may obtain.

* Does a woman conceive when a virgin, or grow great without eating?

* If I put anything down it is snatched away; if I do more than is expected, who will repay me?

* He has dug a well where no water is, he has raised a husk without kernel.

---

* Excerpted from: "*Archeology and The Bible*" (3rd ed.), Philadelphia: American Sunday School, 1920 (pp. 407-408)

* Does a marsh receive the price of its reeds, or fields the price of their vegetation?

* The strong live by their own wages; the weak by the wages of their children.

* He is altogether good, but he is clothed with darkness.

* The face of a toiling ox you shall not strike with a goad.

* My knees go, my feet are unwearied; but a fool has cut into my course.

* His ass I am; I am harnessed to a mule—a wagon I draw, to seek reeds and fodder I go forth.

* The life of day before yesterday has departed today.

* If the husk is not right, the kernel is not right, it will not produce seed.

* The tall grain thrives, but what do we understand of it? The meager grain thrives, but what do we understand of it?

* The city whose weapons are not strong the enemy before its gates shall not be thrust through.

* If you go and take the field of an enemy, the enemy will come and take your field.

* Upon a glad heart oil is poured out of which no one knows.

* Friendship is for the day of trouble, posterity for the future.

*An ass in another city becomes its head.

* Writing is the mother of eloquence and the father of artists.

* Be gentle to your enemy as to an old oven.

* The gift of the king is the nobility of the exalted; the gift of the king is the favor of governors.

* Friendship in days of prosperity is servitude forever.

* There is strife where servants are, slander where anointers anoint.

* When you see the gain of the fear of god, exalt god and bless the king.

ACTIVITY

Armchair Academia: Compare the literal style and interpretive significance of these proverbs with the lines of "*Marduk's Tablet of Destiny*" given in the section titled "*Mardukite Zuism: A Brief Introduction*" (in the appendix).

ART

In ancient Mesopotamia, "art" was a new cultural innovation combining form and function, beauty and practicality. Urbanization permitted permanency and a greater ability to preserve one's property. This developed naturally into a basic desire for things to simply be "nicer." Artisans of every fashion were required for building up the Babylonian empire and everything within it.

From the glazed bricks that lined the processional streets and city-walls, to the very design of the Temples, Palaces, and every symbolic treasure kept inside them—each one contributed something unique to the publicly perceived power of the Babylonian tradition. Artisans and craftsmen were frequently commissioned by the Temple District to fashion various votive objects, ornate wall reliefs, special pottery, "seals," "stamps" and of course, religious statuary.

Due to its archeological longevity, Mesopotamian statues are perhaps the most famous demonstrations of artistic form and religio-political function. Naturally, we find large statues of Anunnaki Gods in the Temples. But others, like the immense human-headed winged-bull *lamassu*, were intended to stand as protective guardians at the entrance of Temples and libraries. In the Palace District, statues and grandiose wall-reliefs were created to venerate royalty and record historical events. Nearly all significant buildings had collections of small statues buried at the corners of its foundation.

There are other connections binding culture and religion in a way that cemented personal "faith" in the security of social systems and world order. A unique "glyptic" micro-sculpting art craft is found throughout the Ancient Near East and it plays an especially significant role in establishing the "legal" legitimacy of one's participation in society. It also required precision skill to carve the imagery on small "seals" and "stamps"—the smallest of which we've found are as tiny as one centimeter in diameter. But, here we find ancient origins of legally recognizable "signet rings" and "official marks."

Most official "*cylinder seals*" were 2-3 centimeters long (with a diameter usually half its length). They were made from a small piece of hard material—such as bone, shell, quartz, chalcedony, lapis lazuli, hematite, marble, agate and other precious stones. Their round cylindrical shape resembles a "bead"—some having holes running through to make it easier to carry or even wear them on a cord.

Intricate sunken or raised designs were carved with flint or copper tools, or a "bow-drill," to make the seal. Because it was used to make an impression in clay, any imagery and writing had to be reversed. Impressions were used to mark something "officially"—such as a personal signature on a contract, or a manufacturers mark—or for more decorative purposes. Imagery usually centered around Gods, their worshipers and other mythological symbolism and motifs. Personal seals might also serve as "amulets" and typically depicted specific deities, trees, animals, and prayers that an individual felt affinity for.

SCRIBES & SCHOOLHOUSES

"Who dwells in the place of scribal art, like sun may they shine."

In ancient Mesopotamia, the word for "school" and "tablet-house" are synonymous: E.DUBBA in Sumerian; *bit-tuppi* in Akkadian. ['E' and 'bit' (spoken 'bet') both mean "house." The Sumerian root 'DUB' for "tablet" is treated as 'tup-' in Babylon.] The purpose of the educational system was to develop young citizens into "scribes" (*tupsharru*, "tablet-keeper"), meaning literate and "learned" members of society.

Prior to *Mardukite Babylon*, the educational system was private and exclusive to children (usually male, unless a daughter of royalty or future priestess) of elite families that could afford it. But, its public standardization during *Mardukite Babylonian* eras led to a greater and more productive society. Being able to *read* the tablets (rather than rely on someone else that could) added to the legitimacy of the structured civic systems represented on those tablets. Oral traditions are universal, but when a citizen could actually read their own contracts, or even the national laws and beliefs carved onto a eight-foot tall *stele* in the center of town, suddenly these "words that stay" took on greater significance.

Students required a strict intensive education if they aspired to walk the path of a *scribe*. They began attending school at tablet-houses around the age of ten (or earlier), then spent the next five years (until adulthood at 15) learning reading, writing, math and music, from sunrise to sunset, 24 days per month. [We don't know if school was held all year or not.] The average farmer, laborer or soldier did not necessarily possess these skills. Not all graduating students stayed on to develop even further learning as "scribes" (or physicians or clergy), but as civilization progressed, more of the serious professions required the ability to read and write.

Sumerian *cuneiform* was originally written using one's thumb nail. But around the Old Babylonian Era, a beautiful refinement of the script occurred for the Akkadian language with the invention of the *stylus* (*urbănu*) or scribe's-pen, cut from a reed plant. A Babylonian student studied both the Sumerian and national Akkadian languages. They retained many Sumerian words as a classical language, much like Europeans had treated Latin.

Archeologists are able to distinguish classroom sites from traditional library tablet-houses due to the sheer amount of tablets displaying "corrections." The teacher would write out tablets for a student to copy and then correct their assignments. Students also recited memorized lines. On a higher level, the standardization of public education in Babylon could also be considered the original inception of systematized social learning or "indoctrination" of a worldview. Such things are so commonplace today that we seldom think of it —but in the ancient world, this innovation allowed for perpetual "domestication" (or civilizing) of an exponentially growing population (and in a region with a constant migrant influx).

Apart from schoolhouse tutoring and serving as clergy, the scribes were historians and lore-keepers responsible for the archival preservation, duplication and certification of critical literature and important documents. In *Mardukite Babylonia*, tablet-scribes developed a cult-like dedication to the Anunnaki scribe-god *Nabu*, inventor of the *stylus*. This "secret society" even maintained *Nabu's* private temple-shrine, library and scribe-college in *Borsippa*, only ten miles away from *Babylon-city*. Where this present book has adopted a "temple-priestess perspective" of Mesopotamia, most other modern Mardukite literature (*by Joshua Free*) takes the "Borsippa scribe-priest of Nabu" approach to the Babylonian tradition.

MAY YOUR EXCEEDING WISDOM
GIVEN BY THE TABLETS OF NABU
NEVER CEASE ON THE CLAY
IN THE TABLET HOUSE.

IN THIS TABLET HOUSE
LIKE A SHRINE
FASHIONING EVERYTHING
MAY IT NEVER COME TO AN END.

TO THE JUNIOR SCRIBE
WHO PUTS HIS HAND TO THE CLAY
AND WRITES ON IT
MAY NABU THE ONE WHO SPEAKS
GIVE WISDOM.

MAY HE OPEN HIS HAND
IN THE PLACE OF WRITIING
MAY HE COME FORTH
LIKE THE SUN FOR THE SCRIBES.

THE STAR RELIGION

When the oldest astronomical observations were recorded by the Sumerians, the Sun still entered the celestial zone of *Taurus* on the vernal/spring equinox (*March 21*), when the "new year" began. The same constellation is still recognized as "the Bull" today—originally in honor of *Enlil*, commander of the Anunnaki Gods during the Sumerian era; what we still refer to as, the *Age of Taurus* (*c.* 4130 BCE – 2160 BCE).

The Anunnaki Assembly (or Council) always intended this early "Sumerian" arrangement of the pantheon as temporary, with *Marduk* awaiting his era to command in the new *Age of Aries*. But 2160 BCE came and went and there was no peaceful transition of power, nor even a recognition of a required forthcoming regime change. To add insult to injury, Sumerian Kings reinvigorated public devotion in their old lunar-cults (dedicated to *Nanna/Sin*) and *Inanna/Ishtar*-cults when establishing a new "Third Dynasty of UR" (UR III, *c.* 2120 BCE – 2000 BCE) in a last-ditch effort to maintain control.

The UR-III attempt at a *Sumerian Renaissance* did not completely thwart an eventual rise of *Mardukite Babylon*—but it required some ingenuity to preserve Mesopotamian civilization in the wake of a Sumerian cultural decline (*c.* 2150 BCE). *Babylon* already existed as a proto-*Mardukite* settlement during UR-III, but it was never recognized as any kind of political center (or capital) during the Sumerian era. A period of chaotic confusion erupted among the population in the absence of a true authority and world order, leaving the region open to militant foreign invasions.

Toward the end of the *"Enlilite"* Sumerian era, the original *Mardukite* population (called *martu* or *amurru*; also *"Amorites"* in many academic texts) still primarily remained "outside" Mesopotamia. These nomadic *Nabu*-tribes awaited the *Age of Aries* in the desert wilderness to the west. Essentially, *"Martu"* is the same as saying *"Mardukite"* today; the population is named (using its own native language) for its chief Anunnaki-deity (*Marduk*).

With the "new age" dawning upon the land, the *Amorites* began a peaceful ethnic invasion, integrating themselves within the general Sumerian population. They shared the same Anunnaki pantheon. They even spoke a *semitic* language, similar to the Akkadians—*Akkadian* being the oldest *semitic* language. Their interests did not include killing, destroying, looting, and leaving Mesopotamia in ruin (the way other foreign invaders did), because this was to be their home and these were to be their people.

On a national (political) level, the *Amorite* cultural invasion was met with strong resistance by the UR-III Dynasty. Even after that dynasty fell (2000 BCE), city-states such as *Larsa* and *Isin* continued to maintain their Sumerian independence (up until the reign of Hammurabi). It would take another hundred years for the *Amorites* to fully infiltrate Mesopotamia and establish the "First Dynasty of Babylon" *c.* 1900 BCE.

The *Mardukite Babylonian* empire thrived for three centuries before its capture by the Hittite military. Kassites from the east drove out the Hittites. They did their best to assimilate the Babylonian tradition, as did the later Assyrians, but after the fall of its First Dynasty (1595 BCE), it took a millennium before an authentic *Mardukite Renaissance* occurred during the "Neo-Babylonian (Chaldean)" era (625 BCE – 539 BCE), which included Nebuchadnezzar II.

An *Anunnaki "Star Religion"* based on astronomical observation propelled Mesopotamian civilization from its start. But that esoteric information was of the Gods—and only served the priestesses and priests. The common person in society only understood the quality of their everyday life, and much of that was based on a strong faith in the Sumerian "systems" they participated. In order for Babylon to prosper in a post-Sumerian *Age of Aries*, the legitimacy for *Marduk*'s reign had to be established firmly in social consciousness.

Babylonians mythologically established *Marduk* as the new "*Bull of Heaven*"—calling him the "*Solar Calf*"—effectively replacing any position formerly held by *Enlil*. For example, in earlier literature, the Sun had been compared to an *ox*, or a farmer yoking his oxen to a shinning plow. A similar title was bestowed upon Marduk as he passed through the twelve zodiac house-signs: *Gudi-bir*, "the bull of light." When the Sun rose on the vernal/spring equinox, backed by one of the zodiac houses (zones), it was called the "directing bull"—"the bull who guides (the year)." Annual observation of a *Mardukite* version of the "New Year" festival in Babylon proved to be the key to perpetuating its religious success.

ANNUAL FESTIVALS

Astronomical and seasonal observation led to the original holidays of most ancient cultures. The "equinoxes" are the first significant dates that would have been recognized by the wise-ones that recorded natural and celestial data. They occur twice each year, in the spring and autumn, traditionally March 21 and September 21 (using modern standards). They are acknowledged on most ancient calendars and mark fundamental transitions in the annual cycle of life on Earth. Seasonal festivals also served an especially important function in agricultural societies and their continued survival.

In Mesopotamia, the spring equinox festival marked the start of the year on the first day of the month *Nisan(u)*. It was the single most important annual holiday. Its name—A.KI.TI in Sumerian; *Akitu* in Akkadian—meant "On Earth, Life," indicating seasonal renewal of the land and a time to begin planting barley. [In fact, an alternate (but less likely) translation of the Akkadian name could be "On Earth, Plant."] On a magical or symbolic level, the collective intention or social consciousness of a spring festival was directed to generate life and encourage abundance—ensuring fertility for the people, animals and natural environment.

As described in the previous section: on this first day of the year, the relative alignment between the Sun and the celestial sphere (or "zodiac"), as observed from Earth, also determined the current "*Age*." This was important for *Mardukite Babylonians* to certify the national rituals and legitimize the position of Marduk. Revising earlier customs, the festival also celebrated the "divine marriage" of Marduk and Sarpanit—an earthling spouse, the daughter of an early Sumerian bloodline seeded directly by the Anunnaki. His selection of a "human" consort (elevated to goddess status in Babylon) only furthered the idea that Marduk sought to maintain a closer relationship with humanity than former Anunnaki Gods.

On a local political level, the annual *Akiti Rituals* cemented "Divine Right" of the king to rule as a representative intermediary between the general population and cosmic order. But, of course, the clergy were responsible for conducting the rites, which included the king temporarily surrendering their royal regalia and kingship to Marduk (or a statue thereof). Priestesses and priests ultimately determined whether or not a king's right-to-rule would be returned to him for another year—presumably based on how well he had ruled the previous year (and perhaps whether or not it aligned with the will of the Temple District). Although mainly symbolic drama, the very fact of its inclusion in a public liturgy is why *anti-Mardukite* and tyrannical usurper kings did not "observe the rites."

Above all, the "New Year" *Akiti-Akitu* festival was a celebration and commemoration of the *Mardukite* pantheon—*Marduk* and *Sarpanit*, and, of course, *Nabu* (his adopted heir apparent) and *Teshmet* (*Tasmit*). A ten-mile procession from *Borsippa* carried the official statue of *Nabu* to attend the festival in *Babylon-city* and participate in the rites. There was also a dramatic reenactment of the *Babylonian* "*Epic of Creation*," displaying Marduk conquering the forces of the Universe (or *Tiamat*, the Cosmic Dragon). The entire festival period lasted twelve days.

From the available cuneiform tablet records recovered and deciphered, we know that a "harvest festival" also occurred each year at the autumn equinox (the first day of the month of *Tashritu*). Early scholars blurred any details about the autumn-harvest festival with the spring festival (or even earlier Sumerian beliefs) that academicians confusingly reference both *Babylonian* festivals as *Akiti*. This is in part because of UR-III tablet interpretations that may refer to an "*A-ki-ti* of seed time" (spring) and an "*A-ki-ti* of barley-cutting" (autumn).

Mardukite Babylonians reserved the "dark half" of the year to acknowledge the "other side" of the pantheon—mainly *Inanna-Ishtar* and *Dumuzi* (*Tammuz*). The symbolic ritual motif for autumn and winter undoubtedly turned toward "death"—hence we find a ceremonial reenactment of "*Inanna's Descent to the Underworld*" and emphasis on other mythological themes concerning her lover, a slain god-king renewed. And to differentiate this autumn festival (from the spring) for an authentic new modern *Mardukite* standard, we have adopted the name "*Zagmuk*" from an archaic Sumerian word for the same.

Additional records refer to other publicly observed "community fire festivals" where consecrated symbols representing the wickedness and iniquities of society would be burned in effigy. Such details are included in a companion volume—"*The Maqlu Ritual Book*" (or "*Anunnaki Rites: New Standard Zuist Edition*"). Whether or not these were assigned to the "solstices" or some other specific dates, we cannot be absolutely certain. In the *Mardukite* tradition of modern "Mesopotamian Neopaganism," it has become a custom to observe the *Maqlu* ritual on the eve of October 31, paralleling the Celtic *Samhain*.

"Let us learn to appreciate there will be times when the trees will be bare, and look forward to the time when we may pick the fruit."

—Anton Chekhov

— 2 —
BABYLONIAN GODS & GODDESSES

"Through Marduk, the power of Eridu — incantation-prayer and 'intention' — was taught to the scribes of Nabu and the Mardukite Priests, who were taught to attract and compel the 'gods' in the name of Marduk, always incanting the word-formula of the highest order: Nabu invoked by way of the name of Marduk; Marduk invoked by way of the name of Enki, Our Father, who in turn would invoke by the name of Anu — and so was born the concept of magical hierarchies, an ideal that was convoluted and obscured when employed later, such as during the Middle Ages and particularly distorted by the Judeo-Christian paradigm as evident in many popular grimoires"
—Joshua Free, Tablet-W, Book of Marduk

BABYLONIAN RELIGION

The Anunnaki pantheon dominated the social and religious consciousness of Mesopotamia for 6,000 years, right up until the arrival of Arabs and Islam. When the Akkadian language and Babylonian tradition replaced the former Sumerian culture, it retained the same Anunnaki pantheon. The names were changed to match the new language; and hierarchical positions were updated to be consistent with the new *Mardukite* emphasis propagated by the capital city of Babylon—in honor of its patron god, Marduk, and in recognition of the *"Age of Aries."*

The rich culture, advanced knowledge and spiritual tradition of Babylon inspired envy and awe by those living in the surrounding areas. While the Sumerians and Babylonians observed what we consider the "original" Anunnaki tradition, that tradition and its lore did not remain exclusive to Mesopotamians. It spread to those cultures emerging along its perimeter and evolved further from there. The *Arameans, Canaanites, Cimmerians, Edomites, Elamites, Gutians, Hittites* and *Hurrians*, all assimilated their own diluted interpretations of Babylonian Anunnaki tradition in their own language, for their own religious purposes and cultural flavors. The *Assyrians* were the most famous example of this—modeling their chief god *Ashur* directly from Marduk. The Assyrian King *Ashurbanipal* was also quite adamant about owning a copy of every piece of significant tablet literature from Babylon for his personal library.

Ancient Mesopotamians shared a unique relationship with the Anunnaki Gods. For a time, they resided on Earth in Sumerio-Babylonian city-states, or at least visited the region frequently. They kept themselves separate from the people—residing in homes elevated high above the general population. There is also evidence to suggest that they "appeared" to other ancient cultures on the planet as well, since we find a consistent pattern represented in many "mythologies."

While some ambiguous recollections are certainly retained in Judeo-Christian *Old Testament* scriptures, most later cultures influenced by this Ancient Near Eastern experience—such as the Greeks and Romans—did not have the same direct contact with their version of the deities. For most ancient religions, the gods are "distant" yet watchful. And while classical-era statues and legends depicted anthropomorphic "humanoid" pantheons, the actual physical presence of a deity is always considered "elsewhere"—often some remote area or inaccessible mountain peak.

The idea of a visible, yet unapproachable, home for gods began in the Ancient Near East. Although mountains can be viewed in the far-off distance, the landscape of Mesopotamia is quite flat. One of the Anunnaki founded each of the original city-states and became its "patron-god." Various temple-shrines, like churches, dedicated to a specific "patron-god" (and their other "family members") were built in the Temple District and elsewhere throughout the city. These were places where citizens could interact with the priestesses and priests serving as intermediaries to the gods, but they were not the actual residence of the deity. Construction of that residence was reserved for the tops of large ominous artificial mountains—called *ziggurats*—constructed from clay bricks and off-limits to the general population (lay persons or non-clergy).

Babylonian priest-astronomers named the seven ancient planets the "wandering gods of the fixed zones"—and in agricultural terms, the seven "bellwethers" (named for the head bell-wearing cattle leading a herd). Note that in the ancient system, the Sun and the Moon are treated as planets.

There is some evidence to suggest that Sumerio-Babylonian clergy were aware of Neptune, Uranus and Pluto—but since they were not visible to the naked eye they were considered too distant to directly influence affairs on Earth, when they could more easily employ "closer" intermediaries (lesser gods). Where the Sumerian religion adopted a twelvefold hierarchy (mirroring arrangements of the original Anunnaki Assembly and the "zodiacal wheel"), the system adopted in *Mardukite Babylon* is sevenfold, with a direct relationship with the planets, days of the week, colors, notes of music, and so forth.

The Babylonian pantheon spiritually aligned Anunnaki roles with the visible planets—but they did not primitively confuse the persona of the deity with the actual planet (in the way most archaeologists interpret). Contrary to popular beliefs supported by contemporary historians: the "star god mythology" at the foundation of Babylonian religion was not a primitive attempt to understand natural forces. Even if that were the case elsewhere, the type of animistic shamanic characteristics found in those cultures are not present in the "urban religion" of Babylon.

Although the clergy acknowledged a "*Divine Spark*" present in all life, they did not believe, for example, that a "*storm-god*" was literally present *in* the wind. When a deity name on a tablet referred to a planet, it was preceded by the MUL.MUL sign (meaning "star-star" or "twin star"); when the personage of a god is indicated, the AN or *ilu* sign precedes it.

THE ANUNNAKI GODS

The Babylonian "*Mardukite*" perspective explored here is different than the original Sumerian pantheon inspired by the Anunnaki "elder tradition." It is dedicated to the "younger pantheon," the offspring of Enlil and Enki (both sons of Anu). The "elders" are still acknowledged in Babylonia during the *Age of Aries*, but their they move on to become more distant historical figures and their hierarchical positions become filled by the "younger" group. Everyone gets a promotion.

In the Babylonian pantheon, the Sumerian "elders"—Anu, Enlil and Enki—form a "Supernal Trinity" that is outside of (or above) the sevenfold "planetary gate" system. Unlike other traditions, the "significant other" or "consort" (husband, wife...) of a god was equally "worshiped" alongside their respective partners. This is why the similarly named singular planets are referred to as "twin stars." The "elder" divine couples are then: Anu and Antu; Enlil and Ninlil; and Enki and Ninki. Their "younger" offspring are represented in the *Mardukite* tradition as follows:

> NINURTA/NINIB (Saturn energy current)
> MARDUK (Jupiter energy current)
> NERGAL (Mars energy current)
> SHAMMASH/UTU (Solar energy current)
> ISHTAR/INANNA (Venus energy current)
> NABU (Mercury energy current)
> NANNA/SIN (Lunar energy current)

However, we again must recognize that these positions are shared with a consort: Ninurta and Bau; Marduk and Sarpanit; Nergal and Ereshkigal; Ishtar (Inanna) and Dumuzi; Nabu and Teshmet; Shammash (Utu) and Aya; and Nanna (Sin) and Ningal.

These same "powers" and "forces" have historically appeared to humans all over the earth. Mankind followed, and fell in with the plan of "deifying" these beings into "gods" complete with religious traditions and beliefs defended by the sword. At first, offerings presented by the public to the temples were literally to feed the Anunnaki themselves. But once the Gods "left" Earth, the offering would continue on to feed the clergy and their families, perpetually increasing the security and wealth of the Temple District—even when distributing it among the "poor." Eventually the shrines and temples were left emptied, seemingly forgotten by humanity as they, themselves, eventually felt empty and forgotten.

CARE AND FEEDING OF THE GODS

If the past fifteen years of modern *Mardukite* literature has established one definitive point, it is that the concept of "magic" is synonymous with (practically indistinguishable from) "religion" in Mesopotamia. Whether a member of the clergy or a lay-citizen, the whole spiritual system in Babylon emphasized one's personal relationship with the Anunnaki Gods (and what they represented).

Essentially, we are talking about the original system of "religious temple magic." It does not require the same intricacy and complexity found in later forms of "kabbalistic magic" (the basis of modern "magick") that became popular during the Middle Ages (and which were actually mutated evolutions of Mesopotamian magic).

To further illustrate just how "basic" such *religious magic* is, it is interesting to note that since the 2009 release of *The Complete Anunnaki Bible*, the suggested "ceremonial formula" for modern *Mardukites* can be reduced to a single paragraph, summarized on the Tablet-B Series:—

> The priest(ess) is always to observe the pious ways, and the *Rites of Offering* at the *Altars of the Gods*. This is traditionally performed by singing praise ("hymns") and intoning "prayers" (requests) recorded on the tablets while making offerings of incense, grain and libations of water, honey and buttermilk (and in some cases, wine); and in some cases stones such as alabaster, gold, and *lapis-lazuli*. Sacred, "blessed" or "holy" oil frequently appears in ancient Babylonian rites, and may have even possessed psychotropic properties, though the exact mixture has been lost—save for one formula which requires the mixture of gold flakes [a stone] with the essences of *"binu"* [a shrub/tree] and *"mastakal"* [an herb]. The offerings were traditionally placed in bowls before icons, images or idols of the deity in the temples.

While the passage serves as an adequate introduction to the subject, we will be providing more details in this present book for those desiring to make a modern practice of this. A modern practitioner may not have access to ancient Babylonian temples, but the tradition was also observed as a "personal religion" by the citizens in their everyday lives. The activities observed at the Temple were duplicated on a personal level in one's own home. The typical religious devotee maintained a special room or area that adequately served one's purposes. Such symbolic personal practices were common even when an individual made their "standard" offerings at the Temple.

"*The Pious Ways*," by Babylonian standards, followed the cliché adage that "cleanliness is next to godliness." No true "divine offering" could be made before first clearing and blessing a space, sleeping in said space, cleansing one's self, wearing clean linens, anointing with oils, and finally, removing one's shoes. Any "intentions" are stated (directed or prayed to the deity) during the act of making the offering. Whether approaching the tradition as a clergymember (accepting and making offerings) working at the Temple, or a citizen practicing in their own home, the basic steps are the same.

Physical components appearing in one's own personal shrine (or prayer room) generally imitated what is found at the Temple, including (but not limited to): an altar, an altar cloth, a statue (idol) or other deity symbol, a censer for incense, and at least one lamp, candle (or tealight). Each of the Temples were dedicated to a specific *divine aspect*, but *Babylon-city* included a separate Temple-shrine for each of the *Seven* (among others).

To provide an example of a basic setup, we present the elements found on the author's own priestess altar—which is a *Teshmet*-dedicated shrine. The altar itself is made of wood, with a copper symbol inlaid on the top; an incense wand (of *myrrh*) rests on a stand (or burner) on the left; a crystal clear goblet of pomegranate wine; a statuette of the intended deities; a bundle of raw wheat; a bronze offering plate for dates, fish, and fine white-flour bread with butter on top; a bowl of honey for the bread; and a candle attached with gum to a small copper plate (to catch the wax).

An individual did not have to choose one particular Anunnaki God in exclusion to the others—although one generally dedicated a single *Rite of Offering* to just one aspect. Also remember that "divine couples" were worshiped together as a single aspect. So, it was not uncommon to find representative images of both the Goddess and the God at the same altar (or shrine). Responses to one's "prayers" and adoration could be interpreted in a variety of ways, such as: contact through dream communication, "*gnosis*" (spontaneous revelation), sense of a divine presence, and/or a physical manifestation of synchronicity (that some might mistake as mere coincidence).

Raw ingredients offered at the Temple were not hand delivered up to the god of the *ziggurat* "as is." It was the responsibility of certain clergy to prepare a meal—or a *täkultu*—which included:

NAQŬ – drink/libation (water, beer, wine).
NINDABŬ – grain (bread, barley).
NISANNU – fruit (dates).
NIQŬ – meats, poultry, fish.

Other nonperishable gifts were also graciously accepted by all the deities—so it was common to see such things being carried to the Temple as offerings. These might include: baskets; colored linen and wool garments; cedar and cypress wood (or items); purple-violet and royal-blue goods; precious metals (silver, bronze, iron and gold); and precious stones, such as *ud* (ash), *lapis lazuli*, *ka* (basalt), *muhu-digili* and *mushgarru* stones.

◊ ◊ ◊ ◊ ◊ ◊ ◊

This chapter goes on to include a basic ritual formula for making offerings, and then a basic description for the primary Anunnaki Goddesses and Gods of the Babylonian pantheon (and spiritual literature of the *Mardukite* period) and their residences. This information supplements data given in another volume available for this series: "*Sumerian Religion*" by Joshua Free, simultaneously released as "*Anunnaki Gods: New Standard Zuist Edition.*"

To truly understand ancient Mesopotamian religion, one thing must be stressed above all else: this tradition was founded when the Anunnaki Gods were still residing on, or openly visiting, the planet. They were not yet all distant memories. They certainly were not primitive anthropomorphic illusions used to understand natural forces. They were not yet restricted to communicating in visions and dreams—or burning hedges. For this reason (and many others described in this book), Mesopotamian religion uniquely stands apart from any others in the ancient world.

In physical forms, occupying biological avatars (regardless of their nature otherwise), the Anunnaki Gods were, in many ways, just like us. They required sustenance and therefore preferred food and drink that was pleasurable to consume. They enjoyed music and dancing. They traveled to various cities for festivals, holidays and commemorations. They required beds to sleep in and enjoyed the pleasures of marital (and at times extramarital) intercourse. They had to wash, dress, and even preferred to wear the pleasant odors of perfumes.

FORMULA FOR MAKING AN OFFERING

1. LIGHT THE INCENSE
(smoke carries speech to the divine)

2. LIGHT THE LAMP/CANDLE
(aesthetics, atmosphere and light)

3. GREET DEITY/STATUETTE/SYMBOL
(address/acknowledge deity)

4. WELCOME THEM TO YOUR SPACE

5. OFFER THE MEAL

6. OTHER OFFERINGS/GIFTS
(any special items)

7. EXPLAIN OFFERINGS
(their intended use)

8. PLACE ON ALTAR
(leave for ten to thirty minutes and when appropriate edibles are consumed, liquids poured into earth)

9. THANK DEITY AND WELCOME BACK AGAIN

TESHMET
Tashmit / Teshmetu / Tasmitu

"While Nabu spoke, Teshmetu listened."

Sometimes called "The Great Goddess" and "Bride of E.SAGILA," she is the wife of Nabu (who is the God of wisdom, writing and learning, representative of the planet Mercury). Her name is derived from the Akkadian *šamû*, which means "the granting (of requests)." Like her husband, she is equally famous for her wisdom—known as a merciful mediator, a protector from evil, and a goddess of love and potency.

Dwelling in the E.KUA or E.ZIDA at *Borsippa* (the cult center of Nabu's clergical scribes), Teshmet is considered benevolent and merciful, interceding with her divine powers on behalf of the people. She is the "One Who Listens" and epitome of what it means to be a "twin star" to her consort. She is the "listener" to his "speaker"—and the "Lady of Hearing and Favor," called upon to act as an intermediary to Nabu (on behalf of those in need). Dedicating a shrine of mulberry and SIDARŬ-wood, with a golden footstool, would be a most acceptable gift for the "Lady of Listening." Her astronomical sign is Capricorn.

According to tablet records, Teshmet is the daughter of Uraš (Urash), the archaic Sumerian name of Enlil's mother (and mother to Ninsun or Bau). Even independent of Nabu, she was the patron goddess of Dilbat, with a cult center also at Kalhu-city. In the Sumerian language she is sometimes referred to as Nana; and in Assyria she is called Nisaba (which archaeological scholars have commonly mistaken for a "female Nabu"). The transliterated name used most commonly in our *Mardukite* literature is as it appears in Old Babylon (Akkadian): Tashmetum.

SARPANIT
Sarpanitu / Zarpanit / Zirbanitu / Erua

In the *Mardukite* Babylonian pantheon, "Queen Zērbānītu" is the "Queen of Totality; of the Whole Universe (All Creation)." As the "twin-star" to Marduk (the "new" Jupiter, replacing Enlil), her husband, she was elevated high in the pantheon as the patron goddess of Babylon; Erua or Belitu—"one who creates the seed," the "lady of ladies" and "beloved spouse"; and, perhaps most literally, the "shinning one from Zarpa."

Sarpanit is represented as the archetypal "mother goddess" in Babylon, the "giver of progeny" often depicted pregnant (as Erua)—supposedly with the Marduk's heir-son, Nabu. *E.dara'anna* is the name of her room-cell within E.SAGILA at *Babylon-city*. As a "creator goddess" she is considered a protector of the country (*Babylonia*). Similar to how Teshmet acted as an intermediary for Nabu, Sarpanit was known as an "interceder of the faithful," often petitioning Marduk on behalf of the people. Her symbol is the rising moon.

ISHTAR (VENUS)
Inanna / Astarte / Ashtoreth / Mylitta

Perhaps the most famous Goddess in the history of Earth, with an ambitious reach that spread from Sumer to virtually every ancient culture—Inanna or Ishtar—the Goddess of Ten-Thousand Names. She is the "exalted lady" and "valiant queen of the gods." She is the "ruler of heaven and earth" and "star of lamentation"; the "lady of battles," the "courtesan of the gods," the "arbitress," and "she who discloses pitfalls (or snares)." She is the "hierodule of heaven" (*Annunitum*) represented by, and sharing a name with, the planet Venus—and her Anunnaki numeric rank is "15."

Starting from the earliest Sumerian era, Inanna is the goddess of sex and war, of gentle rains and thunderstorms, Lady of the evening, and the morning star. She is the *Enlilite* "everymans" goddess—prayed to by men when in battle and when in bed; daughter of Nanna (Sin), the Moon God; brother to Shammash, the Sun God; and sister of Ereshkigal, the Underworld Goddess. She is originally betrothed to Marduk (in an effort to unite the *Enlilite* and *Enki'ite/Mardukite* Anunnaki lineages for the *Age of Aries*), but as both of them ambitiously sought to "*be on top,*" that union never occurred. She is still given the position of Venus in the Babylonian pantheon, but *not* as the "Lady of Babylon" (consort of Marduk).

Evidence of her cult-like worship is found in all Sumerian (*pre-Mardukite*) traditions. Young, beautiful, and impulsive, Inanna is given an exceptional degree of prominence in Sumer for being part of the "younger generation" of Anunnaki. She is called *Annunitum* or "Anu's Beloved"—especially favored by Anu, her grandfather, who gave her the E.ANNA Temple in Uruk to establish her cult center. Of course, she also had many other shrines throughout Mesopotamia, including the E.TURKALAMMA in Babylon (where her Akkadian name is "Ishtar"). Her symbols include the cow, doves, and (as it appears on the walls of *Babylon-city*) lions.

ERESHKIGAL (AND NERGAL)
Allatu(m) / Leluwani / Allani (and Erra)

Ereshkigal is "Queen of the Netherworld" and "Lady of the Great Place (Deep Earth)—the Goddess of Irkallu (*the Underworld*). As a daughter of Nanna (Sin), she is sister to Inanna (Ishtar) and Shamash. Her "divine consort" is the "god of light"—Nergal (represented by the planet Mars). Their daughter was made famous in the "Descent" tablet cycles, the "Black Goddess" and "Goddess of Death"—Namtar (who is sometimes called in exorcism rites to liberate a sick individual presumed to be possessed by spirits.

The other "attendants" of the Underworld and Death served Ereshkigal and operated in specialized groups. The *gallû* were "constables"; the *rabisu*, "deputies"; and the *umu* were "day-demons." Ereshkigal's primary job was to guard the Gates of the Underworld ("Death"/"between-lives" area) and the Fountain-of-Life. Ereshkigal and Nergal shared a cult-center and Temple in the city of Kutha. To the *Mardukite* Babylonians, Nergal was also known as Erra, the "God of Destruction and Pestilence" or Salbatanu, "He Who Keeps Plague Constant"—and his Anunnaki numeric rank was "8."

Gender-roles of the Sumerian Underworld "divine courtship drama" are the opposite of what we find in the Greek recension (of Hades and Persephone) that a reader may be more familiar with. It is the origin of later agricultural traditions where the seasonal/astronomical cycles are aligned with stories to establish a "mythology." The cuneiform tablet-cycle titled *"Ereshkigal and*

Nergal" describes the Goddess at first residing alone and sexually frustrated in her dark and desolate otherworld kingdom. She eventually compels the "god of light" (Nergal) to spend the "dark half" of the year in the Underworld as her sexual partner.

BAU (AND NINURTA / SATURN)
Ninegal / Nungal / Gula / Ninisina / Ugallu / Ninunuga
(and Ningirsu / Pabilsag)

Starting in the Third Millennium BCE, Bau is called Ninisina the "Lady of Isin"—patron-goddess of *Isin-city* and its dynasty—along with her "divine spouse," Ninurta (representative of the planet Saturn). A daughter of Anu and Nammu (Enki's sister), and sister to Nanna, she is of the mid-generation Anunnaki that ranked high in the Sumerian pantheon. In fact, Ninurta is Enlil's heir-son, the pre-Babylonian "Marduk" figure of the *Enlilites*. Their cult-center remained in Isin during the *Mardukite* era, where she was named Gula in the new Akkadian language.

In prayers and rituals, Bau is petitioned as the Goddess of Healing and as a "guardians spirit." She is the "Lady Who Brings the Dead Back to Life." Her religious icons and statues commonly display her seated next to a dog. The act of a dog licking wounds was considered a symbol of healing. In these artistic depictions, her dog is her personal guardian, named *Tuni-iu-sag*. In the Sumerian tradition (as observed in Isin), the son *Damu,* and daughter *Gunura* or *Ninazu,* of Ninisina and Pabilsag are also physicians and healers of renown.

AYA (AND SHAMMASH / SUN)
Sherida (and Utu / Uttu / Uddu)

In Babylo-Akkadian, the cuneiform name *ilu-Šamaš* is transliterated as Shamash or Shammash (Š = "*sh*"). The name *Šamaš* or *Samas* is the same for the Anunnaki God as for the actual Sun-star (though the two could be distinguished either by context or prefixing the word with a "MUL" sign). However, his consort, Aya (or Sherida in the old Sumerian language) is named specifically for the Sun at "dawn"—making her the first individual in recorded history to be named "Dawn" in a native language. In this wise, Mesopotamian tradition is particularly unique for the fact that it acknowledges a prominent "Solar Goddess" to represent feminine aspects of the Sun.

The sun represents the brilliance and radiant energy experienced by lifeforms on Earth—its light allowing the organic life to grow, and by solar cycles we often measure its lifespan. The fiery nature of the Sun-star (and its deities) is frequently called upon during incantations to "incinerate iniquities" and "illuminate truth." Even in *Mardukite* tradition, it is the Sun (Shammash) represents legal justice and ethics. The graphic at the top of the *stele* displaying Hammurabi's famous law in Babylon actually depicts the legal code resulting from an encounter with Shammash, not Marduk.

The Anunnaki numeric rank given to the Sun is "20." Unlike the elder god-couples appearing in the Sumerian pantheon—Anu-60/Antu-55 (Heaven and Uranus), Enlil-50/Ninlil-45 (Air-Space and Jupiter), Enki-40/Ninki-35 (Earth and Neptune) and Nanna-30/Ningal-25 (the Moon)—the positions for "divine couples" representing the Sun-20, Venus-15, Mercury-12 and Saturn-8, apparently share sacred numeric values. Therefore, we might presume that the number "20" applies equally to both Aya and Shammash.

NINGAL (AND NANNA-SIN / MOON)
Nikkal (and Nanna-Suen / Su-en / En-zu)

Ningal—"the great lady"—is the original Sumerian female lunar archetype (the Moon Goddess, a daughter of Enki, Mother to Inanna-Ishtar and Shammash). She was worshiped alongside her divine husband, Nanna (the Moon God, firstborn son of Enlil and Ninlil, Father of Inanna-Ishtar and Shammash), at their city cult-centers in Ur and Harran. In Ur, their temple—E.GISH-SHIR-GAL—translates to mean "House of the Great Light." One might note that in this old Sumerian cosmological lore, the "divine couple" representing the "Moon" is responsible for birthing "Venus" and the "Sun."

Nanna and Ningal are particularly significant deities in the predominantly "lunar" or "dark" Sumerian tradition that predates the Babylonian era—yet they remain in the *Mardukite* system. where Nanna (the Moon) is named Suen or Sin in Akkadian. But these various names do not generically all mean "moon." The full name/word *nannar* indicates "light of the full moon." Another archaic one, AS-IM-BABBAR, is the "light of the new moon." And *su-en* is specifically the "light of the crescent moon."

In Anunnaki numerology, Nanna's rank or value is "30"—the number of days in a month, based on the number of degrees designating one-twelfth of a 360-degree circle. There are some archaic writings that suggest the Moon was intentionally placed in its ancient position (which was much closer than it is today) in order to regulate the months. Ningal's number is "25."

NINKI (AND ENKI)
Damkina / Damgalnuna (and EA / Nudimmud)

Ninki (or Damkina) is called "Mistress of the Incantation of the Deep," a reference to the "Incantation of the Deep" or else the "Incantation of Eridu"—the first "magical incantation" developed in prehistory and recorded on archaic tablets. Her name indicates she is "Lady of the Earth" or "Lady of Earth (Life)," and as such, she is named the consort of Enki, "Lord of the Earth." He is also named Ea (E.A.), the words for "home" and "water"—yet another reference to the proto-Sumerian Anunnaki legacy of *Eridu-city*.

Enki and Ninki governed the power inherent in the spoken word, which is to say the "magic spell" or "incantation." Their domain and cult-center at the "Temple of the Deep" (or "Temple of the Abyss") in *Eridu* earned a reputation as the "City of Magic and Sorcery"—the original "ancient mystery school" of the sciences, magic, technology—and knowledge of the "Arts (Systems) of Civilization," referred to on archaic tablets in plural as the Divine *ME*, pronounced "*may*."

Enki is the eldest son of Anu and half-brother of Enlil (by a different mother). Collectively, these three deities (and their divine counterparts) comprise the original proto-Sumerian Anunnaki religious pantheon on Earth, of which is later treated as the "Supernal Trinity" of the spiritual system. Enki maintains his numeric value of "40" in both Sumerian and Babylonian tradition—and "35" for Ninki.

In Babylon, Ninki is a significant "Mother Goddess"—she is recognized as Marduk's mother. Marduk was raised in Eridu as Enki's heir-apparent, learning the arts of magic and science and the "systemology" of existence. Enki is the original "God of Wisdom and Magic" during the *Age of Taurus*—although as his apprentice, by the *Age of Aries* it is Marduk that is treated as "Master of Magicians."

MARDUK (JUPITER)
Amar-utu / Asar-luhi / Bel / Merodach / Sanda

Marduk is the central deity of the *Mardukite* tradition and patron-god of Babylonia. His cult-center and temple, the E.SAG-ILA, was located in *Babylon-city*. The heir-son and apprentice of Enki. in proto-Sumerian Eridu, he was named *Asar-luhi*, and even *Amar-utu*, the "Solar-Calf"—as he was intended to inherit "*Enlilship*" during the *Age of Aries*. His consort, Sarpanit, was equally elevated in the new Babylonian Anunnaki pantheon as a high status Goddess (and is discussed elsewhere in this volume).

As Mesopotamia entered the *Age of Aries*, its population experienced a Babylonian reformation of the prior Sumerian systems. The Akkadian language and refined cuneiform script became a national standard, even among diplomatic correspondence with other foreign nations of the Ancient Near East, including Egpyt. The "Divine Right" of Marduk to lead the pantheon and become the "Lord of Lords" is spiritually solidified and politically cemented in social consciousness with the document (tablet series) called the *Enuma Elis* or *"Babylonian Epic of Creation."* In that document, Marduk becomes "Lord of the Fifty Names" assuming the powers and personas of all the deities—and upgraded from the Anunnaki numeric rank of "10" to "50" (as previously held by Enlil in the Sumerian pantheon).

Ancient and classical cultures emerging after *c.* 2000 BCE were all highly influenced by the *Mardukite Babylonian* tradition—most of which assimilated a version of Marduk to be at the head of their pantheons, of course, adapting the lore to their own language and flavors. Its unique style of "monaltry" is the closest thing to "monotheism" described in ancient writings. In this case, other deities exist, but are treated as emissaries or ambassadors for a supreme deity, who is really the sum of the others by themselves.

For example, another epitaph for Marduk is Bel, which is meant to signify "Lord" (with a capital "L"). In the nearby *Western Semitic* tradition emerging in Canaan *c.* 1500 BCE, Marduk becomes *"Ba'al"* or *"Baal."* In addition to the *bow*, one of the primary symbols and weapons of Marduk is called the *imhullu*, and it resembles a long three-prong fork-like trident that allegedly produced lightning. Combing this with the astronomical association of the planet Jupiter and the Greeks then had an archetype for *"Zeus."* Closer to home, in another example, the Assyrians—who highly revered the cultural superiority of Babylon and even held an occupation of the dynasty for a time—modeled their own chief-god *"Ashur"* after Marduk.

NABU (MERCURY)
Muduggasa / Tutu (Thoth) / Nebo / Apollo

"As the writer or scribe of the gods, he records their decisions.
As proclaimer or herald of the gods, he announces them.
Trust in the words of Nabu; trust in no other god."

Apart from his father, Marduk, the god Nabu is perhaps the second most significant deity in *Mardukite Babylonian* tradition. His clergical scribe-cult and temple-home was located at *Borsippa*—which was practically a suburb of Babylon, located a mere dozen miles from its city center. He first emerges in religio-political history as a messianic-prophet proclaiming the coming of the *Mardukite* tradition for his father's new *Age of Aries.* His wife, Teshmet or Tasmitu, was the divine "listener" complimenting his role as "speaker" (and she is discussed elsewhere in this volume).

In Babylonian tradition, Nabu is both the embodiment of wisdom and an agricultural nature-god—with "12" being his sacred number (numerologically aligning him with the measure of Space and Time). In many ways he becomes a "junior Enki" of the younger pantheon—a god of water, irrigation and fertility, while also the god of arcane knowledge, oral tradition (unrecorded history) and scribal writing. He is the *Mardukite* "God of Writing" (the "Divine Scribe" or "recorder") and inventor of the reed stylus pen, which allowed for a Babylo-Akkadian refinement of cuneiform script and a standardization of its styling and small characters—the earlier primitive version being inscribed using fingernails and such.

Under the ancient epithet Tutu, he was a reality engineer—a divine artificer and creator—often depicted holding the *Tablet of Destinies*. As such he is the inspiration for the original iconic archetypes behind the *Tahutian* (Thoth) and *Hermetic* (Hermes) wisdom traditions outside of Mesopotamia. In fact, as Thoth, Nabu is one of the few deities directly appearing in the ancient Egyptian pantheon that was not from Egypt. After Babylon made a premature attempt at supremacy in *c.* 3750-3450 BCE, *Mardukite* culture was mostly suppressed during the Sumerian era. Therefore, much of Nabu's pre-Babylonian activity leading up to the *Age of Aries* occurred outside (west) of Mesopotamia.

Much like his father, Nabu continued to more additional titles and his literary-cult gained wider influence as the *Age of Aries* progressed. One of the Neo-Assyrian period warlord kings, Ashurbanipal (*c.* 660 BCE) fancied himself an intellectual and went on to establish the largest royal library of his time in *Nineveh* (called *Ninua* at the time, or *Kuyunjik* today), collecting every writing (or proper copies thereof) in the known world. He was particularly interested in having information from every single Babylonian tablet that could be found and even dedicated his entire library to Nabu.

From letters concerning Neo-Assyrian temple officials and a certain sacred ritual involving Marduk, Nabû and Tašmetu, in the words of Nabû-šumu-iddina (SAA 13 73: 11-21), we read:

> *ana bulu napšate ša mar šarri belija*
> *lušallim u lepušu /*
> *minu ša mar šarri beli išapparanni /*
> *Bel Nabû ša ina Šaba u hašaddašan*
> *uni napšate ša mar šarri belija liṣṣuru /*
> *šarrutka ana šat ume lušalliku*

"For the sake of the life of the crown prince, my lord,
they should perform the rites of their gods to perfection.
What are the written instructions of the crown prince, my lord?
May Bel and Nabû who are betrothed in the month of Shebat,
protect the life of the crown prince, my lord.
May they extend your kingship to the end of time."

TRIADS OF BABYLONIAN DEITIES

THE SUPERNAL TRINITY

ANU + ENLIL + EA/ENKI

{ Heaven + Air-Space + Earth }

THE WATCHERS IN THE SKY

NANNA + ISHTAR + SHAMMASH

{ Moon + Venus + Sun }

THE HOLY FAMILY OF BABYLON

MARDUK + SARPANIT + NABU

{ Jupiter + Mercury }

SOME IMPORTANT CITIES OF THE GODS

"Nippur was not made; E-kur was not built.
Erech was not made; E-anna was not built.
The abyss was not made; Eridu was not built."
[CT. XIII, Tablet 82-5-22, 1048. Plate 35, ln. 6-8]

The first city-states in history developed and spread around a central Temple. While many early homes in Mesopotamia were crafted from reeds and mud, the most permanent structures (for those that could afford it)—such as the Temple District—were constructed of sun-dried clay bricks. Of course, we must say "most permanent" because the long-term survival of these structures without continuous repair was anything but permanent—as the ruins which litter the "Middle East" today would suggest. Kiln-fired and glazed bricks were not commonly used in construction until the Babylonian Renaissance.

Impermanence of early Mesopotamian construction contributed to the appearance and mystique that it later gained at the height of its various eras.

Archaeologists often had difficulty in properly dating various aspects of these sites because of how frequently they were built upon the remains of preexisting ones—and this continued for thousands of years, essentially raising the terrain of urban areas like hills set against the otherwise flat environment. As the earliest Temples and Palaces were repeatedly rebuilt over time, their elevation especially towered over the city. Entire scholarly volumes are dedicated to archeological details of Mesopotamian city-states. Here, we are concerned with formally introducing just a few specifically that most affected the complete Babylonian legacy.

ERIDU

{ *Modern Site: Abu Shahrain* }

"A reed had not come forth,
A tree had not been created.
A house had not been made,
A city had not been made,
When all the lands were sea,
Then Eridu was the first city."

E.RI.DU (or NUN.KI) is the very first known prehistoric Anunnaki settlement in Mesopotamia, settled long before the "Deluge" and predating any established system of writing and civilization there. Some called it "City of the Tree (or Palm)," "The Good City," "The Home Far Away" and "The Deep." Its origins became legendary once history was recorded—for it was not only the oldest, but it was the home of Enki. In a short time, it became a major religious center at the southernmost point of Mesopotamia.

Excavated remains of Eridu extend as far back as *c.* 5500 BCE (as the "Stone Age" ends); though archaic tablet writings—and the famous "*King Lists*"—suggest an Anunnaki presence there for much longer. For example, Eridu is the location serving the first two "legendary" proto-Sumerian kings—Alalum and Alagar—who ruled before the "Deluge" with a reign that spanned *thousands* of years. To put into further geographic perspective: early Sumerians established the ancient city of Ur only fifteen miles northeast of Eridu.

As legend has it: when civilization first started (or *restarted*, depending on your view of prehistory), Enki (E.A./Ea) the *apkallu* ("wise sage") rose up from out of the Persian Sea (now the Persian Gulf) and established his home right on its coastal shores. From there he dispensed wisdom, knowledge, and the "Arts of Civilization." This legend survived many millenniums. The *Mardukite* historian Berossus (*Bel-re'u-sunu*, High Priest of Marduk's Esagila, *c.* 250 BCE) writes of it (in the Greek language of the Hellenistic era) where *Oannes* (*U'anna*), the fish-god, emerged from the Persian Gulf and taught humanity the "*Epic of Creation*" (*Enuma Elis*).

During ancient periods, the Tigris and Euphrates rivers each independently flowed into the gulf, where today they actual converge into a single river before reaching the sea. The Persian Gulf is now nearly one hundred miles away from the ancient site of Eridu, but this was not the case thousands of years ago. The gulf has since "shrunk" in size, leaving behind a marshy silty wetland where the sea once was. The receding waters may have resulted in more land area today, but in *c.* 5500 BCE, Eridu would have been the southernmost point of Mesopotamia along the Euphrates, right on the coastline of the gulf.

Excavations at the site reveal that it originally consisted of a single small structure with a single room—the original home (or shrine) of Enki—measuring a mere 12 feet by 15 feet. This simple temple had only one main doorway leading to a single altar-table in the center and a niche in the wall where a statue may have stood (but which has never been found). These are the humble beginnings from which the *Mardukite-cult* was born. But things did not remain so humble.

By the proto-Sumerian Ubaid period of the early Fourth Millennium BCE, the Temple of Enki had grown tremendously. It now featured a design that would become a basic template for temples and churches ever after: a large hall with many separate cell-like rooms on either side—and at the far end of the hall, the sanctuary-shrine was elevated as much as forty feet high on a terrace (accessible by a stairway).

BABYLON

{*Modern Site: Babil*}

Most academicians and historians begin their account of Babylonian history with the First Dynasty of Babylon *c.* 1900 BCE. And it is true that this is when the *"Amorites"* (*martu, amurru*) or ancient *Mardukites* finally established the supremacy of Babylon for the *Age of Aries*—effectively replacing the old Sumerian "lunar cults" and "elder" version of the Anunnaki pantheon. However, archaic tablets suggest that the actual site of Babylon had already existed, extending back into prehistory. The *Amorites* (or *Mardukites*) spent two centuries infiltrating Mesopotamia with a goal to directly reach and reclaim Babylon. They did not arbitrarily just decide to establish their new dynasty and thriving metropolis there by chance.

Modern *Mardukite* tradition includes esoteric lore that is not necessarily accepted or agreed upon by other contemporary academic sources. A summary of this controversial *Mardukite* and Babylonian prehistory is included in the 'Introduction' of "*The Complete Anunnaki Bible*":

"The mission to unify all of civilization under a *'Mardukite'* banner (to return people to the Source through 'magic' and 'prayer', and not animal and other sacrifices of life, or wretched systematic enslavement) did not bode well for the other gods. Marduk sought to bring the *'Navel of the Earth'* from antediluvian Nippur to Babylon during the *Age of Taurus*. But his 'Star-Gate' at BAB.ILI (*Babylon; "The Gateway of the Gods"*)—the original *'Tower of Babel'*—was destroyed in *c.* 3460 BC. Marduk then went to the Nile Region—where he was known as RA—and a 350-year war between gods ensued there for supremacy before Marduk returned to Mesopotamia for the *Age of Aries.*"

Marduk's great *ziggurat* of *Babylon-city* was named E.TEMEN-AN-KI – *Etemenanki*; "Temple of Heaven and/on Earth" or "Temple of the Universe" or "House of the Foundation of Heaven and Earth," &tc. It towered 300 feet tall in seven stages, starting from a 300-by-300 foot base. Each of its rising stages or levels were accessible by a ramp-like staircase from the preceding one. The sacred "House of Marduk (and Sarpanit)" was at the very top. It is the proverbial *"Tower of Babel"* of legendary renown—built, destroyed, then rebuilt, several times over the course of thousands of years.

The *ziggurat* was off-limits except to clergy and deities. Others seeking to worship or petition the gods would go to the more publicly accessible "Temple of Marduk (and Sarpanit)" called E.SAG-ILA (*Esagila*; "Lofty House," "House of the Lofty Head" or "House That Lifts Its Head")—which was also found in the Sacred Precinct or Temple District that extended 40-60 urban acres at times. Excavations reveal that the "Temple of Marduk" alone measured 470 feet on its longest side (with a total square area much larger than a modern city block). Within the Temple, the shrine of Sarpanit was located in a special "cell" or room called *E.dara-anna*.

BORSIPPA

{*Modern Site: Birs Nimrud*}

Borsippa not only served as the sacred precinct of Nabu and Teshmet, but also was the quintessential college-town of *Mardukite Babylonia*. Located ten miles south of *Babylon-city*, Borsippa was the official home of Nabu and Teshmet, their sacred cult-center, seminary, convent, scribe-school, astronomical observatory, and the Great Library of Babylonia. There is evidence of its occupation from at least the Third Millennium BCE, predating the First Dynasty of Babylon (much like the site of Babylon itself).

Ruined remains of the central *ziggurat*—E.ZIDA—still rise 150 feet above the surrounding landscape today. Presumably it was a half-size model of Marduk's great E.TEMEN-AN-KI in Babylon. While little more a mound and crumbling tower is found there now, it is still more visibly intact than most other ancient sites in that region—perhaps living up to its namesake of "Enduring House" or "True House."

Early academic archeologists of the 19th Century knew the general area to look for ancient Babylon, but not its exact location. When they first began to excavate Borsippa, scholars actually believed they had found Babylon—and even the surrounding populations held a belief that the towering remains were, in fact, the famous *"Tower of Babel."* But, of course, they were wrong—and the actual site of Babylon was finally discovered nearby in the 1880's.

URUK (ERECH)

{*Modern Site: Warka*}

Inclusion of Uruk is unique for our brief study of Mesopotamian cities, because it was not a *Mardukite* center (unlike Eridu, Babylon and Borsippa). It was, however, prehistoric—established on prehistoric and archaic Anunnaki roots—just like the previous sites. Originally it was the sacred city of Anu (and Antu) at the apex of the proto-Sumerian pantheon—but it was soon "gifted" to the goddess Inanna-Ishtar. Combined, Anu and Inanna were the central deities of its spiritual tradition.

Early foundations for Uruk's sacred precinct were constructed along the Euphrates River in the late Fifth Millennium BCE, approximately 60 miles north of Enki's spiritual center in Eridu. It remained mostly a small cult-center until *c.* 3750 BCE, when Mesopotamian culture shifted from the proto-Sumerian "Ubaid" period to the proto-Sumerian "Uruk" period. This transition also coincides with the beginning of the "Bronze Age." [We say "proto-Sumerian" because the early dynastic period that is historically referred to as "Sumerian" really begins *c.* 2900 BCE—at which point there are many city-states throughout Mesopotamia, each ruled by their own dynasty (until they were unified by the Akkadian Empire).]

Esoteric *Mardukite* lore explains the sudden rise of Uruk (and the diminishing cultural significance of Eridu) with a narrative regarding the Anunnaki god Enki and the goddess Inanna-Ishtar. In one version, she gets him drunk; in another, she seduces him. The truth probably lies somewhere in between. But, most importantly, Inanna-Ishtar is able to relieve Enki of the sacred *ME*, the "discs" containing data for the "Arts of Civilization" and other details regarding the systematization of reality. She takes these with her to Uruk and suddenly many of the historical "firsts" are implemented and spread as "civilization."

It is from Uruk that Inanna's "fertility-cult" originated and soon after became a staple of ancient Mesopotamian religions. It is during this period that we find the first ritual expressions of "sacred marriage"—symbolically recognizing a "divine union" between Inanna and her new lover, Dumuzi (*Tammuz*). Uruk is the City of Ishtar that "Gilgamesh" (*Bilgames*) is the King of in the classic epic. Events recorded as Ishtar's "Underworld Descent" likely took place during the Uruk period too. In the beginning of a lament of Ishtar's for her lost city she lists temples and cities by name.

"My faithful house, my E.mahtila,
My faithful house, my E.temenanki,
My faithful house, my E.dara-anna,
My faithful house, my brickwork of Uruk,
My faithful house, my E anna,
My faithful house, my E.gipariminna,
My faithful house, my brickwork of Zabalam,
My faithful house, my Hursagkalamma.
My faithful house, my E-turkalamma."

"As for the lord, in his dirge, he has become alienated from the house of Nippur from the brickwork of Ekur, from the Ki'ur, the Enamtila and the brickwork of Sippar, he moved away, the whole land is in confusion. From the sanctuary Ebabbar, the Edikudkalamma, and the brickwork of Babylon, he moved away, the whole land is in confusion. From the brickwork of Esagil, the sanctuary Eturkalamma and the brickwork of Borsippa, he moved away, the whole land is in confusion From the brickwork of Ezida, from the sanctuary Emahtila.
the brickwork of Etemenanki the sanctuary Edara'anna
he moved away; the whole land is in confusion."

AN ASSYRIAN LITANY OF GODS

"You are sworn by Aššur, king of heaven and earth!
As well by Anu and Antu!
As well by Illil and Mullissu!
As well by Ea and Damkina!
As well by Sin and Nikkal!
As well by Šamaš and Nur!
As well by Adad and Šala!
As well by Marduk and Zarpanitu!
As well by Nabû and Tašmetu!
As well by Ninurta and Gula!
As well by Uraš and Ninegal!
As well by Zababa and Babu!

168

As well by Nergal and Las!
As well by Madanu and Ninĝirsu!
As well by Humhummu and Išum!
As well by Girra, by Nusku!
As well by Ištar, Lady of Nineveh!
As well by Ištar, Lady of Arbela!
As well by Adad of Kurbail!
As well by Hadad of Aleppo!
As well by Palil, who marches in front!
As well by the heroic Sebettu!
As well by Dagan of Musuruna!
As well by Melqarth and Eshmun!
As well by Kubaba and Kurhuha!
As well by Hadad [of ...] and Ramman of [Damascus]!"

—3—
PRIESTS, PRIESTESSES & TEMPLES

*"A Priest or Priestess is always to observe the pious ways
and the Sacred Rites at the Altar of Offering."*

THE RISE OF 'CHURCH AND STATE'

Prehistoric roots of Mesopotamian society—and all civilization thereafter—began approximately 8,000 years ago. By this, we mean what directly became "modern" civilization. Archaic tablets records also indicates nearly half-a-million years of Anunnaki activity on Earth, so we are not disqualifying much earlier societal "attempts" and long-lost civilizations and other sites that may be found.

When someone refers to Mesopotamia as the *"cradle of civilization,"* they mean the literal birth of specific systems of civilization that we now take for granted today as being simply commonplace to any typical "human society."

While some key factors of societal function have merely evolved with an increased population and physical technologies, other aspects have shifted or changed so significantly that they are difficult to accurately conceive of today. This allows us to challenge some of the commonly accepted academic and archaeological interpretations when shaping a "modern-day" *Mardukite* tradition. A modern practitioner must take a holistic approach to conceive the wide-angle view that is ancient Mesopotamia—particularly concerning its origins and development, which have been obscured by time and miscommunication.

At its start—even before *"kings"* and *"empires"* as we would understand them today—there was no separation of *"church and state"* (as they were one and the same entity). What's more: there we find absolutely no distinction between practices of *"religion and magic"*—and any such distinctions may really be the result of outsider interpretation anyway.

In short: the concepts of *religion, government* and *magic*, all began synonymously as a single "systematization" or "paradigm" of "human consciousness." And this impression or imprint on consciousness was installed directly by the Anunnaki Gods—whatever their actual nature may be; whether visitors from outer space, avatars from another dimension, or survivors of a previous advanced civilization—it really makes little difference. The results were the same: *Sumerian civilization.*

These details, and many others, are important for a "practitioner" of the tradition. For modern purposes, we mean specifically an "esoteric" *insiders* understanding as maintained by the "clergy" themselves—the priestesses and priests of the tradition.

Even in ancient times, this "esoteric" understanding would have been superior to the "exoteric" perceptions held by the general population.

It is not surprising then that we find the priestesses and priests as the original "authority-figures" at the inception of human systems.

In previous chapters, we introduced Enki's *Eridu* as the prehistoric model for pre-dynastic proto-Sumerian culture. What developed into the first "city-state," really began with a "god" and his "home"; then grew into a "temple" for a "divine couple"; and then the world's first great institution for magic, science and religion—the "knowledge of the gods" and the "arts of civilization."

All the while, rule of the area rested with Enki directly; then Enki *and* Ninki. But, shortly thereafter we find the very first class emerge that is separate from both "gods" and "humans" (and acting as a direct intermediary between them)—the *High Priestess* and *High Priest* of the Temple...

TEMPLE ROLES & HEIRARCHY

"Give dedication and commitment to the Eternal Source.
Love one another; do not sacrifice animal life—
but celebrate life and sing praises.
For there is no religion higher than the Source."

—Nabu-Tutu Tablets (Esoteric Series-T)
"The Complete Anunnaki Bible"

Although the word *"en"* later came to mean "lord," it originally implied a *High Priest*; the word *"entu"/"entu(m)"* indicated a *High Priestess*. For the original ancient tradition: Enki and Ninki were respectively the first *High Priest of Earth* and *Mistress of Earth*; they established the example or "order" that would be followed by those chosen to represent them to the people. As the local population grew and the social and political affairs became more complex, everyday management of the Temple itself might be turned over to official administrators called *"sanga"* (in Sumerian) or *"shangu"* (in Akkadian) —which means a "bound priest" or one that is fully "duty-bound" to their deity. After Eridu, this same pattern resulted in the formation of several other early city-states throughout Mesopotamia.

For present purposes, we will use the term "priesthood" to denote the class and religious order of both priestesses and priests (in place of the term "clergy"). The Temple-priesthood was divided into three main groups (or classes): the uninitiated ones; the initiated ones with limited privileges, and the initiated ones with full rights. For females specifically, there were five primary roles or functions: *"holy sister," "priestess," "hierodule," "dedicated-woman"* and *"temple-maiden."*

Before long, dozens upon dozens of various titles developed to distinguish specific offices and roles of the many priestesses and priests of the Temple. Most of them lived full-time at the temple complexes, serving the patron gods and performing religious—and sometimes medical—services for the inhabitants of these *Cities-of-the-Gods.* Unfortunately, many scholarly translations simply reduce all of the various titles to simply mean "priest" without understanding their function. But today we know that each meant something unique, such as the *erib biti,* or *"Temple-Enterer."*

The term *erib-biti*—or *Temple-Enterer*—denoted the highest level of priesthood; its members enjoying unlimited access to the Temple District. For example, the actual "shrine-cell" or "cella" was the most protected area of the Temple —of which only *erib-biti* were allowed to enter, and hence their name. Other ritual specialists, the cult-like staff of *šangû* and *ahu rabû,* lamentation hymnists, might have had access—and others, such as goldsmiths or textile workers that maintained the cult statues. For the most part, only those initiated or requiring access to the *cella* (and by extension, the courtyard to reach it), were allowed to pass.

Only initiates were allowed to serve in the Temple-courtyard. Such restrictions were necessary to prevent any "polluting of the offerings." The courtyard included another unique feature of religious significance we might recognize today as a *baptismal-font,* or *tank* containing an accessible supply of standing *"holy water."* In Babylon, this special basin of holy water was symbolically called the *abzu* or *apsû*—a term reflecting the significance of the "deep waters" of Enki's Sea, or even the "Abyss."

Some other specialists within the priesthood included:

patesî, nisakku or *issaku* — "high priest"
nu-es — "exalted priest"
pasisu — "anointer" (responsible for purifying persons and objects with
    sacred oils and pure waters)
asipu, îshippu, zammeru, and *kalŭ* — "wizards" (skilled in "magical arts")
makhkhu — "great one" (a subset of *asipu*)
issipu or *baru* — "soothsayer" (seer/diviner)
nisakku, ramku, or *surmahhi* — received offerings and \divined the will
    (generally the material and dietary needs) of the temple-god(s)

dashishu, mahhŭ, or *hărŭ* — "guardians of the oracle"
kali or *galli* — "eunuch-priests"
masmasu — "ritual assistant" or "purifier" (officiate)
zammaru — "chanters"
isqu — "novitiate" (an apprentice)

Above all else, the chief religious and social function of a priestess (or priest) is to act as the mediator between a deity and its worshiper. They were a distinct high-class of citizen, living in and serving the sacred precincts. These "Temple Districts" grew into large cult communities (on their own) within the greater urban sprawl; and much like government infrastructure today, they required their own secure vested specialists to perform the common everyday tasks.

To be a *"Priestess of Marduk"* (*entu* or *sal-me*) in Babylon required being *ellu,* "clean" or "pure"—or sometimes translated as "blameless." This meant physical cleanliness and grooming, even proper lineage or descent, &tc.; but also (and perhaps more importantly) indicates emotional and psychological clarity. Priestesses were often responsible for dispensing counsel and spiritual advisement—after first having received an appropriate regimen of this themselves.

In Sumerian, KAR.KID is often translated as *"Daughter of God."* This title carried a similar meaning as *hemet neter* or "consort of god" in the Egyptian tradition. And like *the* Sumerians, Babylonian priestesses adopted a new name when officially initiated/ordained. Some classes of priestess could marry and even be a stepmom. For example: a *nadītu* (like a "nun" or "sister" today) of Marduk could marry and have sex, but could not bear children. In this case, a designated *Šug-Ĭtu* (or second wife) could have the man's children, so that the *nadītu* could lead a "pure" and "flawless" life. According to the *Code-of-Hammurabi,* those who dared to touch or kiss a *nadītu* could be burned to death. To approach or even dream of one might warrant punishment.

THE PATH OF THE TEMPLE

priest	priestess
boy	girl
shows talent as scribe/priest	wants to be priestess
literary education	literary education
difficult training	difficult training
great rewards	great rewards
god/goddess	goddess/god

TASKS AND RESPONSIBILITIES

The *en* and *entu* had many duties. They conducted religious rituals and brought offerings to the altars of their Gods. Tending to the altars and shrines included ritual washing, anointing or cleansing of the space and statuary, and any ceremonial setup. They managed the Temple District, performing purification and healing rites, community rituals and seasonal festival ceremonies. They managed urban affairs, helping to keep law and order in their cities. They even had their own military—the very first organized factions of guards and warriors. They sang hymns of praise and played jubilant songs. They promoted fertility in the land, among animals, and the family unit. They were expertly trained in the sexual arts and offered many counseling services at the Temple.

COMMUNICATION
CARE AND FEEDING OF GODS
SERVICE TO THE GODS
OFFERINGS TO THE GODS
RELAYING PRAYERS AND ANSWERS
INSTRUCTING IN PRAYER
PURIFICATION AND EXORCISMS
MEDICAL TREATMENT
MUSIC / SONG / HYMNS

BASIC ATTIRE

"Priestly" or ritual attire distinguished a member of the priesthood from others in the community. It also served a psychological function for the practitioner themselves—for by donning the sacred regalia of their office, the individual also recognized themselves as a representative of the "deity." In time, this was symbolism was equally transferred to represent the power and authority of the "state." And as we have previously suggested, the two were soon identified as one and the same in social consciousness.

Typically the priesthood wore white—but many dressings including ornamental accents and features, sashes, worn seals and other indications of one's position or office. Priestesses often word "flounced" robes and attire—where additional material is attached, or else the material along horizontal seams are gathered up to add more "frill" and "body" to an otherwise "straight" appearance.

It was considered unclean or "impure" for the soles of the feet to touch the ground, so all initiates wore sandals of various designs. A priestess also adorned her head with an *aga*—or else what we might call a "tiara" today.

When they died, priestesses and priests were buried with the attire and symbols of their holy office. They were also buried with other golden objects —crowns and rings—intended as gifts or "dowry" to their deity. These tombs were located in a place called "The Hall Which Brings Sorrow."

ALTAR RITES

"To Speak As One With The Gods,
I ___, Entu of ___ ..."

If a Temple represents a microcosm of the Universe—a smaller version of the same—then an *Altar* is specifically symbolic of the relationship between the "deity" and the "Universe." Likewise, we might say that any religious or spiritual practices involving the altar also represent direct relationships between the "deity" and "self"—and between "self" and the "Universe." The nature of these interactions is what became *"tradition"*—symbolically represented as *"religion."* There is also a possibility that construction of some primitive altars imitated an obscure archaic "control board" or "communication device" that originally served even more "practical" or "technological" functions—which may have only been properly understood by the *"gods."* At present, we are most concerned with their traditional religious use.

We have briefly mentioned the "altar" previously—an upright standing object at, or upon which, the "sacrificial" offerings (mainly food and other fine items) are made to the Anunnaki Gods (and other "spiritual" entities). Babylonians constructed altars from any available materials, including: reed, clay, brick, wood, or precious stones inlaid in gold. At the prehistoric Temple of Eridu, its small shrine first consisted of an altar set into a niche in a wall opposite the doorway. That, combined with a small offering table in the center of the room, completed the simple devotional area of the very first "sacred space" dedicated to an Anuunaki-based religion.

Various emblems and symbols—specific to the tradition or a particular deity —might also be present, either inscribed (or painted) on the altar, or as objects set upon or near it. For example: an altar may be placed on, or next to, a statue of a deity's sacred animal—or, a large enough "statue" of the god's animal could serve as an altar, which the symbolic objects and offerings placed on its "back." The "sacrificial meals" were placed on the altar—or near it, on a pedestal or other basket-like container. Meals consisted of a two-course breakfast in the morning and then a dinner late in the day.

Some basic symbols one might find associated with a Babylonian altar (as appropriate for use by a priestess), includes: the solar disc, "horned" cap (representing the Moon), a "spade" (sacred to Marduk), a sign that resembles the Greek *"Omega"* character, a sign for the *"Aries"* constellation, *&tc.* There are many items one might place on or near the altar, depending on one's intention (or prayer) or nature of the rite, such as: a favorite rock, incense, candles, statue(s), and bowls of various oils.

There are several factions of the priesthood that made regular use of the altar. *Baru* divined the will of, and consulted with, the gods. They also studied the skies for changes and motions; watched bird flight patterns; looked for patterns in smoke and oils dropped in bowls of water—in general, they looked for, recorded, and monitored *patterns.* Records of these observed patterns resulted in the first types of divination and omens. They essentially served as "soothsayers" and "seers" for the Temple and state.

If we classify the *baru* as a seer, then an *asipu* is a wizard. The *"ashippu"* (or IŠIPPU) priests were also spiritual healers, and often responsible cleansing or sanctifying the temples and shrines. They performed the "incantations" and "exorcisms" (such as in the *maqlu, surpu* and *utukku* rites)—and developed *amuletic* plaques to ward the walls and doors of a Temple (and of which were also used frequently in personal homes). They studied divination, dream interpretation, necromancy, and magic. They operated as conjurers, diviners, and enchanters. [In the Temple-District, *Bit-assaputi* means "House of the Oracle," so named from the *"asipu"* root.]

Asipu also made *"house-calls."* This required setting up an "offering table" or "reed altar" (if one was not already present in the dwelling). Sometimes, these *"traveling asipu"* would carry kits that included material to make temporary makeshift altar-shrines. Offerings were made as part of formal religious rites—but these rites also included physical treatments and herbal medicine. *Sabatu* is the act of purifying the area a ceremony is to be held—whether at the Temple or some other designated "sacred space."

Dramatic ritual elements supplemented other physical care, adding a spiritual and psychological component to the healing arts. Incantations were used—usually describing a narrative whereby some god visited some higher god for advice—relaying instructions and setting the tone for "magical work." This directly encouraged a patient to better "get themselves well" or reinforced stronger "belief" in the effectiveness of a physician and their actions. This component is still found today in among modern "health-care" practices, though it is seldom spoken of. Far from primitive, ancient Babylonians even recognized and treated such things as "situational stress," "mental disturbance" and "psychosomatic illnesses."

When an *asipu* made any petitions to a deity (regardless of the type of "magic" they conducted), a small "sacrificial meal" would be offered (and each deity invoked would get their own portion) on or near the altar. The meal typically consisted of small breads—preferably those baked with "fine white flour" (*isq-ūqu*)—vegetables, dates, meat, and a *mersu*-confection (made with ghee and honey). A couple *la'annu*-jars (of water, beer, wine, cow milk) were poured out into an *adagurru*-vessel or *pursıtu*-vessel set out to hold the "libation." [A libation might be either poured out onto the ground (if purely symbolic or appropriate) or poured into a waiting vessel.] During the meal, censers are lit, filling the area with the fragrance of juniper and/or cypress burnt on *asagu*-thorn charcoal. A seating area may be indicated with a *misu*-cloth. Once meal preparations are complete, the *asipu* leaves the area (so that the god can eat in peace). Upon returning (after 10-20 minutes), they present offerings of cedar and/or silver.

CONSECRATING & ANNOINTING

"Consecration"—or the act "to consecrate"—is a religio-magical term meaning "to purify and make holy or sacred." Traditionally, only an initiated member of the priesthood could do this—someone with proper training and skill to "*direct intention.*" All ritual implements, all sacred objects in the Temple, and all offerings made to the Gods, required formal purification or consecration.

We briefly mentioned the *abzu*-font, which held "*holy water*" (blessed by a priest/ess) in the Temple courtyard. Any water intended for such purposes would first be collected from an appropriate source—preferably from "running" (moving) streams and rivers. The "holy water" could also be bottled and dispensed for individual/personal application; but most commonly it was used to "bless" large areas and congregating crowds—lightly sprinkling (flung from a distance) using an *asperges/aspergillum* tool (or dried palm leaves).

To bless water—which is to say "make" *holy water*—an ancient tablet fragment instructs gathering seven sacred plants/herbs (the specific varieties are unknown today), which are set in a bowl of water for three days. Then, the following incantation is repeated three times before the bowl.

"Pure water;
Water from the Euphrates;
Water which has been kept
aright in the Deep,
The pure mouth of Ea (Enki)
hath purified it.
The Children of the Deep,
Seven are they.
They purify the water,
Cleanse it, make it limpid;

Before your father, Ea (Enki);
Before your mother, Damkina (Ninki).
May it be pure, be bright, be clean;
That the evil tongue may stand aside."

Where a congregation or gathering is concerned: *kinetic motion* is a readily available "tool" (or social catalyst) for raising energy, programming energy, and releasing energy. By this, we mean ritual dance (and music) employed for consecrating and "charging" spaces, sacred tools, the people themselves, and other things present. At festivals, it was used for "raising spirits." They held hands and danced clockwise in a circle to build and focus their energy. You can easily imagine a group of beautiful girls holding hands, dancing in a circle, combining their energy like bright orange cords of light. Then the churning clockwise motion would "spiral" the energy up and out.

Fire is also used for ceremonial purification. It is the central component of the "burning rites" or "*maqlu ritual*"—which are described in a companion volume of this series.* But incense smoke (made from blending wood, herbs and/or oil) is present in nearly all Babylonian rites. Whether simply present or burned, most of the sacred Mesopotamian "herbs" and "essences" (cedar, cypress, juniper, frankincense, myrrh, &tc.) were believed to have "purifying" properties.

Fresh herbs and essences are preferred whenever used for ornamental altar dressings, incense resins, and when making oils. Some deities favored certain substances, which could affect what essences and oils might be most appropriate for a particular rite or petition. For example: *tamarisk* is sacred to Anu; *cedar* to Ea/Enki; *acacia* and *juniper* to Inanna/Ishtar; *myrrh, lotus* and *belladonna* were particularly popular among priestesses serving a goddess.

Oils were used for consecrating, anointing and specialized forms of divination. Olive-oil, or any "natural oil" (*vegetable, coconut, grape-seed, &tc.*) or "fat" may be used—either by itself or as a base for an herbal infusion. One one archaic tablet, the recipe for "dream oil" (or "prophet oil) is given. A single batch calls for one half-cup of *olive-oil*, a pinch of *cinnamon*, a pinch of *nutmeg*, and a teaspoon of *anise*. You then: 1) heat and strain the combined ingredients; 2) pour into a clean jar; 3) anoint/apply to the forehead and temples; and 4) store away from heat, light and moisture.

The following incantation may be applied whenever oil is used to anoint an individual—either for healing purposes or as a general blessing for religious rites:

---

* Refer to "*The Maqlu Ritual Book*" (in hardcover), simultaneously released (in pocket paperback) as "*Anunnaki Rites: The Maqlu Ritual Book.*" Some of the information previously appeared as the *Tablet-M Series* in "*The Complete Anunnaki Bible.*"

"Pure oil, clear oil, bright oil,
Oil that purifies the body of the gods,
Oil that soothes the sinews of mankind,
Oil of the incantation of Ea (Enki),
Oil of the incantation of Asalluḫi (Marduk).
I coat you with soothing oil
That Ea (Enki) granted for soothing,
anoint you with the oil of healing,
I cast upon you the incantation of Ea (Enki),
lord of Eridu, Ninšiku.
I expel Asakku, ahḫāzu-jaundice,
and chills of your body,
I remove dumbness, torpor
('lethargy' or inactivity),
and misery of your body,
I soothe the sick sinews of your limbs.
By the command of Ea (Enki), king of the apsû,
By the spell of Ea (Enki),
By the incantation of Asalluḫi (Marduk),
By the soft bandage of Gula,
By the soothing hands of Nintinugga
And Ningirima, mistress of incantation.
On *so-and-so*, Ea (Enki) cast the incantation
of the word of healing
That the seven sages of Eridu soothe his body"

THE 9 PLACES OF ANOINTMENT

1. THE SOLES OF THE FEET

2. THE BENDS OF THE KNEES

3. THE BASE OF THE SPINE

4. THE GENITALS

5. THE WRISTS

6. OVER THE HEART

7. THE BREAST

8. UNDER THE CHIN

9. THE FOREHEAD

SHRINES

Descriptions for the design and function of a "shrine" is found throughout this book. It is listed here in this chapter among other specific "tools" or "components" of religious-magic and the tradition practiced by priestesses and priests of the Temple. However, "personal shrines" were also found in most Babylonian homes, dedicated to both "personal gods" and "ancestral spirits" (departed loved ones and family members).

Design of a shrine ranged from quite elaborate to the most simple—an image and a candle to illuminate the area at night. A shrine might also contain statues, *steles*, and/or basic tablet renderings. A special rug (or "prayer mat") might be placed on the floor; used for prayer and as a clean surface to kneel on. Shrines often included a small altar-like table, a wall-niche (or edge) to place an "offering-plate" (and candles).

By including incense smoke and resonant *tintinnabulation* of a brass bell, the personal intentions (petitions, communications) of the practitioner were carried up to the heavens. Items selected as an offering (and/or burnt as incense, &tc.) were based on personal preference—that of the practitioner and/or the "deity"/"spirit" being honored.

[A list of of commonly chosen offerings frequently recorded on relevant tablet records is provided hereafter.]

Fruits: apricot, cucumber, dates, dried fruits, figs, honey, pomegranates.
Nuts: almond, pine nut, pistachio, walnut.
Grains: barley, cakes, spelt, wheat.
Veggies: arugula, garlic, leeks, onions, turnips.
Liquids: beer, date-palm wine, grape, pomegranate, wine.
Oils: almond, balanos, castor, moringa, poppy seed, safflower, sesame.
Meats: beef, lamb (mutton), pork, seitan (fish).
Incense: cedarwood, fig, frankincense, galbanum, labdanum, lily, lotus, mastic, myrrh, pine, rose, sweetgrass.
Material: cloth, combs, community service, mirror, money, music, reading (scripture), statue.

PHYSICIANS & HEALING

Many priestesses and priests specialized in the healing arts. Healing was, and remains, a trained skill. Its origins extend into prehistory. Any records of prescriptions originating in Eridu have never been uncovered. There are some basic cuneiform "medical textbooks" from the Sumerian period, but the Babylonians made many significant innovations. Assyrian King Ashurbanipal later collected all of these tablets to construct the most complete "medical library" of the Ancient Near East.

Archaic tablets describe two basic names for a physician. Unfortunately, academic scholars are quite confused about their distinction. On the one hand, we have the *asu*, meaning "physician" or "doctor" (not gender-specific); and on the other, the *asipu* (*ashipu*), primitively translated as "witch-doctor." Scholars believe that the *asu* focused exclusively on "physical" remedies, while the *ashipu* applied only "spiritual" ones. This was not the case. Both types applied "holistic" treatments as the situation required. The only real difference is that the *asipu* was also clergy—part of the Temple staff—and more expertly trained.

Learned Babylonians understood how certain "physical" symptoms generally required "physical" treatments—but they also believed that the visible or obvious "physical" manifestation of many ailments possessed underlying "spiritual" causes. In fact, the oldest records describing heart-break, mania, depression, emotional well-being, and psychosomatic effects, are all written in cuneiform.

A professional healer was required to make initial preparations for healing rituals, which an *ashipu* used when applying spiritual and/or physical treatments. Preparations for such a rite included: preparing libations; purifying the "clay pit"/arranging magical encirclements; making and dressing any surrogate figurines, laying out sacred objects, medicinal tools, and herbal ingredients; and finally, helping the patient to ready themselves (both physically and psychologically) for the ritual. [The patient was also instructed to make petitions/prayers to their personal deities.]

Babylonian physicians utilized spiritual knowledge, prayer, magical encirclements, and administered amulets during healing rites. But on a physical level, they also worked with purifying fumigants, linen-bandages, herbal pharmaceuticals, salves/ointments, potions/tinctures, topical-washes, hot-baths, suppositories—and even enemas. The formal nature of a healing ritual contributed to increasing the "faith" or "belief" that the patient had for the procedures (medicine) and skill of the physician; therefore willingly participating "psychologically" as a critical component of the personal healing process.

For most basic applications, cuneiform tablets provide simple procedural instructions describing the deliberate actions made by a physician or *asipu*. It always began by purifying one's self—as is still the standard medical practice today. Herbs and other ingredients were freshly procured. A circle was drawn on the floor with fresh flour. Incantations were recited. Offerings and libations were made to (appease or pacify) the relevant deities. Figurines are held up to the gods. Fumigants were burned. Injuries are washed and dressed. Salves, potions, and other herbal pharmaceuticals were applied.

Fumigants

Fumigants were applied when treating many common complaints—most notably: headaches, gastrointestinal discomfort, ringing of the ears, shortness of breath, a stiff neck, vision issues, and other "unspecific" ailments. The ingredients are collected, crushed (or ground), and/or mixed with a flammable substance, before burning on hot coals. An incense burner (censer) is often, unless directed otherwise as specified on the tablet (for example: using a human skull).

Bandages

Clean linen, cloth, or leather bandages were applied alongside other topical treatments. The skin is lubricated to prevent drying. Herbal/mineral ingredients are crushed and sifted—then soaked in *kasû*-juice, beer, wine, milk, vinegar, or urine (or a combination of these). If it is too wet, flour may be sprinkled on top before applying the bandage, which may be heated or chilled as the situation required. A bandage is applied directly to the hurt area—wherever the "ghostly pain" afflicts the patient. For headaches: the bandage is wrapped around the head or temples. For an earache: bound around the ears.

Salves

For medicinal salves and ointments: ingredients are mixed with an oil (usually cedar), animal fat, resin and/or wax. The specific tablet instructs the healer to char, crush, or grind them. The mixture is often allowed to sit overnight. To ensure that medicinal properties of the salve would penetrate the skin when rubbed on the patient, ancient Mesopotamians included purified crushed stone grit. As with bandages, they are applied directly to the affected area. In addition to "normal" topical applications, special salves were used to treat vertigo, shortness of breath, neurological disorders, and other "unspecific" ailments. [The following list is applicable for bandaging instructions as well.]

Headache salves — rubbed on the temples/eyelids
Eye salves — daubed on eyelids
Neckache salves — rubbed on neck/body/both
Ghostly pain salves — rubbed on sore area
Internal pain salves — rubbed on abdomen
Fever salves — rubbed on head/soles of the feet
Salves to guard against apparitions — rubbed on the head and soles of feet
    before getting out of bed

Most ingredients used to make salves are not considered "magical" in nature, unless their intended purpose is "magical." For example: the magical formula for a *"spirit-apparition salve"* required "dust from a human skull." It is also important to note that salves that have "magical" purposes (such as *"to guard against apparitions"*) are the only ones that *require* a simultaneous offering-rite during preparation—since they pertain directly with the domain of the "spiritual" world. A tablet-fragment reveals part of the instructions, as given here:

"burāšu-juniper and red salt
you mix in erēnu-cedar oil
repeatedly rub it on the foot and head"
—or—
"bur-aˇsu-juniper, kikkir-anu [...]
grind together
mix with aromatics
repeatedly rub on the bottom of feet"

Pharmaceuticals and Potions

Medicinal tablets recovered from the royal library of the Assyrian King, Ashurbanipal, reveal that ancient Mesopotamians assigned medicinal properties to an estimated *120* "mineral" substances and *250* "herbal" ingredients—specific barks, flowers, fruits, leaves, roots, &tc. Today, scholars are still working to properly identify many of the transliterated names for these. Ancient names for *sulfur* and *alum* are found in many healing formulas—as are *potassium nitrate* (an astringent) and *sodium chloride* (an antiseptic).

Many identifiable medicinal "herbs" mentioned on cuneiform tablets are quite recognizable to modern herbal practitioners today, such as: *asafoetida, belladonna, cannabis, cardamon, cassia, cinnamon, coriander, date, fig, fir, garlic, henbane, juniper, licorice, mandragora (mandrake), mint, mustard, myrrh, myrtle, pear, poppy, thyme,* and *willow.* Urban "healing centers" (the Temple) would have maintained a supply of both fresh and dried ingredients—which required either growing them locally or importing them.

Potions, tinctures and extracts were used to treat many of the same ailments as bandages and salves, and were frequently combined with such treatments. Ingredients might be ground, crushed, or sifted—then if necessary, refined further overnight in water or vinegar. Once strained, evaporated, and powdered, the final product was commonly dissolved in, or mixed with, *beer* for consumption (preferably on an empty stomach)—although *honey, milk,* or *wine,* could also be used.

Washes

A "wash" serves both physical and spiritual purposes. On a practical level, it is intended to cleanse and purify the body—or an area of the body—prior to other treatments. [Though in some cases, it may be the treatment for a specific area or affliction.] A wash is applied to the body from the top, moving downward, to prevent contamination. [This is opposite from the practice of anointing with oil, which is applied from the bottom, moving upward—to avoid it dripping on an "un-anointed" area prematurely.]

Ingredients are ground and mixed with pure water, oil, or a combination of oil mixed with other liquids. Washes were used to treat "flashes" in the eyes, "roaring" in the ears, and even gastrointestinal distress, among other things. When indicated, liquid mixtures were poured onto, or blown into, an orifice using a straw (a hollow reed or metal tube)—and/or a lower-body soak-bath might be prepared. These types of treatments are most frequently mentioned on tablets describing certain "venereal diseases"—literally "*Venus diseases*" or being "*touched by the hand of Inanna-Ishtar.*" Note this fragment of a diagnostic tablet:

"*If blood flows out of the penis, it is the hand-of-Shammash;*
a sign of the Underworld (Land-of-No-Return).
If the penis and testicles are inflamed,
the hand-of-Inanna-Ishtar has reached him in his bed.
If the testicles are inflamed and penis is covered in sores,
he has gone into the high priestess of his god."

Suppositories

The ingredients were ground or crushed, sifted, and wrapped in a tuft of wool. This was formed into a finger-shaped pellet using sheep fat. Before being inserted they were lubricated with *erënu*-cedar resin. Suppositories were used to treat "roaring" or inflamed ears (when caused by a blockage it served the same purpose as a cotton-swab) and gastrointestinal discomfort. Enemas could also be included in this category. The ingredients are baked or boiled in beer or urine, filtered, then allowed to cool before use.

SEERS & DIVINATION

"*The Observation of Oil in Water;*
The Secret of Anu, Bel, and Ea;
The Secret Tablet of the Gods,
The Sachet of Leather of the
Oracles of Heavens and Earth;

The Wand of Cedar-Wood
That is Dear to the Great Gods..."

Divination is an esoteric/arcane skill, or mystical art, concerned with "divining" or "discerning" future events or consequences. Babylonians believed a "seer" or *baru* (meaning "inspector" or "one who examines") could literally "see" the future—or that which is otherwise not visible or perceived by that normative senses of the *'Human Condition'*. And while such beliefs are commonly reduced to party-trick fortune-telling and generalized horoscopes today, ancient Mesopotamian society was extraordinarily dependent on specialized clergy that were effective and well-practiced in *divining* the "will" of the gods.

The obvious root of the word "*divination*" is "*divine.*" This denotes recognition of a personal relationship between "humans" and "gods"—or between "earth" (*physical*) and "heaven" (*spiritual*), and how the two are affected by each other. Material (*earthly*) success was thought to be dependent upon direct cooperation of the gods (*the spiritual/ metaphysical cause*)—and their "will" (*Cosmic Law*). This "*divine knowledge*" was sought by priestesses and priests serving as *seers*. [All clergy were required to maintain some level of communication with the *divine*.] Their function was to act as a mediator or interpreter between the deity and the worshipers in order to ensure that the worshipers may obtain guidance in the personal matters of their every day life.

All priests and priestess were trained to deliver petitions, prayers and requests *to* the gods. Even the average citizen in Babylon could accomplish this to some degree. But *seers* and "*diviners*" specialized in mediating (relaying) messages *from* the gods. The Babylonians believed that one's destiny was "written in the skies." They studied the systematic movement of celestial bodies, meteors, and constellations—ascribing to them names (and attributes) of their Anunnaki gods. As such, *true astrology* was born. They were particularly interested in observable patterns of the "wandering stars" that so strongly influenced activity on earth—which we call "planets" today.

Seers and "divination-priests" *looked* for "signs" of the *divine*, often called "*omens.*" They documented systematic patterns in nature, where something was observed to precede the occurrence of something else. They interpreted these *omens* according to records of the past, assuming a principle that "like-circumstances would bring about a like-result."

Archaeologists have recovered literally thousands of cuneiform "*omen tablets*" filled with "if such-and-such, then such-and-such" statements. Ancient "diviners" used this information to guide interpretation (and predictions) of unforeseen changes in nature, the varying appearance of the heavens, and unstable phenomena on earth. It was also used to determine "auspicious timing" for all significant matters of state and military, when certain actions would more favorably lead to a particular desired outcome.

Babylonians recognized two main classifications of divination—roughly translated as "voluntary" and "involuntary," but of which we might consider "intentional" versus "conditional." In the first type, "voluntary" acts of divination involve the *seer* or *diviner* personally and intentional *seek out* some sign or use some object or other medium as a catalyst. For the involuntary type, the *"baru"* observed *conditional* factors and features that manifested unbidden (as if "omens" sent by some god), and in any event *demanding* interpretation.

VOLUNTARY/INTENTIONAL DIVINATION
– *Observing drops of oil in a bowl of water*
– *Interpreting "tea-leaf" remains in a cup*
– *Casting sticks, staffs, rods, and "drawing lots"*
– *Casting bones and "drawing stones"*
– *"Bibliomancy" using cuneiform tablets*
– *Interpreting "dice rolls"*

INVOLUNTARY/CONDITIONAL DIVINATION
– *Observing positions of stars and planets*
– *Destructive tornadoes (violent storms)*
– *Interpreting patterns and motion of clouds*
– *Swarms of locusts (insect pests)*
– *Interpreting flight-patterns of birds*
– *Deformities and health in livestock (cattle)*
– *Birth of twins, triplets, &tc.*

Dream interpretation might apply to either type—but "voluntary" only if the *prophetic dream* is *intentionally* sought out, such as described in Silvestro Fiore's *Voices from the Clay*:

> *"Oneiromancy* is a favored means of knowing the future at the time of Gudea [*c.* 2150 BC]; the *en-si* [transliterated from the logogram PA-TE-SI] went into the temple with an intention of dreaming 'in the god's abode' and gaining knowledge of 'Divine Will'. Assyrian kings sometimes sent 'Dreamers' into the temple, whose dreams were then interpreted as if experienced by the sovereign himself. It is possible that the dreamer partook of a narcotic potion, before lying down to sleep, in order to be favored with a divine message. Many of the dreams favored as omens by the Mesopotamians needed interpretation, since their purpose, 'to reveal the god's intention' was not always clear."

THE TEMPLE DISTRICT & ITS STAFF

The main subject of this book is the religious (vocational) life among Babylonian clergy—and many details seem to overlap between sections and chapters throughout. Here, we will close this present chapter with a concise summation of principle details regarding the Temple-District and its staff.

The "Temple-District" served as the 'chief edifice' of all Mesopotamian cities; a central conglomeration that not only ran a city's business affairs and facilitated it's daily life, but were also cared for by the people of the cities they helped thrive. Cities usually had multiple temples, each one dedicated to a particular deity.

Smaller sanctuaries within a temple were also dedicated and consecrated as spaces to serve 'related' deities. For example: the E.SAGILA temple in Babylon-city dedicated to Marduk also contained a separate sanctuary for his consort, Sarpanit.

Temples prominently became the focus of urban religion. They drew the public to congregate in their outer courtyards, typically sectioned off from the surrounding area by a wall. An inner-courtyard or *kisallu*, existed on the other side of the large wall—considered off-limits and practically non-existent to the "uninitiated." Various other areas of the Temple-District were also restricted to specific grades or classes of clergy.

As an economic (corporate) identity, the Temple was the wealthiest financial institution in ancient Mesopotamia—yes, even surpassing that of the "Palace-District" and the king. The Temple owned one-third of all real estate in Babylon. And since most Mesopotamian cities developed as a response to strong founding religious-center, the Temple was the *oldest original* landowners, and generally took possession of the "best" properties available. They also owned and managed their own livestock (cattle) and gained revenue from endowments and voluntary offerings. They were also the primary money-lenders, with an ability to fund projects and endeavors far greater than any private merchant.

Even apart from specific "offerings" made to the gods, the concept of "tithing" (ESRÂ) originated in Mesopotamia—a form of payment made to support the Temple (by its congregation). This gratuity was a spiritual and civic duty, practically a "religious tax" collected from the urban community, which in return received material support, counsel and protection from the Temple (a tradition that began long before dynastic kings or a political military). Even after the prominent rise of palace-kings, bureaucratic systems, aristocrats and armies, the Temple still served as the primary civic-social governing institution for this religio-centric culture.

Far from public participation in the outer courtyards, the "innermost sanctum" or "Holy of Holy" (*paraku*) of the Temple was curtained off and reserved especially for its patron god—or an appropriate embodiment thereof, referred to as the "*cult statue.*" This was the most important religious "symbol" in Babylonia.

The "*cult statue*" was not simply a "representation" of the deity—such as one might find in their home for a personal shrine. After appropriate consecration and dedication, the *cult statue* of the Temple was considered *to be* "same-and-as" the deity (when otherwise absent). This later gave rise to varying misconceptions regarding "*idol worship*" by outsiders (uninitiated).

Once they were materially created, *cult statues* required consecration and dedication through a series of evening rituals where they were given "life"— their mouth "was opened" (*pet pî*) and "washed" (*mis pî*) so they could see and eat. If the deity approved of its consecrated form, it would accept the "image" and agree to "inhabit" it. A similar "opening of the mouth" rite was used in Egyptian tradition—where the clergy would wash, anoint, pray over and consecrate the statue intended as a physical vessel for the deity.

Last, but certainly not least, in this department: the *ziggurat* of each Mesopotamian city was also built within the Temple-District. Its prominent appearance, visible quite far away, was perhaps the most significant religious symbol. Standing tall, like a mountain peak, among an otherwise flat landscape, these massive multi-tiered buildings became the most famous icon of ancient Babylonian religion. Clergy would ascend its many stairways and levels in imitation of their own spiritual ascension, but also to conduct rituals, recite prayers, sing hymns of praise, make offerings to the shrine (at the top), and make astronomical observations.

The Temple was also the largest employer, requiring many skilled-talents and individuals performing *dullu*—"service to the gods." There were herdsman, butchers, millers, oil-pressers, brewers, cooks, bakers, servers, accountants, treasurers, scribes, messengers, janitors, guards, artisans, weavers, tailors, seamstresses, barbers, singers, acrobats, gatekeepers, candle makers, and reed-workers.

—4—
SYMBOLS, TOOLS & MAGICAL RULES

*"At the command of the Lord and my Lady,
may what I am doing be successful."*

ANCIENT SYMBOLS

Initial development and later advancement of human civilization—and its systems—was dependent on the establishment and communication of *"symbols."* Symbols are (usually) abstract representations (or substitutions) for a *person, place, thing, concept* or *idea.* Symbols become *"tools"* when they are used to relay a shared-meaning between two or more parties/participants. For example, all writing systems are based on symbols with a "shared-meaning" assigned to them. In fact, it is the shared understanding and native use of a certain *language*, far more than geographical location or genetic-ethnicity, that archaeologists use to distinguish one ancient culture from another. Symbols are the very seed from which *culture* grows.

Symbols also become *tools* when an individual uses them intentionally to "evoke" or "conjure" the representative (prescribed) meaning in their own mind—or when treated as an indicator of something personally significant. For example: performing divination; interpretation of dreams; making amulets and sacred implements/tools; incorporation into sacred art; marking property (*kudurru*-stones); and interpreting "omen" signs observed in naturally occurring patterns and manifestations of everyday life.

Ancient Babylonian "Symbols of Power" (generally representing some "divine" or "heavenly" aspect) were used for legal and/or religious purposes. For example: deity symbols (identified with captions) were placed on *kudurru*-stones, which marked real-estate boundaries and royal land grants. Clay images (figurines) of deities and other beneficent spirits were inscribed with incantations for "magical spells."

Celestial and *"zodiac"* symbols were considered as powerful as the original deities they represented. The *apkallu* are representative of the *divine sages* (which are treated as ancient protective guardians)—depicted as griffin-like creatures—as featured on tablets and artistic reliefs, each holding a "pine cone" and a "bucket." [Many other significant symbols are listed throughout this section/chapter.]

"Letters" (as symbols) and *"numeric sequences"* have served an *oracular* function in *divinatory* systems, for many thousands of years. In fact, while the

Babylonians continued to refine their *cuneiform script*, they continued to treat the ancient Sumerian characters (of their Mesopotamian predecessors) with sacred reverence. Symbols, letter-characters and images representing various concepts are given preassigned meaning, then drawn "randomly" and interpreted. The most obvious examples still in use today are "*runes*" and "*tarot cards*." In the past, various oracular symbols have also been placed on tiles, clay coins, and even sticks. Almost any material can be employed for these purposes.

NUMERIC SYMBOLS

Numeric symbols representing the Mesopotamian "base-60" mathematical system are represented by *cuneiform script*. The number "1" is represented by a single wedge-shaped mark. The remaining numbers through "9" are simply composed of individual marks collected in groups. [Seven "1" marks equals "7."] A separate single sign existed to represent "10." [The original ancient system did not have a "*zero.*"]

In many ways, signs for larger numbers are cumulatively arranged in a similar fashion to "Roman Numerals"—where the value "25" (or "XXV") is represented by *two* signs for "10" ("X") followed by a "5" ("V").

In Babylonia, you would use *two* "10" symbols and *five* "1" symbols. One unique peculiarity of the system is that "60" is simply represented by a slightly larger version of "1"—a single *cuneiform* mark. The value of "75" is written by starting with a larger single mark, followed by a "10" sign and *five* "1" marks.

[Less frequently, the "*minus*" sign was used at the end of a number (to lower the total value represented). This means "9" could be written as a group of *nine* "1" marks, or as a "10" plus a "*minus-1.*" Therefore, *subtraction* notation in math calculation first began as "adding a negative value."]

For religious-magic purposes, a number might also be used to represent a specific deity (as a substitute place holder or even an esoteric formula for its name). A tradition began during the Sumerian era where key figures of the Anunnaki pantheon are given a numeric designation. This eventually inspired prescribing additional mystical "correspondences" to numbers (based on a deity's personality or the planet they represented), establishing the earliest known system of abstract "*numerological*" interpretation (used for divination, tablet records, and magical spells, &tc.).

[Numeric ("sacred") values assigned directly to the Anunnaki gods are given in a previous chapter.]

1	11	21	31	41	51
2	12	22	32	42	52
3	13	23	33	43	53
4	14	24	34	44	54
5	15	25	35	45	55
6	16	26	36	46	56
7	17	27	37	47	57
8	18	28	38	48	58
9	19	29	39	49	59
10	20	30	40	50	

CELESTIAL & ESOTERIC SYMBOLS

The following list includes the *most* common imagery and symbolism depicted (or described) on cuneiform tablets, clay amulets, religious statuary, and relief art. [When appropriate, a corresponding deity name is also provided. Note that the consort of a listed deity is likely also being represented.]

- 'Ankh', AN-KI (see *Rod and Ring* and *Beetle*)
- Arrow, Bow (*Ninurta; Marduk*)
- Beetle, Scarab* (*immortality, longevity, wisdom*)
- Bull, Heavenly (*Anu*)
- Bull (*Bel – Enlil*; also *Adad*)
- Cane, Crook (*divine guidance, shepherding*)
- Cone, Pine (*divine blessings/intervention*)
- Crescent, Moon (*Nanna-Sin*)
- Crescent and Disc (*Nanna-Sin* and *Ningal*)
- Crown or Helm of Horns (*Anu*)
- Crown, Royal (*Bel – Enlil* or *Marduk*)
- Cutter, Umbilical (*Ninhursag*)
- Date/Palm Trees (*agricultural deities*)
- Disc, Sun (*Shammash* and *Aya*; also *Marduk*)
- Disc, Winged (*divine, Sun, Nebiru; Marduk*)
- Dog, Domestic (*Bau-Gula*)
- Dots, Seven (*the planet Earth*)
- Dragon, 'mushushu' (*Marduk* and *Nabu*)
- Eye (*deities/divine, Anu, the Sun/Shammash*)
- Fish (*Ea-Enki*)
- Fish-Man (*Ea/Enki*; and the city of *Eridu*)
- Goat-Fish (*Ea/Enki*; and the city of *Eridu*)

---

* The *scarab* is a sacred symbol in both Egypt and Mesopotamia.

- Lamp, Oil (*Nusku*)
- Lightning (*Enlil, Ninurta, Adad* and *Marduk*)
- Lion (*Inanna-Ishtar*)
- Rod and Ring (*divine power, cosmic authority*)
- Rosette and Star (*divine wisdom*)
- Snake, Serpent (*Ningishzidda* and '*genetics*')
- Spade (*Marduk*)
- Staff, Serpent; '*caduceus*' (*Ningishzidda*)
- Star, General (*skygods/deities, spiritual*)
- Star, 4-points, and rays (the *Sun, Shammash*)
- Star, 6-points (*heaven-earth union, Marduk*)
- Star, 8-points (*skygods/heaven, Inanna-Ishtar*)
- Stylus, Reed (*Nabu*)
- Sun Disc (*Shammash* and *Aya*; also *Marduk*)
- Tablet, Cuneiform (*Nabu*)
- Trident, Forked (refer to '*Lightning*')
- 'Tree of Life' (*systems: cosmic, spiritual, life*)
- Trees and Ibexes (*fertility, agricultural deities*)
- Turtle (*Ea/Enki*: and the city of *Eridu*)
- Vase, Water (*irrigation, Ea/Enki*)
- Waves, Water (the '*Waters of Life*', *Ea/Enki*)

SYMBOLS OF "THE SEVEN"

References to "*The Seven*" are found on many Mesopotamian incantation-tablets. They are presumed to be seven specific deities or ancient guardians, though interpretations differ on their identity.

Representative symbols are given for "*The Seven*" on one obscure tablet fragment. We can decipher these symbols as: a *fox*, a *dog*, a *raven*, a *vulture*, a *non-coyote-wolf thing*, a *raptor-bird*, and a *crocodile*.

The original tablet reads as follows:

> *"A fox with a sweeping tail;*
> *A thing that sniffs around like a dog;*
> *Something pecks at caterpillars like a raven;*
> *A giant carrion-eating eagle;*
> *A non-wolf lamb-eating creature;*
> *A thing that screeches like a hawk;*
> *And a shark in the waves."*

FRAGMENTS DESCRIBING SYMBOLS

"The Sages (*apkallû*)
with the faces of birds, and wings,
carrying in their right hands
a 'purifier' (*mullilu*),
and in their left a bucket (*banduddû*);
or another pair of Sages
cloaked in the skins of fishes..."

* * * * * * *

"...the seat and horned crown
of *Anu,* king of heaven;
the walking bird of *Enlil,*
lord of the lands;
the ram's head and goat-fish,
the sanctuary of great *Ea-Enki*..."

* * * * * * *

"...the sickle, water-trough
(and) wide boat of *Nanna-Sin*;
the radiant disc
of the great judge *Shammash*;
the star-symbol of *Inanna-Ištar*,
the mistress of the lands;
the fierce young bull of *Adad*,
son of *Anu*..."

CHECKLIST — A PRIESTESS TOOL-KIT

Generally speaking, the supplies and consumable materials required by a priestess (or priest) to participate in the Babylonian religious tradition (and/or practice its "magic") would be provided for by the Temple. Basic descriptions of the tools appear in various chapter-sections of this book wherever specific instructions call for them (or where matters of the Temple, &tc. are described). However, modern practitioners likely do not have access to a proper Babylonian Temple. Therefore, in order for you to experience this tradition as originally intended (and as described within this book and related *Mardukite* literature), some of the most critical items for you to collect are listed below.

[ ] Censer, Vessels, Vials

Uses: aroma/ambiance; offerings (incense carries prayers skyward); burning releases energy (from the material/substance; area purification; personal purification.

Materials: bottles of perfume, scented oils, anointing oils; containers of herbal incense.

[ ] Jars, Bowls, Aspergillum

Uses: holding, preparing, and sprinkling blessed   waters.

Materials: dried palm leaf; jars; bowls; spoons/ladle.

[ ] Oracular Divination System

Uses: to divine the unknown, or discern answers.

Materials: drops of oil in water (in a bowl); incense (smoke); telescope (astronomical observation); 'lots' – reed straws, twigs, dice, coins; clay tiles (with symbolic runic glyphs/characters inscribed thereon).

[ ] Candles, Lamps, Torches

Uses: ambiance/light to work by (illumination); presence of the sacred fire (element).

Materials: plates with sand or candle holders; charcoal (for censer), flint and tinder (matches or a refillable windproof oil lighter).

[ ] Sacred Art, Statuettes, Reliefs

Uses: focal point; representations of personal god and goddess; presence of the earth element (clay and other substances).

Materials: image of deity(s); statuette; wood, glass, clay; photo, drawing; any deity-specific symbols.

[ ] Blessed Flour

Uses: marking space (boundary of magic circle on the ground); protection/safety; directing energy ('magic dust').

Materials: pouch containing blessed clean fine-white flour (called 'Flour of Nabu and Teshmet'; or on instruction-tablets from Sumerian tradition, 'Flour of Nisaba').

[ ] Magic Carpet

Uses: a barrier between clean garments and the ground; portable consecrated space (for offering rites and incantation-prayers); an area for setting out tools and materials; meditation; 'astral travel'.

Materials: a square or rectangular 'prayer rug' or moderately-sized carpet (handwoven and consecrated).

[ ] Sacred Tablets

Uses: recitation of prayers/incantations; instructions for offering rites and rituals.

Materials: clay tablets (or in modern times, books and scrolls, &tc).

[ ] Ritual Attire / Clothing

Uses: dressing; status/class; rank (in the priesthood); protection; cleanliness (appearances).

Materials: robe, cloak/mantle, conical hat, tunic, skirt, belt-cord, scarves, sashes, diadem, earrings, bracelet, necklace (amulet), sandals.

CASTING & DRAWING LOTS

The term "lot" (as in "lottery") denotes *random selection* from a group. When we say to someone, *"well, that's your lot,"* we mean *"that's what you're getting"* as in the result you are *"allotted."* In ancient Latin, the term is *sortes*, the root of "sortition" (the practice of randomly selecting a representative or political official). The tradition actually extends into Anunnaki prehistory (as recorded after-the-fact). According to cuneiform tablets: *Anu, Enlil* and *Ea-Enki* original chose their positions (or celestial domains) by "drawing lots"—randomly selecting from three different lengths of reed-straw or stick-twigs (which have been the archetypal standard ever since).

Many different kinds of object can also be used to advance a similar type of *cleromantic* divination system. And over the course of thousands of years of human history and cultural variation, just about every type of material and representative-form *has* been used—marked scarabs, painted tiles, beads, buttons, sea-shells, bones, and dragon tears[*] (just to name a few). The only real rules for divination are quite basic: preassigned meaning and random selection. Even the act of "flipping a coin" to assist with making a decision is ancient in origin and falls neatly into this category.

Dice were also commonly used for divination. This practice is traditionally known as *"astragalomancy"* today, because many ancient dice discovered by anthropologists and archaeologists (among various cultures) were actually made from certain bones. However, in Mesopotamia, dice were manufactured from clay—and they were usually *four-sided*; tetrahedral, not cubed. Such dice have been found along with boards to play the *"Game of Twenty-Squares"*— sometimes referred to as the *Royal Game of Ur*, due to its initial discovery while excavating the ancient city.

---

[*] Specifically *Dragon's Blood* – a dried palm-sap resin commonly melted on hot coals for incense.

The most basic form of dice divination is rather like "flipping a coin" to determine "YES" and "NO" (based on "odd" or "even" resulting values). In one Babylonian version, two dice could be rolled. The first represented the "past," while the second one equaled the "present." Then the two were added together for insight on the "future." [e.g., *past* plus *present* equals *future*; ($X+Y=Z$).] To advance this concept further, a third aspect may be included to indicate "MAYBE" (as indicated in the following *Table* and *Activity* based on cuneiform records).

YES	NO	MAYBE
WHITE	BLACK	GREY
HEADS	TAILS	X
ODD	EVEN	X

As a general rule: a single set of 'lots' (whatever material type they are) is stored in a small pouch. Following the advice from elsewhere in this book, a priestess (or *seer*) would cleanse, pray, meditate, and focus on the question or issue at hand. The question is whispered over the bag (sometimes three times). Then, with eyes closed, they reached in, and pulled one element out for interpretation (or else drew them one at a time, if called for, as the case may be.

ACTIVITY

In this activity, you are invited to make your own basic set of *lots*. To begin: choose a material that is readily accessible and to your liking (whether sticks, stones, buttons, *etc*). You can always make more than one set (to experiment with) later on, making each from a different material. Use the guidelines and *Table* in this chapter to assist you.

For our illustrative example, we will use the three stones that the author found on a nature-walk. Three of the same color, size and weight were chosen—essentially indistinguishable from each other when felt inside a bag-pouch.

Since the stones in this example are the same color, the author added basic symbols for "indicators." With a gold-colored permanent marker, they drew an "X" on one for "NO"—and an "O" on a second for "YES" (and the third stone was left blank as the *gray* "MAYBE" aspect).

Then, they are placed in their own clean new pouch. The pouch and materials inside of it are purified, consecrated and blessed as a single unit. Use a preferred method or technique that you have already learned from this tradition. Then, pray, meditate and focus on the oracle. Whisper your question over the bag, close your eyes, draw your *lot*, and divine your answer.

Q1: _____

A1: _____

Q2: _____

A2: _____

WATER DIVINATION

The most basic method of "water divination" (or "pool divination") used in Babylon is performed by throwing a pebble into the water. Then you simply count the number of ripples or rings that appear. An *odd* number indicates "YES"; *even* is "NO." [In this wise, you can see how the simple *Table* given in this chapter may be applied to diverse applications.]

SCRYING

Scrying (or *skrying*) is the method of divination involving "gazing" or "softly looking" at something as a catalyst for "internal visions" and "insight." Alternatively, one might be looking for *patterns* within the medium itself. We will quickly illustrate these two different approaches in a basic example. If one were to use *fire* as the medium, then the hypnotic-trance state that one achieves by gazing into it can be a catalyst to inspire visions, *&tc.* Alternatively, one might also look for physically observable *patterns* within the activity of the actual flames, or even the smoke that trails up from them.

As with any form of divination in Mesopotamia, the practice is a religious rite (however brief it may be) and follows the basic "standard practices" previously described throughout this book. This includes various preparations and purification of self and the area, *&tc.* On a practical level, such rituals allow one to fully commit themselves to the "intentional act." Additionally, one might consecrate and anoint with oils to be in full spiritual receptivity of any "divine" messages and so forth.

There are many mediums available to a *seer* of Babylonian tradition—fire-gazing, watching clouds, observing motions of oil droplets in water, or meditating on some divine symbol. But, beyond any specific "technique" or medium that might be applied, the *real* practice for this skill mostly concerns increasing the ability to "clear" one's mind (or "*mind's eye*") and allow for naturally-occurring imagery or insight to arrive (rather than forcing it or creating it). This is not really achieved by book learning and study; it results only from personal practice and experience.

'CIRCLE-CASTING'

A 'magic circle' for personal rites and rituals can be marked out on the ground with many materials, including (but not limited to): flour, stones, crushed rocks, salt, reeds, leaves, twigs/branches, and fire (made by encircling with alcohol and igniting it). In this wise, the *magic circle* is an abstract (and often impermanent) *tool* that was not included on the earlier "*tool-kit*" checklist. It is used for: centering or focusing; consecrating sacred space; spiritual protection; and as a preliminary to rites and meditation.

In view of the fact that "*all intentional acts are magical acts*" and "*magic and religion are one*" in Babylonia, there was no such thing as an "arbitrary" or "nonchalant" rite or healing or drawing of lots. A priestess or priest treated each activity (described in this book) as a sacred act. When performing the rites, or intoning a prayer, the priestess was not alone speaking to themselves; they considered that they were in the presence of their deity.

The gods expected to be treated as honored guests (even if only attending "in spirit"), invited only to the purest and most consecrated spaces whenever their attention was called upon. The ritual area was swept clean with a *palm-frond* (the original "broom") and sprinkled with water (to settle the dust). In addition to performing any personal preparations (purification, &tc.), a circle is visibly marked around the working area (which includes the bed or another individual in the case of healing). And as such, the *magic circle* is "cast."

[It is important to note that the preferred material used for 'casting a circle' is *blessed flour*; mentioned in the previous "checklist" as the '*Flour of Nabu and Teshmet*' (or '*Flour of Nisaba*' on older Sumerian tablets).]

A TABLET FRAGMENT ON 'GESTURES'

"Lift hands upward — for a prayer;
Cup upward — to bless and name;
Palm outward...
Holding the throat...
Raise the staff — for strength;
Strike the wand — for power and protection."

AMULETS

While there is no literal word for "*amulet*" in Mesopotamia, many token objects (such as "*cylinder seals*") were used for this purpose, and so it is the label many historians and mythographers have applied to this area. Quite simply, for our present purposes, we will define an *amulet* as any object, a

198

natural substance, creation or artifact, that is believed to possess magical and/or protective powers.

Amulets are either carried by a person or placed at the location of desired effect. They might bring good fortune, avert evil, or both depending on the intention placed into their creation and consecration. They are an example of (what anthropologists refer to as) "sympathetic magic"—deriving their power from connections with nature, from religious associations, and from the very rituals of their creation. Depending on their intended purpose, various ingredients—herbs, flour, ground-up stones and oils—might be mixed in with the construction materials and/or used to consecrate the object afterward.

EXAMPLE:
"Carve an image of a sirrush-dragon onto a small slab of alalu-stone (for good luck)."

SIRRUSH — "A FUMING RAGING DRAGON"
WITH A "HAIRY MOUTH OF FIRE"

One medical-tablet describes instructions for using a "healing charm" on a patient. Dip the (*amulet*) in oil and rub it on patient. Then, place it around their neck to absorb the particular "*ailment-entity*" (*spirit, ghost*) that afflicts the body. Then, place it in a leather bag. The leather material the bag is made from should be taken from an animal that has died of natural causes. Alternative, it may be wrapped in a tuft of wool (preferably red-dyed wool). This wool might also be smeared with cedar resin, cedar oil or other oils. These healing "*amulets*" required appropriate names to be inscribed on them. They should also be threaded on a cord made from two contrasting colors (usually red and white wool) to indicate the desired separation between the patient and the "ghost."

During the Neo-Assyrian Babylonian Renaissance era, the kings and clergy often wore a necklace with small metal amulets representing various symbols of the gods (as personally selected by the individual). In this wise, *amulets* served as extensions of one's personality.

'DUB.U.HI.A' – 'A TABLET ON HERBS'

Medieval-era "*sorcerers*" in Europe were known for concealing some ingredients of their 'magical' *formulas* with "code names." Ominous alternate names were often chosen to keep the "uninitiated" (unintended readers) from understanding and using them. We find evidence of this same practice in ancient Mesopctamia. This peculiar tablet fragment lists several "code names" along with their actual substance, serving as a critical *key* for deciphering true ingredients from obscure 'magical' *formulas*. Its reverse side gives an esoteric correspondence-list regarding parts (internal organs) of the body and the planets.

"A Snake's Head: *a leech*;
Blood of a Snake: *hematite*;
Lion Semen: *human semen*;
Semen of Nabu/Thoth/Hermes: *dill*;
Blood From A Head: *lupine*;
Blood of Hephaistos: *artemisia*;
Human Bile: *turnip sap*;
Fat From A Head: *spurge*;
but Blood of Porcupine really means *from a porcupine*."

Heart — *Sun*;
Brain — *Moon*;
Spleen — *Saturn*;
Liver — *Jupiter*;
Gallbladder — *Mars*;
Kidneys — *Venus*;
Lungs — *Mercury*.

KNOT MAGIC

The oldest records of "*Knot Magic*" (also called '*Cord Magic*' in some traditions) are found in the ancient Near East. Its practice may be found among both Babylonians and Egyptians. Preferably one uses a natural cord of wool or cotton, which may even be dyed a particular color to match its use. According to one modern esoteric interpretation: "knots are tied to ritually 'bind' or 'hold' a magical intention for immediate or eventual use; they may be untied to 'release' energy or when an specific 'activated effect' is desired."[†] But, ancient instructions are not necessarily this concise or consistent.

When used for healing purposes (and general well-being), the priestess (or priest) is practicing "transference magic." In this wise, the illness (and/or spiritual cause) is *transferred* and *bound* to the knots of a cord. [By its very nature, '*knots*' are useful for all manners of "binding magic."] In addition to the cord-color, the *number* of knots used for a particular "spell" usually has some numerological significance; usually (but not always) an odd number—often 3, 5, 7, or 9—with *seven* being the most commonly employed.

One example we may draw from a tablet calls for making a cord-necklace or bracelet, which is then worn as a preventative health measure (or blessing), or it may be used directly as part of a healing rite. When making it, the names *ulud* and *lama* (male and female protective/guardian spirits) are evoked to observe. Its intended use/effect will determine the cord-color (if any). When applied for healing (or pain management) it is tied directly onto the affected area. Seven (or *seven times seven*) knots are tied, anointing each one with oil (along the way). The following tablet-incantation may also be recited with each knot:

> "Marduk, the wise sage of the gods;
> Erra (Nergal), warrior of the gods;
> Išum, herald of the street;
> The Sebettu, spiritual warriors without equal;
> Have mercy on me;
> _____ , the offspring of my god,
> Your reverent servant."

After tying the final knot of the cord, recite (the incantation above) and then add to it:

> "Should protection be assured upon the wearer,
> they will sing your praises,
> for all time to come and to all mankind"

From the *maqlu ritual text*[‡] we find many references to "undoing the knots of others"—of the evildoers and evil magicians. However, In one of its rites, an "image" (representation) of one's enemy (or a spell to be undone, or an evil spirit) is prepared as a *cord* with *nine knots*. An incantation-line is recited with each knot and then a final line prepares the "image" for burning.

---

† "*Arcanum: The Great Magickal Arcanum*" by Joshua Free.

‡ Refer to "*Anunnaki Rites: The Maqlu Ritual Book*" or the Tablet-M series given in "*The Complete Anunnaki Bible*" edited by Joshua Free.

"May the mountain cover you!
May the mountain hold you back!
May the mountain calm you down!
May the mountain overpower you!
May the mountain swallow you up!
May the mountain pass reject you!
May the mountain cliff kill you!
May the mountain wastelands make you thin!
May the [mighty] mountain avalanche fall upon you!
Indeed, you shall be shaken from my body!"

ACTIVITY
[*Create Your Own Amulet*]

Materials Required: (*in place of clay, try*) flour, water, salt, plastic bowl, herbs and oils, a pouch, a reed-stylus or sharpened stick.

1. Add the flour and salt to the plastic bowl.
2. Add in any dried herbs and oils, then stir.
3. Add in water and stir until you get a dough-like substance.
4. Form some into a ball the size of your palm.
5. Mold it into a flat rectangle shape.
6. Use your reed/stick to punch a hole through the top.
7. Use the reed/stick to mark out a keyword or name across the top and/or bottom.
8. Mark the central square area with an image/symbol of your choosing.
9. Allow to harden or bake; thread with a cord and place in a pouch.

—5—
PRAYERS, HYMNS & CHANTS

"PETU BABU TEMU"
Open the Gates of Understanding

INCANTATION TABLETS

The purpose of this chapter-lesson is twofold. Most obviously, we are introducing a sampling of actual prayers and hymns translated from incantation-tablets and other recovered Babylonian tablet-fragments. These may be directly used (where appropriate) in conjunction with other training and suggestions provided in this book. But, additionally, we want a reader to gain a basic understanding of the patterned design (or formula) that such historical incantations follow. In this wise, *new* personal prayers specific to personal purposes and personally selected deities can be *newly written* by the modern reader or priestess (while still retaining authentic guidelines of the original tradition).*

There are many examples that could be given. In fact, there are many additional examples found in other *Mardukite* volumes within this series. Naturally, for the present book, we are focusing on the structure and design of prayers used specifically by clergy—priestesses and priests—of the Babylonian Temple. [There is more information on ceremonial-temple incantation-prayers in the next chapter.] Tablets that contain prayers to a specific deity are grouped together. Where a single incantation-prayer petitions multiple deities, the order in which the names appear is usually indicative of the spiritual hierarchy (regarding which deities are most "in one's favor").

An incantation-tablet may or may not include specific instructions. For example, with the *maqlu tablet series*: several tablets detail spoken incantations for dozens of individual rites, whereas most of the instructions are found on a separate final tablet in the series. Aside from a few specific "series" of tablets that have been excavated together and collected, most of the recovered incantation-tablets and fragments do not often provide much instruction. It has been assumed that such details would be instructed separately as part of the priesthood-seminary training (as with the progressive lesson-chapters of this present book). As such, a priestess (or priest) would already know how to apply them.

---

* A perfect example of a collection of incantations newly written for the modern Mardukite Babylonian tradition was published in 2010 by Joshua Free as "*The Complete Book of Marduk*"; also reissued as "*Anunnaki Prayers: The Cuneiform Almanac (New Standard Zuist Edition)*"; and excerpted as the Tablet-W series in "*The Complete Anunnaki Bible.*"

Although the terms are often used interchangeably: *prayers* are *petitions* (on some level) and usually (but not always) contain an *invocation*; *hymns* are generally recited or sung in general celebration or reverence of a deity and may contain an *invocation*, but usually not a situational *petition* or *request*.

Incantations are used to praise the gods, petition them for help, and as an affirmation of faith. People prayed for almost everything. They prayed for the diseased and sick, for family/ancestral spirits, to remove guilt, for the destruction of their enemies, to deflect witchcraft, and achieve worldly success. *Hymns* and *chants* were commonly used to raise energy and as another way to commune with deities. In most cases, an *incantation-prayer* follows a threefold pattern:

First part – an address to (praise of) a deity.
Second part – a petition, request, or lament.
Third part – giving thanks/receive blessing.

Generally, lines *one*-through-*ten* are a direct invocation of the god; line *eleven* (or *one*, if no invocation is present) is where the petitioner states their name (and brief lineage) and describes their need or their complaint; and the conclusion of the prayer contains various petitions and gratuitous rhetoric. When deciphering academic records or raw tablet material, it is important to note:

The colophon-line is the title of the prayer,
INIM.INIM.MA SU IL.LA;
It commences with the phrase
DU.DU BI
(or *ipui innatu*, "do the following")

A *rubric* is the direction or instruction contained in a single line. This line is never found separate by itself, but immediately follows the *colophon-line* and precedes any other directions for the ceremony or ritual. [If the formula line "*lu ina KISDA lit ina SA.NA ipui*" appears, it refers to the manner in which the *preceding* incantation-prayer is to be recited.] In brief, these instructions all indicate that the incantation be recited simultaneous with whatever action(s) the ceremony/rite calls for. [The most common instruction being simply to "*perform the incantation*"—meaning also all accompanying actions.]

CEREMONIAL TABLET FORMULAE

Some incantation-tablets include several instructional lines after a prayer, which describes what should take place during a larger ritual or ceremony. Such directions are brief and simple for shorter/smaller rituals; and the more elaborate a ceremony is, the more elaborate the instructions. However, their design still follows basic formula-patterns.

204

EXAMPLE ONE
(*three lines*)
"the offering of incense;
the pouring out of a libation;
the reciting the incantation three times."

EXAMPLE TWO
(*three lines*)
"In the night before Ishtar thou shalt sprinkle a green bough with pure water.
The [...] drink-offering shalt thou present. Seven times the food shalt thou [...]
A [...] of incense shalt thou offer. Place thou there a garment and a gift."
(or cleanse the area, the offering/incense and the gift)

EXAMPLE THREE
"directions for making certain offerings;
the commencement of an incantation."

EXAMPLE FOUR
(*two lines*)
"directions for ceremonies;
commencement of a second prayer or incantation."

PRAYER AND PETITIONING

*"Have mercy on me, and, O Lord, hear my prayer!
Destroy my foes and drive away the wicked!
Never let there approach me the poisons,
the enchantments [...]: [...]!
[...] pity me and command favor!
O my god and my goddess,
may peace be my portion!
[...] may thy heart have rest,
may thine anger be loosened,
and do thou establish prosperity!
Thy greatness let me praise,
let me bow in humility before thee!"*

EXAMPLE ONE
line one: the goddess (*Bilit*) is addressed;
the next line: the god (*Bel-Marduk*);
then: examples of the god's power and mercy;
then: stating the petition before deity(s).

EXAMPLE TWO
"petitioner states they have offered a present,

and poured out a libation;
and then prays for removal of their sorrow
and sighing for the length of their days;
concluding with the desire that to declare the
greatness of the god unto distant peoples."

ADDITIONAL NOTES ON INVOCATIONS

"Anu, above me, the King in Heaven;
Enki, below me, the Lord on Earth;
The power of Marduk is within me;
It is not I, but Marduk, that performs the incantation."

Traditionally, a Mardukite *"priest"* conducts the (incantations) ceremonies as though they are the original *"high priest"* of *Eridu*-city—*Marduk* and *Nabu*—as an extension of the power passed to them by *Enki*. Here, the operator literally *invokes* or *"calls in"* that specific spiritual current or flavor of energy. The priest asks for the *'god-form energy'* (reportedly *'cherry-flavored'*) and conducts the remainder of the ceremony *as* that requested *form*.

ADDITIONAL NOTES ON PURIFICATION

Prepare a bowl of fresh water; add oil and salt; add fresh herbs; Then pass your hand over the water and make your incantation-prayer. Flick the water (using your fingers or a plant) around the room and on yourself; rinsing your hands in water; finally pouring the remaining contents of the bowl into the earth. This same procedure is followed with sacred oil, but you can store it in a bottle (rather than pouring out an unused portion). Dip your fingers in herb-infused water containing also olive oil and myrrh. Water and oil may be dispersed by using the *tamarisk* branches, reed or a date-palm stalk. Salt is considered pure and sacred by itself (even without formal consecration). Fire can also be used to purify.

ADDITIONAL NOTES ON "THE RIGHT WAY"
(BASED ON BABYLONIAN NABU-TUTU TABLETS)

"Worship your god daily—with offerings, prayers, and appropriate incense. Bend your heart to your god; to that which befits the office of your personal god—prayers, supplication, pressing (the hand to) the nose (as a greeting). Each morning, shall you offer up to your personal god. Then your power will be great; and you will, through your god, have enormous success."

206

ADDRESS TO THE SUPREME DEITY
(ASSYRIAN / NEO-BABYLONIAN)

"In the heavens, who is great?
Thou alone are great!
On earth, who is great?
Thou alone are great!
When thy voice resounds in heaven,
the gods fall prostrate!
When thy voice resounds in earth,
the genii kiss the dust."

TO THE CREATIVE GOD
(AKKADIAN / OLD BABYLONIAN)

"O lord of charms, illustrious one;
Who gives life to the dead, the merciful!
Thou who didst create mankind in tenderness;
Thy love surrounds us!
Oh wind! The merciful!
The god whose life establishes us! O lord!
In darkest strife,
Oh never may thy truth forgotten be!
May the race of (Akkad) forever worship thee!"

PRAYERS TO ISHTAR

"Queen of Heaven, goddess of the universe;
you are the holy one of women and men.
The one who walked in terrible chaos;
and brought life by the law of love.
And out of chaos brought us harmony;
and from chaos, she has led us by the hand.
Women of women, goddess with no equal;
she who decrees the destiny of people.
Highest ruler of the world;
sovereign of the heavens.
Goddess, even of those who live in heaven.
With Ishtar, there is counsel and wisdom.
The fate of everything,
she holds in her hand.
Joy comes from her every glance.
She is the power, the magnificence;

She is the deity who protects.
She is the spirit that guides;
be it maiden or mother,
women remember her, and call her by name.
Oh, Shinning One!
You stop the anger of all other deities;
You care for the oppressed and the mistreated.
Each day offering them your help.
You are the one who gleams the brightest
in the midst of all other deities."

◊ ◊ ◊ ◊ ◊ ◊ ◊

[A prayer containing an invocation of the goddess and description of her power.†]

"O Ishtar, heroine among goddesses!
Thy seat is in the midst of the bright heavens!
Thou are [...], and like the Sun-god [...]!
Lady of the sky, the mountains and the seas!
Thou [...] the handiwork of creatures of the ground,
thou beholds [...]!
Thou scatters the nations [...], thou directs [...]!
[...] all of them […] creation [...]!
Thou, O Ishtar, are powerful and great,
And thy seat is in the midst of the bright heavens!"

PRAYERS TO TESHMET

"O goddess Tašmitu, whose command is mighty!
Who causes her word to be obeyed, who establishes [...]!
Who appeases the anger of god and [...]!
Who hears prayer and supplication!
Who accepts petition and sighing!
Oh seed of Izida (E.ZIDA),
House of the living creature of the great gods!
Queen of Borsippa, Lady of the Dwelling!
Oh lady Tašmitu, whose command is mighty!"

[The petitioner prostrates themselves before the (image of the) goddess; describing (and appealing to) her merciful character (as giver of peace and prosperity); once more addressing her by name; then proceeds to make a request.]

"O Tašmitu, goddess of supplication and love, lady of [...]!

---

† *Kuyunjik* tablet #32 (*British Museum*); *K-3358.*

I ___, the son/daughter of ____,
whose god is ____, whose goddess is ____,
Have turned towards thee, O lady!
Hearken to my supplication!"

◊ ◊ ◊ ◊ ◊ ◊

[*On the ceremonial tablet: the first line directs sprinkling of pure water; an offering of incense (of fyarru-wood); and a recitation of the incantation. The second directs to employ the knotted-cord rite (tying nine knots, one for each of the "May..." lines of the incantation.*]

"Before Nabu thy spouse, the lord, the prince;
the first-born son of Isagila (E.SAG-ILA),
intercede for me!
May he hearken to my cry at the word of thy mouth!
May he remove my sighing, may he learn my supplication!
At his mighty word may god and goddess
deal graciously with me!
May the sickness of my body be torn away!
May the groaning of my flesh be consumed!
May the consumption of my muscles be removed!
May the poisons that are upon me be loosened!
May the ban be torn away may the [...] be consumed!
May mercy be established among men (and their) habitations!
May god and king ordain favor
At thy mighty command that is not altered,
and thy true mercy, Oh lady Tašmitu."

◊ ◊ ◊ ◊ ◊ ◊

[*On a tablet describing a lunar eclipse ritual: after addressing the goddess by name her suppliant continues.*]

"I ____, son/daughter of ____, whose god is ____,
whose goddess is ____,
In the evil of an eclipse of the Moon,
which in ____ a month on _____ a day has taken place
In the evil of the powers, of the portents,
evil and not good, which are in
my palace and my land,
I have turned towards thee! I have established thee!
Listen to the incantation!
Before Nabu, thy spouse, the lord, the prince,

the first-born son of Isagila (E.SAG-ILA), intercede for me!
May he hearken to my cry at the word of thy mouth;
may he remove my sighing, may he learn my supplication!
At his mighty word may god and goddess
deal graciously with me!
May the sickness of my body be torn away; may the
groaning of my flesh be consumed!
May the consumption of my muscles be removed!
May the poisons that are upon me be loosened!
May the ban be torn away, may they be consumed!
May that with thy command, mercy be established!
May god and king ordain favor
at thy mighty command that is not altered
And thy true mercy that changes not, O lady Tašmitu!"

A PRAYER TO SARPANIT
(OLD BABYLONIAN)

"She is mighty, she is divine, she is exalted among the gods.
Zarpanit, brightest of the stars, dwelling in *E-ud-ul*.
Shining Beltia, exalted and most high.
Among the goddesses, there is none like her.
She accuses and intercedes.
She abases the rich and vindicates the cause of the lowly;
She overthrows the enemy,
he who does not revere her godhead;
She delivers the captive, she takes the hand of the fallen;
Let them tell of thy glory, let them exalt thy kingdom;
Let them speak of the prowess, let them glorify thy name;
Have mercy on thy servant who blesses thee.
Take their hand, those in need and suffering
Those in disease and distress, give them life.
May they go forever in joy and delight.
May they tell of thy prowess to the people of
the whole world."

PRAYERS TO NABU

"Nabû, prince of heaven and of earth,
who controls harmony [...]
Ninurta, heir to the god Enlil [...]
The one who breaks up mountains [...]

[…] for her (Ištar's) great divinity,
the Sebettu, the supreme gods who,
for the king who reveres them,
they stand at his side,
and make his weapons
prevail over all enemies."

◊ ◊ ◊ ◊ ◊ ◊

"Oh prince, preeminent, first born of Marduk;
Oh prudent ruler, offspring of Sarpanit;
Oh Nabu, bearer of the tablet
of the fate of the gods;
Director of E.SAGILA;
Lord of E.ZIDA, protector of Borsippa;
Beloved of Ea-Enki, granter of life;
Patron of Babylon;
Protector of the living god,
of inhabited hills, of the fortress, of the people;
Lord of temples; thy name is [...]
in the mouth of the people, Oh Shedu!*
Son of the great prince Marduk,
in thy mouth is truth;
in thy illustrious name;
by command of thy great divinity!"

[*The incantation continues for use in healing rites.*]

"I, ____, son/daughter of ____,
who am grievously ill, am thy servant;
whom the hand of the demon
and the poison of […].
May I live and prosper [...]
Establish (your) truth in my mouth;
Put kindness in my heart.
May the Anunnaki return and be established.
May they proclaim favors to me.
May my god stand at my right hand.
May my goddess stand at my left hand.
May the favorable Shedu and
the favorable Lamassu, [...] with me."

---

* *Sedu* or *si-du*, "*spirit*"—read/spoken as "she-du"

◊ ◊ ◊ ◊ ◊ ◊ ◊

"O hero, prince, first-born of Marduk
O prudent ruler, offspring of Zarpanitu
O Nabu, Bearer of the tablet of the destiny of the gods,
Director of Isagila (E.SAGILA)
Lord of Izida (E.ZIDA), Shadow of Borsippa!
Darling of Ia-Enki, Giver of life!
Prince of Babylon, Protector of the living!
God of the hill of dwelling, the fortress of the nations,
the Lord of temples!
Thy name is in the mouth of the peoples, O Shedu.
O son of the mighty prince Marduk,
in thy mouth is justice!
In thy illustrious name, at the command
of thy mighty godhead,
I ____, the son/daughter of ____,
who am smitten with disease, thy servant,
Whom the hand of the demon
and the breath of the [...]
May I live, may I be perfect [...]
Set justice in my mouth! [...] mercy in my heart!
May the Anunnaki return and be established!
May they command mercy!
May my god stand at my right hand!
May my goddess stand at my left hand!
May the favorable Shedu,
the favorable Lamassu, (stand) with me!"

[*Directs to make offerings with commencement of incantation. When used for a healing rite, the sick person makes a formal statement using their own name and lineage. The prayer then concludes with specific requests.*]

"At this time [...] I stand before thee!
Good is thy shadow [...]!
May my way be propitious [...]!
Set a pleasant path for my feet!
O lord, my god, deal graciously with me!
O lord Nabu, my god, deal graciously with me!
In the night season may my dreams be propitious!
Mercy, compassion, (and) life, O Shedu,
Command, grant my petition and establish me!
At the command of thy mighty godhead let me live,

let me have knowledge!
In the sight of wide-spread peoples,
may I bow in humility before thee!"

PRAYERS TO MARDUK

"Marduk, great lord, prince,
into whose hand the decrees of
Heaven and Underworld are entrusted.
May the servant who reveres you
be well favored in your presence.
May they have a personal god
and a protecting angel."[†]

◊ ◊ ◊ ◊ ◊ ◊ ◊

"Oh, Eternal Ruler,
Lord of everything that exists;
to the king whom thou loves,
and whose name thou last mentioned,
grant that their name may flourish
as seems good to thee.
Guide them on the right path,
I am the prince, thy favorite
creation of thy hand;
Thou created me and entrusted me
rule over everything,
according to thy mercy, O lord,
which thou bestows on all.
Make me to love thy exalted rule.
Cause the fear of divinity
to exist in my heart.
Grant to me whatever
may seem appropriate to thee
since thou has created my life."

◊ ◊ ◊ ◊ ◊ ◊ ◊

"Oh Lord of wisdom, ruler in your own right.
Oh Bel[‡], Lord of wisdom, ruler in your own right.
Oh father Bel, Lord of the lands;

---

†   Kassite *cylinder seal, c.* 1600 BCE.
‡   In Babylon, "*Bel*" is a reference to "*Marduk.*"

Oh father Bel, Lord of truthful speech;
Oh father Bel, shepherd of the [Babylonians*].
Oh father Bel, who yourself opens the eyes.
Oh father Bel, the warrior, prince among soldiers;
Oh father Bel, supreme power of the land;
Bull of the corral, warrior who leads
captive all the land.
Oh Bel, proprietor of the broad land;
Lord of creation, you are chief of the land;
The Lord whose shining oil is food
for an extensive offspring.
The Lord whose edicts bind together the city;
The edict of whose dwelling place
strikes down the great prince.
From the land of the rising
to the land of the setting sun.
Lord of life, you are indeed Lord!
Oh Bel of the lands, Lord of life,
you, yourself are Lord of life.
Oh mighty one, terrible one of heaven,
you are guardian indeed!
Oh Bel, you are Lord of the gods indeed!
You are father, Bel, who cause the plants
of the gardens to grow!
Oh Bel, your great glory may they fear!
The birds of heaven and the fish of the deep
are filled with fear of you.
Oh father Bel, in great strength you go,
prince of life, shepherd of the stars!
Oh Lord, the secret of production you open,
the feast of fatness establish, to work you call!
Father Bel, faithful prince, mighty prince,
you create the strength of life!"

◊ ◊ ◊ ◊ ◊ ◊ ◊

[*The following is self-titled as a "Tablet of Ea-balassu-iqbi. the son of Bel-apla-iddin, the son of Nanna-u-tu (. . .) Hand of Marduk-zera-ibni, his son, the kalu apprentice of Marduk. Babylon, the 10th day of the month (. . .) in Year 178 of the Seleucid era (when Arsakes was king)."*]

"May the heavens quiet you! May the earth appease you!

---

* "*Sang-Ngiga*" is the original transliteration.

O lord, may the heavens quiet you!
May your beloved spouse, Zarpanitum,
utter a prayer to you!
May the faithful vizier Nabu utter a prayer to you!
May the daughter-in-law, the first born of Uras
utter a prayer to you!
May the faithful princess Tasmetum
utter a prayer to you!
May the supreme princess, the lady, Nana,
utter a prayer to you!
'You should not reject your city!'
may they say to you!
May they utter a prayer to you!
For how long again?
'You should not reject Babylon!'
May they say to you!
May they utter a prayer to you!
[*uninterpreted lines*]"

A PRAYER TO SAMAS (SHAMMASH)

"O Samas, judge of heaven and earth,
that burns the broad earth!
O Lord, that opens the ear,
the darling of Bil!
Exalted judge,
whose command is not altered;
Whose mercy no god has ever annulled!
A lord art thou, and mighty is thy word!
Thy command is not forgotten,
thy intercession is unequaled
Like Anu, thy father, thy word is exalted!"

PETITIONING THE PANTHEON
(ASSYRIAN / NEO-BABYLONIAN)

"Assur, Marduk.
Nabû, who holds the stylus;
who carries the tablet
of decrees (fates) of the Gods.
Šamaš, the king of heaven and earth;
Sîn, luminous;

Adad, the canal inspector.
Ea-Enki, Lord of wisdom;
who forms all things of every kind,
who fashions creation.
Ištar, Lady of the battle; Ištar my lady;
who loves the king who pleases her,
who subdues (her enemies).
The Sebettu, mighty lords (gods);
who lead my troops;
who strike down my enemies.
Amurru, who carries the curved staff
(and) the bucket;
Sumukan, who sets right [...]
The (Anunnaki) great gods;
who dwell in heaven and earth [...]
guard my kingship."

SMALL PRAYERS & BLESSINGS

[*"May the good udug and the good lama stand (as guardians)."*]

udug sa-ga lama sa-ga
he-em-da-su-su-ge-eš

◊ ◊ ◊ ◊ ◊ ◊ ◊

[*"Grant that in the mouth of the magician's son thy servant a word may hasten."*]

izib Sa i-na pi mar ambari
ardi-ka ta-mit up-tar-ri-du

◊ ◊ ◊ ◊ ◊ ◊ ◊

[*"O Lord, I will sing a song of your divinity."*]

belu luzmur zamar ilutika

◊ ◊ ◊ ◊ ◊ ◊ ◊

[*"May Ea-Enki speak for your life."*]

Ea-Enki bala ka liqbi

◊ ◊ ◊ ◊ ◊ ◊ ◊

"When you cast the incantation of Eridu,
The evil udug, evil ala, evil ghost, evil galla,
Lamaštu, Laballu, Evil man, evil eye,
evil mouth, evil tongue.
Then they all shall stand aside!
Then the good udug and good lama
shall stand (beside you) as guardians.
Then it shall be adjured by the heavens,
and it shall be adjured by the earth."

A HYMN TO INANNA-ISHTAR

Lady [...]! Returning heroic youth, Inanna [...]
At the shrine, in *Nibiru*, in the *E.dul.kug* [...] by An,
with the holy crown of An placed on her head,
the most holy *ba* garment of An draped around her torso,
and the holy scepter of An placed in her hand
—seated on a seat in the assembly,
rendering great judgments in the mountains,
and reaching majestic decisions in all the lands!

Holy Inanna gazes as she shines [...]
down from heaven like a light.
Together with father *Suen* (Nanna-Sin),
the mistress issues commands to the *E.kur.nu.gal* of Urim.
In her hands she holds prosperity for all the lands.
The lady [...] Holy Inanna [...]
[...], you are endowed with beauty [...]

You are she who raises [...] in their prayers.
You are she who displays shining *carnelian*
from the mountains to be admired.
Bringing shinning *lapis lazuli*
from the bright mountain in special baskets,
you are she who, like fire, melts gold from *Harali*.
You are she who creates apples in their clusters.
You are she who demands [...]
(and) creates the *date* spadices in their beauty.

(*Inanna speaks*)
"When I was living in my dwelling place,
when I was living in An's dwelling,
my lover *Ucumgal-ana* called upon me to be his wife.
In *Bad-tabira*, from the *E.muc.kalama*, [...] for his crown."

[...] his assembly, and brought [...] into her holy shrine
for her brother *Ucumgal-ana*.

(*Inanna speaks*)
"[...] stands [...] *Dumuzid* stands in beauty like an *ildag*-tree.
I will fill my heart with joy.
The one who makes food plentiful [...] on the bright mound.
My heart is filled with joy, [...] in heaven and earth.
The house of *Arali* [...]."

[...] the houses in the broad streets [...]
Holy Inanna, your august [...]!
[...] Inanna be praised!

A HYMN TO MARDUK

"Of Bĕl, mighty hand,
Who lifts up glory and splendor; day of power.
Fearfulness he establishes.
Lord of DUN.PA.UD.DU.A, mighty hand.
The catch-net he throws over the hostile land.
Lord, great warrior, mighty hand.
A firm house he raises up; the enemy he overthrows.
The shinning one, lord of Nippur, mighty hand.
The lord, the life of the land, the *massŭ*
of heaven and earth."[†]

◊ ◊ ◊ ◊ ◊ ◊ ◊

"Famed mighty one, chieftain of Eridu;
Exalted prince, first-born of Nudimmud;
Raging Marduk, restorer of rejoicing to E'engura;
Lord of *E.sag-ila*, hope of Babylon;
Lover of *E.zi-da*, preserver of life;
Lone one of *Emahtilla*, multiplier of the living;
Protector of the land, savior of the multitudes of people;
The single great one of chapels everywhere,
your name is sweetly hymned by the people in all places."

A GREAT HYMN TO MARDUK
(ASHURBANIPAL PERSONAL COLLECTION)

I praise your name, Marduk,

[†] *British Musuem.* [K.4980. IV R. 27, No.4]

the most powerful of the gods,
the canal inspector of heaven and earth [...],
who was well engendered, and alone is most high [...]!

You bear Anuship, Illilship, Ninŝikuship,
lordship, kingship [...]!
You gather all wisdom, total strength [...]!

Honored ruler, exalted monarch,
overpowering, magnificent [...]!
They glorified his lordship,
prepared battle, [...] Anu!

You are exalted in the heavens, king on earth,
the skillful counselor of the great gods [...],
establisher of all habitations,
grasper of the discs of the celestial firmament
and all the lands!

You are magnificent among the gods,
Nudimmud beautified your features [...];
the great gods made you hold fast in your hand
the tablet of destinies and gave you the power
to raise and lower; they kissed your feet
and proclaimed, blessing you:
"He alone is king!"

To [...] the enemies, Illil made magnificent
for you the decrees [...]!
Great [...] of the gods, bright radiance,
[...] sheen, [...] who goes about
amidst the heavens [...]!
[...] smiter of the skull of Anzū,
defeater of [...], [...], the mad dog,
the bison, the fish-man [...];
[...] divided them [...]

Heir of Nudimmud, [...] your eyes [...]
You [...] a bow, merciless arrows,
swords, weapons of war [...]
You vanquished broad Tiamat,
[...] Qingu, her spouse.

May Babylon exult in you and *E.sagila* rejoice over you,
wherein you pass just and rightful judgment,
decide the decisions for [...],

let loose water from the underground sources,
cause copious rains, raise huge floods.

The greatness of Bel, canal inspector of heaven,
is truly great, he is much mightier than the gods, his fathers!
He excels in form, is most high in stature,
magnificent in his lordly apparel.

He summoned the *Igigi* and the *Anunnaki*,
they kneel before him, and the gods who begot him
repose in silence at his feet.
To take advice, to consult in lordly consultation,
their attention is directed towards Marduk alone.

Offerings, incense, censers,
stringed *inu*-instruments, harps and [...]
are set out; they glorify the builder of *E.sagila*,
Babylon rejoices, [...] is exuberant!

The *Igigi, Anunnaki*, the gods and goddesses
of cult centers, shrines and daises submit to you!
The governors and advisers pray to your majesty.

Eldest son of Nudimmud,
primordial, brave, strong, the merciless storm,
raging fire, scorching flame burning the enemy,
who in the midst of battle does not fear
the clash of weapons and engagement in combat.

The most lofty in stature, Marduk, the flaring sun,
light-giving lantern, who in his magnificence
[...], who purifies the unclean,
and makes the [...] to shine.

May all the gods and every goddess,
Anu, Illil-Enlil, the constellations, the Abyss,
the solid ground, Nudimmud along with the
[...] Lahmu gods, Cancer and Pisces,
witness the deeds of the lord of the gods,
Marduk and may they constantly [...] everlasting [...].

Forever present me with the *bursag*-offerings, pure [...],
[...] which the irascible* god [...]
by his exalted command established to give vigor
to those endowed with life.

---

* "*Irascible*" — easily angered.

Your shining name is Jupiter, the first-ranking god,
the foremost of the foremost,
the highest god, who [...], who at his rising
makes manifest a sign, [...] the Pleiades [...].

Noble, magnificent, Egišgalanna,
the lord who [...] the celestial positions
of the *Anunnaki*, who [...] purification rites,
rituals, and offerings [...].

Your utterance is most great, Marduk, raging [...]!
You are the greatest among all the gods,
your divinity [...] the gods [...].

Prince, praiseworthy, shrouded one!
In your net [...]; on your right is [...],
on your left is Erragal, the strongest one of the gods,
in front of you go the valiant Pleiades!
Fire burns to the right and left [...],
wherever you have raged.

Most honored, most splendid
—how splendid he is, the god to whom [...]
subject themselves, [...] his divinity!
To all the gods who occupy daises,
he munificently endows food
and cereal offerings [...].

Marduk made firm and grasped in his hand
the lead ropes of the *Igigi* and *Anunnaki*,
the mainstay of Heaven and the Underworld.
In the east and west he set up constellations
gave them roads and passages [...].

Judge of the four regions
is your weighty sworn name,
the circumspect one, Illil-Enlil of the great gods,
who establishes the rules of the Abyss,
gives allotments and food offerings to the great gods.

Receive my supplications,
accept my humble entreaties, [...];
may the god who pleases you
constantly speak favorably to you of me!

May Anu, Illil-Enlil, Ea-Enki,

make your mood jubilant
and your heart exuberant!
May Damkina, your great mother,
command you to be at peace in *E.sagila*,
the place which you love.

She is venerable, queenly, strong;
she is mistress, spouse, goddess, lady,
proud, great, lofty, beautiful, Zarpanit!
Great lady, beloved consort of Marduk;
O beloved mother of Nabu-Tutu,
let me live and I will sing your praises!

Let me glorify your mighty deeds,
O majestic princess, queen of *Esagila*,
goddess of goddesses, queen of queens,
elevated queen of all [...],
merciful goddess who loves prayers!

I pray to you, proud, raging loud:
May your angered heart find rest,
may your enraged mind relent and be appeased!
May I find life in your breath,
lofty sage of the gods, Marduk!

—6—
RITES, RITUALS & CEREMONIES

"I am the priestess of Marduk and Sarpanit.
I am the daughter of E.ri-du
and the high priestess in Babylon.
I am the priestess of Nabu and Teshmet.
I am the daughter of E.zi-da
and the high priestess in Borsippa."

INITIATION & ORDINATION

Initiation to the "inner-circle" priesthood of ancient Mesopotamia was far more exclusive than what we would find in modern practices today. Of course, not all members of the priesthood required such an initiation to hold their office. For example, the 'unconsecrated lamentation hymnists' (*kalû la gul-lu-bu*) and 'diviners' (*baru*) could operate as clergy without achieving high-level initiation. However, only true initiates were permitted to enter the "inner sanctum" of the Temple and/or attend to needs of the gods.

It was the responsibility of high ranking priestesses and priests to choose their own successors and guarantee perpetual continuity of the Mardukite cult. But these selections had to be approved. An individual candidate (or their sponsor) had to formally petition the Temple with a written application. In all cases, the procedure leading to a priesthood initiation began with a formal written request addressed to the *šatammu*—the highest administrative authority of cult affairs (at the local level).

Upon receipt of an application, the Temple-courts (*šatam-mu*) began their preliminary investigation of the candidate. But, officially consecrating new clergy was also a state affair. Therefore, royal permission had to be obtained. The Temple and Palace cooperated in handling all civil affairs. Certain clergy held specialized offices in the Palace and frequently accompanied the King (and court) in their endeavors. The *šatammu* expertly protected the regulations and interests of the Temple; yet, officially, the King still retained the final word regarding new clergy, internal promotions, and removing administrative staff.

Becoming an "ordained" (officially recognized) priestess or priest did not happen all at once. Often, the process unfolded in three stages. In the first stage, divination is employed to select an interested candidate—and therefore demonstrating by some oracular means that they are truly "chosen" for this role (by divine ordinance)—"separate from the profane/mundane world."

Secondly, the "novitiate" had to learn more details about the religious tradition and its rituals—much like what you find in this book. The final step is to actually "incorporate the individual into the spiritual world" via formal initiation and vocational practice.

The actual initiation ceremony begins with preparation of the candidate with an elaborate 'Purification Rite' [see next section] prior to ever entering the inner Temple for the the first time. Any attending priestesses, priests and officiates, had to be clean and oil-anointed (as per their own standard rite) before entering the Temple as well. Formal initiation (or ordination) into Babylon's "secret society" carried three additional qualifications or requirements, which were tested (or attested to) during the rite: *purity of body*, *purity of blood*, and *purity of mind*.

The first qualification for initiation was 'purity of the body'. [Refer also to 'Purification Rite' section that follows.] But this included elements that one had little normal control over. For example, one could not suffer from poor eyesight, kidney-stones, or even bare an asymmetrical face. They were to be as "pure as a golden statue"—a perfect "outward" portrayal or reflection of the "divinity" represented.

The second requirement was to be of the right family (genetic) descent. This is perhaps the first time in history we find a reference to a 'purity of blood'. This was verified by checking on one's parental lineage. [This also means that two of three qualifications were beyond one's ability to change.] We cannot be certain exactly what standards were followed—but we might assume that an individual could not publicly/politically represent a deity if they notoriously came from a scandalous or criminal family.

The third and final check was mental in nature--'purity of mind'. By this, we of course mean a test of mental fortitude, emotional clarity, and the ability to retain adequate vocational training.

Some might argue that a candidate had to prove aptitude or intelligence; but most of what was necessary could be learned or developed (if one were able and willing). Thereafter, formal tests of one's "cultic suitability" continued to occur regularly throughout one's vocational career.

Apart from the notes detailing the 'Purification Rite', we cannot be absolutely certain what kind of actions or rhetoric is applied to this over-night 'Initiation' process. However, at the end of the ceremony, the initiate emerges from their experience as the sun dawns. They speak:

> "At dawn my hands are washed.
> May a propitious beginning start for me.

May happiness and good health
ever accompany me.
Whatsoever I seek, may I attain it.
May the dream I dreamed
be made favorable for me.
May anything evil, anything unfavorable;
The spittle of warlock and witch,
not reach me, not touch me;
By the command of EA-Enki, Šamaš,
Marduk, and the princess Bēlet-ilī."

'PURIFICATION RITE' (NOTES)

"Not only perfect of body, but perfect of mind;
When one becomes pure, they become god-like;
They become acceptable servants of the gods."

Only clergy "prefects" (ex: *erib-biti, nešakku, pašišu, &tc.*) were allowed to enter the innermost sanctums of the Temple, or given the task of *qurrubu sa naptani* —the privilege of bringing food to, caring for, or otherwise being at all near, the gods themselves. All high-level priestesses and priests were required to follow a strict regimen or self-care (regarding hygiene and appearances).

All clergy were required to maintain themselves all the time, but were required to cleanse and purify immediately before entering the sacred areas of the Temple. However, the day of their initiation would have been the first time that an individual was subjected to these higher standards. Hence the *'Purification Rite'* (or *gullubu*; "ritual shaving") attached to the *'Initiation'* is a much lengthier "cosmetic make-over" process than one would normally require to simply maintain it thereafter.

The *'purification'* segment took place during the day; the *'initiation'*, at night (and lasting until the following dawn). The candidate is prepared with the *'purification rite'* in a private bath-house (within the Temple District) before they are permitted to enter the actual Temple for the *'initiation'*. The *'rite'* begins with a full physical examination (by the *ašipu*, or physician-priest). Determining that there are no physical blemishes, disfigurements, poor eyesight, chipped teeth, damaged hands, or skin disease, and so forth, the candidate is ready to proceed with their ritual purification.

During the ritual, an *ašipu* recites a repetitive series of (sixteen) incantation-prayers over the candidate while they are completely shaven (*gullubu*), washed /cleansed (*ramku*), and their nails are trimmed. [Priestesses were permitted long-hair; but it was separated into two braided parts or *plaits* on either side, with their lengths wrapped across and secured/pinned over the crown of the head—known today as a 'heidi'/*milkmaid* (braided) '*up do*'.] This clean-cut appearance distinguished high-ranking members of the priesthood from the otherwise mundane animal-like appearance of common humans.

During the course of this day-long event, the candidate was not permitted to eat meat and could only drink water. Toward the end, they are anointed with oil and their mouth is washed. They are given the *kubsu* (bleached white wool turban of their office). And after all of this, they are finally ready for service of the highest order—ready to present themselves (and speak) to a god!

'PRIESTESS INSTALLATION' (NOTES)

"The (high priestess) of EA-Enki am I.
The (high priestess) of Damkina am I.
The messenger of Marduk am I.
My spell is the spell of EA-Enki.
My incantation is the incantation of Marduk.
The circle of EA-Enki is in my hand.
The tamarisk, the powerful weapon of Anu;
In my hand I hold,
The date-spathe, mighty in decision;
In my hand I hold."

Ceremonial '*installation*' of a priestess is treated very similar to an elaborate wedding—and it marked a sacred marriage between the initiate and the divine. On the *first* day, a girl is selected from the elite by divination (presumably 'drawing lots'). She is anointed and purified at her father's house.

On day *two*, there is a procession to the Temple of their deity. Her hair is cut and she is anointed in the courtyard before returning home. The *third* day requires making personal offerings to the deity, which must be "accepted" in order for an '*installation*' (*malluku*) to be approved. On the *fourth* day there is a procession to various holy shrines, including more offerings, and finally, a banquet.

During the '*installation*' she received golden rings and bracelets, serving as her own personal '*dowry*' from the gods—given directly to (and owned by) the priestess (unlike in traditional marriages). She is given a red-dyed wool head-dress bearing an insignia appropriate to her office/role within the priesthood.

On days *five* to *eleven*, a local seven-day celebration occurred in the Temple

District. On the (final) *eleventh* day, she was dressed in bleached-white garments of a bride. She is carried in procession by her 'brothers'; her 'sister' washes her feet. She is given a bedchamber with a chair or footstool by the elders. She gracefully descends up the bed, lying in wait for arrival of the deity...

PREPARATORY OPENING RITES
(TABLET FRAGMENTS)

"Do the following.[†]
Before Marduk, set a SA.NA of incense,
a SA of oil, a drink-offering, water;
Honey (and) butter shalt thou offer,
[...] the seed of the *mastakal*-plant;
in the middle of the oil cast [...];
recite the incantation and anoint with oil."

[Similar instructions from another tablet source.]

"Pure water shalt thou sprinkle.
The [...] drink-offering shalt thou present.
Dates and [...] shalt thou heap up.
[...] oil and drink-offering, water,
honey (and) butter shalt thou offer.
An incense-burner shalt thou set there.
The [...]-drink shalt thou pour out."

INCANTATION OF ERIDU (THE DEEP)
(MARDUKITE GRAND INVOCATION)[*]

"Anu, above me, King in Heaven.
Enlil, Commander of the Airs.
Enki, Lord of the Deep Earth.
I am Nabu; hear my words.
I am the priest(ess) of Marduk and Sarpanit.
Born of EA-Enki and Damkina.
I am the priest(ess) in E.ri-du.
I am the magician in Babylon.
My spell is the spell of Ea-Enki.
My incantation is the incantation of Marduk.
The Tablets of Destiny, I hold in my hands.

---

†   *Siptu bit nu-ru* ritual tablet.

*   *Tablet-W* translation in "*The Complete Anunnaki Bible*"; originally derived from "*The Complete Book of Marduk by Nabu*" (*Liber-W*).

The [Sign]‡ of Anu and Antu, I hold in my hands.
The wisdom of Enlil and Ninlil, I call to me.
The Magic Circle of EA-Enki and Damkina,
I conjure about me.
Shammash and Aya are before me.
Nanna-Sin and Ningal are behind me.
Nergal and Ereshkigal are at my right side.
Ninurta and Ba'u are at my left side.
Blessed light of Ishtar and Dumuzi shines favorably upon my sacred work.
It is not I, but Marduk, who performs the incantations."

THE ASHIPU RITUALIST (TRAINING)
(EXORCISM RITES & SPIRITUAL HEALING)

The two primary means of expelling evil spirits are *water* and *fire*. These two elements can cleanse everything from "evil"—even entire worlds. So, when gods are called upon, they are the gods of *water* and *light*. One might note, from prior information in this book, that *water* is the essential foundation of most religious ceremonies (and magical rites) in Babylon—but especially those concerned with the removal of "*evil spirits.*" All other means utilized toward this purpose were subordinate to *water*. Above all, *spring-water* was most sacred; many temples even maintained their own springs.

The *maqlu* series or "*burning*" rites—purification by *fire*—are treated in a separate volume in this series. Those tablets pertain to countering "magic spells" of evil witches and warlocks operating against the well-being of the community (or civilization) as a whole. In this section, we will treat the *siptu* incantation-tablets, or "spiritual exorcisms" that banish "evil spirits" (from the body) with blessed *water*.

Mesopotamian knowledge of "magic" and "religion"—which is also to say, science and medicine—originated with the prehistoric cult in Eridu, dedicated to EA-Enki (not surprisingly, the Anunnaki god of *water*). In ancient times, the city of Eridu was located near the mouth of the Euphrates and Tigris rivers, directly on the shores of the *abzu*, or *apsu*, or "the Deep"—the "Persian Gulf"—which the Babylonians perceived as a direct connection between *this* material world and the *Celestial Abzu*.

Cuneiform tablets often read like brief narratives when offering "magical" (or "medicinal") wisdom. In many cases, a 'younger god' will go and appeal to an 'elder god' for advice on a specific matter. Within the context of the dialogue, some prescription or instruction will be found. Such tablets were collected in

---

‡   This word is translated to mean "*tamarisk*," "*scepter*," or "*ankh*" (or "*rod and ring*") in different versions.

228

libraries and used as references for treating present issues. [The "*omen tab-lets*" are also based on past observations of synchronicity, which are then later referred to for advice when similar conditions occur again—a practice Babylonians eventually standardized as "*astrology.*"]

For a most basic example (on one tablet citing a narrative from Eridu): EA-Enki is revered as the God of Absu; Marduk as a young Lord of the Springs. Marduk asks for advice on healing the "sick man." EA-Enki directs him to take water from the mouth of the two rivers (the Tigris and Euphrates) and sprinkle it on the "sick man." The direction to "perform the incantation" led to the basic practice of a priest(ess) sprinkling a sick (or unclean, impure) individual with water while reciting a prayer.

"When one has become sick, they are under the influence of grievous spirits." As primitive as that belief may seem to a modern reader, it does not really pro-pose anything different than "*germ theory.*" The truth is that while physical symptoms may be recessed in a person, modern ("western") medicine does not have a clear understanding on the underlying nature of disease—particu-larly where it concerns other living organisms acting upon the body. That living cells or viruses may have their own center of consciousness or a "spir-itual awareness" (and therefore intelligence or even intentional third-party programming) is barely even considered when treating and handling such things today.[†] ["Evil spirits" were also thought to hide in dark corners, stale dusty environments, and even ritual objects—which is why the tools and sac-red spaces are always purified before any magical/religious ritual/ceremonial work is conducted.]

In Babylon, the "sick person" prays with (and through) the *asipu* (*ashipu*) or *mas.masu* (*mashmashu*) to be freed from "evil" that has come into his body. The priest(ess) then sprinkles them with blessed "holy water" (*mū ellu*) while reciting a *siptu*-exorcism to expel the "evil spirits." If they "win" this "spiritual battle" against the spirit, then health is renewed; but if they "fail" there will be "death" (or unconsciousness)—they journey to the "*underworld*" (or else the domain of "evil spirits") for an indeterminate period of time until being sprinkled by the gods (there) with the '*waters of life*'.

The "magical force" or "spiritual authority" of the *siptu*-incantation is tied to vocalization of the god-names. Babylonians attached "power" to *divine names* —something which continued thereafter in most cultures and spiritual tradi-tions. ['*Kabbalistic*' and '*hermetic*' traditions inherited the knowledge directly from Babylon.] The "power" of the deity was believed to be connected (in some way) to their various titles and names—each carrying a very specific

† Refer to either "*Entities and Fragments: Systemology Advanced Training Course Manual #5,*" "*Keys to the Kingdom (Volume 2)*" or "*The Complete Keys to the Kingdom (Workbook Edition)*" by Joshua Free.

meaning. The literal frequency-vibration (or sound) and cuneiform appearance of these titles was of such importance that *divine names* from the older Sumerian language were also retained (for their "power") in Babylonian tradition.

A *siptu*-incantation may be spoken once; but more often it was recited three times for a stronger effect. Its context is similar to what is found with more modern "exorcisms" today—such as the verbiage used by the Catholic Church —*e.g.* "*The power of Christ compels you,*" "*In Jesus' name...*" &tc. A few tablet-fragments are included below as examples of basic formulae. It is not uncommon to end the incantation with a simple roll-call of *names* and *titles* of the various gods invoked within the prayer. But, perhaps of all the possible lines that can be included, the most paramount is usually the most direct:

NĪŠ IL ___ LŪ TAMĀTU

or

NĪŠ IL ___ UTAMMËKA

"In the name of ___, I exorcise thee."

◊ ◊ ◊ ◊ ◊ ◊ ◊

EXAMPLE 1
(*long formula*)

"In the name of Heaven, be thou exorcised!
In the name of Earth, be thou exorcised!
In the name of Bel, lord of the world, be thou exorcised!
In the name of Beltis, mistress of the world,
be thou exorcised!
In the name of Ninib, mighty warrior of Bel,
be thou exorcised!
In the name of Nuzku, the exalted messenger of Bel,
be thou exorcised!
In the name of Istar, mistress of mankind,
be thou exorcised!
In the name of Adad. the lord whose thunder is good,
be thou exorcised!
In the name of Samas, lord of judgment,
be thou exorcised!
In the name of the Anunnaki, the great gods,
be thou exorcised!"

◊ ◊ ◊ ◊ ◊ ◊ ◊

EXAMPLE 2
(usual formula)

In the name of Heaven, be thou exorcised!
In the name of Earth, be thou exorcised!

◊ ◊ ◊ ◊ ◊ ◊

EXAMPLE 3
(simple)

In the name of the great gods, be thou exorcised!

◊ ◊ ◊ ◊ ◊ ◊

EXAMPLE 4

I exorcise thee by Anu, father of the great gods!

◊ ◊ ◊ ◊ ◊ ◊

EXAMPLE 5

In the name of the Anunnaki, I exorcise thee!
That thou are commanded to depart.

◊ ◊ ◊ ◊ ◊ ◊

EXAMPLE 6
(siptu closing)

In the name of Heaven, be thou exorcised!
In the name of Earth, be thou exorcised!
Šedu *(shedu)*; Lama—Lamma—Lammasu!

AN EXAMPLE EXORCISM TABLET
(BABYLONIAN)

"Marduk, the son of E.ri-du,
placed his hand upon him;
He performed the incantation:
Bring a censer and a torch (and say)
'May the plague demon Namtar,
who is in the body of this person,
trickle away like water.'
Take the copper of might of the hero Anu,

which by the roar of its splendor
removes the evil (and say)
'An evil demon art thou;
a god who walks in the night;
whose unclean hands
do not know reverence.
An evil demon art thou
who lies down in wait for the man,
resting like an ass.
An evil demon art thou;
who knows not sacrifice,
and who has no gifts.
Disease is all you know;
snare and burden is all you have.
But in mercy, the god gladly
vindicates good for him,
unto Shammash […]'."

REASONS FOR HEADACHES, DISEASES AND POSSESSION
('SURPU' DIAGNOSTIC-LIST TABLET)[†]

The person who has...
...sinned against their God
...sinned against their Goddess.
...misconducted themselves before the God.
...misconducted themselves before the Goddess.
...made their God and Goddess angry with them.
...sought undue secrets of the Gods of Heaven.
...sought undue secrets of the Temple-Shrines of Earth.
...slighted what is due to the Gods.
...sought undue favor of the Gods at the Temple-Shrines.
...offered impure sacrifice at the Altar of Offering.
...offered sacrifice [to the Gods] and taken it back.
...destroyed the sacrifice made at the Altar of Offering.
...obstructed the sacrifices made by another.
...caused obstruction between [friends or family].
...eaten flesh of a sacrifice at the Altars of Offering.
...held hatred towards an elder.
...shed his neighbor's blood.
...propositioned their neighbor's wife.

[†]   Excerpt from *Mardukite Tablet-H* series; reprinted in "*The Complete Anunnaki Bible*."

...propositioned their neighbor's husband.

...used a false balance in business affairs.

...removed or misplaced a boundary or landmark.

...unjustly entered their neighbor's house.

...taken their neighbor's garment.

...stolen or caused another to steal.

...said "no" for "yes" and "yes" for "no." [*lying*]

...been straight in the mouth but not true in the heart.

...promised pleasure and joy but not given it.

...spoken of what is unholy.

...spoken wickedness.

...caused a judge to receive a bribe.

...wronged their city.

...opposed one in authority under Marduk.

...give in small things but refused in great.

...transgressed the righteous.

...offended the righteous.

...set their hand to evil acts.

...set their hearts to follow after evil.

...stopped a neighbor's canal. [*water supply*]

...been banned of weapons but seeks them.

...set their hand to evil sorceries and witchcraft.

...pointed at the holy fire.

...taken a prolonged seat in the sun. [*sun-stroke*]

...struck the young of an animal.

...tearing up plants in the desert.

...tearing of plants and trees.

...raised a fire and falsely sworn by a god.

...has tasted from the unclean cup.

...has tasted from the unclean plate.

...has tasted from the unclean dish.

...performed an unknown sin against their God.

...performed an unknown sin against their Goddess.

THE ASHIPU 'GHOST RITE'
(ARCHAIC EXAMPLE)

"Šamaš, king of Heaven and Earth;
Šamaš, judge of the lands;
Šamaš, foremost of the gods;
Šamaš, mighty and resplendent one;
Šamaš, lord who makes things go aright."

Based on descriptions given on tablets, we can interpret "ghost-pains" or "phantom pains" as those which are not connected to an (visible) injury or illness—such as a painful "stinging" sensation, &tc. Mesopotamians believed that "demons" and their diseases (or apparent 'side-effects') could be caught using knots, bands, threads, strings, and amulets (tied around the affected area). In many regards, the same "religio-magical" principles apply to handling "ghost-pains."

To provide an example: one tablet provides instructions for a ritual procedure (to combat "ghost-pains") that directs the priest(ess) to scatter *burašu*-juniper on *ašagū*-thorn charcoal in a censer before (an image of) Shammash. Then beer is offered in libation. Some hair from a virgin she-goat and some hair from a virgin lamb are twined together into a *cord*. Then *three knots* are tied *seven times.** Whenever one is tied, the (above) incantation is recited three times before (the image of) Shammash. Then the *knotted-cord amulet* is tied onto the patient wherever they feel the stinging. If the condition doesn't subside within a month, the process is repeated (where the knots are loosened and then tied again).

THE ASHIPU 'PASASU RITE'
(ARCHAIC EXAMPLE)

Pasasu is the '*Rite of Anointing*'—which is referenced in virtually every ritual text and ceremony (and throughout this book) wherever "oil" and/or "anointing" is mentioned. This practice was so paramount to the religio-magical (and medical) tradition that the terms *pasisu* and *asipu* became virtually synonymous. An anointing rite may be applied by a priest(ess): to themselves; to each other (clergy); to common citizens; to idols/statuary (and other religious tools/ implements); and to a home (or any space consecrated for ritual purposes).

While *olive oil* or *palm oil* served as the most common base, other substances and oils might be mixed with it—either according to some special "secret" recipe, or as indicated on instruction-tablets. The most common additives were raw herbs and essential oils, such as: myrtle, myrrh, frankincense, cedar, marjoram, hyssop, coriander and cinnamon. *Note that essential oils are not for internal consumption.*

The following is a standard example of the '*Rite of Anointing*', which begins with a preliminary invocation. It is unclear whether this first incantation is used while the *cnointing-oil* is being prepared, *or* prior to entering the house (as this is describing an *asipu* house-call), *or* both.

---

* The ambiguous writing is unclear whether *3-x-7*, or *21* individual knots, are tied along its length—or if the same three knots are loosened and retied.

"Ea-Enki, King of the Deep,
I, the magician, am thy slave.
March thou on my right hand;
Assist me on my left.
Add thy pure spell to mine;
Add thy pure voice to mine.
Vouchsafe (to me) pure words.
Make fortunate the utterances of my mouth.
Ordain that my decisions be happy,
Let me be blessed wherever I tread.
Let the man whom I now touch be blessed,
Before me may lucky thoughts be spoken,
After me may a lucky finger be pointed.
Thou are my guardian genius,
And my guardian spirit!
Oh, Marduk, the god that blesses.
Let me be blessed, wherever my path may be!
Thy power, shall god and man proclaim;
This [...] shall do thy service,
And I too, the magician, thy slave."

◊ ◊ ◊ ◊ ◊ ◊ ◊

[Incantation, upon entering the house...]

"Shammash (is) before me,
Nanna-Sin (is) behind me,
Nergal (is) at my right hand,
Ninib-Ninurta (is) at my left hand.
When I draw near unto the sick one;
When I lay my hand on the head of the sick one;
May a kindly Spirit, a kindly Guardian, stand at my side."

◊ ◊ ◊ ◊ ◊ ◊ ◊

[Incantation, for each time the oil is applied.]

"Pure oil, clean oil, bright oil,
Oil that brings abundance to the gods,
Oil that eases the sinews of men,
Oil of the exorcism of Ea-Enki,
Oil of the exorcism of Marduk;
I have made thee abundant with the oil of easing,
Which Ea-Enki has given for easing;

I have anointed thee with the oil of life;
I have pronounced the exorcism of Ea-Enki,
the lord of Eridu, and Nin-[...];
I have expelled the *asakku*, the *ahhazu*,
The trembling of thy body;
I have driven out the cry of pain
and anguish of thy body,
I have eased the sinews of thy afflicted limbs;
By command of Ea-Enki, king of the deep,
By the spell of Ea-Enki,
And By the conjuration of Marduk;
By the binding of the of [...]-la,
By the two easing hands of Nin-[...];
Of Ninahakuddu, mistress of the holy-water-bowl;
___ the son/daughter of ___ is restored to life
[...], Ea-Enki, exorcism [...]
[...] of Eridu may ease the body [...]"

'BEDCHAMBER RITES' (NOTES)
(SACRED MARRIAGE)

"Carry the ceremonial bed down the river,
to the sacred Temple of Aššur.
As long as the bed is aboard,
watch over it day and night;
and make regular offerings in front of it."

The most complete surviving Mesopotamian records of a 'sacred marriage' reenactment ('love ritual' or *quršu*) involving actual 'copulation' ('coitus', or *garašu*) are Assyrian (or at best, for our purposes, from the Neo-Assyrian Babylonian Renaissance era). Other than "healing rites" (involving a 'sick bed'), the 'love ritual' is practically the only time a 'bed' (*eršu*) is referenced on religio-magical tablets. In this case, a specific 'ceremonial bedchamber' (*bet erši*) provides the setting.

Assyrian tablets refer to an elaborate week-long 'love ritual' celebrated in Assur-city (at the 'Temple of Aššur') each year during the eleventh month (*Shebat*). The 'bet erši' became a major part of royal festivities during the reign of King Assurbanipal, after the reconstruction of *Ešarra*. Letters written by religious officials at the 'Temple of Nabû' in Calah-city suggest a similar annual rite (dedicated specifically to Nabû and Tašmetu) took place there in the beginning of the second month (*Iyyar*).

LOVE RITUAL OF NABU & TESHMET

"Tašmetu, the Great Lady,
your beloved spouse who intercedes for me daily,
is before you in the sweet bed;
who never ceases demanding
that you protect my life.
Oh Nabû, the one who trusts in you
will not come to shame."

Aside from the romantic epics and cult-literature dedicated to Inanna-Ishtar and Dumuzi (Tammuz), *"The Love Ritual of Nabû and Tašmetu"* is perhaps the best documented Anunnaki 'sacred marriage' (and more appropriate for *Mardukite Babylonian* tradition).

Our primary source for this information comes from discourse (correspondence letters) exchanged among '*temple administrators*' (*hazannu*) and kings. We have collected some of the best preserved examples below. Some details differ between accounts, mainly regarding which day a thing happens. It is also possible that the version used in Assyria was different from the version in Babylon (as described by Mardukite *priest-king*, Nabû-šumu-iddina, *c.* 880 BCE).

The *"Nabû and Tašmetu Quršu Festival"* takes place during the first 11-12 days of the second month, *Iyyar* (or *Airu*). Presumably, all preparations are completed on the first day of the month (*1-Iyyar*) because the tablets indicate that the first day of the actual ritual is *2-Iyyar*. That day (*2-Iyyar*) is approximately April 22nd. This is one month after the *Akiti* "*New Year*" is celebrated on March 21st when the "*Sun entered Aries*" (*1-Nissanu*).

What the Mesopotamian *Quršu* provides us with, is a Mardukite parallel tradition to the European-pagan "*Beltane*" (literally, '*Fires of Bel*') fertility festival— which coincides with the '*May-flower blossoming*' period (approximately April 20 – May 1).

Astronomically, both of these annual festivals—*Beltane* and *Quršu*—began when the "*Sun entered Taurus*." The religio-magical purpose behind these "love rituals" or "sacred marriage ceremonies" is the bestowal of fertility and divine blessing upon the land and its people.

On the *first* day of the festival-ritual (*2-Iyyar*), a fresh *erši*-bed (apparently freighted to the site via the river) is carried to the inner temple—to the sacred "bedchamber" (*bet erši*) or "nuptial chamber" (*hammutu*). The chamber is "prepared for the erotic rendezvous of Nabû and Tašmetu."

All of the "wedding guests"—the attending 'gods' (or at least their 'statues')—arrive at the Temple on the second festival day (3-*Iyyar*).

> *Ša 4 Ajjaru Nabû Tašmetum ina bet erši errubu*
> "On the 4th day of Iyyar,
> Nabû and Tašmetu will enter the bed chamber."

> *ana badi Nabû Tašmetum ina bet erši errubu*
> "Tomorrow (on the 4th day), in the evening,
> Nabû and Tašmetu will enter the bed chamber."

Some versions suggest that Nabû enters the bedchamber alone on the third festival day (4-*Iyyar*) and that Tašmetu arrives on the fourth day for the "wedding night" and "intercourse" (start of the 'honeymoon'). Others say that Nabû and Tašmetu entered the bedchamber together on the fourth festival day (5-*Iyyar*). Whichever day they do travel the streets to enter the bedchamber, it is marked by a grand public procession to the Temple—Tašmetu emerging from her '*holy workshop*' (*mummu*) and Nabû from his '*tablet house*' (*bet tuppi*). Praises and hymns are sung and chanted, inviting the "divine couple" to "come and enter the bedchamber."

The tablets ambiguously direct for the "wedding feast" (*šakussu ša šarri*) to occur on either the fifth ritual day or the fifth day of *Iyyar* (which is the fourth ritual day); after which the couple stayed in the bedchamber for five (or six) days before emerging again. For the duration of their intimate rendezvous, they are nourished by repeated bedside '*Rites of Offering*' performed only by the highest temple administrators. Food for the wedding feast, and other offerings and gifts, are donated by the royal family and other high ranking members of the community—but really, all citizens were invited to participate. The correlating instructions from Nabû-šumu-iddina's correspondence continue:

> *niqiatišunu u[bbalina] pan Nabû Tašme[tum]*
> *ina bet er[ši] eppaš*
> "I will bring the offerings before Nabû and Tašmetu,
> and will perform the rites in the bedroom."

> *šakussu ša šarri ušakkulu hazannu uššab*
> "On the 5th day, they will serve the royal banquet.
> The administrator will attend."

> *hazannu ša bet Nabû anaku lallik [ina] Kalhi*
> "I am the administrator of the temple of Nabû.
> I should therefore go to Calah"

> *šamallû ša niqîšu ibaššuni eppaš ša 1 qa*
> *aklišu ušella ina bet Nabû ekkal*

> "Of the apprentice priests, whoever has a sacrifice
> to make will do so; and whoever brings even one
> bit of food may eat it in the Temple of Nabû."

> *issu libbi UD.5.KAM adi UD.10.KAM [il]ani ina*
> *bet erši šunu u hazannu [k]ammus*
> "From the 5th to the 10th, the gods will be in
> the bed chamber, and the administrator will sit by."

From the 5th until the 10th day, Nabû and Tašmetu stay in the bedchamber (with the temple administrator in their presence). The tablets make obvious implications that intimate relations occur for the duration. The goddess Tašmetu, while gratifying her beloved in the '*sweet bed*', makes appeals to him based on the king's petitions (made on behalf of the greater community of citizens/worshipers). The insinuation here is that Nabû is most receptive to the requests when he is properly 'appeased'.

On the 11th day, Nabû emerges from the bedchamber to "stretch his legs" with a walk through the royal gardens. A chariot transports him through the city—and this post-wedding procession from the Temple through the city (which ends with his returning the '*tablet house*') is the final phase of the festival-ritual. There final details regarding Tašmetu (from this point) do not appear on any surviving examples. We are perhaps led to assume that she remains in the bedchamber on the final day, 'resting' from her week of 'activity'.

A DIVINE MENAGE-A-TROIS

Obscure Mardukite tablet records and a recovered *kudurru* text allude to the god Nabu sharing a "sacred marriage" with two different goddesses—Nanaya and Tašmetu—forming a divine '*love triangle*'. This is unique for the Mardukite lineage, which mainly consisted of Marduk and Nabu; but it was a common practice in the older Anunnaki pantheon. Male deities would typically have both an "official" and an "unofficial" female consort in order to beget two distinct bloodlines. [Anunnaki "half-siblings" (by the same father) could be betrothed to each other *only if* they were born from different mothers.]

Fragments of an '*Old-Babylonian*' (*Akkadian*) era love-poem/narrative, dated to approximately 1700 BCE, define Nanaya and Mu'ati—a variant name for Nabu—as a divine couple. This would, in fact, predate the "sacred marriage" between Nabû and Tašmetu that is strongly emphasized a thousand years later during the '*Neo-Assyrian*' (*Babylonian Renaissance*) period. Nanaya and Tašmetu definitively maintained separate residences in Babylon; so we know the two aren't different names for the same persona. It is quite possible that Nanaya was Nabu's original consort during the Sumerian (*Enlilite*) era, when their *Amorite/Amurru/Martu* (pre-Babylonian Mardukite) cult still confined itself west of Mesopotamia and in Egypt.

'*Old-Babylonian*' era Mardukites celebrated a '*love-ritual*' (*hadašš utu*) for Nabû and Nanaya that parallels the "*Nabû and Tašmetu Quršu Festival*" observed during the '*Babylonian Renaissance*'. That the two are so similar is of benefit to us, since we have far fewer details for the older one. They both were celebrated in the second month (*Iyyar*). Nabu is prepared by dressing in the garments of "*Anuship.*" There is a public procession for each deity from their shrine leading up to entering a bedchamber, where they spend several days in seclusion 'consummating' until (as the other rite) Nabu emerges to walk in the gardens.

Gaps in our understanding between surviving records of Old-Babylonian and Neo-Assyrian periods might be filled by some intriguing documentation of this tradition in Egypt, of all places. In this prose describing a '*bedchamber-rite*', the name Nanaya is written "Nana" (or *Nanai*). However, all of the poetry-dialogue is presumably spoken by her (unidentified) "male beloved"—and it reads:

Nana, you are my wife.
The bed of rushes they have laid down,
perfumed fragrances for your nostrils.
Our goddess, may you be carried,
escorted to your dear one,
let them bear you to the dear one.
In your bridal chamber a priest sings.
Nanai, bring near to me your lips.

[*Before entering the bedchamber,
the lovers stay together for a lengthy while.*]

We dwelt here in the morning;
we shall dwell here in the evening.
The chosen lad too has come.
A sound keeps you awake in the evening;
into our shrine, my […], who is coming?
A sound of harps keeps you awake in the evening;
in the grave of my ancestor, a dirge.
A sound of lyres from the grave
keeps you awake in the evening.

[*At the appointed hour, they enter the chamber.*]

My beloved, enter the door into our house.
With my mouth, consort of our lord, let me kiss you.

And I go and enter.
In my nostrils it is sweet;
Come, enter the perfumed hideaway.
Horus-Bethel will lay you on the bedspread;
El, on embroidered covers.
In his heavens, Mar from Rash blesses;
Mar, a blessing before Bethel everlasting:
'My sister, Marah, blessed are you, our lady.'
'Blessed are you, Had, with a blessing fit for El.'
'Blessed are you, Baal of Heaven.'
'Rebuild humanity; A cursed land rebuild;
A city of ruins rebuild.'
'Keep alive the pauper; bless the poor man.'

DEFILEMENT OF THE RITES

Periods of Babylonian glory, fertility, abundance and prosperity, were often offset by the reign of *anti-Mardukite* rulers and usurpers. During such times of political turbulence, the "rites were not observed" and civilization suffered. When they were not sabotaging Mardukite religious tradition by oppressing temples or reinstalling archaic (*Sumerian*) cults, some of these tyrannical kings went as far as to blatantly defile the sacred 'bedchamber rites' for their own sexual gratification (and outright confuse the spiritual nature of such traditions, and the proper identity of deities, in social consciousness).

Nabû-šumu-iškun ruled Babylonia from *c.* 760 to 748 BCE. According to historical records, he "removed the gods from their proper places" in order to directly interfere with the Nabu – Nanaya – Tašmetu 'love triangle' (during an era when *all three* were recognizably worshiped as a 'triad'). He detained Nabu in Babylon, meanwhile making Nanaya "the lover of Nabû" enter the "workshop" (*bit mummu*). He "covered the 'garment' of Nabu with the 'garment' of Bel (Marduk)" in the eleventh month (*Shebat*). Then he, *himself*, dressed up as Bel and—*aššuta ša Bel ana Tašmetum ušatriš*—"as Bel, proposed marriage to Tašmetu!"

Nabû-šumu-iškun made it appear as though Nanaya had replaced Tašmetu in the "workshop" (presumably in Borsippa); whereas Nabû, impersonated *by* the king and falsely dressed *as* Marduk, was betrothed to Tašmetu in Babylon. Thus, Nanaya was left alone in Borsippa; whereas Tašmetu was married off to quasi-Marduk (the king in disguise) and forced to play out the role of consort to the patron god of Babylon; all the while their actual 'true love' was imprisoned and helpless to intervene. In this wise, Nabû-šumu-iškun blurred the divine roles and identities, cheated the goddesses of their proper worship, and publicly desecrated the sacred rituals of divine love.

—7—
CUNEIFORM TABLETS, EPICS & POEMS

The following is a brief collection of translated cuneiform tablet-records selected as a reference for this volume. Most of these do not already appear in the 'Mardukite Tablet Catalogue' (Esoteric Library). A couple of them appeared in 'The Complete Anunnaki Bible', but were not included in any previous 'New Standard Zuist Editions'. [A serious student or practitioner should refer to 'The Complete Anunnaki Bible' for a more comprehensive source book of ancient cuneiform literature.]

ENKI'S JOURNEY TO NIBRU

In those remote days, when the fates were determined; in a year when Anu brought about abundance, and people broke through the earth like green plants—then the lord of the *abzu*, King Enki; Enki, the lord who determines the fates, built up his temple entirely from silver and lapis lazuli. Its silver and lapis lazuli were like shining daylight. Into the shrine of the *abzu* he brought joy.

Anu artfully made bright crenellations rise out from the *abzu*, for Lord Nud-immud (another title for Enki) it was erected. He built the temple from precious metal, decorated it with lapis lazuli, and covered it abundantly with gold. In *E.ri-dug* (Eridu), he built the house on the bank. Its brickwork makes utterances and gives advice. Its eaves roar like a bull; the Temple of Enki bellows. During the night the temple praises its lord and offers its best for him.

Before Lord Enki, Isimud, the minister praises the temple; he goes to the temple and speaks to it. He goes to the brick building and addresses it: "Temple, built from precious metal and lapis lazuli; whose foundation pegs are driven into the *abzu*; which has been cared for by the prince in the *abzu*! Like the Tigris and the Euphrates, it is mighty and awe-inspiring. Joy has been brought into Enki's *abzu*."

"Your lock has no rival. Your bolt is a fearsome lion. Your roof beams are the bull of heaven, an artfully made bright headgear. Your reed-mats are like lapis lazuli, decorating the roof-beams. Your vault is a wild bull raising its horns. Your door is a lion who seizes a man. Your stairway is a lion coming down on a man."

"*Abzu*, pure place which fulfills its purpose! *E.engura*! Your lord has directed his steps towards you. Enki, lord of the *abzu*, has embellished your foundation pegs with carnelian. He has adorned you with [...] and lapis lazuli. The Temple of Enki is provisioned with holy wax; it is a bull obedient to its master, roaring by itself and giving advice at the same time. *E.engura*, which Enki has surrounded with a holy reed fence, in your midst a lofty throne is erected; your door-jamb is the holy locking bar of heaven."

"Abzu, pure place, place where the fates are determined—the lord of wisdom, Lord Enki; the lord who determines the fates, Nudimmud, the lord of *E.ri-dug* lets nobody look into its midst. Your abga priests let their hair down their backs."

"Enki's beloved *E.ri-dug*; *E.engura* whose inside is full of abundance! *Abzu*, life of the Land, beloved of Enki! Temple built on the edge, befitting the artful divine powers! *E.ri-dug* your shadow extends over the midst of the sea! Rising sea without a rival; mighty awe-inspiring river which terrifies the Land! *E-engura*, high citadel standing firm on the earth! Temple at the edge of the *engur*, a lion in the midst of the *abzu*; lofty Temple of Enki, which bestows wisdom on the Land; your cry, like that of a mighty rising river, reaches King Enki."

"He made {the lyre, the *aljar*-instrument, the *balaj*-drum (of your *sur*-priests) with the drumsticks}, the *harhar*, the *sabitum*, and the [...] *miritum*-instruments offer their best for his holy temple. The [...] resounded by themselves with a sweet sound. The holy *aljar*-instrument of Enki played for him on his own and seven {singers sang and} *tigi*-drums resounded."

"What Enki says is irrefutable; [...] is well established." This is what Isimud spoke to the brick building; he praised the E-engura {with sweet songs} duly. As it has been built, as it has been built; as Enki has raised *E.ri-dug* up, it is an artfully built mountain which floats on the water. His shrine spreads out into the reed beds; birds brood (at night) in its green orchards laden with fruit. The *suhur*-carp play among the honey-herbs, and the *ectub*-carp dart among the small *gizi*-reeds. When Enki rises, the fish rise before him like waves. He has the *abzu* stand as a marvel, as he brings joy into the *engur*.

Like the sea, he is awe-inspiring; like a mighty river, he instils fear. The Euphrates rises before him as it does before the fierce south wind. His punting pole is Nirah {or Imdudu *in some versions*}; his oars are the small reeds. When Enki embarks, the year will be full of abundance. The ship departs of its own accord, with tow rope {held} by itself. As he leaves the Temple of *E.ri-dug*, the river {gurgles} to its lord: its sound is a calf's mooing; the mooing of a good cow.

Enki had offering laid lavishly. Where there were no *ala*-drums, he installed some in their places; where there were no bronze *ub*-drums, he dispatched some to their places. He directed his steps on his own to Nibru and entered the temple terrace, the shrine of Nibru. Enki (reached for) the beer, he (reached for) the liquor. He had liquor poured into big bronze containers, and had *emmer*-wheat beer (pressed out). In *kukuru*-containers which make the beer good, he mixed beer-mash. By adding date-syrup to taste, he made it strong. He [...] its bran-mash.

In the shrine of Nibru, Enki provided a meal for Enlil, his father. He seated Anu at the head of the table and seated Enlil next to Anu. He seated Nintur (Nintud) in the place of honour and seated the *Anuna* (*Anunnaki*) gods at the (adjacent places). All of them were drinking and enjoying beer and liquor. They filled the bronze *aga*-vessels to the brim and started a competition, drinking from the bronze vessels of *Urac*. They made the *tilimda*-vessels shine like holy barges. After beer and liquor had been libated and enjoyed, and after [...] from the house, Enlil was made happy in Nibru.

Enlil addressed the Anuna gods: "Great gods who are standing here! Anuna, who have lined up in the *Ubcu-unkena* (Palace of the Assembly)! My son, King Enki has built up the temple! He has made *E.ri-dug* {rise up} {come out} from the ground like a mountain! He has built it in a pleasant place, in *E.ri-dug*, the pure place, where no one is to enter—a temple built with silver and decorated with lapis lazuli, a house which tunes the seven *tigi*-drums properly, and provides incantations; where holy songs make all of the house a lovely place—the shrine of the *abzu*, the good destiny of Enki, befitting the elaborate divine powers; the temple of *E.ri-dug*, built with silver: for all this, Father Enki be praised!"

ENKI AND NINMAH

In those days, in the days when heaven and earth were created; In those nights, in the nights when heaven and earth were created; In those years, in the years when the fates were determined; when the *Anuna* (*Anunnaki*) gods were born; When the goddesses were taken in marriage; When the goddesses were distributed in heaven and earth; When the goddesses became pregnant and gave birth; When the gods were {obliged} their food [...] dining halls. The senior gods oversaw the work, while the minor gods bore the toil. The gods were digging the canals and piling up the silt in Harali. The gods, crushing the clay, began complaining about this life.

At that time, the one of great wisdom, the creator of all the senior gods, Enki lay on his bed, not waking up from his sleep, in the deep *engur*; in the subterranean water, the place inside of which no other god knows. The gods said, weeping: "He is the cause of the lamenting!" Namma, the primeval mother who gave birth to the senior gods, took the tears of the gods to the one who lay sleeping, to the one who did not wake up from his bed, to her son: "Are you really lying there asleep, and not awake? The gods, your creatures, are smashing their [...] My son, wake up from your bed! Please apply the skill deriving from your wisdom and create a {substitute} for the gods, so that they can be freed from their toil!"

At the word of his mother Namma, Enki rose up from his bed. In *Hal-an-kug*, his room for pondering, he slapped his thigh in annoyance. The wise and intelligent one, the prudent, [...] of skills, fashioner of the design of everything brought to life {by birth-goddesses}. Enki reached out his arm over them and turned his attention to them. And after Enki, the fashioner of designs by himself, had considering the matter, he said to his mother Namma: "My mother, the creature you planned really will come into existence. Impose on him the work of carrying baskets. You should knead clay from the top of the *abzu*; the {birth-goddesses} will nip off the clay, and you shall bring the form into existence. Let Ninmah act as your assistant; and let Ninimma, Cu-zi-ana, Ninmada, Ninbarag, Ninmug, [...] and Ninguna stand by as you give birth. My mother, after you have decreed his fate, let Ninmah impose on him the work of carrying baskets."

[...] she placed it on grass and purified the birth. Enki [...] brought joy to their heart. He set a feast for his mother Namma and for Ninmah. All the courtly {royal} birth-goddesses ate delicate [...] and bread. Anu, Enlil, and Lord Nudimmud (Enki) celebrated the offering feast. All the senior gods praised him: "O lord of wide understanding, who is as wise as you? Enki, the great lord, who can equal your actions? Like a corporeal father, you are the one who has the ME of deciding destinies, in fact you are the ME."

Enki and Ninmah drank beer, their hearts became elated. Then Ninmah said to Enki: "Human bodies could either be made good or bad; and whether I make its fate good or bad depends on my will." Enki answered: "I will counterbalance whatever fate—good or bad—you happen to decide."

Ninmah took clay from the top of the *abzu* in her hand and she fashioned it: First, a man who could not bend his outstretched weak hands. Enki looked at the man and decreed his fate: he appointed him as a servant of the king.

Second, she fashioned one who {"turned back the light"(?)}, a man with permanently opened eyes. Enki looked at the man and decreed his fate: allotting to it the musical arts, making him as the chief [...] in the king's presence.

Third, she fashioned one with both feet broken, with paralyzed feet {*or* "born as an idiot" *in some versions*}. Enki looked at him, and decided the work of [...] and the silversmith [...]

Fourth, she fashioned one who could not hold back his urine. Enki looked at this one and bathed him in enchanted water; he drove out the *namtar*-demon from his body.

Fifth, she fashioned a woman who could not give birth. Enki looked at the woman and decreed her fate: he made her serve in the queen's household as a weaver.

Sixth, she fashioned one with neither penis nor vagina. Enki looked at this one and named it {eunuch}, and decreed as its fate to stand before the king.

Ninmah {or Enki *in some versions*} threw (all) the pinched-off clay to the ground and was greatly [...] The great lord Enki said to Ninmah: "I have decreed the fates of your creatures and given them their daily bread. Now come, I will fashion somebody for you, and you must decree the fate of this newborn one!"

Enki devised a shape with head, [...] and mouth in its middle, and said to Ninmah: "Pour ejaculated semen into a woman's womb, and the woman will give birth from the semen." Ninmah stood by for the newborn [...] and the woman brought forth in the midst [...] As a result, this was *Umul*: its head was afflicted, its place of [...] was afflicted, its eyes were afflicted, its neck was afflicted. It could hardly breathe, its ribs were shaky, its lungs were afflicted, its heart was afflicted, its bowels were afflicted. With its hand and its lolling head, it could not not put bread into its mouth; its spine and head were dislocated. The weak hips and the shaky feet could not {carry} it on the field [...] Enki fashioned it in this way.

Enki said to Ninmah: "For your creatures I have decreed a fate, I have given them their daily bread. Now, you should decree a fate for my creature, give him his daily bread too." Ninmah looked at *Umul* and turned to him. She went nearer to *Umul*, asked him questions, but he could not speak. She offered him bread to eat, but he could not reach out for it. He could not lie on [...], he could not [...] Standing up; he could not sit down, could not lie down, he could not [...] a house, and he could not eat bread. Ninmah answered Enki: "The man you have fashioned is neither alive nor dead. He cannot support himself."

Enki answered Ninmah: "I decreed a fate for the first man with the weak hands, I gave him bread. I decreed a fate for the man who turned away from the light (who could not close his eyes), I gave him bread. I decreed a fate for the man with broken, paralyzed feet, I gave him bread. I decreed a fate for the man who could not hold back his urine, I gave him bread. I decreed a fate for the woman who could not give birth, I gave her bread. I decreed the fate for the one with neither penis nor vagina on its body, I gave it bread. My sister, [...]"

{Tablet damage; indecipherable lines omitted.}

Ninmah answered Enki: "You entered [...] [...] Look, you do not dwell in heaven, you do not dwell on earth, you do not come out to look at the Land. Where you do not dwell, but where my house is built, your words cannot be heard. Where you do not live, but where my city is built, I myself am {silenced}. My city is ruined, my house is destroyed, my child has been taken captive. I am a fugitive who has had to leave the *E.kur*, even I myself could not escape from your hand."

Enki replied to Ninmah: "Who could change the words that left your mouth? Remove *Umul* from your lap [...] Ninmah, may your work be [...], you [...] for me what is imperfect; who can {oppose} this? The man whom I shaped [...] after you [...], let him pray! Today let my penis be praised, may your wisdom be {confirmed}! May the *enkum* and *ninkum* [...] proclaim your glory [...] My sister, the heroic strength [...] The song [...] the writing [...] The gods who heard [...] let *Umul* build {*or serve ?*} my house [...]" And Ninmah could not rival the great lord Enki; Father Enki, your praise is sweet!

NINGISHZIDA'S DESCENT TO THE UNDERWORLD

"Arise and get on board; Arise, we are about to sail; Arise and get on board!" -- Woe, weep for the bright daylight, as the barge is steered away! -- "I am a young man! Let me not be covered against my wishes by a cabin, as if with a blanket; As if with a blanket!"

Stretching out a hand to the barge, to the young man being steered away on the barge; Stretching out a hand to Lord Ningishzida being taken away on the barge; Stretching out a hand to *Ictaran* of the bright visage, being taken away on the barge; Stretching out a hand to *Alla*, master of the {battle-net}, being taken away on the barge; Stretching out a hand to *Lugal-cud-e* being taken away on the barge.

Stretching out a hand to Ningishzida being taken away on the barge--his younger sister was crying in lament to him in the cabin at the boat's bow. His older sister removed the cover from the cabin at the boat's stern: "Let me sail away with you; Let me sail away with you, my brother. My brother, let me sail on your barge with you; My brother, let me sail away with you. Let me sail on your splendid barge with you, my brother." She was crying a lament to him at the boat's bow: "My brother, let me sail away with you. The *gudug* priest sits in the cabin at your boat's stern. Let me sail away with you, my brother; Let me sail away with you."

"My young man, *Damu*, let me sail away with you, my brother; let me sail away with you. *Ictaran* of the bright visage, let me sail away with you, my brother; let me sail away with you. *Alla*, master of the {battle-net}, let me sail away with you, my brother; let me sail away with you. *Lugal-cud-e*, let me sail away with you, my brother; let me sail away with you. *Lugal-ki-bura*, let me sail away with you, my brother; let me sail away with you. Ningishzida, let me sail away with you, my brother; let me sail away with you. My brother, let me sail on your barge with you; my brother, let me sail away with you. Let me sail on your splendid barge with you, my brother; let me sail away with you."

The evil-demon who was in their midst called out to Ningishzida: "*Lugal-ki-bura*, look at your sister!" Having looked at his sister, *Lugal-ki-bura* said to her: "He sails with me, he sails with me; Why should you (want to) sail to the underworld? Lady, the demon sails with me; Why should you sail to the underworld? The thresher sails with me; Why should you sail to the underworld? The man who has bound my hands sails with me; Why should you sail? The man who has tied my arms sails with me; Why should you sail?"

"The river of the underworld produces no water, no water is drunk from it; Why should you sail? The fields of the underworld produce no grain, no flour is eaten from it; Why should you sail? The sheep of the nether world produce no wool, no cloth is woven from it; Why should you sail? Even for me, even if my mother were to dig a canal, I shall not be able to drink the water meant for me. The waters of springtime will not be poured for me as they are for the tamarisks; I shall not sit in the shade intended for me. The dates I should bear like a date palm will not reveal their beauty for me. I am a field threshed by my demon; you would scream at it. He has put manacles on my hands; you would scream at it. He has put a neck-stock (around) my neck; you would scream at it."

Ama-cilama then said to her brother, Ningishzida: "The ill-intentioned {or evil} demon may accept something; there should be a limit to it for you. My brother, your demon may accept something; there should be a limit to it for you. For him let me [...] from my hand the [...]; there should be a limit to it for you. For him let me [...] from my hand the [...]; there should be a limit to it for you. For him let me [...] from my hips the dainty lapis lazuli beads; there should be a limit to it for you. For him let me [...] from my hips the [...] my lapis lazuli beads; there should be a limit to it for you."

"You are a beloved [...]; there should be a limit to it for you. How they treat you; Oh, how they treat you! There should be a limit to it for you. My brother, how they treat you, how haughtily they treat you! There should be a limit to it for you. (You say) 'I am hungry, but the bread has slipped away from me'; there should be a limit to it for you. (You say) 'I am thirsty, but the water has slipped away from me'; there should be a limit to it for you."

The evil-demon who was in their midst, the clever demon, that great demon who was in their midst, called out to the man at the boat's bow and to the man at the boat's stern: "Don't let the mooring stake be pulled out, so that she may come on board to her brother; that this lady may come on board the barge."

When *Ama-cilama* had gone on board the barge, a cry approached the heavens, a cry approached the earth, that great demon set up an enveloping cry before him on the river: "*Urim*, at my cry to the heavens lock your houses, lock your houses; city, lock your houses! *Urim*, against your lord who has left the [...] city, lock your houses!" [...] a holy sceptre. [...] a holy robe of office. [...] a holy crown. [...] a lapis-lazuli sceptre.

He [...] to the empty river, the rejoicing river: "You (*Ama-cilima*) shall not draw near to this house, [...] to the place (*or* palace) of *Ereshkigal* (*Eres-ki-gala*). My mother [...] out of her love. As for you (demon), you may be a great demon [...], [...] your hand against the office of the underworld's throne-bearer."

"My king will no longer shed tears in his eyes. The drum will [...] his joy in tears. Come! May the fowler utter a lament for you in his well-stocked house, lord, may he utter a lament for you. How he has been humiliated! May the young fisherman utter a lament for you in his well-stocked house, lord, may he utter a lament for you. How he has been humiliated! May the mother of the dead *gudug* priest utter a lament for you in her empty [...], utter a lament for you, lord, may she utter a lament for you. How he has been humiliated! May the mother high priestess utter a lament for you who have left the [...], lord, may she utter a lament for you. How he has been humiliated!"

"My king, bathe with water, your head that has rolled in the dust. [...] in sandals, your feet defiled from the defiled place." The king bathed with water his head that had rolled in the dust. [...] in sandals, his feet defiled from the defiled place. "Not drawing near to this house, [...] your throne [...] to you 'Sit down'. May your bed [...] to you 'Lie down'." He ate food in his mouth; he drank fine wine. Great holy one, Ereshkigal, praising you is sweet.

THE EPIC OF NERGAL & ERESHKIGAL
[Akhenaton's (Amarna) Fragments]
(*From 'The Complete Anunnaki Bible' Tablet-U Series*)

When the gods organized a banquet, they sent a messenger to their sister Ereshkigal.
"We cannot come down to you, and you cannot come up to us. So, send someone to fetch a share of the food for you!"

Ereshkigal sent Namtar, her vizier:
"Go up, Namtar, to high heaven!"

He went into where the gods were sitting, and they bowed and greeted NAMTAR, the messenger of their eldest sister. They bowed respectfully when they saw him and the great gods. [. . .] food for the goddess his mistress. [. . .] wept and was overcome. [. . .] the journey.

[6+ *lines missing*]

Ea-Enki [. . .] and went to Namtar and sent him back.
"Go and tell my word to our sister. She will say, 'Where is the one who did not

rise to his feet in the presence of my messenger? Bring him to me for his death, that I may kill him!'"

Namtar came back and spoke to the gods, the gods summoned him and discussed the death with him.
"Look for the god who did not rise to his feet in your presence, and take him before your mistress!"

Namtar counted them. The last god was crouching down.
"That god who did not rise to his feet in your presence; he is not here!"

Then Namtar went and gave his report,
"My mistress, I went and counted them. The last god was crouching down. The god who did not rise to his feet in my presence was not there."

Ereshkigal addressed Namtar, her messenger, "[. . .] month."

[*several lines missing*]

"Identify the one," [. . .] to the hand of Ea-Enki.
"Take him to Ereshkigal!"
He was weeping.

Before his father ENKI, he pleaded:
"He will see me! He will not let me stay alive!"

"Don't be afraid for I shall give to you seven [and seven] demons. To go with you I send: Lightning-Bolt, The Bailiff, The Croucher, Explosion, Terrible Wind, Fits of Sickness, The Stagger, The Stroke, The Lord of the Roof, The Fever, The Scab and [. . .] Ereshkigal will call out, 'Gatekeeper, [. . .] open your door.'"

[*several lines missing*]

Nergal approaches the gates:
"Loosen the lock, that I may enter into the presence of your mistress, Ereshkigal. I have been sent from above!"

The Gatekeeper said to Namtar:
"A god is standing at the entrance of the door. Come, inspect him and let him enter."

Namtar came out, saw him and called: "Wait here!"
He went to his mistress and said:
"My lady, here is the god who in previous months had vanished, and who did not rise to his feet in my presence above!"

Ereshkigal replied:

"Bring him in. As soon as he comes, I shall kill him!"

Namtar came out and addressed Nergal: "Come in, my lord, to your sister's house and [. . .]"
Nergal said, "You should be glad to see me. . ."

[*several lines missing*]

...At the seventh, the Terrible Wind. At the eighth, Fits of Sickness. At the ninth, The Staggers. At the tenth, The Stroke. At the eleventh, The Lord of the Roof. At the twelfth, The Fever. At the thirteenth, The Scab. At the fourteenth Gate, he managed to seal her in. In the forecourt he cut off Namtar.
He gave his troops the orders:
"Let the doors be opened! Now I shall race past you!"

Inside the house, he seized Ereshkigal by her hair, pulled her from the throne to the ground, intending to cut off her head.
"Don't kill me, my brother! Let me tell you something."

Nergal listened to her and relaxed his grip, he wept and was overcome when she said:
"You can be my husband, and I can be your wife. I will let you seize Kingship over the wide Earth! I will put the Tablet of Destiny in your hand! You can be the master; I can be the mistress."

Nergal listened to this speech of hers, and seized her and kissed her. He wiped away her tears.
"These things have you asked of me? After so many months, it shall certainly be so!"

THE COURTSHIP OF ISHTAR & DUMUZI
(From 'The Complete Anunnaki Bible' Tablet-U Series)

The brother spoke to his younger sister.
The Sun God, Shammash {Utu}, spoke to Inanna {Ishtar}, saying:
"Lady, the flax in its fullness is lovely.
Inanna {Ishtar}, the grain is glistening in the furrow.
I will work the ground for you.
I will bring the grain to you.
But a piece of linen-cloth, big or small, is always needed.
Inanna {Ishtar}, I will bring it to you."

Inanna {Ishtar} said:
"Brother, after you've brought me the flax,
Who will comb it for me?"
Shammash {Utu} replied:

"Sister, I will bring it to you combed."

Inanna {Ishtar} said:
"Shammash {Utu}, after you've brought it to me combed,
Who will spin it for me?"
And Shammash {Utu} responded:
"Inanna {Ishtar}, I will bring it to you spun."

Inanna {Ishtar} said:
"Brother, after you've brought the flax to be spun,
Who will braid it for me?"
And Shammash {Utu} responded:
"Sister, I will bring it to you braided."

Inanna {Ishtar} said:
"Shammash {Utu}, after you've brought it to me braided,
Who will weave it for me?"
And Shammash {Utu} replied:
"Sister, I will bring it to you woven."

Inanna {Ishtar} said:
"Shammash {Utu}, after you've brought it to me woven;
Who will bleach it for me?"
And Shammash {Utu} responds:
"Inanna {Ishtar}, I will bring it to you bleached."

Angered now, Inanna {Ishtar} demanded:
"Brother, after you've brought my bridal sheet to me,
Who will go to bed with me!?
Who, Shammash {Utu}—who will sleep with me!?"
Shammash {Utu} calmly replied:
"Sister, your bridegroom will go to bed with you.
He who was born from a fertile womb,
He who was conceived on the sacred marriage throne,
Dumuzi, the shepherd! He will go to bed with you."

Inanna {Ishtar} spoke:
"No, brother!
I want the farmer!
He is the man of my heart!
He gathers the grain into great heaps.
He brings the grain regularly into my storehouses."
Shammash {Utu} said:
"Sister, you should marry the shepherd.
Why are you unwilling?
His *cream* is good; his *milk* is good.

Whatever he touches shines brightly.
Inanna {Ishtar}, marry Dumuzi.
You who adorn yourself with the agate necklace of fertility alone,
Why are you unwilling?
Dumuzi will share his rich *cream* with you.
You who are meant to be the king's protector,
Why are you unwilling?"

Still angry, Inanna {Ishtar} then spoke:
"The shepherd?!
I will not marry the shepherd!
His clothes are course; his wool is rough.
I will marry the farmer.
The farmer grows flax for my clothes,
The farmer grows barley for my table."

Then Dumuzi arrived and said:
"Why do you speak about the farmer? Why do you speak about him?
If he gives you black flour, I will give you black wool.
If he gives you white flour, I will give you white wool.
If he gives you beer, I will give you sweet milk.
If he gives you bread, I will give you honey cheese.
I will give the farmer my leftover cream.
I will give the farmer my leftover milk.
Why do you speak about the farmer?
What does he have more than I do?"

Laughing, Inanna {Ishtar} replied:
"Shepherd-boy, without my mother, Ningal, you'd be driven away;
Without my grandmother, Ningikugga, you'd be driven to the *Abyss*,
Without my father, Nanna-Sin, you'd have no roof,
Without my brother Shammash {Utu} [...]"

Dumuzi interrupted:
"Inanna {Ishtar}, do not start a quarrel with me.
My father, Enki, is as good as your father, Nanna.
My mother, Sirtur, is as good as your mother, Ningal.
My sister, Geshtinanna, is as good as yours, Ereshkigal [...]
So, Queen of the palace, let us talk it over, shall we?"

The words they had spoken between them were words of passion and desire.
From the start of the heated quarrel came the lovers' desire for each other.

Dumuzi, The Shepherd, went to the royal house with cream.
He went to the royal house with milk.
Before the door, he called out:

"Open the house, My Lady, open the house!"

Inanna {Ishtar} ran to the arms of Ningal, her mother.
Ningal counseled her daughter, saying:
"My child, this young man will be your father.
My daughter, this young man will be your mother.
He will treat you like a father.
He will care for you like a mother."

Still Dumuzi called:
"Open the house, My Lady, open the house!"

Inanna {Ishtar}, at her mother's command,
Bathed and anointed herself with scented oil.
She covered her body with the royal white robe.
She readied her dowry.
She arranged her precious lapis lazuli beads around her neck.
She took her seal in her hand.
Dumuzi waited expectantly.
Inanna {Ishtar} opened the door for him.
Inside the house she shined before him.
Like the light of the moon.
Dumuzi looked at her joyously.
He pressed his neck close against hers.
He kissed her.

Inanna {Ishtar} then said:
"What I tell you, let the singer weave into song.
What I tell you, let it flow from ear to mouth,
Let it pass from old to young:
My vulva, the horn,
Is The Boat of Heaven,
Is full of eagerness like the new moon.
Who will plow my vulva?
Who will plow my high field?
Who will plow my wet ground?
I am a young beautiful woman;
Who will plow my vulva!?
Who will station the ox there!?
Who will plow my vulva!?"

Dumuzi smiled and said:
"Great Lady, the king will plow your vulva!
I, Dumuzi the King, will plow your vulva."
Inanna {Ishtar} screamed:
"Then plow my vulva, man of my heart! Plow my vulva! Do it now!"

◊ ◊ ◊ ◊ ◊ ◊

When after the king's lap stood the rising cedar.
Plants grew high by their side.
Grains grew high by their side.
Gardens flourished luxuriantly.

Inanna {Ishtar} sang in delight:
"He has sprouted;
He is fertile growth planted by the water.
He is the one my womb loves best.
My well-stocked garden in the plains,
My barley growing high in its furrow,
My apple tree which bears fruit up to its crown,
He is fertile growth planted by the water.
My honey-man, my honey-man sweetens me always.
My lord, the honey-man of the gods,
He is the one my womb loves best.
His hand is honey, his foot is honey,
He sweetens me always.
My eager man who caresses my navel,
My man who caresses my soft thighs,
He is the one my womb loves best.
O, how I love him!
He is my fertile growth planted by the water."

And Dumuzi sang:
"O Great Lady, your breast is your field.
Inanna {Ishtar}, your breast is your field.
Your broad field pours out the plants.
Your broad field pours out grain.
Water flows from on high for your servant.
Bread flows from on high for your servant.
Pour it out for me, Inanna {Ishtar}.
I will drink all you offer."

Inanna {Ishtar} said passionately:
"Make your milk sweet and thick for me, my bridegroom.
My shepherd, I will drink your fresh milk.
My wild bull, Dumuzi, make your milk sweet and thick.
I will drink your fresh milk.
Let the milk of the goat flow in my sheepfold.
Fill my holy churn with honey cheese.
Lord Dumuzi, I will drink your fresh milk.
My husband, I will guard my sheepfold for you.
I will watch over your house of life, the storehouse,

The shining quivering place which delights;
The house which decides the fates of the land,
The house which gives the breath of life to the people.
I, the queen of the palace, will watch over your house."

Dumuzi spoke:
"My sister, I would go with you to my garden.
Inanna {Ishtar}, I would go with you to my garden.
I would go with you to my orchard.
I would go with you to my apple tree.
There I would plant the sweet, honey-covered seed."

Inanna {Ishtar} sang:
"He brought me into his garden.
My brother, Dumuzi, brought me into his garden.
I strolled with him among the standing trees,
I stood with him among the fallen trees,
By the apple tree I knelt as is proper.
Before my brother coming in song,
Who rose to me out of poplar leaves,
Who came to me in the midday heat, before my lord, Dumuzi,
I poured out plants from my womb.
I placed plants before him,
I poured out plants before him.
I placed grain before him,
I poured out grain before him,
I poured out grain before my womb."

She sang louder:
"Last night as I, the Queen, was shining bright,
Last night as I, the Queen of Heaven, was shining bright,
As I was shining bright and dancing,
Singing praises at the coming of the night;
He met me! He met me! My lord Dumuzi met me!
He pushed his hand to my hand.
He pressed his neck close against mine.
My high priest is ready for the holy loins.
My lord Dumuzi is ready for the holy loins.
The plants and herbs in his field are ripe.
Dumuzi! Your fullness is my delight!"

She called for it, she called for it, she called for the bed!
She called for the bed that rejoices the heart.
She called for the bed that sweetens the loins.
She called for the bed of kingship.
She called for the bed of queenship.

Inanna {Ishtar} called for the bed:
"Let the bed that rejoices the heart be prepared!
Let the bed that sweetens the loins be prepared!
Let the bed of kingship be prepared!
Let the bed of queenship be prepared!
Let the royal bed be prepared!"

She spread the bridal sheet across the bed.
She called to the king:
"The bed is ready!"
She called to her bridegroom:
"The bed is waiting!"
He put his hand in her hand.
He put his heart to her heart.
Sweet is the sleep of the hand-to-hand.
Sweeter still is the sleep of heart-to-heart.

Inanna {Ishtar} said:
 "I bathed for the wild bull,
I bathed for the shepherd Dumuzi,
I perfumed my sides with ointment,
I coated my mouth with sweet-smelling amber,
I painted my eyes with coal.
He shaped my loins with his fair hands.
The Shepherd, Dumuzi filled my lap with cream and milk,
He stroked my pubic hair,
He watered my womb.
He laid his hands on my holy vulva,
He smoothed my black boat with cream,
He quickened my narrow boat with milk,
He caressed me on the bed.
Now I will caress my high priest on the bed,
I will caress the faithful shepherd Dumuzi,
I will caress his loins, the shepherdship of the land,
I will decree a sweet fate for him."

'SUMMER' & 'WINTER'
(Sumerian 'Emesh & Enten' Cycle)

Anu lifted his head in pride and brought forth a good day. He laid plans for
[...] and spread (wide) [...] the population. Enlil set his foot upon the earth like
a great bull. Enlil, the king of all lands, set his mind to increasing the good
day of abundance: to making the [...] night resplendent in celebration; to
making flax grow; to making barley proliferate; to guaranteeing the spring

floods at the quay; to making [...] lengthen their days in abundance; to making Summer close the sluices of heaven; and to making Winter guarantee plentiful water at the quay.

He copulated with the great hills; he gave the mountain its share. He filled its womb with Summer and Winter, the plenitude and life of the land. As Enlil copulated with the earth, there was a war {like a bull's}. The hill spent the day at that place and at night she opened her loins. She bore Summer and Winter as smoothly as fine oil. He fed them pure plants on the terraces of the hills like great bulls. He nourished them in the pasture of the hills.

Enlil set about determining the destinies of Summer and Winter. For Summer: founding towns and villages; bring in harvests of plenitude for the Great Mountain, Enlil; sending laborers out to the large arable tracts; and working the fields with oxen. For Winter: plenitude; the spring floods; the abundance and life of the land; placing grain in the fields and fruitful acres; and gathering in everything. Enlil determined these as the destinies of Summer and Winter.

Winter guided the spring floods, the abundance and life of the land, down from the edge of the hills. He set his foot upon the Tigris and Euphrates (like a big bull) and released them into the fields and fruitful acres of Enlil. He shaped lagoons in the water of the sea. He surrounded all the reed-beds with mature reeds, reed shoots and [...] reeds.

Summer, the heroic sun of Enlil, drained the large arable tracts. He [...] cool water on the fields and fruitful acres like [...] [...] Holy winter [...] The ox [...] its head in a yoke. Ninurta, Enlil's son, [...] the fruitful acres. He [...] grain in the large arable tracts. He fills the fields and fruitful acres of Enlil.

Winter made the ewe give birth to the lamb; he gave the kid to the goat. He made cows teem together with their calves; he provided butter and milk. On the high plain he made the deer and stag glad of heart. He made the birds of heaven set their nests in broad spaces. The fish of the lagoons laid eggs in the reed-bed. In all the orchards he made honey and wine drip to the ground. He made the trees, wherever planted, bear fruit. He established gardens and provided plants. He made grain abundant in the furrows. He made *Ezina* appear radiant as a beautiful maiden. The harvest, the great festival of Enlil, rose heavenward.

Summer founded houses and farmsteads, he made the cattle-pens and sheepfolds wide. He multiplied the stacks of sheaves in all the arable tracts. At their edge he made [...] flax [...] ripen. He brought a plentiful harvest into the temples; he heaped up piles of grain. He founded towns and villages; he built the houses of the land. He made the houses of the gods grow like the hills in a pure place. In *E.namtila*, the holy seat of kingship, fit for high daises; he established abundance for the Great Mountain, Enlil.

Summer, the heroic son of Enlil, decided to bring offerings to *E.namtila*, the house of Enlil. He brought animals, cattle and sheep of the hill, fully grown wild rams, deer and stags, [...] sheep, long-fleeced barley-fed sheep, thick-tailed sheep. Pigs grown fat in the midst of the reed-beds, porcupine, tortoise, turtle, birds brooding in their nests, taken together with their eggs, harvest crops, flour and malt for mixing, butter and milk from cattle-pen and sheepfold, wheat, [...] beans, small beans and large beans gathered in piled-high baskets, onions [...] in their furrows, *zahadin*-onions and shallots, seed turnips, saffron, [...] [...]. Summer, the heroic son of Enlil, offered.

Winter, lordly son of Enlil, [...], released the water of life and [...] opened. He gathered the [...] oxen and [...] the oxen. The disputed sheep was provided, barley-fed but with a scorpion at its side. Quartz, gold and silver found in leather pouches, cedar, cypress, [...], boxwood, [...], [...] tribute of the land, figs from Mari, [...], strings of dried fruit, cool water, the tribute of the hills, [...] thick honey, *dida*-beer, [...], village [...], *bibra*-birds *esig*-birds, *buru-bacur* birds, fattened ducks, carp, [...] which Winter made grow up, large pomegranates gathered from the orchards, big bunches of grapes on high, winter cucumbers, [...] empty [...], brought forth [...] in the early rain, large turnips, large [...] cut down with the knife, long leeks. Winter himself brought the tribute he had collected.

Summer and Winter set about organizing the animals and offerings for *E.namtila*, the house of Enlil. The two of them, like huge butting bulls, reared themselves triumphantly. But Winter, because his limbs had grown tired from the grain grown heavy in the furrows, and the wheat and *emmer* which he had been watering by hand, turned away as from an enemy and would not draw near.

Consequently, Winter was overcome by anger and he started a quarrel with Summer: "Summer, my brother, you should not praise yourself; whatever harvest produce you bring as gifts to the palace has not been made by your toil: you should not brag. As if you were the one who had done the hard work; as if you had done the farming; as if you had taken care of irrigation control during the spring floods; as if you had brought forth the [...] grain in the arable tracts with the dew from heaven: how much through my toil is it that you enter the palace!"

"Whatever animals, cattle and sheep of the hill, you bring to my [...] [...] Your gardener [...] the palace [...]; Honey and wine in the orchard [...]; Its destructive hoe [...]; Your gathered vegetables, the purslane, [...]; Whatever you [...] at the gate of the palace. In the field your arm [...]. The straw of your grain you bring [...]"

"After you have threshed it at your threshing floor, and have [...] the cattle's dung, your carrying nets are to hand, [...] bearing your straw. [...] the animals, the storehouses and their contents. After your houses and farmsteads [...] sheep, [...] from your cattle, after [...] their reed-beds, after [...] green briars and cut [...] thorns, [...] storehouse [...] the dung of unyoked oxen -- the slave, Summer, the duly-appointed laborer who will never rest from his toil, a hired man who has to return to the fields of the land for his own sustenance!"

On that day Winter taunted Summer, the hero whom one does not challenge, searched for rude insults. He was confident in himself, considering the harvest time, and turned aside. Like a great bull eating rich grass, he raised his head.

Next, Summer replied to Winter: "Winter, you may have to stay by the side of the oven, [...]; but you should not launch such serious insults against someone who does not lead a {sedentary life}. [...] for the work of tilling the land, with its difficulties; you do not raise a cry in the [...] cult center; you do not look after the house. The young scribe is neglectful, which is an abomination, and no rushes are plucked for the beds. The singer does not embellish the banquet, [...] at its side."

"Winter, don't launch such insults! [...] to the desert. I will make the strength of my power come forth in the house so that you recognize it. In my working term of duty, which is seven months of the year, [...] does not speak softly. [...] [...] Tirelessly and constantly I place abundance upon the fields."

"After they [...] my seed, Winter, do not [...] noise, when water is cut off from the arable tracts, when the bowls lie placed, when the fishing place has been prepared, when the fish have been piled up, I am father Enlil's great comptroller. I harrow the fields into fruitful acres. When the oxen have stopped working in the fields, when you have concentrated your efforts on the damp areas and given the sign for the field work, I do not work for you in the large arable tracts and fruitful acres early in the season. If the spring grain bends its neck in the hollow of the furrows, no one provides a fence. Whatever your farmer brings to the oxen, he will not make the oxen angry with me. Winter [...] in the uplands [...]. The man of the bedroom [...]." Then Summer taunted Winter: "Wise [...], serious insults [...], not [...]."

Thereupon Winter replied to Summer: "Summer, the donkey grazing on grass at the harvest {ground} and braying noisily; the mule [...]; the harvest ox chafing its neck in the pegs and tossing its head in the lead rope; the innkeeper going to the harvest {ground} carrying a bowl in his hands; the flour [...] playing [...]; the bragging fieldworker who does not know the extent of the field. Summer, my brother, after you have gone out boasting about my toil, when at the turn of the year grain is brought into the houses and granaries are packed full, when you bring the surplus, your *bardul*-garment and your *niglam*-garment are [...]. When some one gives a {great axe} to you, you go off to your steppe."

"Summer, my brother, the wet spots must not be [...] when tilling the field. A man from the storehouse stands in front of you and instructs you. When on the high plain [...] the ash tree [...], [...] yourself [...]. [...] When tribute is brought in your freight boats [...]. When the grass has arrived in the storehouse, [...] before me. What will the penned sheep eat? Your [...] reeds are exhausted. The reed-cutter who sets about pruning with the {machete} and splitting older reeds, the builder who places laborers in houses, never resting from his efforts, the potter who digs out clay, lights a fire and stokes it with wood [...] the pot! Weaver, weave your *bardul*-garment with the strength of your *aktum*-cloth. Brewer, bake your beer bread at the harvest {ground} as your assignment! Cook, produce great banquet loaves in summer! The building supervisor [...] the [...] of the roofs. People [...] boots and shoes [...]."

"Summer, my brother, as long as you go with my term of duty, great and small shall order you about and your string is not cut. Although you have gathered all things in the land and filled the storehouses, in all my strength, I am their owner when your limbs become tired. When the clouds have brought down the abundance of heaven, and the water of the first greening has descended from the hills, and the new grain has been put in the granary to be added to the old grain; the good farmer, having seen to his fields, shouts for joy, the carrier donkeys stand ready and he sets out confidently for the city."

"My brother, when you have put the holy plow away in the barn, the storehouse, everything you have gathered, you make a roar like fire. You sit down to plentiful food and drink. You obtain the choicest goods from the land. For my king named *Nanna*, the son of Enlil, *Ibbi-Suen*, when he is arrayed in the *cutur*-garment and the *hasag*-garment; when you have taken care of the *bardul*-garment and the *nijlam*-garment; when you have made a perfect feast for the gods; when the *Anuna* {or Anunnaki} have placed garments on their holy bodies; in his *E.namtila*, the holy abode of kingship founded by Anu, at the place of content they prepare a choice banquet."

"When the *cem* and *ala* drums, [...] and the other instruments play together for him, he passes the time with your heart-gladdening *tigi* and *zamzam*-instruments. But it is I who have made the wine plentiful and made much to eat and drink. I perfect the garments with fine oil. I bring up the [...], the *cutut* and *aktum*-garments. As for safeguarding, the best in Sumer, in the oppressive heat of Summer, where they had put away in the bedrooms amongst the 'black-haired people' {or humans}, moths destroy the blankets and make the *aktum*-cloth perish because of you. [...] exhausts itself for you [...]. The wooden chest [...]. I am Ninkasi's help; for her I sweeten the beer, with as much cold water, the tribute of the hills, as you brought."

"After [...] pots, after [...] pots, after the plump grapes have been laid out in the cool breeze, I make my king's great palace [...] pleasant. I am the one who cools down my king. I fill the fish-hook. My comrade, grasp your leather bag, go out [...]. The farmer [...] hardship. The farmer [...] the rain. The gardener does not know how to plant purslane, your [...] basket [...]. How can you compare yourself to me while seeking a roof under which to rest?"

For a second time Winter has taunted Summer. Summer, the heroic son of Enlil, was convinced of his own strong power and consequently trusted in himself. He acted as if in a friendly manner to the insults that Winter had spoken to him.

Then Summer replied to Winter: "Winter, you should not boast about your superior strength after you have explained the grounds for your boasting. I shall speak about your abode in the city which I shall [...] You seem like a man of (high) office, but you are an inept one. Your straw bundles are for the oven-side, hearth and kiln. Like a herdsman or shepherd encumbered by sheep and lambs, helpless people run like sheep from oven-side to kiln, and from kiln to oven-side, in the face of you. In sunshine [...] you reach decisions, but now in the city people's teeth chatter because of you."

"When the day is half done, nobody walks about the streets. The servant, basking by the side of the oven, is in the house until sunset. The maid, not attending to the flow of the water-container, passes the day (resting) on garments. As for the fields not worked in winter, their furrows are not cut straight; and their grain, having not been cast into a wholesome place, is taken away by huge flocks of rooks. The vegetable cutter [...] does not [...] those vegetables at the market. Carrying old reeds, the laborer is halt and lame. Don't speak with a gaping mouth of your superior strength; I will make known its shape and {substance}."

For a second time Summer had taunted Winter. On that day of the *E.kur*'s festival and (celebrating) *Sumer*'s plenty {or abundance}, the two of them stretched their legs and stood combatively. Summer and Winter, like great bulls about to tear at each other's horns, bent forward like wild bulls in the main courtyard and took their positions.

Like a great bull Winter raised his head to speak: "Father Enlil, you gave me control of irrigation; you brought plentiful water. I made one meadow adjacent to another and I heaped high the granaries. The grain became thick in the furrows. *Ezina* came forth in splendor like a beautiful maiden. Summer, a bragging field-administrator who does not know the extent of the field, [...] my thighs grown tired from toil. [...] tribute has been produced for the king's palace. Winter admires the heart of your [...] in words."

Summer pondered {or considered} everything in his head and calmed down. Summer spoke respectfully to Enlil: "Enlil, your verdict is highly valued, your holy word is an exalted word. The verdict you pronounce is one which cannot be altered; who can change it? There was quarreling of brother and brother but now there is harmony. For as long as you are occupying the palace, the people will express awe. When it is your season, far be it from me to humiliate you; in fact I shall praise you."

Enlil answered Summer and Winter: "Winter is the controller of the life-giving waters for all the lands; the farmer of the gods produces everything. Summer, my son, how can you compare yourself to your brother, Winter?"

The importance of the exalted word (that) Enlil speaks is skillfully made; the verdict he pronounces is one which cannot be altered; who can change it? Summer bowed to Winter and offered him a prayer. In his house he prepared *emmer*-beer and wine. At its side they spend the day at a succulent banquet. Summer presents Winter with gold, silver, and lapis lazuli. They pour out brotherhood and friendship like (the) best oil. By bringing sweet words to the quarrel they have achieved harmony with each other. In the dispute between Summer and Winter: Winter, the faithful farmer of Enlil, was superior to Summer; praise be to the Great Mountain, father Enlil.

HYMN OF THE TEMPLES
(Sumerian—Archaic Translation)

E.unir ('House Which is a Ziggurat'), grown together with heaven and earth, foundation of heaven and earth, great banqueting hall of *E.ri-dug*! *Abzu*, shrine erected for its prince, *E.du-kug* ('House which is a Holy Hill/Mound') where pure food is eaten; watered by the prince's pure canal; mountain, pure place cleansed with the potash plant; *Abzu*, your *tigi*-drums belong to the divine powers. Your great [...] wall is in good repair. Light does not enter your meeting-place where the god dwells, the great [...], the beautiful place. Your tightly constructed house is sacred and has no equal. Your prince, the great prince, has fixed firmly a holy crown for you in your precinct; *E.ri-dug* with a crown placed on your head, bringing forth thriving thorn-bushes, pure thorn-bushes for the *susbu*-priests; O shrine *Abzu*, your place, your great place!

At your place of calling upon *Utu* [*Shammash*]; at your oven bringing bread to eat; on your ziggurat, a magnificent shrine stretching toward heaven; at your great oven, rivaling the great banqueting hall, your prince, the prince of heaven and earth [...] can never be changed; the [...], the creator, the [...], the wise one, the [...]; Lord *Nudimmud* {another name for EA/Enki}, has erected a house in your precinct, *E.engura* ('House of the Subterranean Waters'), and taken his seat upon your dais. [...] the house of *Enki* in *E.ri-dug*.

O [...], shrine where destiny is determined, [...], foundation, raised with a ziggurat, [...], settlement of *Enlil*, your [...], your right and your left are *Sumer* and *Akkad*. House of *Enlil*, your interior is cool, your exterior determines destiny. Your door-jambs and architrave are a mountain summit, your projecting pilasters a dignified mountain. Your peak is a [...] peak of your princely platform. Your base serves heaven and earth. Your prince, the great prince *Enlil*, the good lord, the lord of the limits of heaven, the lord who determines destiny; the Great Mountain, *Enlil*, has erected a house in your precinct, O shrine *Nibru*, and taken his seat upon your dais. [...] the house of *Enlil* in *Nibru*.

Tummal, exceedingly worthy of the princely divine powers, inspiring awe and dread! Foundation, your pure lustration extends over the *abzu*. Primeval city, reed-bed green with old reeds and new shoots, your interior is a mountain of abundance built in plenitude. At your feast held in the month of the New Year, you are wondrously adorned as the Great Lady of *Ki-Ur* rivals *Enlil*. Your princess, Mother *Ninlil*, the beloved wife of *Nunamnir*, has erected a house in your precinct, *E.Tummal* ('Tummal House'), and taken a place upon your dais. [...] the house of *Ninlil* in Nibru.

E.melem-huc ('House of Terrifying Radiance') exuding great awesomeness, *Ec-mah* ('magnificent shrine'), to which princely divine powers were sent from heaven; storehouse of Enlil founded for the primeval divine powers, worthy of nobility, lifting your head in princeship, counselor of *E.kur*, parapeted buttress, your house [...] the platform {of} heaven. The decisions at its place of reaching the great judgment, the river of the ordeal, let the just live and consign to darkness the hearts that are evil. In your great place fit for pure lustration and the rites of *icib*-priests, you dine with Lord *Nunamnir*. Your prince, the prince who is the counselor of *Enlil* and worthy of *Ec-mah*, the *udug*-demon of *E.kur* the leader *Nuska*, has erected a house in your precinct, O house of Enlil, and taken his seat upon your dais. [...] the house of *Nusku* in *Nibru*.

E.me-ur-ana ('House Which Gathers the Divine Powers of Heaven') standing in a great place; the just divine powers which the warrior [...], strength of battle, heroic mace, carrier of the quiver, mighty bustling brick building, your foundation is eternal. Founded by the primeval lord, with decisions which belong to the princely divine powers, holy soil filling the mountain, lifting your head among the princes; magnificent house, the wonder coming from you is like the sun whose glow spreads. *E-cu-me-ca* ('House Which [...] the Divine Powers'), *Enlil* has instilled your name with terrifying awesomeness.

Your prince, the great [...], the warrior whose strength is boundless, the great ruler for Enlil, the noble who rivals heaven and earth, the provisioning seal-keeper of Father *Enlil* who makes the great divine powers perfect, the [...], the leader for Father *Enlil*, the foremost, the lion engendered by the Great Mountain, who destroys the hostile lands for *Enlil*, Lord *Ninurta*, has erected a house in your precinct, *E.cu-me-ca*, and taken his seat upon your dais. [...] the house of *Ninurta* in *Nibru*.

E.ja-duda {or *E.ga-duda*} ('House, Chamber of the Mound'), [...]; crown of the high plain, holy place, pure place, house, your foundation is a great princely mooring pole. *Du-saj-dili* {or *Du-sag-dili*} (singular mound), your lady, the singular woman who keeps the chamber and the dais full, gladdens your platform in princely style. Your princess who avoids anger and is exceedingly wise, the princely daughter who prospers together with the Great Mountain, *Cu-zi-ana*, the junior wife of Father Enlil, has erected a house in your precinct, O *Du-saj-dili*, and taken her seat upon your dais. [...] the house of *Cu-zi-ana* in *Ja-gi-mah* {or *Ga-gi-mah*}.

O mighty *Kec*, form of heaven and earth, arousing terror like a great horned viper, house of *Ninhursaga*, built in a terrifying place! Respected *Kec*, your interior is a deep interior while your exterior is tall. Great lion [...] on the high plain and roving about on the plain, great hill established by incantations, twilit interior in which moonlight does not shine, Nintur has made you beautiful; O house *Kec*, your brickwork and your molding of it! Your terrace! Your exterior, a lustrous *suh*-crown, and your building of it! Your princess, the silencing princess, the true and Great Lady of heaven, when she talks heaven trembles, when she opens her mouth a storm thunders, *Aruru*, the sister of Enlil, has erected a house in your precinct, O house *Kec*, and taken her seat upon your dais. [...] the house of *Ninhursaga* in *Kec*.

O *Urim*, bull standing in the wet reeds, *E.kic.nu.jal* {or *E.kic-nu-gal*} ('House Sending Light to the Earth'), calf of a great cow, [...] light of holy heaven, [...], trap laid in a nest, *Urim*, container feeding all lands, you are a shrine in a pure place, earth of *Anu*. House of *Su-en* {or *Nanna-Sin*}, at your front a prince, at your back a ruler, your dining hall with *adab*-songs, your great, holy banqueting hall with *cem* and *ala*-drums! The light coming from you and your true lordship is a precious destiny.

Jipar, princely shrine of the holy divine powers, shining like the [...] sun, *E.kic.nu.jal*, beaming moonlight which comes forth in the Land, broad light of midday which fills all lands, house, your platform is a great snake, a marsh of snakes. Your foundation is the *abzu*, fifty in number, and the *engur*, seven in number, a shrine which looks into the heart of the gods. Your prince, the prince who makes decisions, the crown of wide heaven, the sovereign of heaven, *Acimbabbar*, has erected a house in your precinct, O shrine *Urim*, and taken his seat upon your dais. [...] the house of *Nanan* {*Nanna*} of *Urim*.

E.mu-mah ('House with a Magnificent Name'), rising mountain of heaven, your holy sides and your great foundation are a precious destiny. Interior full with princely divine powers, a beaming light which shines, shrine with your back to the blue sky and your prominent front to all people, in the Land it represents a binding agreement and a single track. Magnificent river with open mouth gathering together your [...] divine powers, your base is great in awe-someness, a righteous hill grown in a broad place. Your lofty dwelling-place of magnificence with all the divine powers of princeship, [...], shouting [...]; house of celebration, your platform gladdens the settlements.

House, your prince *Culgi* has made it great and most princely. The perfect and magnificent [...], the mighty and great wind, adorned with the divine powers, determining destiny, *Culgi* of *Anu*, has erected a house in your precinct, *E.husag* ('House Which is a Hill/Mound'), and taken his seat upon your dais. [...] *E.husag* of *Culgi* in *Urim*.

O city, [...] from the *abzu* like barley, cloudy plain, taking the divine powers from its midst; *Kuara*, your foundation and just banqueting hall, the lord who does not hold back his goods stands ready for admiration. The Seven Sages have enlarged it for you from the south to the uplands. Your prince, the most precious prince *Asarluhi* {another name for *Marduk*}, the most precious one, is a warrior, born a noble prince, a leopard who seizes prey. He is like an onrushing storm battering the rebel land. As long as it remains disobedient, he pours spittle upon it. *Asar-alim-nuna*, the son of the *abzu*, has erected a house in your precinct, O house *Kuara*, and taken his seat upon your dais. [...] the house of *Asarluhi* in *Kuara*.

E.gud-du-car ('House with Many Perfect Oxen') of holy *nir*-stone in which its sovereign sits, raising a magnificent door decoration for the princely son, whose best fine oil is holy and well-prepared; *Ja-bura* ('chamber of bowls'), holy cattle-pen pasturing cows with *munzer*-plants, your prince is a great wild bull, an elephant rejoicing in its own strength, a wild cow growing horns and and delighting in its shining horns. The incantation priest of opposed languages who put clouds in the sky, the storm which roars in the sky, as the sunlight giving [...] to the earth, *Ningublaga*, the son of *Nanna*, has erected a house in your precinct, *Ki-abrig*, and taken his seat upon your dais. [...] the house of *Ningublaga* on *Ki-abrig*.

O shrine, great sanctuary founded at a cattle-pen, small shining city of *Su-en* (*Nanna-Sin*), *Kar-zida* ('pure quay'), your interior is a mighty place, your foundation is holy and clean. Shrine, your *jipar* is founded in purity. Your door is of strong copper set up at a great place. Lowing cattle-pen, you raise your horns like a bull. Your prince, the lord of heaven standing in joy, [...] at midday and [...], *Acimbabbar*, has erected a house in your precinct, O *Kar-zida*, and taken his seat upon your dais. [...] the house of *Nanna* in *Gaec*.

O 'House Which Comes Forth From Heaven', resplendent in *Kulaba*; shrine *E.babbar* ('shining house'), shining bull, lift your neck to *Utu* (*Shammash*) who [...] in the sky! Your shining horns are aggressive, holy and lustrous. Bearing a beard of shining lapis lazuli, [...], your prince, the mighty sunlight, the lord who [...] the true word, who lightens the horizon, who lightens the sky's [...]

vault, *Utu*, the sovereign of *E.babbar*, has erected a house in your precinct, O house *Larsa(m)*, and taken his seat upon your dais. [...] the house of *Utu* in *Larsa(m)*.

E.negir, great libation pipe, libation pipe to the underworld of *Ereshkigal*; *Gudua* (the '*Entrance to the Underworld*') of Sumer where mankind is gathered; *E.gida* ('long house'), in the land your shadow has stretched over the princes of the land. Your prince, the seed of the great lord, the sacred one of the great underworld, given birth by *Ereshkigal*, playing loudly on the *canaru-*instrument, sweet as the voice of a calf, *Ninazu* of the words of prayer, has erected a house in your precinct; O house *E.negir*, and taken his seat upon your dais. [...] the house of *Ninazu* in *E.negir*.

O primeval place, deep mountain founded in an artful fashion, shrine, terrifying place lying in a pasture, a dread whose lofty ways none can fathom, *Jicbanda* (?), neck-stock, meshed net, shackles of the great underworld from which none can escape, your exterior is raised up, prominent like a snare, your interior is where the sun rises, endowed with wide-spreading plenty. Your prince is the prince who stretches out his pure hand, the holy one of heaven, with luxuriant and abundant hair hanging at his back, Lord *Ningishzida*. *Ningishzida* has erected a house in your precinct; O *Jicbanda*, and taken his seat upon your dais. [...] the house of *Ningishzida* in *Jicbanda*.

O house with the great divine powers of *Kulaba*, [...], its platform has made the great shrine flourish. Green fresh fruit, marvelous, filled with ripeness, descending from the centre of heaven, shrine built for the bull, *E.ana* (or *E.anna*; 'House of Heaven'), house with seven corners, with seven fires lifted at night-time, surveying seven pleasures, your princess is on the pure horizon. Your lady *Inanna* {or *Ishtar*} who [...], who adorns the woman and covers the man's head with a cloth, the one with a lustrous [...] *suh*-crown, the dragon of *Nijin-jar* (?), the queen of heaven and earth, *Inanna*, has erected a house in your precinct, *E.anna*, and taken her seat upon your dais. [...] the house of *Inanna* in *Unug*.

'House Where Lustrous Herbs are Strewn Upon the Flowery Bed', the bed-chamber of holy *Inanna*, where the lady of the plain refreshes herself! Brick-built *E.muc* ('House Which is the Precinct') is flowery and holy, its [...] clay established for him who tends the ewes on the high plain. Your [...] house of *Arali* ('House Which is the Nether World') gives shade to the shepherd. Your prince, a raging lion on the plain, the *cuba*-jewel of the 'Mistress Whose Breast is Holy and Marvelous', the lord who is holy Inanna's husband, *Dumuzi(d)* {*Tammuz*}, the sovereign of *E.muc*, has erected a house in your precinct, O *Bad-tibira*, and taken his seat upon your dais. [...] the house of *Dumuzi* in *Bad-tibira*.

E.igizu-uru ('House, With a Mighty Face'), with plenty coming from within, your well-stocked chamber is a mountain of abundance. House, your fragrance is a mound of vines. Your true minister is a leader in heaven. House, your princess is prominent among the gods, the true minister of *E.ana*, who holds a holy-sceptre in her hand. *Nincubur* {*Ninkubar*}, the true minister of *E.ana*, has erected a house in your precinct, O *E.akkil* ('house of lamentation'), and taken her seat upon your dais. [...] the house of *Nincubur* in *Akkil*.

O city, founded upon a dais in the *abzu*, established for the rites of *icib*-priests, house where incantations of heaven and earth are recited [...] [...] [...] lustration water in the holy heaven and on the pure earth. *Ningirim*, the lady of the shining lustration water, has erected a house in your precinct, O house *Murum*, and taken her seat upon your dais. [...] the house of *Ningirim* in *Murum*.

E.ninnu ('House of Fifty'), right hand of *Lagac*, foremost in *Sumer*; the *Anzu(d)*-bird which gazes upon the mountain, the *car-ur* weapon of [...] *Ninjirsu* {*Ningirsu*}; [...] in all lands, the strength of battle, a terrifying storm which envelops men, giving the strength of battle to the *Anuna* {*Anunnaki*}, the great gods; brick building on whose holy mound destiny is determined, beautiful as the hills, your canal [...], your [...] blowing in opposition at your gate facing towards *Iri-kug*, wine is poured into holy Anu's beautiful bowls set out in the open air. Whatever enters you is unequaled, whatever leaves endures. [...], terrifying facade, house of radiance, a place of reaching judgment which Lord *Ninjirsu* has filled with great awesomeness and dread! All the *Anuna* gods attend your great drinking-bouts.

Your prince, a raging storm which destroys cities in hostile lands, your sovereign, a terrifying wild ox which will manifest its strength, a terrifying lion which smashes heads, the warrior who devises strategies in lordship and attains victory in kingship, the mighty one, the great warrior in battle, the lord without rival, the son of Enlil, Lord *Ninjirsu*, has erected a house in your precinct, *E.ninnu*, and taken his seat upon your dais. [...] the house of *Ninjirsu* in *Lagac*.

O *Iri-kug* ('holy city'), shrine of holy *Anu*, which caused the human seed to come forth, called by a good name, within you is the river of ordeal which vindicates the just man. *E.jalga-sud* {*E.galga-sud*} ('House Which Spreads Wisdom Far and Wide'), storehouse which eternally possesses silver and lapis lazuli; *E.tar-sirsir*, from which decisions and the divine powers come forth, where the hero performs obeisance, your princess, the merciful princess of the Land, is the mother of all lands. The lady, the great healer of the black-headed who determines the destiny of her city, the first-born daughter of holy *Anu*, the maiden, Mother *Bau*, has erected a house in your precinct, O house *Iri-kug* and taken her seat upon your dais. [...] the house of *Bau* in *Iri-kug*.

O house, wild cow [...], city which appears in splendor adorned for the princess, *Sirara*, great and princely place, your [...] by the shrine, your lady *Nance*, a great storm, a mighty flood, born on the shore of the sea, who laughs on the foam of the sea, who plays on the water of the flood, who [...], *Nance*, the [...] lady, has erected a house in your precinct, O house *Sirara*, and taken her seat upon your dais. [...] the house of *Nance* in *Sirara*.

E.ab-caga-la ('House Which Stretches Over the Midst of the Sea') built in a holy place; *Gu-aba*, your interior produces everything and is a well-established storehouse. Holy shrine, wild cow for which everything endures, your princess is *Ninjagia* (?), the magnificent [...] stewardess, the mighty [...] of Father *Enlil*, who takes counsel with Lord *Nunamnir* (*Enki*). Born in [...], [...] in the flood of the sea, like her [...] father a controller of the pure sea, holy *Ninmarki* has erected a house in your precinct, O house *Gu-aba*, and taken her seat upon your dais. [...] the house of *Ninmarki* in *Gu-aba*.

O house *Kinirca*, suited for its lady, [...], beautiful as a hill, standing by the ziggurat, house, [...], place resounding loudly with happiness, house, your princess is a storm, riding on a lion, [...]. Exalted in holy song and antiphony, singing with a loud voice, the child, the true wild cow, taken care of at the holy breast of the mother who begot her, *Dumuzi-abzu*, has erected a house in your precinct, O shrine *Kinirca*, and taken her seat upon your dais. [...] the house of *Dumuzi-abzu* in *Kinirca*.

E.bur-sigsig ('House With Beautiful Bowls') set up under heaven, mighty banqueting hall, fulfilling the commands, abundance of the midst of the sea in [...], at whose holy [...] there is entreaty and joy. The faithful man has enlarged *E.mag* {*E.mah*} ('magnificent house'), the house of *Cara*, for you in plenty. Your house *E.mah*, whose prince is the princely son of the Mistress, continues in good fortune, an area of abundance and well-being. The one who arranges the hair at the nape of the neck, with the gaze of a wild cow, *Cara*, who [...] good things, the son who allots the divine powers to his mother, has erected a house in your precinct, O house *Umma*, and taken his seat upon your dais. [...] the house of *Cara* in *Umma*.

E.cerzi-guru ('House Dressed in Splendor'), dressed with ornaments of *cuba*-stone; great awesomeness, *Nijin-jar* (*Ningingar* ?) of holy *Inanna*, adorned throughout with the divine powers which are true; *Zabalam*, shrine of the shining mountain, shrine of [...] dawn, which has resounded with pleasure; the Mistress has founded your good banqueting hall for you in pleasure. Your Lady, *Inanna*, the [...], the singular woman, the dragon who speaks hostile words to [...], who shines in brightness, who goes against the rebel land, through whom the firmament is made beautiful in the evening, the great daughter of *Su-en* (*Nanna-Sin*), holy *Inanna*, has erected a house in your precinct, O house *Zabalam*, and taken her seat upon your dais. [...] the house of *Inanna* in *Zabalam*.

O 'House Inspiring Terror Like a Great Lion', making as clear as day the decisions for those on the high plain, house of *Ickur*, at your front is abundance, at your rear is celebration. Your foundation is a horned bull, a lion. Holy staff, teat of heaven with rain for fine barley, the pilasters of your house are a wild bull with outspread horns, your [...], foundation and wall rising high [...], thick cloud, [....] snake, [...] moonlight, [...] *Ickur*, a sweeping flood, [...] a storm and seven raging winds, [...], blowing raging winds, [...] running from the [...], splits the [...] hillside, diorite, stones and [...] [...] the seed of the Land, the [...], the [...] prince, the canal inspector of heaven and earth, the [...] living, the numerous people, the [...], *Ickur* has erected a house in your precinct, O house *Karkara*, and taken his seat upon your dais. [...] the house of *Ickur* in *Karkara*.

O [...], bolt founded by *Anu*, [...] [...] [...] [...] [...] has erected a house in your precinct, O [...], and taken a seat upon your dais. [...] the house of [...] in [....].

Anu has [...] your platform. *E.mah* ('exalted house'), 'House of the Universe', suited for its lady, your front inspires great awesomeness, your interior is filled with radiance. Mother *Nintur*, *Enlil*, and *Enki* have determined your destiny. *E.suga* ('joyous house') which [...], life of the black-haired people, *Anu* has given you the magnificent divine powers from the interior of heaven. As in *Kec*, *Ninhursag(a)* has blessed your priests maintaining the shrine in the holy *uzga*-precinct. 'House with Great Divine Powers', a pure platform and cleansing lustration; *Acgi* {*Akgi*}, the god of *Adab*, has erected a house in your precinct, *Adab*, house situated at a canal, and taken his seat upon your dais. [...] the house of *Ninhursag(a)* in *Adab*.

Isin, city founded by *Anu*, which he has built on an empty plain; Its front is mighty, its interior is artfully built, its divine powers are divine powers which *An* has determined. Shrine which Enlil loves, place where *Anu* and *Enlil* determine destinies, place where the great gods dine, filled with great awesomeness and terror: all the *Anuna* gods attend your great drinking-bouts. Your princess, the mother, the Mistress adorned with jewels of *cuba*-stone, who maintains the holy place's *Nijin-jar*, who binds the *suh*-crown on the *nugig*-priestess, who causes the seven teats to flow for the *nubar*-priestess, has resounded with seven pleasures. Your lady, the great healer of the Land, *Ninisina*, the daughter of Anu, has erected a house in your precinct, O house *Isin*, and taken her seat upon your dais. [...] the house of *Ninisina* in *Isin*.

Kazallu, your crown reaches to the center of heaven, shining, [...] an object of admiration. Your prince is the seed of a bull, engendered by a wild bull in [...], a magnificent [...] with sparkling eyes, a lord with the teeth of a lion, who snatches the calf with his claws, who snatches [...] who snatches [...], the [...] who gives strength to the [...], the great lord *Numucda*, has erected a house in your precinct, O *Kun-satu* ('Threshold of the Mountain'), *Kazallu*, and taken his seat upon your dais. [...] the house of *Numucda* in *Kazallu*.

E.igi-kalama ('House Which is the Eye of the Land'), your foundation is firmly laid, growing hill which stands broadly on the earth, [...] the enemies' land, [...] [...] [...] has erected a house in your precinct, O [...], and taken a seat upon your dais. [...] the house of *Lugal-marda* in *Marda*.

Der {*an archaic Akkadian name*}, taking extreme care of decisions, [...], on your awesome and radiant gate a decoration displays a horned viper and a *muchuc* embracing {seized in a trap}. Your prince, a leader of the gods, fit for giving counsel and grand speech, the son of *Urac* who knows thoroughly the true divine powers of princeship, *Ictaran* the [...] sovereign of heaven, has erected a house in your precinct, *E.dim-gal-kalama* ('House Which is the Great Pole/Axis of the Land'), and taken his seat upon your dais. [...] the house of *Ictaran* in *Der*.

O *E.sikil* ('pure house') whose pure divine powers are supreme in all lands, whose name is high and mighty, magnificent dwelling of the warrior, holy house of *Ninazu*, house of the holy divine powers! House, your divine powers are pure divine powers, your lustration is a cleansing lustration. The warrior refreshes himself in your dwelling. *Ninazu* dines on your platform. Your sovereign, the great lord, the son of Enlil, is a towering lion spitting venom over hostile lands, rising like the south wind against enemy lands, snarling like a dragon against the walls of rebel lands, a storm enveloping the disobedient and trampling on the enemy.

When he strides forth, no evil-doer can escape. When he establishes his triumph, the cities of the rebel lands are destroyed. When he frowns, their people are cast into the dust. House, your prince is a great lion from whose claws the enemy hangs. Your sovereign is a terrifying, mighty storm, the vigor of the battle, in combat [...] like a [...] with a shield on his lofty arm, a net over the widespread people from whose reach the foe cannot escape. When the great lord is resplendent, his magnificence has no equal. The true seed born of the Great Mountain and Ninlil, your sovereign, the warrior *Ninazu*, has erected a house in your precinct, O *E.sikil*, O *Ecnunna*, and taken his seat upon your dais. [...] the house of *Ninazu* in *Ecnunna*.

'House Built in Plenitude', *Kic*, raising its head among the princely divine powers, established settlement, your great foundation cannot be scattered. Your plinth is a vast oppressive cloud floating in the midst of the sky. Your interior is a weapon, a mace decorated with [...]; Your right hand makes mountains tremble, your left thins out the enemy. Your prince, mighty and magnificent, a great storm overpowering the earth, inspiring great and terrifying awe, your sovereign, the warrior *Zababa*, has erected a house in your precinct, O *E.dub* ('storage house'), O house *Kic*, and taken his seat upon your dais. [...] the house of *Zababa* in *Kic*.

E.kecda-kalama ('House Which is the Bond of the Land'), bull [...] great strength among the gods, terrifying wild cow, wild bull which causes lament; *Gudua*, your quay is a low quay which bestows water, your interior is artfully built, your mace is a [...] mace released from heaven, your platform is a lustrous platform spreading over *Mec-lam* {'Underworld'}. Your prince, the mighty god, the sovereign of *Mec-lam*, the fierce god of the underworld, the sovereign of *Ud-cuc* {sunset}, *Nergal*, *Mec-lam(ta)-ea*, has erected a house in your precinct, and taken his seat upon your dais. [...] the house of *Nergal* in *Gudua*.

O mighty *Urum* where *Su-en* (*Nanna-Sin*) pronounces judgment; *E.ab-lua* ('House With Teeming Cattle'), wide cattle-yard, *Acimbabbar* acts as your shepherd. House, my sovereign, your sceptre reaches to heaven, [...] to the earth, moonlight [...], celebration, your [...] may [...] the light. Your prince, the prince of holy celebration, [...], who appears in the lapis lazuli colored sky, a celebration, to whom the hero pays homage [...], who brightens the Land, [...]. *Su-en*, has erected a house in your precinct, O house *Urum* and taken his seat upon your dais. [...] the house of *Su-en* in *Urum*.

Zimbir, dais upon which *Utu* (*Shammash*) sits daily, *E.nun-ana* ('House of the Prince of Heaven'), star of heaven, crown given birth by *Ningal*, house of *Utu*, your prince, the [...] of the universe, fills heaven and earth. When the lord sleeps, the people sleep; when he rises, the people rise. The bull [...] and the people prostrate themselves. Before *Utu* the herds pasture [...]. The black-haired humans have bathed before him, the Land has [...] before him. He measures out the divine powers; your shrine is a flood. Pronouncing judgment where the sun rises, mighty sunlight, wearing a beard, tying on the *suh*-crown at night, *Utu*, the sovereign of *E.Babbar* ('shining house'), has erected a house in your precinct, O house *Zimbir*, and taken his seat upon your dais. [...] the house of *Utu* in *Zimbir*.

E.hursag ('House Which is a Mountain') beautiful as greenery, [...] your interior is plenitude. At the place where destiny is determined, you determine destiny. May the crown bring joy to your platform. May your roots glisten like an immense *sajkal*-snake in your holy foundations. Mother *Nintur*, the lady of creation, performs her task within your dark place, binding the true *suh*-crown on the new-born king, setting the crown on the new-born lord who is secure in her hand. The midwife of heaven and earth, *Ninhursag(a)*, has erected a house in your precinct, O house [...], and taken her seat upon your dais. [...] the house of *Ninhursag(a)* in [...].

O *Ulmac*, upper land, [...] of the Land, terrifying lion battering a wild bull, net spreading over an enemy, making silence fall upon a rebel land on which, as long as it remains insubmissive, spittle is poured! House of Inanna {or Ishtar} of silver and lapis lazuli, a storehouse built of gold, your princess is an *arabu*-bird, the Mistress of the *Nijin-jar*. Arrayed in battle, jubilantly beautiful, ready with the seven maces, washing her tools for battle, opening the door of battle and [...], the extremely wise one of heaven, Inanna has erected a house in your precinct, O house *Ulmac*, and taken her seat upon your dais. [...] the house of Inanna of *Ulmac*.

O house [...], right arm, battle-axe cutting down the rebel lands, digging up their green fields, [...] [...] Your prince, the warrior who [...], who defeats all in battle, exulting [...], *Aba*, the god of *Agade* {Akkad}, has erected a house in your precinct, O house *Agade*, and taken his seat upon your dais. [...] the house of *Aba* in *Agade*.

'House of Stars', bright *E.zagin-guna* ('House Dressed in Lapis Lazuli'), reaching into all lands, establishing [...] in the shrine, *Eresh*. The primeval lords raise their heads to you every month. [...] the potash plant, great *Nanibgal, Nisaba* {*Teshmet*} has brought divine powers from heaven and added to your divine powers.

Sanctuary established for [...]! To the true woman who possesses exceeding wisdom, soothing [...] and opening the mouth, always consulting a Tablet-of-Lapis-Lazuli, giving advice to all lands, the true woman, the holy potash plant, born of the stylus-reed, applies the measure to heaven and places the measuring-rope on the earth, to Nisaba, be praised! The compiler of the tablets was *En-hedu-ana* {presumably *Nabu*}. My king, something has been created that no one has created before. [...] the house of *Nisaba* in *Eresh*.

'BEFORE ALL BEFORES'
(Ancient Poetic Hymn of Creation)

Before all befores, there was Nammu,
she the origin, ever flowing beginning.

Nammu was the first, the source,
the mother of the universe,
the self-procreating womb of abundance,
alone and all-in-one;
Nammu was primal matter,
the deep fertile waters of the sea.

Before all befores,
for time was yet to be;
Nammu revolved and flowed,
squeezed, coiled, and rushed
like a double-helix spiral.

Nammu's waters then opened up:
she had given birth to Ki-An,
creation's first born;

she the mountain, he the sky.

Before all befores,
wrapped around the liquid body of the mother,
Ki the mountain, An the sky
held each other close
in a most tender embrace.

Ki the mountain, An the sky
lay in each other's arms
before all befores;
when An was an empty sky,
Ki a stony earth,
laying barren and unfulfilled
within Nammu's fecund body fluid
as Ki and An lay closer still,
something stirred, deep from within.

Love that bound An and Ki together
brought into being a sigh,
a wind, a first breath;
and so was Enlil, Infant Lord Air, manifested.

Thus, life throbbed in cheerful continuation,
as An, the mighty bull of heaven,
made love fifty times (and more)
to Ki, his beloved,
the all-powerful cow of earth.

Ki responded to An's enthusiasm
and passion in kind.

She made herself resplendent;
for (her brother-spouse) she beautified her body
with the most precious metals,
fuels and lapis lazuli;
she adorned herself with diorite,
chalcedony and shiny carnelian.
So did the skyfather An array himself
in a cloak of purest azure
to greet his dearest Ki.

Then in great joy and reverence
An, who called himself heaven then,
approached Ki, whom he called earth.

An-heaven dived into Ki's welcoming expanse.

Then (sky) kissed Ki, pouring the semen of trees,
reeds and pastures into the beloved's womb.

Ki, fecund, brave, sweet earth,
was impregnated with the rich semen of heaven,
and joyfully gave birth to the planets of life.
Luxuriantly did Earth bear the rich produce,
generously did she exude wine and honey.

Gleefully, she invited the skies
into herself over and over again.
Fifty times (and more),
sky came into the earth.
Fifty times (and more),
An's seed met Ki;
fifty times (and more),
An's seed grew in Ki;
fifty times (and more),
An and Ki made love;
and so the Anunnaki,
in Ki's womb was formed,
as yet unnamed,
waiting to be born.

Only Enlil, Infant Lord Air was there
within An's and Ki's lap,
all surrounded by Nammu's depths.

Nammu feels and sees everything.
She must now create space for her offspring.
Under Ki, surrounding Enlil, above An,
Nammu arches and stretches her watery form;
to further depths, she directs.

Nammu defines herself as the first ocean,
cradle of other life forms to come.
"Mine are the depths reaching out to the surface,"
decrees (the fates) Nammu;
"Mine is the process of becoming out of nothing's embrace.
Mine is the nurturing womb, life's first mystery;
Mine is the silence that all life created."

'LOVE SONG OF NABU AND TESHMET'

The fragrance of cedar is your love, O lord!
The shade of the cedar, the king's shelter.

His stature is like Lebanon, select as the cedars.
How gorgeous she is, how resplendent!
Tašmetu, looking exuberant, enters the bedroom.
How beautiful you are, my darling, how beautiful!

Rejoice, Nanaya,
in the garden of Ebabbar that you love!
Let my Tašmetu come with me to the garden.
I have come to my garden, my sister and bride.

By night I thought of you.
She got onto the bed, into a bowl her tears flow.
On my bed at night I missed him whom I love.
After I lay in the bosom of the son,
Tašmetu fondles a bunch of gold in the lap of Nabû.
A bundle of myrrh is my lover to me,
Between my breasts he lies.

A quarter of you is lapis lazuli.
Whose whole being is a tablet of lapis lazuli.
His belly is a plaque of ivory
overlaid with lapis lazuli.
Come and rejoice, O king!
Let me make you happy in the tablet house!
Bring me to your chamber, O king!

COSMIC LAW :
AS DESCRIBED ON ARCANE TABLETS*

The *Arcane Tablets* reveal that the *Cosmos* is regulated by a "Cosmic Law"—actually *Seven Cosmic Laws*—superimposed over the *Universe*. It constitutes the most basic level of *reality-agreement* concerning experience of manifestation at the level of *Beta-Existence*.

An understanding of "Cosmic Law" is inherent in ancient "*Hermetic philosophy*" in addition to "*New Thought*" teachings predating our modern *Mardukite NexGen Metahuman Systemology*.

I. *The Law of Orderly Trend.*
"Under this law, there is always manifested law and order in the Cosmos, from suns to atoms; from the highest to the lowest; matter, energy and consciousness."

II. *The Law of Analogy.*
"Under this law, there is found a correspondence and agreement between all of the various forms of manifestation. What is true of the atom, is true of the sun. What is true of matter, is true of energy and mind. To know one is to know all."

III. *The Law of Sequence.*
"Under this law, there is included the activities of what is generally known as 'cause and effect'. Nothing in existence happens by pure chance. Nothing happens without a precedent manifestation, and a subsequent manifestation. Nothing stands alone in exclusion."

IV. *The Law of Rhythm.*
"Under this law falls a variety of phenomena, the most important of which is 'vibration'. Everything in existence is in constant vibration—everything material, mental, or of 'energy'. Upon this fact depends the variety, degrees, states, and conditions, of the manifestations in the Cosmos. To control vibration is to control all forces in the Universe."

V. *The Law of Balance.*
"Under this law, there is to be found an explanation for the universal equilibrium, compensation, and balance, observed in all manifestation in the Cosmos. One thing balances another; everything has something set opposite it, to balance it."

---

* Excerpted from "*Fundamentals of Systemology*" by Joshua Free.

VI. *The Law of Cyclicity.*

"Under this law is found the cyclic—or circular—trend of all things, physical, mental and spiritual. Everything moves in circular systems. The wise convert the circles into upward spirals. Instead of traveling and endless circle, or downward, the wise rise in spirals to attainment and advancement."

VII. *The Law of Opposites.*

"Under this law is to be found the explanation of the fact that everything has its opposite; everything is and is-not at the same time; everything has its other side—also the fact that opposite things are alike, in the end, for the extremes meet and contradiction may be reconciled."

ENUMA-ELIŠ :
THE SEVEN TABLETS OF CREATION
(SUMMARY)*

TABLET I.

a.)—ABZU (*the Abyss*) and TIAMAT (*the Cosmic Dragon*) are first forms; form the One (*All*).

b.)—Generations of "gods" are born and begin to make too much noise.

c.)—TIAMAT entrusts her vizier KINGU the power to fight for her.

d.)—TIAMAT creates calamity and a horde of monsters as ammunition.

TABLET II.

a.)—Enki reveals the plot against the gods to ANSAR.

b.)—A primary discourse from Tablet-I is repeated.

TABLET III.

a.)—Anu, Enlil and Enki do not stand fit to battle against TIAMAT.

b.)—Marduk is petitioned to champion the Anunnaki gods.

c.)—Marduk asks for supreme divinity if successful; to be *Chief God*.

TABLET IV.

a.)—The Anunnaki agree to Marduk's terms and prepare him for battle.

b.)—Marduk receives a "cloak of invisibility."

c.)—Marduk enchants his favored weapon: a bow.

d.)—Marduk destroys KINGU with a thunderbolt.

e.)—TIAMAT is slain; her minions are scattered and sent to "secret places."

f.)—Marduk fashions a "*Gate*" to seal these energies separate from the material universe

---

* Excerpted from "*Babylonian Myth & Magic*" by Joshua Free.

TABLET V.

a.)—Marduk seals the cosmic systems of "Lights," "Spheres" and "Degrees" under himself.

b.)—A material-matix *below* is fragmented by "seven," while the *heights* remain divided into "twelve."

c.)—The "*Anunnaki Star-Gate*" system is sealed throughout the Universe.

d.)—Marduk sets up a throne for himself next to Anu.

TABLET VI.

a.)—The Anunnaki praise Marduk for his feats.

b.)—The "Key to the Gate" (of the *Abyss* or *Dragon*) is "hidden" in genetic memory of the "*Race of Marduk*," including humans upgraded by Enki.

c.)—Babylonian systematization begins.

TABLET VII.

a.)—Having slayed TIAMAT and granted power over material creation, Marduk takes fifty names and the "number" of Enlil.

b.)—Marduk takes the "signs" and esoteric knowledge ("magic") of Enki.

c.)—Marduk fractures then seals all systems on Earth under his name.

THE WITCH'S HANDBOOK

A TREASURY OF TRADITIONAL 20TH CENTURY WITCHCRAFT

an introduction by Rowen Gardner

Once intended a sequel to *"The Sorcerer's Handbook"* by Joshua Free (while writing as "Merlyn Stone") in the 1990's, his "notebooks" composing the historically legendary *"1998 Book of Shadows"*—and eventually *"The Witch's Handbook"*—were only released privately to members of his own *Coven* operating in Colorado, and other groups he networked with, during a peak period of development for the modern "New Age."

Within these pages, you will also encounter the complete structure of the original century-old *"Book of Shadows,"* illuminated for the first time with a new revolutionary *never before published* presentation of concise descriptions and references that uncover influential sources behind-the-scenes of many contemporary *Wiccan* and traditionalist *Witchcraft* movements. It's all here. From the *Key of Solomon*, to the *Rites of the Golden Dawn* and *OTO*, to the *Aradian Gospel of Witches*, to the relatively modern innovation of a "Neopagan Eightfold Year" by three men: a Druid (Ross Nichols), a Magician (Aleister Crowley) and a Witch (Gerald Gardner); no stone or pentacle is left unturned in this effective, yet candid, complete practical guide to the *Arts of Witchcraft.*

Long before the public inception of the *Systemology Society*, or even the *Mardukite Research Organization*, Joshua Free maintained an underground occult presence in the 1990's as "Merlyn Stone." Thousands of copies of his works began circulating during an era prior to the type of commercialized self-publishing and "print-on-demand" distribution prevalent throughout the "New Age" market today. At the time, it was still quite a prestigious feat to see hundreds of hand-made books reaching new readers each month—but what's more amazing is that Joshua Free (then "Merlyn Stone") was *only* a high school teenager.

Although it is quite common for writers to maintain an archival stock of unpublished notebooks and manuscripts, *"The Witch's Handbook"* is unique for the fact that its existence as the *"1998 Book of Shadows"* is not altogether unknown. But since it was rarely referred to and never officially circulated outside the personal contact of its author, we can now finally treat this complete version of the work as a "lost classic restored" more than two decades since its first underground presentation. It is also unique fro the fact that it is the *only* book ever written by Joshua Free dedicated exclusively to *Wicca* and *Witchcraft.*

Some readers and long-time Seekers following along with Joshua Free's metaphysical literary releases over the past twenty years may recall sparse
allusions to the "*1998 Book of Shadows*" or a secret unpublished "*Sorcerer's Notebook*" appearing throughout his works, including the recent reissue of
"*Elvenomicon*" (formerly "*Book of Elven-Faerie*") and "*The Great Magickal Arcanum: A Master Course in Magick for Modern Wizards.*" But very little is known
about the original work, in spite of excerpts appearing in an Appendix for the
latest 21st Anniversary Collector's Edition of "*The Sorcerer's Handbook*," with a
footnote that simply reads:

> "Commissioned in 1998 by the 'Outer Court' (or training coven) of the
> *Elven Fellowship Circle of Magick* (*EFCOM*) in Denver, which was integrated
> into their Book of Shadows."

Much like Joshua Free's *Draconomicon*—which I was also called on to produce a
Foreword for when it was recently reissued in an expanded and enhanced
25th Anniversary Collector's Edition—originally "*The Witch's Handbook*" was
not written or even intended for mass circulation when it first appeared underground as penned by "Merlyn Stone," a name the author primarily
operated with in the "New Age" from 1995 until 2005, prior to the launch of
"Mardukite Ministries" (Mardukite Zuism) or founding the "Systemology Society."

It is due to the circulation of *Draconomicon* in the 1990's during the "Merlyn
Stone Era" that I was able to be acquainted with the prodigious work of
Joshua Free, much of which is only now being given its due attention and
credit by the more mainstream contemporary "New Age" community. And
there are a few others that were privileged to experience similar encounters
with the author during his early period of development in the 1990's—yet
many of us surprisingly and cautiously alarmed when coming around to face
a *teenager* not even out of high school. However, these many decades later, I
have resolved that my faith was well-placed in the young *lad*.

Yet, "faith" is something that has never been requested by Joshua Free in all
of his deliveries and apprenticeships. Where it comes to "magick" and "metaphysics," he always provides a certain flavor of candid blatant pragmatism
that is generally not seen in most presentations of the occult—and of which it
is apparent over the past decade that many have borrowed heavily from his
examples of establishing an "internet presence" long before such was commonplace. As a result, he stands apart from the growing numbers of pseudo-
gurus and flashy web-based occult niches that really have provided little of
true value to anyone—and the subject of "Witchcraft" is no exception.

A strange sensation comes over me, given my background, when given this
opportunity to assist in editing the first ever public release of "*The Witch's

Handbook" for what is assumed to be a predominantly North American readership. For one thing: I am writing from Wales, or what many across the pond refer to simply as part of "England" or "Britain"—and it is not very far from where I sit that Gerald Gardner (of no known family relation to me, by the way, though I've never looked into it very closely) was first "initiated" into what was, at the time, "*English Witchcraft*," and of which has become quite popular in America as "*Wicca.*"

It is, however, curious to me that now—twenty years into the new millennium—so little of our traditional *Witchcraft* from England remains in the poorly copied watered-down rehashes pushed in the "New Age" market today, and which when compared to the literature available and traditions active during the 1900's, offer far less genuine substance for a Seeker, or in this case: *Aspiring Witch.* It is for this very reason that when the pages resurfaced again in discussion—as Joshua Free was preparing to deliver 48 lectures for the "*Mardukite Master Course*" in September 2020—I pressed the idea for the work to finally be published and even volunteered to edit and arrange the contents.

The reluctance to publish this book, according to my discussion with Joshua Free, has never been concerning the validity or merit of the work itself. However, shortly after initial commercial novelty of "*The Sorcerer's Handbook*" began to wane in 2001, Joshua Free's continuing underground pursuits—up to the point of launching the "Mardukite" movement—were dedicated exclusively to Druidism and tracking its evolution back to Mesopotamia.

Even after his return to the public scene in 2008, with the exception of *Sorcerer's Handbook* and *Great Magickal Arcanum*, all of his published books indeed surrounded the Druids and/or Babylon—leaving out his little know work on *Witchcraft* as an anomaly. As he said to me, "quite frankly, it's been two decades since I've had any interaction with the *Wiccan* community directly and I'm not sure that they would even take serious notice of this work." Yet, after seeing what passes for "*authentic Witchcraft*" these days, I beg to differ.

This premiere edition of *The Witch's Handbook* is based on the original notebooks, offering far greater detail than the literal hand-written hardcover "*1998 Book of Shadows*" that was copied and circulated nearly a quarter-of-a-century ago. It is already established in other works that the "*1998 Book of Shadows*" was intended primarily for "Outer Court" or "training" purposes of the *Elven Fellowship Circle of Magick* and other networking groups; but Joshua Free also prepared and released each of the main sections—as it appears in *The Witch's Handbook*—separate from one another as incremental installments throughout 1993 for inclusion in the greater body of the "EFCOM" *Book of Shadows.*

Those readers familiar with the literary works by Joshua Free will more readily recognize some of the elements found within this background for *The Witch's Handbook*, which otherwise may be otherwise misinterpreted as "just another *Wicca* book on the shelves." This one is different; and it already has its own place within a long prestigious legacy of occult instruction by one of the most profound voices on the planet today—and it is that unique quality of voice that is able to bring a new illumination to a subject that has been all but beaten to death by just about every writer that has had a stab at it.

The Witch's Handbook is also an unknown (yet integral) part of early developmental work that others are likely to recognize, including: *The Sorcerer's Handbook* and *Great Magickal Arcanum*. Although distinctions have blurred in recent reissues: facets of the first edition *Sorcerer's Handbook* (Spring 1998) and the second edition (as "*The Witch's Handbook*" or "*1998 Book of Shadows*") were combined for the *Sorcerer's Notebook*, released publicly as the third edition *Sorcerer's Handbook* (Autumn 1998), which received the greatest circulation of all versions of the *Sorcerer's* Handbook, with nearly two-thousand copies in print by 2001. But aside from the title, none of these early editions actually resembled one another—and only two have ever been released publicly before now.

The Witch's Handbook is the "missing link" of a once proposed "Merlyn Stone" trilogy that includes *The Sorcerer's Handbook* and *The Druid's Handbook*—both of which have been widely accepted in the underground "New Age" scene already. When one considers that yet another remnant of Joshua Free's unpublished 1990's occultism reemerged, revised and expanded, five years ago under a pretense of *The Vampyre's Handbook*, it has become increasingly clear to me that it is high time that *The Witch's Handbook* also receive inclusion among the rapidly expanding catalog of his works.

◊ ◊ ◊ ◊ ◊ ◊ ◊

Within the pages of *The Witch's Handbook*, an underlying story unfolds beneath and back of the 20th Century revival of *Witchcraft*—and yet the elements of its nature may not become obvious to the reader until the first complete pass through its entirety. True, there are many "Elders of the Craft" still alive that may find no new surprises or "secrets" embedded within this tome; yet even these folk will assuredly enjoy refreshing amusement in the candid *authenticity* present in its relay—something all but lost today in the endless pop-art rehashes of *Wicca* or *Witchcraft* "new releases" now marketed to curious Seekers.

The Witch's Handbook presents a "Traditionalist" approach to *Wicca* and *Witchcraft*—once more prominently visible in America during revivals of the 1900's as "*Gardnerian*" and "*Alexandrian*" traditions were imported. Of course, once they reached the states, the scene changed from "*Traditionalist Wicca*" to

"*American Witchcraft*"—particularly as the "New Age" movements progressively expanded during the 1960's through the 1970's. By the 1980's, traditions of "*American Witchcraft*" hardly resembled flavors of the original "*Wiccan*" contributions—as sparse as they may be—from those like Gerald Gardner, Aleister Crowley, Ross Nichols and Doreen Valiente through the 1950's and early 1960's, once the "Anti-Witchcraft Laws" were repealed in England in 1951.

In Ireland and Britain, the phrase "Old Religion" refers to remnants from Celtic culture and customs indigenous to our lands—and its people—long before the rise of traditional Christianity. In many respects, this work is considered "Druidic" or *of the Druids*; a class of superior learned individuals responsible for maintaining functional "systems" of ancient "*Keltia*"—the Celtic territories they governed, which at one point extended from our familiar Western Isles all the way to "Anatolia" (or present-day Turkey). There are many ways in which the "Old Religion" reflects what is found in other ancient societies—such as with the Ancient Near East—and their practice of using mystical religion as a backbone to civic systematization.[*]

But *times do change* and a tradition must be able to synchronously evolve for it to remain relevant to its practitioners and their environment... and also *survive*.

During the 20th Century, considerable P.R. ("public relations") efforts and other "New Age" publicity assistance ushered in a new era where the idea of "*Wicca*" and "*Witchcraft*" would be looked upon more favorably in the mainstream. Of course, many of the same dogmatic stigmas still apply when treating "paganism" in contrast to two millennium of orthodox opposition.

Ancient "magical societies" were often "temple-centric." The governing "religious" institutions worked closely with ruling powers and the general populace in establishing a cohesive civic and cultural system. Here we see "esoteric knowledge" preserved within the ranks of "*Priestcraft*"—which includes quite elaborate traditions of *Priestesses* serving in dedication of a *Starry Goddess*. But all of this was strictly maintained by "*Initiates*" of the Temple within an urban environment and infrastructure. The seepage of this lore into the hands of "outsiders" and "exiles" took place *afterward*, the likes of which were treated as anathema by the "State."

Unlike what we might encounter with the last 2,000 years of history—where practice of all "magic" is "evil"—the "negative connotations" first attached to the terms "*Witch*" and "*Sorcerer*" in ancient Mesopotamia related to a much

---

[*]   For additional details and background regarding information in this paragraph, refer to the "*Druidic*" material by Joshua Free, including "*Draconomicon*"—which is also reprinted in the Master Edition anthology: "*Merlyn's Complete Book of Druidism.*

deeper standard regarding "unsanctioned magic" practiced *outside* the Temple for personal gain *separate* from the societal system.

Therefore, even at its semantic inception, practice of "*witchcraft*" is a demonstration of *personal* spiritual and magical "religious" tradition that detours the governing infrastructure of its cultural knowledge source. We can even assume that many such individuals were once proper *Initiates* themselves —"sanctioned" *Priests* and *Priestesses* of these famous ancient civilizations, but later left these Temple ranks (and perhaps urban life altogether), taking their knowledge with them into the rural countryside and wilderness.

Of course, were it not for these rebellious efforts throughout the past several millennium, we would perhaps find far fewer genuine traces and active practices of the ancient legacy surviving into present time. While the political structure of civilizations has risen and fallen—and new gods replaced the old —remnants of the "Old Religion" and its folklore continued onward only in far distant reaches of the human population; among those who were not satisfied to accept sweeping societal changes taking place at the whims of a few war generals and tyrant emperors. Because, since when did the masses ever know best for the greater whole—and since when did "might become right"?

The Wheel turns...

◊ ◊ ◊ ◊ ◊ ◊ ◊

To our benefit today, it is both curious and practical that Joshua Free would archive so many citations of source material in his notebooks of "*Traditional European Wicca,*" when the practical demonstrations and advisement to *Covens* and *Groves* found throughout his better known works on "Western Magical Tradition" would suggest a personal background and propagation of "*American Witchcraft,*" of which he was certainly immersed in during the mid-1990's. This is why the esoteric scholarship collected within our newly restored version of *The Witch's Handbook* is worthy of attention, perhaps even more so now in the 21st Century. It will undoubtedly also be of special interest to those Seekers that have been closely examining the timeline of developments for his unique brand and "*gradient path,*" which is now instructed formally from the *Mardukite Academy.*

Wishing you the best, from the arms of the Dragon.

—Rowen Gardner
Winter Solstice 2020
Wales, U.K.

ROLE & POWER OF WITCHES
(Aradian Tradition)

And then it came to pass that *Diana*, once her daughter *Aradia* had accomplished her mission (or completed her allotted time) on the Earth planet among the Humans, recalled her back to the Other. And *Aradia* was given powers to bestow upon those deserving mortals—and that a Witch conjuring her, one that has performed good deeds and invokes her name, may be granted the power:

—To be successful in love.˜
—To do good or evil.‡
—To converse with spirits.
—To find hidden treasure (in ancient ruins).
—To understand the voice of the wind.
—To change water into wine.
—To divine with cards.
—To know the secrets of the hand.*
—To cure diseases.
—To beautify those who are ugly.
—To tame wild beasts.

And if ye be in the favor of *Aradia*, whatsoever ye ask shall be granted. The Witch invokes *Aradia* in dedication and devotion when calling out... *I Seek Aradia, Aradia, Aradia!*

—THE BOOK OF ARADIA

∞ (And grant others to be successful in love.)
‡ "To bless friends with power or curse enemies."
* "Palm reading" (*palmistry*).

RITES OF CONSECRATION
(Merlyn Stone, Autumn '98)

Here we discus "consecrations." To *consecrate* is *"to make sacred"*—an ability entirely within the personal domain; spiritual (or mental, if you prefer) creative faculties of the *Witch*. It is within the power of the *Priestess* or *Priest* to *sanctify*, to *"make clean and holy"* and to treat the instruments and things necessary to be used in the *Art of Witchcraft*.

> *"The virtue of this Consecration primarily consists of two things; to wit, in the power of the person consecrating, and by virtue of the prayer by which the Consecration is made. For in the person consecrating, there is required holiness of Life, and power of sanctifying—which are acquired by priestly offices and initiation. And that the person should, with a firm and undoubted faith, believe the virtue, power and efficacy hereof.*
>
> *"There is also use of the invocation of some Divine names, with the consignation of holy Seals, and things of the sort, which are conducive to sanctification and expiation; such as are the sprinkling with Holy-Water, unctions with Holy-Oil, and odoriferous burning of incense—all appertaining to holy Worship—used everywhere with holy Wax-lights or Lamps burning; for without Lights, no sacrament is rightly performed."*[1]

All significances of "things" are attributed from *Self*—and it is only by definitive—or Self-determined—*attentions* (directed *intentionally* as "actual" *Awareness*) that a "thing" *is realized* as "sacred"; and by this term "sacred" we mean: that which is acknowledged to represent or reflect the "Divine"—or else, "higher" *spiritual* truths behind all *apparent* existence. This is subject only to the very *considerations* held by *Self*, a spiritual (primary) *action* projected as *thought* (subsequently demonstrated as material *action*). Observance of "Causal Law" or "Natural Law" is paramount to the *Craft*.

OF THE WATER & SALT

The Elements (and conditions) of *Water* and *Salt* (*Earth*) are indicative of physical solidity and substance—or *"form"*—manifest in *apparent* existence on the *Earth Planet* (represented as the "Mother" in most traditions). *Water* and *Earth* are also the most "feminine" aspects of the Divine when we derive core "magickal correspondences" from "elemental" knowledge (concerning Nature and natural philosophy).

---

1 Quoting from Henry Cornelius Agrippa, *Of Magical Ceremonies: The Fourth Book of Occult Philosophy.*

Traditionally, this *Water* and *Salt* (once consecrated) become ingredients for baking a simple bread or cake during the ritual, to be shared in "communion" among those present in the *Coven* or *Grove* gathering.

A *Bowl of Water* and *Bowl of Salt* are set on the *Altar*—or, the *Salt* (or *Sea-Salt*) may be cupped in a *Seashell*. During the consecration, each *Bowl* may be respectively placed on the *Pentacle* or a "consecration stone" (used as a *focal*; an assist to concentrate mental focus).

Original suggestions from the "*Book of Aradia*" promoted the *Athame* (or ritual *Dagger*) as the traditional "active" elemental ritual tool for *witchcraft*, although many practitioners exclusively use a *Wand* during ceremonial applications. As practical needs for personal (physical) "protection" increased amongst practitioners, it is quite possible that *Witches* began carrying a *Dagger/Athame* to substitute *Wands* as their key implement of the "air element."

Many ritual suggestions that appear in *The Witch's Handbook* are derived from the *Gardnerian Book of Shadows* from the early 20th century—which was itself based heavily on the "*Book of Aradia*" and "*Key of Solomon*" (and other "*grimoires*" from the Middle Ages), but with a removal of many complicated formulas, including use of *Kabbalah* and other lengthy roll-calls of *Hebrew-Semitic* "Names" for spirits or the Divine.

As opposed to a strict "folk charm" variety of spells and potions that is often conjured to mind in regards to the *Craft*, traditional modern *Wicca-Witchcraft* (since the early 1900's) often incorporates and simplifies "ceremonial magic" notebooks (equally set within a Judeo-Christian worldview), which are then overlaid with a particular "religious mythographic semantic set"—such as with *Gardnerian* traditions, which include *Aradia* and *Kernunnos* (or *Cernunnos*) as primary representatives of the "Divine" ("Goddess" and "God").‡ In older "*grimoires*," as many as 72 names of spirits (or deities) might be intoned for any one "conjuration" or "incantation." In many modern traditions, long lists of deities from various cultural mythologies are often substituted.

The *Witch* (or *High Priestess*) dips the point-tip of the *Athame* into the *Bowl of Water*, saying:

> "I conjure° thee, O Creature of Water, that thou cast out from thee all the impurities and uncleanness of the spirits of the world of phantasm;

---

‡   Particularly a *lunar* or *crescent-horned* "*goddess*" and a *horned* or *antlered-headed* "*god*," of which *Kernunnos* also represents in Celtic/Druidic traditions as "Forest God of the Wilds" shown with *antlers* for *horns*.

∞   The original word here, from the *Key of Solomon*, is "*exorcise*."

in the names of ... and ..."[2]

The *Witch* (or *High Priest*) then dips the point-tip of the *Athame* into the *Bowl of Salt*, saying:[∫]

> "Blessings be upon this Creature of Salt; let all malignity and hindrance be cast forth thencefrom, and let all good enter therein. Wherefore I bless thee and invoke thee, that you may aid me; in the names of ... and ..."[3]

In some traditions, a pinch of consecrated *Salt* is sprinkled at the four corners of the *Altar*. Incorporation of the *Water* and *Salt* in the *Chalice* is treated as part of the "Great Rite."

OF THE GREAT RITE

Traditionally, the "Great Rite" signifies "sexual magic" and "alchemical union"—the creative generative force represented by the *"hiero gamos"* or "sacred marriage" of the *Divine* (*God* and *Goddess*) in this universe. Many archaic sources also allude to physical acts (between the *High Priest* and *High Priestess*) subsequent to symbolic rites utilizing the *Chalice* and *Athame* (*Dagger*). Of course, observation of the original practice among clergy now varies widely between traditions. Additional aspects of the "Great Rite" practice are also applied to the "Third Degree Initiation" (in *Gardnerian* tradition).

The "Great Rite" is integral to a traditional "ritual feast of communion." A portion of *Water* and *Salt* is removed for the "cakes"/ "sweetbreads" (or "cornbread") dough. Then, *Salt* is poured into the remaining *Water* within a *Chalice*—demonstrating an "alchemical marriage" (chemical fusion) of basic elements, while speaking:

> "By this alchemical expression, I do transform and purify my being

---

2   "May all which is evil, all which is negative, all which is base and harmful, be cast forth from this creature of earth, never to return. May only that which is, that which is clean and noble, remain within."—Ed Fitch, *Grimoire of Shadows*. "Element of water, I do banish and cast from thee all that is impure and unclean, that thou may be a fitting tool for our magickal use; and I do charge thee in the names of the God and Goddess."—Mary Kay Simms, *The Witch's Circle*.

∫   Some traditions simply apply a variation of the incantation for *Water* to the *Salt/Earth*, and then tools representing *Air* and *Fire*, &tc.

3   "Take a goblet of water, holding it up to the west and say, 'May the Spirits of Water bestow their blessing and remember.' Take the bowl of salt and hold it up to the northern direction and say, 'May the Spirits of Earth bestow their blessing and remember.'"—Joshua Free, *Elvenomicon*.

unto the highest. Blessed be the alchemical change. Blessed be the Elements of Water and Earth and all that makes contact with them. Elements Unite; energies swirl. Fusion and transformation generate creation."[∞]

This *"Salted Water"* may be used to consecrate the "sacred space," *Witch's Circle* or *nemeton* area, using an *asperger.*[‡] In another tradition, the *Chalice* is taken to the north (or east) and poured out slowly, moving clockwise, around the boundary of the circle. [*Witchcraft* is best performed outdoors.]

Once its contents is mostly emptied, the *Chalice* may be filled with *Wine*, because afterward, in one version of the "Great Rite" from the "*Book of Shadows,*"[*] the *High Priest* holds up the *Chalice* (with *Wine*) while kneeling before the *High Priestess*; and she holds the *Athame* (*Dagger*), lowering the point downward into the *Chalice*, as he says:

"As the dagger is to male; so the chalice is to female—and joined together, they become one united truth."[4]

OF THE CAKES & WINE

The *"Book of Aradia"* provides instructions of consecration (or ingredient preparation) for *"Cakes* and *Wine"* shared by a *coven* during rituals. A tradition of basic "communion" continues in modern *Wicca* for both *"esbats"* (monthly lunar observations; i.e. *full moon*) and *"sabbats,"* referring to eight key annual holidays (seasonal festivals) of "paganism" or "neopaganism." Once the small cakes are baked, the *High Priestess* serves one to each member, saying:—

"May you never hunger."

∞ These lines are absent in the original "Merlyn Stone" notebooks. The first part is adapted from *"Elvenomicon"* by Joshua Free; the second from *"The Druid's Handbook"* by Joshua Free. [Both volumes are contained in the Master Edition anthology: *"Merlyn's Complete Book of Druidism: A Master Course in Druidry for Modern Druids."*]

‡ An *asperger* disperses sprinkles of water across a distance—easily constructed by attaching a pinecone to one end of a rod (or branch). Held like a wand, the pinecone end is dipped briefly into water, then drawn out and dispersed by making flicking motions in the air.

* In an alternative version, the *High Priestess* (*HPS*) holds the *Chalice* between her breasts and the *High Priest* (*HP*) holds the *Athame/ Dagger*; in another modern example, both the HPS and HP share the role of holding both items together, with one's hand over the other's.

4 "HP: *Athame to Chalice.* HPS: *Spirit to Flesh.* HP: *Man to Woman.* HPS: *As the God and Goddess within.* All: *Conjoined they bring blessedness to life."*—Mary Kay Simms, *The Witch's Circle.*

Each member breaks a small piece off to leave in the *Offering Dish*.[†] The *Priest* fills a separate *"Communal Chalice"* to serve a sip of consecrated *Wine*[5] to each member, saying:—

"May you never thirst."

Aradian tradition indicates ingredients of the *cakes* as: *meal, salt, honey* and *water*. The *"Book of Aradia"* substitutes previously given steps (concerning *Water and Salt*) with incantations or "conjurations" directed to the *Meal* (corn meal or another grain flour) and *Salt*, followed by a *"Conjuration to Cain."* The dough is then divided and fashioned into "lunar" shapes (a *horn* or *crescent*) before baking, over which is spoken a *"Conjuration of Diana."* [Some modern traditions draw a *pentacle* (star) across a circular cake/cookie.] Finally, an *"Invocation to Aradia"* is employed for requests of magical power.[*]

Concerning specific recipes: they seldom appear in older grimiores.[6] Baking traditional breads, cakes and cookies—particularly using meal of a local region (*i.e. oats, corn, &tc.*)—was once a common self-sufficient knowledge, especially in more rural communities where "folk traditions" survived.[∫] From the recension delivered by Charles Leland (*in 1899*), the original "conjurations" and "invocations" are as follows:—

---

† The intention of a true *"offering"* given up at the beginning is more significant than simply donating *leftovers*.

5 "I conjure thee, O wine! Though who at first didst grow from nothing, by light of sun and light of moon. The swelling, ripened grape; the blood of the earth pressed soon! I conjure thee, O wine! That as we drink of thee, We drink of the power of the gods; Of fire, and lightning, and rain; Of things that are wild and free!"—Ed Fitch, *Magical Rites from the Crystal Well*.

* See also the section titled: *"Role and Power of Witches."*

6 The following suggestion is copied in the side-notes of Merlyn Stone's notebook: "¼ cup butter; ½ powdered sugar; 1 egg; 1 tsp. vanilla extract; ¼ cup milk; 1 cup ground almonds; 1 cup flour; 1 tsp. baking powder; ¼ tsp. salt. Preheat oven to 350 degrees. Grease cookie sheet. Cream butter and sugar. Add egg and vanilla, beat well. Add milk. Stir in ground almonds. Sift flour, baking soda and salt together. Beat these ingredients in to the butter mixture. The dough may be stiff; gently knead it on a floured board four or five times and then roll out the dough. Cut into crescent shapes or full moon shapes. Bake 8-10 minutes, until very lightly browned. Yield: 15-24 cakes."—Yasmine Galenorn, *Embracing the Moon*.

∫ Another side-note regarding 'Crescent Cakes' quotes: "This is the best recipe I've been able to find. Most of the other published ones taste foul—1 cup finely ground almonds; 1¼ cups flour; ½ cup confectioner's sugar; 2 drops almond extract; ½ cup softened butter; 1 egg yolk. Combine almonds, flour, sugar, and extract until thoroughly mixed. With the hands, work in the butter and egg yolk until fully blended. Chill dough. Preheat oven to 325 degrees. Pinch off pieces of dough about the size of walnuts and shape into crescents. Place on greased sheets and bake for about 20 minutes." Scott Cunningham, *Wicca: A Guide for the Solitary Practitioner*.

Conjuration of the Meal

I conjure thee, O Meal!
Who are indeed our body, since without you
We could not live, you who—at first as seed—
Before becoming flower, went in the earth,
Where all deep secrets hide, and then when ground[∞]
Did it dance like dust in the wind, and yet meanwhile
Did it bear with thee in flitting, strange secrets!
Yet all the while, when thou were in the ear,
Even as a (golden) glittering grain, even then
The fireflies came to cast their light on you
And aid your growth, because without their help
You could not grow nor become beautiful;
Therefore though does belong unto the race
Of witches or fairies, and because
Fireflies do belong to the sun...

Queen of the Fireflies: hurry apace,[‡]
Come to me now as if running a race,
Bridle the horse as you hear me now sing!
Bridle, O bridle, the son of the king!
Come in a hurry and bring him to me!
The son of the king will ever set you free;
And because you are forever brilliant and fair,
Under a glass I will keep thee; while there,
With a lens I will study your secrets concealed,
'Til all their bright mysteries are fully revealed—
Yes, all the wondrous lore perplexed
Of this life to bear and of the next.
Thus to all mysteries I shall attain,
Yes, even to that, at last, of the grain;
And when this at last I shall truly know,
Firefly, freely I'll let thee go!
When Earth's dark secrets are known to me,
My blessing at last I will give to thee!

Conjuration of the Salt

I do conjure thee, Salt, lo! here at (noon),
Exactly in the middle of a stream
I take my place and see the water round,
Likewise the sun, and think of nothing else

∞ As "*flour*."
‡ This portion of the incantation involving the presence of a firefly may have originally
   denoted a subordinate ritual.

While here, besides the Water and the Sun:
For all my soul is turned in truth to them;
Indeed, I do desire no other thought,
I yearn to learn the very truth of truths,
For I have suffered long with the desire
To know my future or my coming fate,
If good or evil will prevail in it.
Water and Sun, be gracious to me!

Conjuration to Cain

I conjure thee, O Cain, as you can never
Have rest or peace until you shall be freed
From the (sun)‡ where you are imprisoned, and must go
Rubbing thy hands and running about quickly:*
I pray thee let me know my destiny;
And if it is evil, change its course for me!
If you will grant this grace, I'll see it clear
In the water, in the splendor of the sun;
And you, O Cain, shall tell by word of mouth
this, whatever my destiny is to be.
And unless you grant me this,
May you never know peace or bliss!∫

Conjuration to Diana

[*The Witch will put the cakes to bake, then say:*]
I do not bake the Bread, nor with it, Salt,
Nor do I cook the Honey with the (Wine);
I bake the body and the blood and soul,
The soul of (great) Diana, that she shall
Know neither rest nor peace, and ever be
In cruel suffering until she will grant
What I request, what I do most desire,
I beg it of her from my very heart!
And if the grace be granted, O Diana!—
In honor of thee, I will hold this feast,
Feast and drain the goblet deep,
We will dance and wildly leap,
And if you so grant the grace I require,
Then when the dance is wildest, all the lamps

---

‡ The "planet" or "sun" denoted here is actually *The Moon* (*Luna*).
* Alluding to attempts to "keep warm" on the cold Moon.
∫ Prevalent practice of threatening "intermediary spirits" appears increasingly throughout the Middle Ages and particularly among *Solomonic*-style grimoires.

Shall be extinguished and we will freely love!~

Invocation to Aradia

Aradia! O my Aradia!
You who are the daughter of him—
Most evil of all spirits, who of old
Once reigned in hell when driven away from heaven,
Who by his sister were you sired,
But as your mother did repent her fault,
She wished to mate you to a spirit who
Should be benevolent,
And not malevolent.

Aradia, Aradia! I implore you,
By the love which Diana did bear for thee!
And by the love which I too feel for thee!
I pray you grant the grace which I require!
And if this grace be granted, may there be
One of three signs distinctly clear to me:
    —the hiss of a serpent;
    —the light of a firefly; or
    —the sound of a frog!
But if you do refuse this favor, then
May you have no future peace or joy,
And be obliged to seek me from afar,
Until you come to grant me my desire,
In haste, and then you may return again
Unto your destination. And so it is!

OF THE HOLED-STONE & PENTACLE

Chapter IV of the "*Book of Aradia*" is dedicated to consecration of sacred stones (to *Diana*)—applied when a *Witch* discovers either one of two types: a "holed-stone" or "holey-stone" (which may be seen through; corded and hung around the neck); and/or a flat round "disc-like" stone (upon which one could trace out a five-pointed star) appropriate as a *focal* tool—called a "*Pentacle*" in modern rituals. The *Witch* is instructed to hold the "holey stone" in the air while speaking an incantation; the round stone is to be thrown up and caught three times "with eyes raised to heaven."*

∞ In many "Aradian/Dianic" and "Gardnerian" traditions, "men and women" of the *Coven* feast together *naked* ("*skyclad*") before celebrating with music and dance; after which, once firelight has dimmed, couples share sexual congress as an extension of the "Great Rite."

* Yes, we would hope that if you *are* throwing a rock up in the air to catch that you

Invocation of the Holey-Stone

I have found a holey-stone upon the ground.
O Fate! I thank you for this happy find,
Also the spirit who upon this road
Has given it to me;
And may it prove to be for my true good
And my good fortune!

I rise in the morning by the earliest dawn,[†]
And I go forth to walk through (pleasant) vales,
All in the mountains or the meadows fair,
Seeking for luck while onward still I roam,
Seeking for *rue* and *vervain* scented sweet,
Because they bring good fortune unto all.
I keep them safely guarded in my bosom,[‡]
That none may know it—it is a secret thing,
And sacred too, and thus I speak the spell:
'*Vervain*, ever be a benefit,
And may thy blessing be upon the witch
Or on the fairy who did give thee to me!'

It was *Diana* who did come to me,
All in the night in a dream, and said to me:
'If you would keep all evil folk afar,
Then ever keep the *vervain* and the *rue*
Safely beside thee!'

Great *Diana*! You
Who are the queen of heaven and of earth,
And of the infernal lands—yes, you who are
Protectress of all unfortunate men,
Of thieves and murderers, and of women too
Who lead an evil life, and yet has known
That their nature was not evil; you, *Diana*,
Has still conferred on them some joy in life.

Or I may truly at another time
So conjure thee that you shall have no peace
Or happiness, for you shall ever be
In suffering until you grant that
Which I require in strictest faith from thee!

---

would be looking skyward...

[†] This portion of the incantation seems to present a subsequent related ritual consecration of the talisman (or a separate amulet blessing) that involves (the herbs) *vervain* and *rue*.

[‡] Alternatively for *Priests*, "Around my neck" or "At my chest/breast" &*tc.* denoting use of the holed-stone as a necklace.

Conjuration of the Round Stone[*]

Spirit of Good Omen,
Who has come to aid me,
Believe I had great need of thee.
Spirit of the Red Goblin,
Since you have come to aid me in my need,
I pray of thee 'do not abandon me':
I beg of thee to enter now into this stone,
That in my pocket I may carry thee,
And so when anything is needed by me,
I can call unto thee: be what it may,
Do not abandon me, by night or by day.

Should I lend money unto any man
Who will not pay when due, I pray of thee,
Red Goblin, make them pay their debt!
And if they will not and is obstinate,
Go at them with your cry of *'Bree! Bree!'*
And if they sleep, awake 'em with a twitch,
And pull the covering off and frighten 'em!
And follow them about wherever they go.
So teach them good with your ceaseless *'Bree! Bree!'*
That: 'He who obligation ever forgets
Shall be in trouble until he pays his debts.'
O my Red Goblin, come unto my aid!

Or, should I quarrel with her whom I love,[∞]
Then Spirit of Good Luck, I pray you go
To her while sleeping—pull her by the hair,
And carry her through the night unto my bed!
And in the morning, when all spirits go
To their repose, shall you, when you return
Into thy stone, carry her home again,
And leave her there asleep. Therefore, O Sprite!
I beg thee, in this stone make thy home!
Obey in every way all that I command.
So in my pocket, you shall ever be,
And you and I will never part company!

Having considered these two previous examples from the *Aradia* book, the origins for these following instructions for the "Holy Stone Talisman" should be well understood—as given, for example, in *The Grimoire of Lady Sheba*

---

[*] This incantation/ritual does not mention *Diana, Aradia, &tc.*

[∞] Gender is supplied here verbatim from "*Book of Aradia*" as the original author/poet intended for its audience; implications of which we will leave up to the reader to consider.

(1972), where the following "chant" (and action) is undertaken in a field or park before "12 o'clock" on the "first day of May" (Beltane). The being referred to above as the "Red Goblin" is evoked and the stone with a natural hole in it (when found) is covered in red silk.

"Walked I forth on May Day Morning,
Search I faithful, for the Round Stone.
Ask I help of Great Diana,
Ask I help of Great Arida,[‡]
Found I the Round Stone.
Held within my hands, the Golden Round Stone.
Lo, I cast my eyes toward Heaven,
Then tossed I the Round Stone toward the heavens; thrice
I tossed the Stone toward Heaven,
Caught I the Round Stone,
Held I fast the Round Stone,
Lest the falling Round Stone
Return to Earth, from whence I took it.

I conjure thee Red Goblin:
I conjure thee by Diana,
I conjure thee by Aradia,
Beautiful and Beloved Mother,
Lovely Goddess of all Witches,
Lovely Goddess of all Earthlings,
By them did I conjure thee.
By the word of my Moon Mother,
Lovely Goddess of the Moonbeams,
By them did I conjure thee.

Now I pray thee, Red Goblin,
Do not abandon, or forsaken me,
For I have great need of thee.
Covered I the round stone,
With silk of red I wrapped it,
Prepared for thee a warm abode.
Rest thou inside my pocked,
Until I have need of thee.
Be thou willing to assist me,
For thou shalt do my bidding
When I call thee forth, Red Goblin.
Reside now within the Round Stone,
Until the day, when by Diana,
I release thee, to return to the Nether,
From the place whence I called thee. So mote it be."

[‡] Spelled as given in the text; obviously "Aradia."

OF THE AIR & FIRE

Censers generating incense smoke and beacon-lamps (or candles) are basic ceremonial representations of the *Air* and *Fire* elements. Traditionally, once *Salt* and *Water* are consecrated at the start of a ritual, next steps include lighting the burner (often charcoal) and consecrating the *Incense* (the *Air* element). As like the *Salt* (*Earth*) and *Water* mixed together, an "alchemical change" (transformation) occurs when introducing *Incense* to *Burner*. And similarly, the result (smoke) from this fusion is used to consecrate objects (and spaces) with the blessings of *Air* and *Fire*. A variation of the incantation from "Of the Water & Salt" (section) is usually applied.[7]

OF ELEMENTAL & RITUAL TOOLS

Some traditions apply *more* elements of "ceremonialism" to the "consecration" of "ritual tools" than others. The purpose of such rites is for the *Witch* or *Wizard*—*Priestess* or *Priest*—to apply Self-determined attention very deliberately to all objects, actions and vocal expressions (incantations, &tc.) present during ritual. For some, acts of "recognition" and "thanksgiving" simultaneous with discovery (or construction) of a magical item is enough—on the basis that the object will receive an increased "charge" of intention (energy) during ritual operations.

Within *Witchcraft* tradition: whether a magical tool is exclusively "consecrated" in a formal ceremony or simply "charged" by repeated ritual appearances, it maintains a status of "enchanted" thereafter (by consideration of the *Witch* or practitioner); cumulative consecrations are not necessary. The basic "elemental tools"—*Pentacle Stone, Athame/Dagger, Wand* and *Chalice*—are always present and therefore actively charged from the *Witch's Circle* (again, by consideration).

There are special cases of heavy concentrated/focused energy on an object, such as the creation of a "magickal artifact," "talisman" or an appropriated vessel to "house a spirit." However, these are all particular *applications* of "ritual magic" (or "magick"), which is performed within an already consec-

---

7   "Hold your hands over the incense and burner, and say: 'I ask the Air Spirits to come and bless this incense. I ask the Fire Spirits to come and bless this burner. [In the names of ... and ...] Blessed be the Elements of Air and Fire and all that makes contact with them.'"—Joshua Free, *Druid's Handbook*. "Take the incense and hold it up to the east, saying: 'May the Spirits of Air bestow their blessing and remember.' Hold up the burner to the south and say: 'May the Spirits of Fire bestow their blessing and remember. Add some incense resin to the coals (or light the stick you are using) and affirm: 'By this alchemical expression do I transform and purify my being; stripping away old skin, leaving my mortal body.'"—Joshua Free, *Elvenomicon*.

rated *Witch's Circle*, while surrounded by (and often including use of) previously "charged" or "consecrated" ritual tools. For this reason, a *Witch* emphasizes prerequisite (preparatory) ritual work and construction or discovery of tools (in addition to theory and history) during preliminary levels ("grades" or "degrees") of initiation prior to incorporating the lot of it into further applications of "directed intention" (otherwise referred to as "spells," "spellwork" or "spellcraft") from traditional lore. Knowingness and the ability to "construct" and "consecrate" tools (energy-matter) and space(-time) naturally should come first. From the *Gardnerian Book of Shadows:*—

> *"There are no magical supply shops,~ so unless you are lucky enough to be given or sold tools, a poor witch must extemporize. But when made, you should be able to borrow or obtain an Athame. So having made a circle, erect an Altar. Any small table or chest will do. There must be fire on it (a candle will suffice) and your book. For good results, incense is best if you can get it, but coals in a chafing dish burning sweet-smelling herbs will do. A cup, if you would have cakes and wine, and a platter with the signs drawn into the same in ink, showing a pentacle. Get a white-hilted knife and a wand (a sword is not necessary). Cut the marks with the Athame. Purify everything, then consecrate your tools in proper form and ever be properly prepared. But ever remember, magical operations are useless unless the mind can be brought to the proper attitude—keyed to the utmost pitch.*

> *"Affirmations must be made clearly, and the mind should be inflamed with desire. With this frenzy of will, you may do as much with simple tools as with the most complete set. But good and especially ancient tools have their own aura. They do help to bring about that reverential spirit, the desire to learn and develop your powers. For this reason, witches ever try to obtain tools from sorcerers, who being skilled men, make good tools and consecrate them well, giving them mighty power. But a great witch's tools also gain much power; and you should ever strive to make any tools you manufacture of the finest materials you can obtain, to the end that they may absorb your power the more easily. And of course, if you may inherit or obtain another witch's tools, power will flow from them."*

Many have assumed that there is some hidden long-running unbroken archaic literary record of *Wiccan* rites and ceremonies, but the standards observed today are, perhaps, a century old at best.*

∞ Gerald Gardner is writing prior to repeal of Witchcraft laws in England (1951); before the rise of New Age marketplaces.

* Slightly longer now: the author is originally writing this document in 1999. Samuel MacGregor Mathers (a founding member of the *Golden Dawn*) translated the *Key of Solomon* to English in 1888 from manuscripts in the British Museum. Public "anti-witchcraft laws" were not repealed in England until 1951.

Apart from minimal folklore provided in *"Book of Aradia,"* the primary source behind "consecration of ritual tools" found in the *Gardnerian Book of Shadows* is the *"Key of Solomon"* and other *kabbalistic* lore borrowed from the *"Hermetic Order of the Golden Dawn"* and the *"Ordo Templi Orientis"* (OTO).[‡] In fact, Aleister Crowley contributed significantly to Gerald Gardner's original presentation of *Wicca*, prior to revisions of the *Book of Shadows* by Doreen Valiente during the 1950's and 1960's, when even more "Hebrew names" (from *Kabbalah*, etc.) and facets of "ceremonial magic" were removed.

The most efficient way to "communicate increased power"[8]—or "consecrate" an item in ritual—is to bring it into contact with manifestations previously considered "sacred." For example, the sequence observed in (previous) rites often begins with consecration of basic elements—such as *Salt* and *Water* or the *Incense* and *Burner*—which are then used to consecrate other objects or spaces. The next example given—the *Pentacle Stone*—is also significant here, because once consecrated by the elements, it too becomes a focal device for "charging" other objects placed upon it later. [This is particularly important when a *Witch* is just starting out; when they do not yet have consecrated tools in which to consecrate more tools.]

OF THE SWORD & DAGGER

The *Key of Solomon* describes a "white-hilt knife" consecrated for use in all magical practices except drawing (casting) of the ritual circle, which is performed with a "black-hilt knife,"[†] or what Gerald Gardner referred to as the *Athame*. Sigils and symbols carved (or painted) onto the handle for the *Book of Shadows* are exactly as they appear in the *Key of Solomon*. As objects representative of the Fire element, operations for consecrating an *Athame* are identical to a *Sword*.

According to original instructions from *Solomonic grimoires*: the white knife (and/or ceremonial sword) is constructed/consecrated "in the day and hour of Mercury," and when Mars is in the Sign of the Ram [*Aries*] or of the Scorpion [*Scorpio*]." The black-hilt knife or *Athame* (used for "making the Circle,

---

‡ Henry C. Agrippa's *"Occult Philosophy"* (*4 vols.*) is another commonly consulted reference for early ritual and ceremonial magic, along with a simplified plagiarized extrapolation of the same, titled: *The Magus.*

8 Referring to a phrase used in Gerald Gardner's *"High Magic's Aid."*

† The associated use of "blood" (and other diabolical) operations from the *Key of Solomon* (and similar *grimoires*) is entirely unnecessary and included only to keep the uninitiated from successfully employing the magic.

∞ The first, eighth, fifteenth or twenty-second hour of Wednesday. Some begin the count at dawn; others right after midnight of the preceding day. Another tradition observes the start of a new day at the dusk of a previous.

wherewith to strike terror and fear into spirits") is crafted "in the day and hour of Saturn."*

The blade is sprinkled with consecrated *Salt-Water* and then passed through the *Incense/Smoke* and then set on the *Pentacle* or *Stone*. An incantation for blade-consecration is given in the *Book of Shadows* as derived from the *Key of Solomon*—except only the first three "Hermetic" names from the *Key* are invoked, the "Tetragrammaton" (YHVH) is removed and all Hebrew Divine Names are replaced with *Aradia* and *Cernunnos*.

> "I conjure thee, O [*Sword, Athame, &tc.*], by the Names—*Abrahach, Abrach, Abracadabra*—that you serve me as a strength and defense in all magical operations against all my enemies, visible and invisible. I conjure thee anew by the Holy Name *Aradia* and the Holy Name *Cernunnos*. I conjure thee, O [*Sword, Athame, &tc.*], that you serve me as a protection in all adversities; so aid me now!"[9]

The blade is sprinkled and passed through the smoke a second time, giving the following prayer (which may be varied for consecrating other ritual tools):

> "I conjure thee, O [*Sword, Athame, &tc.*] of Steel, by the Great Gods and Gentle Goddesses, by the virtue of the heavens, of the stars and of the spirits who preside over them, that you may receive such virtue that I may obtain the end that I desire in all things wherein I shall use thee, by the power of *Aradia* and *Cernunnos*."[10]

---

* The same as the previous note (∞) but for Saturday.

9 "I conjure thee, O Sword, by these Names, *Abrahach, Abrach, Abracadabra, Yod He Vau He,* that thou serve me for a strength and defense in all Magical Operations, against all mine Enemies, visible and invisible. I conjure thee anew by the Holy and Indivisible Name of *El* strong and wonderful; by the name *Shaddai* almighty; and by these Names *Qadosch, Qadosch, Qadosch, Adonai Elohim Tzabaoth, Emanuel,* the First and the Last, Wisdom Way, Life, Truth, Chief, Speech, Word, Splendor, Light, Sun, Fountain, Glory, the Stone of the Wise, Virtue, Shepherd, Priest, Messiah Immortal; by these Names then, and by the other Names, I conjure thee, O Sword, that thou servest me for a Protection in all adversities. Amen."—trans. S.L. MacGregor Mathers, *Key of Solomon.*

10 "*Asophiel, Asophiel, Asophiel, Pentagrammaton, Athanatos, Eheieh Asher Eheieh, Qadosch, Qadosch, Qadosch*; O God Eternal, and my Father, bless this Instrument prepared in Thine honor, so that it may only serve for a good use and end, for Thy Glory. Amen."—trans. S.L. MacGregor Mathers, *Key of Solomon.* This basic prayer, excluding the Hebrew names, appears in the *Book of Shadows* for consecrating other ritual tools.

OF THE WAND & STAFF

The *Key of Solomon*[11] instructs that the *Staff* should be constructed of *elderwood*, or *cane* or *rosewood*; and the *Wand* of *hazel* or *nut* tree. The wood being *virgin*,[12] meaning "of one year's growth only" and cut from the tree in a single stroke, "on the day of Mercury, at sunrise."[‡] Where an *Athame* often substitutes the *Sword* of "ceremonial magic," the *Wand* may serve in place of a *Staff*; in some traditions, a *Staff* can also substitute symbolism of a *Sword*.

Witches often prefer *Wands* of *hazel* or *willow*; considerably more details regarding tree/wood types and corresponding energies may be found in Druid lore.[†] Some archaic sources suggest a 21-inch long *Wand*, although 12-to-18 inches is more workable length. A popular guide-rule is the "length of your elbow to your fingertips. Another *Wiccan* tradition describes removing two limbs from a *Willow* tree at night during a *full* moon: the *Wand* is 13-inches long and a companion *Staff* is 39-inches. The *Witch* then treats the wood several times with a *chamomile* tincture.[13]

Although often simplified and bastardized from their true sources, many elements of other *Solomonic-cycle* "grimoires" frequently appeared in *Wicca* during the 20th century. One example, found in a popular *Witchcraft* tome from the 1970's, actually incorporates construction of a *"Blasting Rod"*[*] exactly as suggested in a diabolical sorcerer's handbook known as the *"Grand Grim-*

---

11 *"Adonai*, Most Holy, deign to bless and consecrate this Wand, and this Staff, that they may obtain the necessary virtue, through Thee, O Most Holy *Adonai*, Whose kindgom endures unto the Ages of the Ages. Amen."—trans. S.L. MacGregor Mathers, *Key of Solomon.*

12 "...grimoires seem to have differing opinions of *virgin wood.* In one description, the wand comes from a branch that has no other shoots; in another, the tree must be less than a year old or not yet having bared any fruit."—Joshua Free, *The Great Magickal Arcanum: A Master Course in Magick for Modern Wizards.*

‡ Wednesday is the "Day of Mercury"— by some counts of planetary hours, *sunrise on a Wednesday* is also the "Hour of Mercury."

† Refer to *"Elvenomicon -or- Secret Traditions of Elves and Faeries: The Book of Elven Magick & Druid Lore"* by Joshua Free; also found in the Master Edition anthology: *"Merlyn's Complete Book of Druidism: A Master Course in Druidry for Modern Druids."*

13 "Another method of preparing a Magic Rod ordains that it shall be a branch of the hazel-tree born during the year of operation. It must be cut on the first Wednesday after the new moon, between 11 P.M. and midnight. The knife must be new and the branch severed by a downward stroke. The rod must then be blessed; at the stouter end must be written the word AGLA †, in the center ON †, and towards the point TETRAGRAMMATON †. Lastly say over it: *Conjuro te cito mihi obedire—I conjure thee to obey me forthwith."*—A.E. Waite, *The Complete Book of Ceremonial Magic.*

* Traditionally used by sorcerers to threaten spirits that do not arrive when evoked, or attack entities that do not submit to the magician's bidding.

oire"∞ as given below, paraphrasing the original source text described by Arthur Edward Waite (*in 1911*):—

> *"The 'Grand Grimoire' devotes an entire chapter to the true composition of the Mysterious Wand, otherwise the Destroying or Blasting Rod. It mentions no other instrument, and ascribes to it all the power in diabolical evocations... On the eve of the great enterprise, says this Ritual, you must go in search of a wand or rod of wild hazel which has never borne fruit; its length should be nineteen and a half inches. When you have met with a wand of the required form, touch it only with your eyes; let it stay until the next morning, which is the day of operation. Then you must cut it absolutely at the moment when the sun rises; strip it of its leaves and lesser branches, if there be any, using your ritual blade or knife...*

> *"Having pronounced the incantation[14] and still keeping your eyes turned towards the region of the rising sun, you may finish cutting your rod, and may then carry it to your abode. You must next go in search of a piece of ordinary wood, fashion the two ends like those of the genuine rod and take it an ironsmith to weld two pointed caps that will affix to said ends. This done, you may again return home, and there, with your own hands, affix the steel caps to the genuine rod. Subsequently, you must obtain a lodestone and magnetize the steel ends, pronouncing the second incantation."[15]*

∞ Medieval grimoires of "kabbalistic sorcery" include not only the *Key of Solomon the King*, and it's *Lesser Key: The Goetia*, but also the *Grand Grimoire (Red Dragon)*, *Grimoirum Verum* and *Grimoire of Honorius (Black Dragon)*. Interest in other popular grimoires—*The Sacred Book of Magic of Abramelin the Mage*, the *Enchiridion, &tc.*—also increased at the end of the 19th century, and continuing during public revival of the *Craft*.

14 "Begin cutting it when the sun is first rising over the hemisphere and pronounce the following words: 'I beseech Thee, O Grand *Adonay*, *Eloim*, *Ariel*, and *Jehovam*, to be propitious unto me, and to endow this Wand, which I am cutting, with the power and virtue of the rods of *Jacob*, of *Moses*, and of the mighty *Joshua!* I also beseech Thee, O Grand *Adonay*, *Eloim*, *Ariel*, and *Jehovam*, to infuse into this Rod the whole strength of *Samson*, the righteous wrath of *Emanuel* and the thunders of mighty *Zariatnatmik*, who will avenge the crimes of men at the Day of Judgment! Amen.'"— *Grand Grimoire*.

15 "By the Grand *Adonay*, *Eloim*, *Ariel*, and *Jehovam*, I bid thee join with and attract all substances which I desire. By the power of the sublime *Adonay*, *Eloim*, *Ariel*, and *Jehovam*, I command thee, by the opposition of fire and water, to separate all substances, as they were separated on the day of the world's creation. Amen."— *Grand Grimoire*.

A SUMMARY OF RITUAL TOOLS‡

The *Cup* or *Chalice* holds drinkable liquids: water, wine, ceremonial mead and other ritual libations. It naturally represents the *Water* element and is placed in the *west* during rituals. A *Cauldron* is simply another version of the *Cup*, used for brewing fusions, potions and tinctures—and likewise makes stereotypical appearances in *Witchcraft.* Alcohol may also be burned within it.

Pentacles symbolize the *Earth* element and come in a variety of styles and sizes —from circular plates of wood, metal, wax or clay, to the traditional stones— used as a focal point of the *Altar,* which is placed in the *northern* quadrant of the working area. The tool is so named for the five-pointed star engraved or drawn across its surface.

The *Magic Blade*—a *Dagger/Athame* or *Sword*—symbolizes a *Witch's* sheer cutting will (and the force or desire necessary for traditional magic) and representative of the *Fire* element (and thus placed in the *south* during ritual). Herbalists will also keep a separate knife used only for cutting plants and

The *Wand* represents the *Air* element in ritual and the action that is transmitted in thought. In folk traditions and *Witchcraft,* they are often made of wood —such as *Hazel* or *Willow.* Other tree associations include *Apple* for love, *Ash* for healing, *Pine* for prosperity, *Rowan* for protection and *Birch* for purification. A *Wand* averages about fifteen to eighteen inches long and half an inch thick. They are placed in the *east* during rituals.

---

‡ Paraphrased from the text of the *"Sorcerer's Handbook."*

THE WITCH'S CIRCLE
(Merlyn Stone, Autumn '98)

Here we discuss the *"Witch's Circle"* or *Magic Circle* of the Arts, where all "ritual magic" (or *magick*) is performed. Each tradition and *grimoire* suggests its unique style and methodology behind "creation of sacred space" or "temple erection."

Originally, the *Craft* of *Witches* was practiced and disseminated in rural areas by folk with little access to national temples, ceremonial chambers and elaborate (and often expensive) tools maintained by the *Priests* and *Priestesses* practicing magic *within* the system and urban domain (or "realm") of ancient magical cultures (and their religions). This accounts for the various differences in carrying out physical practices of *"paganism"* and *"magick."*

Sources of "magical lore" and "ritual texts" for *Witchcraft* were often imported by preexisting members of larger (and nationally sanctioned) organizations—*Orders*, *Lodges*, *Guilds* and *Temples.*

We then see—starting in ancient Mesopotamia—a clear dividing line (regarding social class) between those practicing magic *within* the "system" (acting as "religio-government" officials, *&tc.*) of historic *Temples* in urbanized society, versus those operating independently on the "outskirts" of said social order; and which were able to bring various elements from the sanctioned "Ancient Mystery School" with them into the wilds—where they undoubtedly mirrored facsimiles of religious hierarchy, knowledge grades and initiation structures, while establishing *Witchcraft* traditions of their own design.

MAGICAL PREPARATIONS (APPRENTICE PRIMER)

Methods of *"casting a circle"* or conducting *"ritual magic"* are as personal and varied as interpretations of mythology, religion and "deity" can be. Contrary to styles of "ceremonial magicians"—those that operate elaborate rites indoors, within a highly decorated temple—*Witches* are accustomed to working exclusively outdoors (and in seclusion) with simpler tools and techniques. There are obvious advantages to both routes. For our present purposes, we will focus only on those "ceremonial" elements traditionally incorporated into *Wiccan* practices since the original circulation of Gerald Gardner's *"Book of Shadows"* (and other similar versions) during the 20th century.

Much like consecration of "objects" or "masses," the consecration (or "creation") of "space" is accomplished by *consideration*—meaning the Self-determined "thought" directed by a *Witch.* Basic principles applied to the

Witch's Circle (for purposes of understanding and practicing modern *Wicca*) are generally applicable to all forms of "ritual magic," particularly where they are often borrowed from the same lore—and this reason, the two areas of esoteric study often blend as a modern "applied spiritual/metaphysical philosophy."

It is the basic principles, such as set forth in the current series of handbooks,[*] that renders the "magick" effective at all, regardless of the cultural flavor or mythological personality that is superimposed over it for individuality. These other religious flavors are *added* to the basics—to the benefit or detriment of the practitioner—based on one's own interests and inclinations. Of course, one of the allures of the "magical path" is that it practically demands that an individual construct their own "personal universe" in which to operate from, independent (yet connected by considerations of *Self*) to the "physical universe."

It is from a "higher" vantage point as the *True Self*—and gradients of spiritual clarity along the way—that a *Witch, Mystic, Magician, Priestess* or *Wizard* is able to glean *any* "true knowledge" of *this* "physical universe"—and which has otherwise been considered somehow "supernatural" as an incredible misnomer.[‡]

Although modern *Witchcraft* rightly places an emphasis on "operative circles" (magical workings meant to invite positive change), the "occult history" reveals a long-standing tradition of *magic-users* that applied extensive efforts into fashioning "protective circles" and "blasting rods"—components of "psychic" (or "psionic") warfare with the same "forces" they are threatening for assistance. Such practitioners operate in a state of *fear* and validate low-level considerations that properly handling energy flows is an unknown mystery.

Prior to consecration rites—or any work within the Cirlce—a *Witch's* magic begins with "purification." This is a natural integral of "magical lifestyles," but more attention is given to it immediately prior to ritual. In some ancient traditions, particular regimens and practices precede the ceremonies with a "purification bath." While this may have once been conducted in a more elaborate manner in grandiose temples, there are modernized and more personal versions observed in *Wicca*. Even apart from *'Circle Magic,'* the basic rules of intention (and, if desired, affirmation or incantation) may be applied to the *bath-water* and *bath-salts.* But the step is critical in any true "*priestcraft*" and even appears in the basic instructions from the "*Book of Shadows*":—

---

[*]   Referring to the original 1990's (proposed) "Merlyn Stone" trilogy—*Sorcerer's Handbook, Witch's Handbook* and *Druid's Handbook* (all of which are now restored and available in hardcover collector's editions).

[‡]   *Misnomer,* as in: improperly named, and therefore, improperly defined (and misunderstood).

To practice the Art successfully, you need the following five things—one for each point of the Witch's Pentacle:

1. Intention—You must have the absolute will to succeed, the firm belief that you can do so and the determination to win through against all obstacles.

2. Preparation—You must be properly prepared.

3. Invocation—The Mighty Ones must be invoked.

4. Consecration—The Witch's Circle must be properly cast and consecrated and you must have properly consecrated tools.

5. Purification—You must be purified.

THE PURIFICATION BATH

Of course, purification rites, ceremonial baths and sweat-lodge traditions are not unique to the *Witch,* or the ceremonial magician. This is one instance of commonality that we respect as an underlying truth behind magical work—although frequently overlooked. Esoteric instructions, such as those suggested by *Franz Bardon,*[16] describe acts that we would today refer to as "skin and pore exfoliation." Modern *Wiccan* traditions often borrow from the *Key of Solomon.*[17] The *grimoire* explains that when a practitioner enters the waters of a "river or running stream" or a "tub in thy secret cabinet," they are to say:—

"I conjure thee, O Creature of Water, by [the God and Goddess] who has created thee and gathered thee together into one place so that the dry land appeared, that thou uncover all the deceits of the Enemy, and that thou cast out from thee all the impurities and uncleanliness of the Spirits of the World of Phantasm, so they may harm me none, through the virtue of the Almighty [God and Goddess] who live and reign unto the Ages of the Ages. So shall it be."[∞]

---

16 "...brush yourself with a soft natural brush until your skin becomes slightly pinkish. This will open your pores and allow them to breathe better. Through this, for the greater part, your kidneys are relieved. After this, wash your entire body with cold water, then give your body a rub-down with a rough terry towel until you feel comfortably warm. Make this procedure a daily routine and maintain it for the rest of your life..."—Franz Bardon, *Initiation Into Hermetics.*

17 "The bath often becomes a ritual itself. Candles can be burned in the bathroom, along with incense. Fragrant oils or herbal sachets can be added to the water. My favorite purification bath sachet consists of equal parts of rosemary, fennel, lavender, basil, thyme, hyssop, vervain, mint, with a touch of ground valerian root. (This formula is derived from *The Key of Solomon.*) Place this in a cloth, tie the ends up to trap the herbs inside, and pop it in the tub."—Scott Cunningham, *Wicca: A Guide for the Solitary Practitioner.*

∞ The additional Hermetic names repeated "twice or thrice, until thou art completely washed and clean" are: *Mertalia, Musalia, Dophalia, Onemalia, Zitanseia,*

Having washed clean with a preliminary bath, the *Witch* emerges (from the tub, *&tc.*) and is sprinkled with consecrated waters (infused with hyssop), saying:

"O [God and Goddess], purge me, and I shall be clean; wash me, and I shall be whiter than snow. Cast from me all impurity, that I may accomplish all things."

Then the *Witch* shall robe; and taking up the *Bath-Salts* (or an appropriate herbal sachet) says:

"The blessing of the Almighty [God and Goddess] be upon this Creature of Salt [*or Earth, for sachets*], and let all malignity and hindrance be cast out, and let all good enter herein."[‡]

And saying this, the *Witch* takes the *Bath-Salts* (or sachet) and casts it into the waters/bath, disrobes and enters to bathe a second time before adorning proper ritual garments.

RITUAL DRESSINGS & ATTIRE

A discussion of "ritual tools" and "elemental weapons" appears in another essay,[*] but there is still the matter of a *Witch's* dressings and garments—such as "robes" and "cloaks"—to attend to. Use of "ritual attire" is a standard practice in any *Witchcraft* tradition. The most commonly adopted color is black, especially when practicing lunar magic and other "nighttime" rituals. Some practitioners celebrate the "Wheel of the Year"—as festival ceremonies called "sabbats"—by wearing colors (or accenting with scarves) that correspond with the seasons. There are also traditions that distinguish various "degrees" or "levels" of initiation with a particular color[†] or accent—such as stripes on the cuff of a sleeve, *etc.*

To fully treat the subject of "ritual attire" for *Witchcraft*, we must also include

---

Goldaphaira, Dedulsaira, Ghevialaira, Gheminaira, Gegropheira, Cedahi, Gilthar, Godieb, Ezoiil, Musil, Grassil, Tamen, Pueri, Godu, Huznoth, Astachoth, Tzabaoth, Adonai, Agla, On, El, Tetragrammaton, Shema, Aresion, Anaphaxeton, Segilaton, Primeumaton.

‡ The additional Hermetic names are: *Imanel, Arnamon, Imato, Memeon, Rectacon, Muoboii, Paltellon, Decaion, Yamenton, Yaron, Tatonon, Vaphoron, Gardon, Existon, Zagveron, Momerton, Zarmesiton, Tileion, Tixmion.*

* See chapter on "Rites of Consecration."

† For example, in a traditional *Druid Order*—"Ovate" novitiates wear green; "Bards" wear blue; "Druids" wear white; and "High Druids" and "Arch Druids" often also wear red (and gold).

a consideration of what may refer to as *"skyclad"*—"dressed by the sky"—which is to say *naked*. This is a traditional practice directly expressed in the *Aradian (Dianic)* lore and Gerald Gardner's original *Book of Shadows.*ʃ In modern times, it is generally reserved for solitary rites and close groups or "closed covens." There is also the idea of simply being naked beneath *robes* and/or *cloaks*. One recent example, observed by the current author, involved practitioners wearing only very sheer (almost see-through) black *robes*, which the *High Priestess* even left open in the front. Of course, as a general rule, no one should ever be forced to operate outside of their comfort level.[18]

As a simplification for our purposes, we find another suggestion supplied to initiates in Ed Fitch's *Outer Court Book of Shadows*, where: although it notes that the *"Inner Court of Witchcraft"* practices "sky-clad, where the "Outer Court" (those who have not been initiated to the "Third Degree" or "Third Circle") is concerned, there is a "lesser degree of Magical experience, and to maintain the proper control, the members must wear robes." It is further noted that "shoes and underclothes" are not worn beneath except where weather requires.

There is one additional matter to consider when one is working toward spiritual goals via the magical lifestyle: whether or not emphasis on using various "symbols" and adornment of additional "layers" is truly the route toward higher realizations of Self-actualization—or else true empowerment. The ritual aspects of "magick" and *Witchcraft* are intended as a tool, not a crutch. As a "source-point," a *Witch* intends to *create* effects with magic; not *be* the effects of their creations. Here, the Farrar's point out in *The Witches' Bible*:

> *"A final advantage to skyclad working is particularly important with some personalities; the ones who have genuine occult potential but are glamourized by the appeal of splendid robes and trappings (a by-product, of course, of the Persona problem."*

It is true that practice of "naturism" differs greatly, by comparison, to tradit-

---

ʃ Several sources suggest strongly that, *Wicca* aside, Gerald Gardner was a naturist (nudist), which may have also played a role in the inclusion of *skyclad* practices.

18 "A good reason for skyclad working—and the one most quoted—is a very practical one: experienced opinion holds that it is easier to raise psychic power with an uncovered body than with a covered one... psychic power-raising is a two-sided process of input and output (increased awareness and increased psychic energy amplifying each other by mutual feedback)... the naked body is more responsive not only to sensory impressions but also to psychic ones. An interesting biological footnote: 'pheromones' or external chemical messengers... the air around us is full of... information which we emit and which we receive from others; much of it unconsciously, but we react to it all the time."—Janet & Stuart Farrar, *The Witches' Way*.

ions of "high magic" (of the temples) and the "ceremonial arts" observed by *Priests* and *Priestesses* on public display or even in the Orders and Lodges working from *grimoires* and other arcane magical notebooks. Even the ritual formula so often borrowed from the "*Key of Solomon*" is practiced robed (with special signs and sigils sewn thereon), after having performed the purification bath rite. It goes on to instruct:—

> "*The exterior garments which the Master of the Art should wear ought to be of linen, as well as those which are worn beneath; and if means allow, they should be of silk... (If they are linen, the thread of which they are made should have been spun by a young maiden.) The characters should be embroidered on the breast with the Needle of the Art° in red silk. The shoes should also be white (leather), upon which the characters should be traced in the same way. Besides this, the Master of the Art should have a Crown made of virgin paper, upon which should be four names—one on each side—written in the Pen and Ink of the Art* and marked in scarlet red. Take notice that if the linen garments were vestments of the Levites or of the Priests, and had been used for holy things, that they would be all the better.*"‡

Basic magical attire can be crafted fairly easily and inexpensively. I constructed my own first *cloak* with a few yards of bargain fabric—which is usually sold in 45-inch or 60-inch widths. There are also more involved costume patterns available at these same outlets. But even a new initiate with elementary sewing skills can make their own *robes* and *cloaks*. To close this primer, we should also distinguish between a "*robe*" and a "*cloak*" as general terms.

For our purposes: a "*robe*" generally has sleeves and is tied off at the waist—whereas a "*cloak*" often does not have sleeves and either covers an individual wearing a "*robe*" ¾ or all of the way. A ½ or ¼ *cloak* might be considered a "cape." A "*robe*" may or may not have a hood, whereas the "*cloak*" usually does. It is not uncommon to have a simple white or black robe pulled over as a one-piece and tied about the waist that is then accented by an appropriate (black) "cloak" (which is usually attached or closed at the neckline).

∞ "*...of the Art*" meaning: "ceremonially consecrated."

* The *Key of Solomon* uses the Hebrew names: *Yod He Vau He* in front; *Adonai* behind; *El* on the right; and *Elohim* on the left.

‡ The *Key of Solomon* suggests a prayer while dressing with the garments: "*Amor, Amator, Amides, Ideodaniach, Pamor, Plaior, Anitor*; through the merits of these holy Angels will I robe and indue myself with the Vestments of Power, through which may I conduct unto the desired end those things which I ardently wish, through Thee, O Most Holy *Adonai*, Whose Kingdom and Empire endures forever. Amen."

CASTING THE WITCH'S CIRCLE

Creating sacred space concerns both a personal mental projection of "anchor points" in this universe and marking or defining the physical boundaries of a "Magic Circle." Rather than being a further *agreement* to the "reality" of *this* physical universe (as a microcosm), the Ritual Circle is actually a "macrocosm" of the personal universe or worldview directed by Self and reflected outwardly.† It is from within a consecrated personal workspace—whereby Self operates exterior to this physical universe—that a *Witch* directs their intentions into affecting or manifesting changes *in* the physical universe.

Rather than being a source of "protection" against the spirits and energies evoked, the "Magic Circle" can be better treated as a "portal" between worlds; or at the very least, the boundaries of a time-space. There are no dangers to evoking true magick, but there is still the matter of the "individual" themselves and their own ability to command and control magickal forces and energies—hence within a "Magic Circle" and projected "anchor points" of Self-Awareness as *focal points*, the "Mind-System" can be better brought and maintained under Self-control.

One of a *Witch's* most stereotypical icons—the *broomstick*—appears frequently in modern practices of "clearing" or "purifying" the ritual space, whereby the *Witch* literally "sweeps" the area clean prior to any ceremony, which is a treatment of the ground or earth.∞ This practice—and others for "casting a circle"—emphasizes rendering preexisting energy *null*, while expanding Self-determined management of one's own personal considerations of the space. Additional "purification" operations are employed any time a rite or tradition calls for a space to be "smudged" or "incensed" ("*censed*")—which is a treatment of the air. Use of incense is common in all modern *witchcraft*.

A sacred circle may be physically prepared when appropriate. It is common for *Witches* to gather in "groves" of trees and "henges" of stones—such as is referred to in Druidic traditions of Europe. A small "stone circle"may be erected, either permanently or temporarily. It's not uncommon to prepare several (typically three) concentric circles (within one another). A solitary practitioner often uses their own height as the diameter for the inner most circle for temporary purposes. Most "ceremonial magic" (and suggestions from *grimoires*) require much larger spaces, especially if utilized by several participants.

---

†   See also the newly recorded audio lectures for the "*Mardukite Master Course*" by Joshua Free—esp. Volumes I and II.

∞   Update: practices involving a *broomstick* have dwindled in modern revivals. Once stereotypically aligned to "flying" (riding) or dancing about like a May Pole, some have interpreted the "broom and cauldron" motifs to be a bit too "cute," while other traditionalists cling to them as timeless icons of *witchcraft*.

The following instructions are given in the "*Key of Solomon*" and are included to illustrate the most basic source of casting a *Witch's* circle available to Gerald Gardner and Aleister Crowley in the construction of the original "*Book of Shadows.*"

> "*Having chosen a place...take your [sickle or scimitar] and stick into the centre of the place where the Circle is to be made; then take a cord of nine feet in length, fasten one end to the [sickle] and with the other end trace out the circumference of the Circle, which may be marked with the Sword or the [Athame]. Then, within the Circle, mark out four regions, namely, towards East, West, South and North, wherein place [symbols]; and beyond the limits of this Circle describe with the [Athame] or Sword another Circle, but leaving an open space in the North whereby you may enter and depart beyond; and beyond that you shall describe another Circle at a foot distance with the aforesaid instrument...*"

A similar operation may be found in Druidic lore regarding use of a "*Rod*" to trace the circle—which was technically two "rods" connected by a cord. By fixing one of the ends or "rods" into the ground, the other end could be used —like a geometerist's "compass"—to draw a circle.[19] Given that *Witchcraft* traditions were first observed in secret, any physical trace of a "Magic Circle" had to be temporary—and thus a circle would have to be marked newly with each rite. This is not always the case any more, such as when repeatedly using a site that has a more permanent boundary marked with trees or stones. In either case, ceremonially speaking, a Magic Circle is still "ritually cast" before any operations are performed, as an intentional "consecration of space."

THE FOUR QUARTERS

To the same extent that the Magic Circle is the microcosm/macrocosm of the Greater Universe, the four directions define the "ends" of the Universe—and are often called "*Watchtowers.*" The concept of the *Watchtowers* was adopted into *Wicca* via traditional dissemination of Gerald Gardner's *Book of Shadows*. It is included within modern *Witchcraft* tradition exactly as it appears in rites of the "Hermetic Order of the Golden Dawn" (founded in 1888), of which Gerald Gardner may have been a member of, or if not, had direct access to variations used by the "Ordo Templi Orientis" (via Aleister Crowley).[20]

---

19 "The complete *Druid's Rod* is composed of three measured parts (two rods and a cord)—each 2.72 (or 3) feet in length—making the total length 9 feet (or 8.16 if strictly using the Megalithic Yard)."—Joshua Free/Merlyn Stone, *The Druid's Handbook.*

20 "...what old Gerald told me, and on the rather disjointed state of the rituals which he had when I first knew him: they were heavily influenced by Crowley and the O.T.O., but underneath there was a lot which wasn't Crowley at all, and wasn't the Golden

Ritual observance of the *Watchtowers* predates revival traditions of ceremonial magic and even Semitic Kabbalah lore (which is also frequently incorporated into *Wicca*). This concept is found in ancient Mesopotamia many thousands of years ago—particularly in rites attributed to the Babylonians and Chaldeans—and then later alluded to in the "*Chaldean Oracles of Zoroaster.*" It is surprisingly curious just how little attention is given to the origins—or even the idea or subject—of the *Watchtowers*, based on the widespread use of such semantics throughout the rituals of the Golden Dawn and *Wicca.*

Popular use of *Watchtowers* in modern *Wiccan* rituals and ceremonial magic is primarily a result of "Enochian Magic"[21]—which, combined with the "*Kabbalah,*" served as the major cornerstone of the late-19th century magical revival as observed by groups such as "The Hermetic Order of the Golden Dawn," "Aurum Solis" and "Ordo Templi Orientis" (among others)—all of which contributed in some part to the *Book of Shadows* on which 20th (and 21st) century *Wicca* (and other forms of "operative neopaganism") are based... even if acknowledgment and recognition of this fact has since waned.

The "quarters" or "corners" of the Universe are addressed as "opening rites" or during the "circle casting" of all traditional ritual magic—even when not addressed as "*Watchtowers.*" For example, in one text, it may speak of *calling* to the "Watchtower of the North" whereas another speaks of "Guardians of the Earth Plane" (addressed toward the northern direction)—both essentially serve the same function.

This concept of "addressing" or "anchoring" personal realizations of *six directions* is as ancient as magic, or at least the languages able to describe magical rites. On some of the oldest cuneiform tablet records surviving from ancient Mesopotamia—and particularly Babylon—we discover frequent mention of an "*Incantation of Eridu,*"* where specific names and attributes for the *four* cardinal directions are conjured in addition to "*above*" and "*below.*" Thousands of years later, via the path of Kabbalistic Magic, a version of this same rite (very closely approximating the original) is among the most popular workings used by the Golden Dawn—*and* even early traditions of *Wicca*—known as the L.B.R.P. or *Lesser Banishing Ritual of the Pentagram.*

Dawn or ceremonial magic either—and I had been studying all three of these traditions for years. Yes, I am responsible for a lot of the wording of the present-day rituals; but not the framework of those rituals or the ideas upon which they are based."—letters from Doreen Valiente, quoted by Margot Adler in *Drawing Down The Moon.*

21 "There are four Watchtowers and thirty Aethyrs with a Tablet of Union uniting all. They are located between the lofty realms of divinity and our physical Earth."— Gerald Schueler, *Enochian Physics.*

* Also referred to as the *Incantation of the Deep* (or *Enki*).

In ceremonial magic operations, banners may be hung in each direction and/or correlating "elemental tablets"—or representative objects—are similarly placed at the boundary of the ritual circle. Some grimoires recommend use of beacons or candle-lit lamps, appropriately arranged, to signify the four quarters. In traditional *Witchcraft*, a single candle (of corresponding elemental color) is set out at each cardinal point. These are lit in turn, as the "Guardians" of each *Watchtower* (or "Elemental Realm") are conjured during the initial "casting" of the Magic Circle.

ELEMENTAL CANDLE SUGGESTIONS[‡]
North—Earth—Green (or Brown)
East—Air—Yellow (or Purple)
South—Fire—Red (or Orange)
West—West—Blue (or Grey)

"Circle-casting" rites from various *Wiccan Book of Shadows*, and other ceremonial magic sources, instruct use of an *Athame* (magic dagger) to *trace* the Magic Circle (and any of its "signs"), whereas another variation uses a *Wand*. [By this we mean, "mental" or "astral" *tracing*; not the physical boundary, which would have been marked out already.] Another variation suggests strongly that the Circle is *traced* and *consecrated* with each of the elements— meaning also "clockwise" or "sunwise" movement around the boundary of the Circle, for example, with *incense*, the *salt-water* fusion, marked by a *blade* and traced with a *Wand.*

"Elemental" or "directional" orientation of a ritual is typically indicated in texts, however this is not always the case. Some rites are written with an assumption that the *Witch* already operates within a particular tradition regarding this—but as with many aspects of *Witchcraft*, there are differing practices (instructed or suggested) in various sources. The traditional modern standard is to orient/align altars, and make the first address to the elements, in the eastern direction; others strongly encourage north—I've often split the difference by setting the altar to face the northeast.[†]

The *Witch* goes to the eastern point of the Magic Circle[∞] and lights the eleme-

---

‡ Original elemental color suggestions from *Sorcerer's Handbook*—Earth, green/black (white); Air, yellow (purple); Fire, red (green); Water, blue (orange).

† Of course, when addressing visible planets, a *Witch* operating in the United States will note that the "celestial arc" or horizon line where all planets stream across the sky is southerly, arcing from a line of sight in the east to the south and over to the west.

∞ This text is written with the solitary practitioner as a consideration. In another variation, a particular member of the *coven* is "stationed" at each representative quarter to address that element; and another suggests that members of the *coven* each move together around the Magic Circle to each "station."

ntal candle for Air,* saying:

> "Hail to the Guardians of the Watchtower of the East, Spirits of Air; I summon and stir thee, Powers of Wind; I call thee forth to witness this rite and guard this Magic Circle."[22]

And in the South:

> "Hail to the Guardians of the Watchtower of the South, Spirits of Fire; I summon and stir thee, Powers of Flame; I call thee forth to witness this rite and guard this Magic Circle."

And in the West:

> "Hail to the Guardians of the Watchtower of the West, Spirits of Water; I summon and stir thee, Powers of Sea; I call thee forth to witness this rite and guard this Magic Circle."

And in the North:

> "Hail to the Guardians of the Watchtower of the North, Spirits of Earth; I summon and stir thee, Powers of Stone; I call thee forth to witness this rite and guard this Magic Circle."

This being completed, the *Witch* completes their pass around the circle back to the east, then returns to the altar to commence the remainder of the ritual.

THE WITCHES' RUNE & CHANT

After Doreen Valiente worked with Gerald Gardner to revise his *Book of Shadows*, a particular incantation began appearing in future versions of the "Opening Rites" of *Wicca* through the 1970's.‡ A version of it also appears in Gerald

---

* Some modern *Wicca-Witchcraft* traditions continue to supplement this rite with "tracing a pentagram in the air" from the Golden Dawn "*L.B.R.P.*" (see *The Sorcerer's Handbook*).

22 In ceremonial magic, various archaic names are intoned and then, "By the Names and Letters of the Eastern Quadrangle, I invoke thee Spirits of the Watchtower of the East." Alternatively from the *Book of Shadows*—"Ye Lords of the Watchtowers of the East, ye Lords of Air; I do summon, stir and call you up, to witness our rites and to guard the Circle." Alternatively from *The Witch's Circle*—"Guardian of the Eastern Sphere, now we seek your presence here. Come, East, come. Be here this night. [*Bell rung three times.*] All hail the Watchtower of the East."

‡ For example, it appears in Farrar's *Witches' Bible* (1981, 1984) and *The Grimoire of Lady Sheba* (1972, 1974).

Gardner's novel: *High Magic's Aid*.

Lines containing "Arida"/"Aradia" and "Kernunnos"/ "Cernunnos" were later added to the archaic version. These may be replaced by different ones for a patron "Goddess" and "God" of personal choice. This chant also employs two other names of unknown significance, named "Azarak" and "Zomelak."

According to available research, the "*Eko, Eko*" lines (employing deity names) were absorbed into the "Witches' Rune" from from older sources,[23] which are also used in the *Book of Shadows*—the full text of which has since been equated (perhaps inaccurately) to a "rallying" for the Samhain (Halloween) festival—although it appears common in every standard rite.[24] This rite is essentially a preliminary to general "magick" work—but it is used within the *Religion of Witchcraft*, which is to say *Wicca*, as a prelude to the invocation or "drawing down" of "Gods and Goddesses" (deities).

The first four lines (repeated three times):

"Eko! Eko! Azarak!
Eko! Eko! Zomelak!
(Eko! Eko! Aradia![†]
Eko! Eko! Kernunnos!)"

A possible continuation from original sources:~

"Zod-ru-koz e Zod-ru-koo,
Zod-ru-goz e Goo-ru-moo!
Eko! Eko! Hoo! Hoo! Hoo!"

---

23 The "*Eko Eko*" lines were first published in in the 1921 issue of *Form* (an art periodical published by ceremonial magician and mystic, Austin Osman Spare); reprinted later in *The Occult Review* (April 1926). The words were originally provided (without any additional explanation) by Major General J.F.C. Fuller, a British officer, occultist, historian and apprentice of Aleister Crowley. *Eko! Eko! Azarak! Eko! Eko! Zomelak! Zod-ru-koz e Zod-ru-koo, Zod-ru-goz e Goo-ru-moo! Eko! Eko! Hoo' Hoo! Hoo!*

24 The remainder of the text may be found in the French play written by Jean Bodel in 1261 titled: *Le Miracle de Théophile* (The Miracle of Theophilus)—in which it is used by a Sorcerer to "invoke the devil": *Bagahi laca bachahé, Lamac cahi achabahé, Karrelyos. Lamac, lamec bachalyos, Cabahagi sabalyos, Baryolas. Lagozatha cabyolas, Samahac et famyolas, Harrahya.* Interestingly, another French play by Bodel (titled *Le Jeu de saint Nicolas*) also contains a supposed "invocation to the devil": *Palas aron ozinomas, Baske bano tudan donas, Geheamel cla orlay, Berec hé pantaras tay.*

† Additions in parenthesis appear in the *Book of Shadows* only.

∞ This portion does not appear in the original *Book of Shadows*.

Additional lines used from a French play:[*]

> "Bagahi laca bachahé,
> Lamac cahi achabahé, Karrelyos.
> Lamac, lamec bachalyos,
> Cabahagi sabalyos, Baryolas.
> Lagozatha cabyolas,
> Samahac et famyolas, Harrahya."

And finally, the Gardnerian additions:[‡]

> "Darksome night and shining moon,
> East, then South, then West, then Noon;
> Hearken to the Witches' Rune—
> Here we come to call ye forth!
>
> Earth and Water, Air and Fire,
> Wand and Pentacle and Sword,
> Work ye unto our desire,
> Hearken ye unto our word!
>
> Cords and Censer, Scourge and Knife,
> Powers of the Witch's Blade—
> Waken all ye into life,
> Come ye as the Charm is made!
>
> Queen of Heaven, Queen of Hell,
> Horned Hunter of the Night—
> Lend your Power to this Spell,
> And Work our Will by Magic Rite!
>
> By all the Power of Land and Sea,
> By all the Might of Moon and Sun—
> As we Will, so mote it be;
> Chant the Spell and be it done!"

THE GODDESS & THE GOD
(AN APPRENTICE PRIMER)

A "Religion of Witchcraft and Magic" was referred to as *Wicca* by Gerald Gardner and thereafter has represented a standard for variegated modern revivals of "neopaganism"—spiritual pathways and personal lifestyles that are intended to reflect "ye olde tyme religion," "the old ways," ...the *pagan ways*.

---

[*]   Used in the *Book of Shadows* and *Grimoire of Lady Sheba*.

[‡]   Written by Gerald Gardner and Doreen Valiente; when applied by the solitary *Witch*, the "*we*" and "*us*" can be changed to "*I*" and "*me*" where appropriate.

Of course, the concept of "religion" does not mean the same thing to all people—and it is the treatment of the "magical lifestyle" and "grimoire practices" of *Witchcraft* as a "religion," which separates *Wicca* from other types of occult and metaphysical pursuits.

By definition, when we refer to "religion" we are evoking the idea of "Divinity," which is to say an individual's personal identification with, or personification of, "Deity." And by this we mean that which is representative of a "Supreme Being" or "Supreme Beingness" and even "Infinity." Since such is so incredibly "awesome" that it would be difficult to actually behold or appropriately represent directly, the various principles of "Cosmic Law," the observed cycles of action in Nature and Life, *&tc.* were all treated as the very *"deity archetypes"* personified in the ancient religions being revived today.

In contrast to many other popular religions of the common era—denominations of *Christianity*, factions of *Buddhism* and even *Islamic* practices—the revival of *Wicca-Witchcraft* has set itself apart from the rest with a reintroduction of the "Goddess." Heavy emphasis on "superiority" of the Goddess is really only strictly observed in certain traditions—"Dianic Covens" *&tc.*—where participation is reserved primarily to females practitioners. Otherwise, the deep contrast of a public religion involving a "Goddess" is really only so boldly distinguished in our mainstream perspective when compared to its blatant absence in the last several thousand years.

Ancient pagan traditions did not place any greater religious emphasis on one or another of the genders. The oldest pantheons—such as those in Mesopotamia from 6,000 years ago—did not even emphasize a "union of opposites" so much as they did an "absence of opposites," with each aspect or property of the Cosmos equally represented by, what we would define as, a "God" *and* "Goddess." This means that rather than observing solely a "Moon Goddess" in contrast to a "Solar God," ancient Babylonians (and Sumerians) perceived (and cataloged) "masculine" and "feminine" representations of *each* within the original "pagan" religions.

Duality and polarity are simply necessary factors or conditions for manifestation to occur—for action and movement to occur. The "division" of this is emphasized more strongly in modern *Wicca* than in other forms of neopaganism—lending to its reputation of being primarily a "Goddess Tradition" or "Goddess Worship." Although this is not as blatantly dominant in ancient pagan traditions as many in the New Age suggest, the emphasis seen today is most likely due to a corrective pendulum swing of extremism or revolt to an age of "patriarchal-dominant" presentations of "religion" and Divinity.

"Traditional Witchcraft"—which is essentially *"Celtic Witchcraft"* mixed with *"Italian Witchcraft"*—often focuses on the "Horned Goddess" and "Horned

God," which is to say a "Crescent-crowned Lunar Goddess" and the "Antlered-headed God of the Wild." It is for this reason we see an emphasis on the Moon Goddess in the "Aradian Tradition" and why the Celtic-Druid deity Kernunnos (or Cernunnos) is so frequently invoked in *Wicca-Witchcraft* as the archetypal "Goddess and God of Witches."*

When it comes right down to it: aspects of *true* "religion" are seldom discussed in contemporary "New Age" literature or popular *"grimoires of witchcraft."* In fact, although treated within the context of "neopaganism" or "religion"—with emphasis on all various pantheons of deities drawn out of ancient mythologies—even the true and utmost highest considerations of "Divine" worship, as relayed in the deepest laden traditions of the most distant past, are often nonexistent in modern interpretations.

There are differences between actions taken for "religious prayer" versus "ritual spellcraft" and yet the goals and purposes are so similar: an individual is seeking to communicate an intention to something "greater than" this material existence, however that is perceived. A *Witch* believes that there is another realm overlapping, encompassing and yet intertwined with the Physical Universe; and "magical acts" are the mean of contacting or connecting with this "higher plane" and through it, having a greater effect on the events of the Physical Universe—tipping the scales of "quantum uncertainty" in their favor.

Most traditions will invoke specific archetypes or *Names* for those treated as one's own personal "patron deities." These are usually selected from a particular cultural paradigm or mythic pantheon that personally resonates with the practitioner. Alternatively, using rites as given (or derived) from the *Book of Shadows* employ a hybrid blend of Italian (*Strega*) and Celtic (*Druid*) lore for its "theology." Application of "religious dedication" to *magic* replaces any archaic ritual requirements, such as those found in grimoires, which may suggest threatening, exorcising or coercing dead spirits and demons to attain positive results.

When the Altar is appropriately oriented to the North, North-East or East: the *left side* is considered sacred to the *feminine*, the Moon, the Earth, the Waters and the Goddess; meanwhile the *right side* is treated as predominantly *masculine*, governing the Sky (or Airs), the Sun, Fire and the God.

Within a *Witch's Circle*, Divine forces—dualistic qualities of the Goddess and God—are represented and acknowledged during rituals. This may be as simple as having a *Candle* present on the *Altar* to symbolize each. You may wish to even obtain or fashion an appropriate *Image* or *Statue* to go with it.

---

* Another example lists "*Diana*" and "*Pan*" as predominant.

The following general invocations[‡] may be made before the *Images* or *Signs* while lighting the *Candles*.

A Witch's Call to the Goddess

Goddess of the Starry Skies;
Goddess of the Fertile Plain;
Goddess of the Ocean Sighs;
Goddess of the Gentle Rain.
Hear my calling to you this hour.
Open wide the Gate of Mystic Light.
Awaken me with your graceful Power.
Aid me in my Magical Rite.

A Witch's Call to the God

Great God of the Forest Deep;
Master of the Animals and Sun.
Here in a world lost to sleep,
Now that the day is done [just begun].
I call to you in the Ancient Way,
Here in this Circle round.
I desire my Will to be displayed,
I call you to send your Powers down.

EXAMPLE OF CASTING THE CIRCLE (GROUP LITURGY, VERSION 1998)[†]

The following ritual text is one example of "Casting the Circle" and this part of the rite does not include elements found in other parts of the *Handbook*; such as "Initiations into the Circle" or "Consecrations." As is common in a *Book of Shadows* or "secret grimoire," this script features only a dialogue formula, but not *what* to "visualize" or *how* to handle "energy" or any other ritual "actions"—as it is assumed that a *Witch* keeping written records of ceremonial verbiage, such as these, has been instructed in the basic magical applications elsewhere. Application of this "group liturgy" may be modified for solitary practitioners. [All four formulae are typically used.]

UNIVERSES FORMULA

Leader: "As Above..."

---

‡ The present editor was unable to locate the source of these.
† Revised for Merlyn Stone's "*1998 Book of Shadows*" (the original version of *The Witch's Handbook*) used by the "Elven Fellowship Circle of Magick" (EFCOM) in Denver, Colorado.

Respondents:	"...So Below."
Leader:	"As Within..."
Respondents:	"...So Without."
Leader:	"As the Universe..."
Respondents:	"...So the Soul."

MAGIC CIRCLE FORMULA

East/Leader:	"We consecrate this Circle of Power to *Menw* and *Awen*."[∞]
South:	"May they hear our call and bless us with their grace."[√]
West:	"May the Elder Gods—the Ancient and Shinning Ones—aid and protect us."
North:	"We stand at a threshold between worlds veiled in secrecy."[*]

WATCHTOWERS FORMULA

East:	"ORO IBAH AOZPI—Oh-roh; Ee-bah; Ah-oh-zod-pee[25]—In the names and letters of the Great Eastern Quadrangle, I invoke thee Spirits of the Watchtower of the East."[26]
South:	"OIP TEAA PDOKE—Oh-ee-peh; Teh-ah-ah; Peh-doh-key—In the names and letters of the Great Southern Quadrangle, I invoke thee Spirits of the Watchtower of the South."
West:	"MPH ARSL GAIOL—Em-peh-heh; Arr-ess-el; Gah-ee-oh-leh—In the names and letters of the Great Western Quadrangle, I invoke thee Spirits of the Watchtower of the West."
North:	"MOR DIAL HKTGA—Moh-arr; Dee-ah-leh; Heh-keh-teh-gah—In the names and letters of the Great Northern Quadrangle, I invoke thee Spirits of the Watchtower of the North."

∞ "*Menw*" and "*Awen*" are the Divine Names—or "God and Goddess" (respectively)—used in the original rites of the "Elven Fellowship Circle of Magick" (EFCOM).

√ In *Sorcerer's Handbook*, this reads: "...bless us with power."

* In *Sorcerer's Handbook*, this reads: "...in a veil of mystery."

25 The alternate version in the "*1998 Book of Shadows*" adds the name "*Shem-ham-phor-ash*" to the calls for each Watchtower.

26 This formula-type employs elements from the "Watchtower Ceremony" (used by the Golden Dawn, O.T.O., Aurum Solis and other magical orders) based on a combination of the Chaldean Tablets of Zoroaster and John Dee's Enochian Magic.

East:	"May the presence of the Four Watchtowers be among us within this Magic Circle."

GUARDIANS/MASTERS FORMULA[27]

South:	"Then let us now conjure up and call forth the presence of the Four Masters to stand as Guardians at the Watchtowers and protect this Magic Circle."‡
West:	"And may their powers come with the wisdom to use it."
North:	"From the Northern City of *Falias*, I summon *Master Morfessa*. Bring the *Stone of Fal* and stand as Guardian of the North."
Respondents:	"Hail to the Guardian of the Watchtower of the North."†
East:	"From the Eastern City of *Gorias*, I summon *Master Esras*. Bring the *Spear of Lugh* and stand as Guardian of the East."
Respondents:	"Hail to the Guardian of the Watchtower of the East."
South:	"From the Southern City of *Finias*, I summon *Master Uscias*. Bring the *Sword of Nuada* and stand as Guardian of the South."
Respondents:	"Hail to the Guardian of the Watchtower of the South."
West:	"From the Western City of *Murias*, I summon *Master Semias*. Bring the *Cauldron of Dagda* and stand as Guardian of the West."
Respondents:	"Hail to the Guardian of the Watchtower of the West."
North:	"May the powers of the Four Masters gather here among us."

RITUAL FINALE & CLOSING RITES

If we are to fully treat the subject of a "Magic Circle" or *Witch's Circle* in the traditional sense, then there are a few more points-of-fact to advise in, before

---

27 The alternate version in the "*1998 Book of Shadows*" includes an additional formula for calling the Dragon's Breath from the spirit of the four elemental dragons: "*Grail*" (Earth); "*Sarys*" (Air); "*Fafnyr*" (Fire) and "*Nalyon*" (Water).

‡ In *Sorcerer's Handbook*, this reads: "Let us now conjure the powers of the Masters."

† This formula-type evokes names and attributes specific to the "Elven-Druid" or "Celtic-Faerie" traditions that regard the "Tuatha d'Anu" (Tuatha de Dannan); see *Elvenomicon* by Joshua Free, also available in the anthology: *Merlyn's Complete Book of Druidism: A Master Course in Druidry for Modern Druids.*

closing out this notebook. For starters, there is the matter of "Breaking the Circle" once it is cast, whether that is for emergencies during the ritual or even at the end of a rite. But, in order to discuss this properly, some semantic (vocabulary) clarification is required.

In this *Handbook*, "opening rites" or "starting procedures" are indicative of what we have consistently referred to as "Casting the Circle"—in the same sense as someone might "cast" some sticks or stones on the ground to divine an omen, or the way in which an artist "casts" the form of their creation. In some other literary sources, this same step may also be referred to as "Closing the Circle," which is to say "sealing" it shut as a "closed-system."

Separate from procedures used at the start of a ceremony, there will also be mention of "Opening the Circle." In this instance, we mean breaking the "hermetic seal" that separates the two conceptions of a "universe." In most spellbooks and grimoires, a *Witch* is instructed to *never* break the Circle—and the danger of this is imposed rather heavily in archaic work, such as the verbatim methodology of even the *Key of Solomon* and *Goetia*-type manuals that now seem wholly inappropriate to the Wise.

However, given that a Circle is "cast" as a mental image—or personal energetic creation that is set to "remain solid" for the duration of a ritual—it is highly appropriate that a *Witch* should knowingly "dissolve" or "extinguish" their creation until it is needed again. There are no concerns here over "lost" energy; and the individuals that would speak of such are not really *Aware* of the true properties of energy and its ability to be generated, at Will, by the *Self* as Spirit—the actual "I" or "I-AM" that is *using* a body to conduct the rituals.

If the Circle must be "opened" temporarily during a rite, it is customary to use a Ritual Blade (*Dagger* or *Athame*) and "cut" (acknowledge/postulate) an energetic "opening" (gateway) in the circle (traditionally in the East), which is then "resealed" before continuing the ceremony.

There is also the matter of the Code of Honor, seemingly long-forgotten in today's society, which is fully executed in traditional ceremonial and ritual magic. This means that if energies are summoned or presences are individually called to the Circle, then these should likewise be cordially thanked and dismissed—regardless of whatever *has* or *has not* taken place during the "working" portion of a ritual.[*] According to the original *Sorcerer's Handbook of Merlyn Stone:*—

---

[*] The "working" portion of the ritual includes all work other from chapters/notebooks of *The Witch's Handbook*, conducted in between "Casting the Circle" and "Dissolving the Circle" as covered within the present chapter/notebook.

At the end of a rite, it is customary to work the preliminaries backwards: beginning with the thanking and dismissal of the God and Goddess (*Deities*); followed by the Elementals (*Guardians* and *Watchtowers*); and finally, the Extinguishing of the Circle. For the Elementals: go to the North and dismiss them at each direction in turn, working counter-clockwise to the West and so forth. Ask them to 'return to return promptly to their place of dwelling but to come to the Magic Circle when again called'.

The final necessary part of the ritual is extinguishing and grounding any energies used to "Cast the Circle." This could be accomplished in multiple ways. Some practitioners move counter-clockwise around the boundary *retracting* the band or ring of the Circle. Alternatively, a *Witch* could simply ground the energies with a single postulate—and if ritual actions are desired: stand in the center of the Circle with arms upraised, visualizing energies of the circle being sent down, deeper and deeper in to the ground, down to the fiery center of the Earth to be recycled and reformed.

EXAMPLE OF DISSOLVING THE CIRCLE (GROUP LITURGY, VERSION 1998)[†]

MAGIC CIRCLE FORMULA

East/Leader:	"As we have come to this Magic Circle in love and friendship..."
South:	"...So do we leave the same way."
West:	"May we spread the peace and love that we have known here..."
North:	"...And radiate it outwardly to the world."

GUARDIANS/MASTERS FORMULA

East:	"So now we ask the Elemental Guardians called here to return to their duties in Nature."
South:	"We thank you for attendance, watching over us and protecting this Magic Circle."
West:	"Lords and Ladies of the Elves, Sylphs, and all Creatures of Faerie..."

---

† Revised for Merlyn Stone's "*1998 Book of Shadows*" (the original version of *The Witch's Handbook*) used by the "Elven Fellowship Circle of Magick" (EFCOM) in Denver, Colorado.

North: "...Our thanks and blessing go with you for sharing this time with us."

WATCHTOWERS FORMULA

East: "Guardians of the Watchtowers of the East, Lords and Ladies of the Air Element, thank you for attending our rites. As you depart to your pleasant realms, we bid you a cordial hail and farewell."

Respondents: "Hail and farewell."

South: "Guardians of the Watchtowers of the South, Lords and Ladies of the Fire Element, thank you for attending our rites. As you depart to your pleasant realms, we bid you a cordial hail and farewell."

Respondents: "Hail and farewell."

West: "Guardians of the Watchtowers of the West, Lords and Ladies of the Water Element, thank you for attending our rites. As you depart to your pleasant realms, we bid you a cordial hail and farewell."

Respondents: "Hail and farewell."

North: "Guardians of the Watchtowers of the North, Lords and Ladies of the Earth Element, thank you for attending our rites. As you depart to your pleasant realms, we bid you a cordial hail and farewell."

Respondents: "Hail and farewell."

UNIVERSES FORMULA

East: "The magick work is done."

South: "The mystic web has been woven of mortal mind, heart and soul."

West: "Helpful to they who choose to follow the ways of the mighty spirits of our ancestors."

North: "Baneful to those that choose to oppose the Elder Gods— the Ancient and Shinning Ones."

FINALE

Leader: "The Circle is open but never broken. So Mote it be."

Respondents: "So Mote it be."

Leader: "The Rite is ended. Go in peace, love and unity. Blessed be."

Respondents: "Blessed be All."

SABBATS & GROVE FESTIVALS
(Merlyn Stone, Spring-Summer '98)

A *Witch* will discover a wide diversity of flavors in the last hundred years of fundamental ritual texts concerning "Seasonal Festivals" or *Sabbats*—more so than any other aspect of *Witchcraft Tradition.* This is primarily due to a minimum of "ceremonial rites" or "*coven* specifics" in the Gardnerian *Book of Shadows*;[28] no mention at all in the *Book of Aradia* or other popularly excerpted "classical" *grimoires*; and since the *Sabbats* are religious elements of *Witchcraft* —rather than ritual aspects of "practical magick"—only miniscule amounts of suggestion are put forth by esteemed "Magical Orders" (such as the Golden Dawn, &tc.) and even that usually only pertains to the "equinoxes."

It *is* true that there *are* ancient traditions and cultural folk-practices to support what is given in today's "New Age" presentations of "*Sabbats*" for *Wicca* and *neopaganism*—such as the "*Greater Sabbats*" (*Samhain, Imbolc, Beltane, Lughnassadh*)—which are drawn directly from Irish-Celtic customs and Druidic lore. This lends to the notion that practicing contemporary "*Wicca*" is essentially "*Celtic Witchcraft*." The two "equinoxes" and two "solstices" constitute "*Lesser Sabbats*" each year. Revival observance of "equinoxes" in England began primarily with a reincorporation of modern Druidism by John Toland in 1717. But, we can be quite certain that the ancients were well aware of these cosmic events based on their astronomical arrangement of megalithic sites.

THE STANDARD WHEEL OF THE YEAR

There is a dual significance to pagan observations of the "Wheel of the Year"—a standardized "eightfold model" of the annual cycle—which are: *agricultural* and *astronomical*; elsewhere one might consider the division as *agricultural* (pertaining to *Land/Earth*) and *mythographic* (*mythological*) or else *Solar*. Although a *Witch* may certainly examine the histories and folk traditions of their own preferred culture to find correlative customary rites for seasonal festivals, those that are observed in the "standard model" of modern *Neopaganism* are especially "Celtic"—if not "Druidic"—in origin.

Use of the word "*Sabbat*" seems to have originated in Western Europe during the 13th Century as a term to indicate a "seasonal meeting of *witches.*" Modern *Wiccan* traditions continue to refer to their festival observations of the

---

28 "The *Book of Shadows* is surprisingly inadequate in one aspect: the Eight Sabbats. For some reason, the rituals which the Book lays down for the Eight Sabbats are very sketchy indeed—nothing like as full and satisfying as the rest."—Janet and Stewart Farrar, *Eight Sabbats for Witches.*

"Wheel of the Year" as "*Sabbats.*" The word does not necessarily appear in *all* "New Age" or "neopagan" revivals—such as traditions oriented more heavily toward "Celtic" and "Druidic" overtones, which refer to the same days as "Grove Festivals"[29] or "Fire Festivals."[30] And of course, the term has an obvious relationship with the word "*Sabbath,*" meaning[‡] "a time of worship."[*]

When Gerald Gardner set down the original *Book of Shadows* (with assistance from Aleister Crowley and possibly Ross Nichols) as a foundation for modern *Wicca*: four traditional "Celtic Fire Festivals" were combined with the "solstices" and "equinoxes" to present *Eight Sabbats* for the "Wheel." Coupling these with observance of *thirteen* annual Full Moon "*Esbats*" provided this newer "standardized" 20th Century *Witchcraft religion* with "*21 Days of Power*" each year.

Ancient "Celtic" seasonal festivals—and similar ones observed throughout most indigenous cultures—marked key points in the year indicating *agricultural* significance (and similarly the breeding patterns of animals), which were relevant to farming communities. This was of particular importance to personal survival for these predominantly rural-country self-sufficient "pagan" lifestyles. With annual patterns in Nature on Earth being both easily observable and carrying practical significance, it would be easy to trace and incorporate historic "folk traditions" for each of the "*Greater Sabbats*"—Samhain, *Imbolc*, *Beltane* and *Lughnassadh*—with more numerous examples than space is allotted for in this notebook.

Rather than observing growth cycles and animal behavior, monitoring "solstices" and "equinoxes" as "*sabbats*" requires potentially more detailed calculations, knowledge of astronomical data and even access to "Solar Temples" and/or observatories (ruins of which are found scattered all throughout Western Europe). This supports what many have suggested regarding *Witchcraft* and folk traditions: that observations of the "summer solstice" and "equinoxes" were likely imported from a Celestial-oriented "solar cult" (such as the Druids), rather than an "agricultural" one.

---

29 The phrase "Grove Festival" appears in *Book of Pagan Rituals* by Herman Slater and in the works of Douglas Monroe.

30 The term "Fire Festival" was popularized in *The Golden Bough* by Sir James Frazer.

‡ Also from the Greek *sabatu*, meaning "to rest." As a result, "magick work" is not typically conducted on a Sabbat.

* This paragraph appears in *The Great Magickal Arcanum*.

THE CELTIC FIRE FESTIVALS[†]

The Celtic year was not at first regulated by the solstices and equinoxes, but by some method connected with agriculture or with the seasons. Later, the year was a lunar one, and there is some evidence of attempts at synchronizing solar and lunar time. But time was mainly measured by the moon, while in all calculations night preceded day. Thus "*oidhche Samhain*" was the night preceding *Samhain* (November 1), not the following night.[∞] Usage survives in our "*sennight*" and "fortnight."

In early times the year had two, possibly three divisions, marking periods in pastoral or agricultural life, but it was afterward divided into four periods, while the year began with the winter division, opening at *Samhain*. A twofold, subdivided into a fourfold division is found in Irish texts, and may be tabulated as follows:

Geimredh (winter half)

1st Quarter, *Geimredh*, beginning with the festival of *Samhain*, November 1st.

2nd Quarter, *Earrach*, beginning February 1st. (Sometimes called *Oimelc*).

Samhradh (summer half)

3rd Quarter, *Samradh*, beginning with the festival of *Beltane*, May 1st. (Also called *Cet-samain*, 1st day of *Samonos*; Welsh *Cyntefyn*)

4th Quarter, *Foghamhar*, beginning with the festival of *Lughnassadh*, August 1st (Sometimes called *Brontroghain*).

None of the four fire festivals is connected with the times of equinox and solstice. This points to the fact that the original agricultural Celtic year was independent of these. But Midsummer day was also observed not only by the Celts, but by most European folk, the ritual resembling that of Beltane. The festivals of Beltane and Midsummer may have arisen independently, and entered into competition with each other. Or Beltane may have been an early pastoral festival marking the beginning of summer when the herds went out

---

[†] Selected excerpts from J.A. MacCulloch's *Religion of the Ancient Celts (1911)*; reprinted in the anthology *Book of Pheryllt: A Complete Druid Source Book*. It is included here, as per the original notebooks, "to provide greater legitimacy to the 'pagan wheel' than is found in the *Book of Shadows* or the brands of ceremonial magic that inspired its practicality."

[∞] Many of these older traditions observe a "day's end" at sundown; meaning the period of a day is marked by one sundown until the following sundown—thus Samhain celebrations begin on the evening of October 31.

to pasture, and Midsummer a more purely agricultural or astronomical festival.

The Celtic festivals being primarily connected with agricultural and pastoral life, we find in their ritual survivals traces not only of a religious but of a magical view of things, of acts designed to assist the powers of life and growth.

THE EIGHT SABBATS FOR WITCHES[†]

NOVEMBER EVE (OCT 31 – NOV 1)

—Traditional Names: Samhain/Samhuinn [*sow'en*] ("Summer's End"), Festival of Ancestors and Spirits, Calen Gaeof, Samana/Samonios, Feast/Day of the Dead, Night of the Wild Hunt, All Saint's Day, All Soul's Day, All Hallows Eve/Halloween.

—Astrological: Sun is 15° of Scorpio.

—Summary/Symbols: Often treated as the "Pagan New Year"; a time to honor "dead names" (our ancestors); circles of skulls; dressing up in costumes; carving gourds/pumpkins into candlelit heads; bobbing for apples.

—Elements: Earth, Northwest, Midnight, Winter.

—Celtic Deities: Gwyn ap Nudd, Samhan, Kerridwen, Morrigan.

—Essence & Incense: Apples, applewood, belladonna (nightshade), catnip, datura, hemp, mugwort, pomegranate, pumpkin/gourds, wormwood.

—Altar Candles: 2 black, 1 white.

—Sabbat Incantation: *"Dread Lord of the Shadows, God of Life and Giver of Life. Yet is the knowledge of thee, the knowledge of Death. Open wide, I pray thee, the Gates through which all must pass. Let our dear ones who have gone before, return this night to make merry with us. And when our time comes, as it must, O thou the Comforter, the Consoler, the Giver of Peace and Rest, we will enter thy realms gladly and unafraid; For we know that when rested and refreshed among our dear ones, we will be reborn again by thy grace, and the grace of the Great Mother. Let it be in the same place and the same time as our beloved ones. And may we meet and know and remember, and love them again. Descend, we pray thee, in thy servant and priest (name)."*[*]

WINTER SOLSTICE (DEC 21 – DEC 22)

—Traditional Names: Yule, Midwinter, Alban Arthuann ("Light of Arthur"), Jul, Saturnalia, Finn's Day, Rebirth of the Sun King, Vigil Festival, Christmas.

---

† Collected from the original Merlyn Stone notebooks. Additional suggestions for ceremonial application may be found in *The Druid's Handbook* and *Elvenomicon* by Joshua Free—both of which are contained in the anthology, *Merlyn's Complete Book of Druidism: A Master Course in Druidry for Modern Druids*.

* Gerald Gardner, *Book of Shadows (1949)*.

—Astrological: Sun enters 0° of Capricorn.

—Summary/Symbols: Rebirth of the Sun God; the Yule-log; kissing under mistletoe, "holly and ivy"; decorating evergreen trees, bells, sunrise service.

—Elements: Earth, North, Midnight, Dark to Light.

—Celtic Deities: Kernunnos, Mabon.

—Essence & Incense: Bay/laurel, cedar, cinnamon, ginger, holly, ivy, juniper, mint, mistletoe, myrrh, nutmeg, pine, rosemary, sandalwood, valerian.

—Altar Candles: 1 green, 1 red, 1 white.

—Sabbat Incantation: " *Queen of the Moon, Queen of the Sun, Queen of the Heavens, Queen of the Stars, Queen of the Waters, Queen of the Earth, bring to us the Child of Promise! It is the Great Mother who giveth birth to Him; It is the Lord of Life who is born again; darkness and tears are set aside when the Sun shall come up early! Golden Sun of hill and mountain, illumine the land, illumine the world, illumine the seas, illumine the rivers, sorrows be laid down, joy to the world! Blessed be the Great Goddess, without beginning, without ending, everlasting to eternity. IO EVO HE![31] Blessed be! IO EVO HE! Blessed be! IO EVO HE! Blessed be!"[*]*

FEBRURY EVE (JAN 31 – FEB 1)

—Traditional Names: Imbolc/Imbolg, Brighid's Day, Calen Geaef, Oimelc, Candlemas, Festival of Lights, Lupercalia, St. Blaise's Day, St. Valentine's Day, Snowdrop Festival, Groundhog's Day.

—Astrological: Sun is 15° of Aquarius.

—Summary/Symbols: Anticipation/conception of spring; hearth lighting; candle festival; corn-dolls.

—Elements: Air, Northeast, Dawn, Spring.

—Essence & Incense: Clover, dill, mace, rosemary, rowan, sea weed, snowdrop, white flower, willow.

—Celtic Deities: D'Anu, Brighid, Epona.

—Altar Candles: 2 white, 1 green.

—Sabbat Incantation: *"Dread Lord of Death and Resurrection, Of Life and the Giver of Life. (Lord within ourselves, whose name is Mystery of Mysteries, encourage our hearts, let thy Light crystallize itself in out blood),[32] fulfilling us with resurrection; For there is no part of us that is not of the Gods. Descend, we pray thee, upon thy servant and priest (name)."[*]*

---

31 Concerning the Calls: "Many of these have been forgotten by us here; but we know they used cries of *IAU, HAU,* which seems much like the cry of the ancients: *EVO* or *EAVOE.* Much depends on the pronunciation if this be so. Other calls are: *IEHOUA* and *EHEIE.* Also: *HO HO HO ISE ISE ISE.* 'Tout tout, through and about' and 'rentum tormentum' are probably mispronounced attempts at a forgotten formula..."— *Gardnerian Book of Shadows.*

* Gerald Gardner and Doreen Valiente, *Book of Shadows (1957).*

32 From Aleister Crowley's "*Gnostic Mass.*"

* Gerald Gardner, *Book of Shadows (1949).*

SPRING EQUINOX (MAR 21 – MAR 22)

—Traditional Names: Ostara, Akiti/Akitu (Mardukite Babylonian), Festival of Life, Alban Eiler, Vernal Equinox, Sheelah's Day, Bacchanalia, St. Patrick's Day, Easter/Eoster (Celtic festival of Ishtar-Inanna).

—Astrological: Sun enters 0° of Aries.

—Summary/Symbols: Rebirth of Earth Life; egg hunts and coloring; bird-watching; pastel colors.

—Elements: Air, East, Dawn, Light.

—Celtic Deities: Taliesen, Epona, Kerridwen.

—Essence & Incense: Broom, crocus, daffodil, fragrant flowers, Irish moss, jasmine, lavender, maple, narcissus, olive, woodruff.

—Altar Candles: 2 green, 1 white.

—Sabbat Incantation: *"We kindle fire this day. In the presence of the Holy Ones, without malice, without jealousy, without envy, without fear of aught beneath the Sun but the High Gods. Thee we invoke, O Light of Life: be thou a bright flame before us; be thou a shining start above us; be thou a smooth path beneath us. Kindle thou within our hearts, a flame of love for our neighbors, to our foes, to our friends, to our kindred all, to all (Life) on this broad Earth. O merciful son of Kerridwen, from the lowliest thing that lives, to the Name which is highest of all."*[*]

MAY EVE (APR 30 – MAY 1)

—Traditional Names: Beltane/Bhealltainn, Calen Mai ("First Light of May"), Festival of Flowers and Fire, Tana's Day, Walpurgisnacht (Walpurgis Night), Rudemas, May Day.

—Astrological: Sun is 15° of Taurus.

—Summary/Symbols: The Fires of Bel (bonfires); flower-gathering; Maypole (World Tree).

—Elements: Fire, Southeast, Noon, Summer.

—Celtic Deities: Bel/Belinos, Flora, Blodduwedd.

—Essence & Incense: Apple blossoms, birch, hawthorn, heather, honeysuckle, lilac, May blossoms, primrose, rosemary.

—Altar Candles: 2 white, 1 red.

—Sabbat Incantation: *"Oh, do not tell the (Priests) of our Art, for they would call it sin. But we shall be in the woods all night, a'conjuring Summer in. And we bring you good news by word of mouth, for women, cattle and corn: the Sun is coming up from the South, by Oak and Ash and Thorn. I invoke thee and call upon thee, O Mighty Mother of us all, Bringer of all Fruitfulness. By seed and root, by stem and bud, by leaf and flower and fruit, by Life and Love, do we invoke thee, to descend upon the body of thy servant and priestess here."*[*]

---

[*] Gerald Gardner and Doreen Valiente, *Book of Shadows (1957).*

[*] Gerald Gardner, *Book of Shadows (1949),* with borrowings from Rudyard Kipling's poetry.

SUMMER SOLSTICE (JUN 21 – JUN 22)

—Traditional Names: Litha, Alban Heruin or Alban Hefin, Feill-Sheathain, Midsummer, Festival of Oaks and Stones, St. John's Day.

—Astrological: Sun enters 0° of Cancer.

—Summary/Symbols: Height of the Sun, Needfires (bonfires), Faerie-calling, herb-gathering.

—Elements: Fire, South, Noon, Light to Dark.

—Celtic Deities: Arianrhod, Oghma/Ogmios, Huon.

—Essence & Incense: Copal, daisy, fern, frankincense, lavender, lemon, oak and mistletoe, red rose, saffron, St. John's Wort, sandalwood, vervain, yarrow.

—Altar Candles: 1 red, 1 white, 1 yellow.

—Sabbat Incantation: *"Great One of Heaven, Power of the Sun, we invoke thee in thine ancient names: Michael, Balin, Arthur, Lugh, Herne; come again, as of old, in this thy land. Lift up thy shining spear of light to protect us. Put to flight the powers of darkness. Give us fair woodlands and green fields, blossoming orchards and ripening corn. Bring us to stand upon thy hill of vision and show us the path to the lovely realms of the Gods. (The Spear to the Cauldron, the Lance to the Grail, Spirit to Flesh, Man to Woman, Sun to Earth.)*∞ *Dance ye about the Cauldron of Kerridwen the Goddess, and be ye blessed with the touch of this consecrated water; even as the Sun, the Lord of Life, arises in his strength in the sign of the Waters of Life."**

AUGUST EVE (JUL 31 – AUG 1)

—Traditional Names: Lughnassadh/Lughnasa ("Marriage of Lugh"), Grain Festival, Festival of Bread, Calen Awst ("First Light of August"), First Harvest, Lammas.

—Astrological: Sun is 15° of Leo.

—Summary/Symbols: "Wedding Festival," grain harvest begins, "Lammas Towers" (bonfires competitions), spear-tossing (athletic competitions).

—Elements: Water, Southwest, Sunset, Autumn.

—Celtic Deities: Lugh/Lug/Llew, D'Anu.

—Essence & Incense: Blackberries, corn/grain sheaf, furze, ginseng, heather, marigold, oats, rice, rye, straw, strawberry, sunflower.

—Altar Candles: 1 red, 1 yellow, 1 green.

—Sabbat Incantation:[†] *"O Mighty Mother of us all, Bringer of all Fruitfulness, give us fruits and grains, flocks and herds, and children to the tribe, that we may be mighty. By (the rose of thy love),*[33] *do thou descend upon the body of thy servant and*

∞ "Incantation of the Great Rite for Midsummer."

* Gerald Gardner and Doreen Valiente, *Book of Shadows (1957)*.

† Also known as "Drawing Down the Moon for Lughnassadh."

33 "Thy rosy love" (Gardner); "rose of thy love" (Valiente).

*priestess here."**

AUTUMN EQUINOX (SEPT 21 – SEPT 22)

—Traditional Names: Mabon, Alban Elved, Harvest Equinox, Cornucopia, Festival of the Vine, Dionysus, Rosh Hashanah, Thanksgiving Day.

—Astrological: Sun enters 0° of Libra.

—Summary/Symbols: Produce harvest, the corn harvest, stalk-bundling, harvest feast, thanksgiving.

—Elements: Water, West, Dusk, Dark.

—Celtic Deities: Mabon, Bran, Branwen.

—Essence & Incense: Acorns, Balm of Giliad, grape, hops, iris, mugwort, myrrh, pine-cone, sage, squash/melon, vines.

—Altar Candles: 1 red, 1 green, 1 black.[34]

—Sabbat Incantation: *"Farewell, O Sun, ever-returning Light, the Hidden God, who ever yet remains. He now departs to the Land of Youth through the Gates of Death to dwell enthroned, the judge of Gods and men, the horned leader of the hosts of air. Yet, as he stands unseen without the Circle, so dwelleth he within the sacred seed; the seed of new-reaped grain, the seed of flesh; Hidden in Earth, the marvelous seed of the stars. In him is Life, and Life is the Light of man, that which was never born and never dies. Therefore the (Wise Ones)‡ weep not, but rejoice."**

* Gerald Gardner, *Book of Shadows (1949)*.
34 *The Druid's Handbook* lists "1 red, 1 white, 1 black."
‡ "Wise Ones" reads as "*Wicca*" in the original version.
* Gerald Gardner and Doreen Valiente, *Book of Shadows (1957)*.

THE ARTS OF SPELLCRAFT
(Merlyn Stone, Spring-Summer '98)

"Spells" are magically imbued intentions "cast" by a *Witch* to cause a change in the manner that energy manifests in the Physical Universe. Actual practice of the *Art* is far different than its portrayal in popular medias—but *real magic* can be very effective in tipping the scales of quantum uncertainty in the favor of the *Witch*. Operation of "spellcraft" is also referred to as "low magick," "sympathetic magic," or "ritual magic," depending on the source—and methods are far different than "prayer" or "meditation."

Purpose and function of the "Arts of Spellcraft" are precisely to apply dramatic representations, symbols and imagery in ritual to direct the personal energies of *desire* or *Will*. Though this says nothing regarding the nature of the inclinations and compulsions fueling such—and a *Witch* would be wise to execute the utmost care in treating any worldly matters, such as "wealth," "love," "fertility," &tc. But these things are freely given to that most cunning *Witch* that knows how to manifest them.

A *Witch* will practice the "Religion of *Witchcraft*" (*Wicca*) and likewise operate in service to one or another patron deities, often reviving various related cultural practices, and supplementing with some flavor of religious honor and regimen of *prayer*. This does not replace the function of "magick." Those who flocked to the *Craft* during the Middle Ages were Seekers of "Self-Help" and no longer satisfied with a dependency on religious institutions to serve as intermediaries for "divine intervention."

The *Witch* is not dependent on "Divine intervention," for we have been charged by the Creator Gods to carry all of the faculties necessary for success along our Pathway right within us. The teachings of the Ancients reveal that the individual is the only one that can be truly responsible for their life—and part of that responsibility includes an understanding of the orchestration of forces at work in this Game of Life, and just exactly what part you have to play in it. That is yours to decide. The Gods are notorious for "helping those who help themselves" and grow weary at the ceaseless wails raised up by the ignorant.

Traditionally "spellcraft" is defined simply as generating any transformation or manifestation to occur, in accordance with Will and Intention, in the Physical Universe. In the original *Sorcerer's Handbook*, it is taught that even the act of tying your shoes because you want them tied, is an example of Spellcraft. It doesn't matter what means are used: setting and meeting goals for change is a unique quality of the Human Condition that demonstrates reasoning on a higher level than what we are taught concerning the "nature of man as an animal." Yet, even animals have often demonstrated greater reason and sense than the average Human, when operating on automatic reactive mechanisms alone.

The idea that you can affect the future by acting in the present is an amazing point of Awareness that puts an individual at "Cause" in the universe and in the Game. This is no small realization, because it has allowed the Human Condition to elevate itself to the utmost on this planet—even if seldom tempered with the wisdom to properly carry out such a responsibility and stewardship of Earth. But the truth is: if your intention is to see something through, it doesn't really matter if you accomplish this by some form of esoteric telepathy or simply applying some old fashioned elbow grease, the result is the same (and this is even one of the tenets of "Freemasonry").

When practiced within the concentration of a Magic Circle, "spells" are energetically charged by focused and directed attentions of the *Witch.* Basic steps of consecrating "sacred space" (or the "Magic Circle") are employed; and such ritual forms of "spellcraft" include the magical and elemental objects and representations (discussed prior in *The Witch's Handbook*). The working area can be as simple or elaborate as desired; but be certain that additional tools are included in the rite only if they actually help you to connect with the desired currents of energy and focus on the appropriate target.

Virtually every tradition in the "New Age" demonstrates ritualism differently, and this also applies to teaching the "Arts of Spellcraft." Starting in the 1980's, it seems to have become a growing trend to publish a personal "spellbook," "Book of Shadows" or "magical recipe book." A modern *Witch* will find no shortage of supplemental and complimentary materials on the market in this regard. However, by following the general guidelines of "magic" and "ritual" and developing a comfortable familiarity with the practice of ceremonious rites within the *Witchcraft* tradition, a *Witch* can also just as effectively develop their own "spells."

It is actually far more empowering to develop your own "rituals" and "spells." One of the reasons is that many "spellbooks" will suggest the incorporation of specific "tools," "herbs," "objects" and "words" that may be quite effective for the individual that wrote them down and presumably understood the significance behind the selection of each, but this may not be the case for a newcomer that happens upon the book. Such individuals tend to follow to closely to "instruction" and apply very little of their own "intention" to the operations—and the results speak for themselves.

We are fast approaching the 21st Century and there is an entire esoteric library of background information and applicable lore now available to any

Witch that seeks a greater understanding of the "hows" and "whys" of the occult and practical mysticism. But, even without such rigorous studies, the practice of "magick" has been demonstrated effective when instructed properly—as was discovered to be the case with our earlier version [in *The Sorcerer's Handbook*]. In this present edition, we have simply placed an even greater emphasis and focus on the legacy of *Wicca* and the *Witchcraft* tradition than the earlier publication.

Basic skills and ritual techniques of the former *Sorcerer's Handbook* all still apply to practice of "spellcraft" within the *Witchcraft* tradition. Quite simply: "magick is magick." Whatever works in one application does so because it follows the basic principles governing all workable magic, regardless of what flavor or patina it may be given.

It was quite customary for *Witches* and *Wizards* to keep "Magical Diaries" and notebooks to record the details of their "rites" in order to figure out these "governing workable principles" for themselves. Too often a modern practitioner will simply surround themselves with piles of notebooks and grimoires from *others* without ever actually holding any *personal* reality on the nature of the true magic alluded to—such as can only be worked out and experienced by an individual for and as *Self.*

THE SEVENFOLD SPELLCRAFT FORMULA

Basic prerequisites for "spellcraft" include a practiced ability to be grounded, focused, use breathing techniques, operate rituals within a Magic Circle, apply visualization and handle energy. [In some *covens* and training groups, the application of "spellcraft" is not introduced to an *Initiate* until after a proper mastery of these former techniques is demonstrated.]

Ritual "spells" tend to also include objects and graphic representations of the intention (and/or target)—pictures, symbols, statuary, candles, herbs, stones, talismans, personal items, hair, nail-clippings, &tc.

All other considerations being made, the "Sevenfold Spellcraft Formula"* is given as follows:

1. Casting a Circle (conjuring the "Magic Circle")
2. Calling the Corners (Elementals, Guardians, &tc.)
3. Raising Energy (personal mixed with summoned)
4. Visualization (seeing the change as taken place)

---

* Developed for the "*1998 Book of Shadows*" and "*Sorcerer's Handbook*" used by the "Elven Fellowship Circle of Magick" (1997-2000).

5. Releasing Energy (send toward the "target")
6. Dismissal of Spirits (closing rites and formalities)
7. Extinguishing the Circle (neutralizing residual)

MAGIC AND THE MOON

A "*lunar cycle*" is an observed period of time that it requires for the Moon to complete an orbit around the Earth. In fact, the word "month" would seem to be semantically connected to "moon" and its cycles. These cycles can be measured as both "sidereal" or "synodic" periods. A *sidereal* month is approximately 27.3 days—marking the time it takes the Moon to physically complete an orbit. A *synodic* month also takes into consideration the rotation/ spin and orbit motions of the Earth, which is measured out to be approximately 29.5 days. The average between these two is what the *Witch* observes as a "*Lunar Month*" of 28 days.

There are lunar-oriented calendars dating back to the ancient Sumerians and Babylonias, which consist of 29 and 30-day months. Although common *Witchcraft* "spellbooks" emphasize the "*Full Moon*" as an energetic apex of the monthly cycle, other various "magical lore" exists ascribing properties or correspondences also to the "*New Moon*," "*waning phase*," "*waxing phase*," the "*Gibbous*" (or three-quarter moon), the "*Quarter*" (or half-visible moon) and the "*Crescent.*"

A "*New Moon*" is the energetic "low-tide" threshold of the monthly or lunar cycle, when the Moon is perceived to be invisible or darkened, at least from the perspective of the Earth planet. The "*New Moon*" is a peak point that ends the "*waning*" phase. The *ol' wives' tales* of Europe reveal that a "*New Moon*" is the time of month when a *Witch's* power is "weakest" (as opposed to the "*Full Moon*"), because it has spent two weeks "*waning*." After a "*New Moon*," the *Witch's* power "*waxes*" ("grows") until the next "*Full Moon.*"

Aside from properties attributed to "Dark Power" (which may be associated with the "*New Moon*"), there are relatively very few "magickal practices" (other than meditation, divination and passive exercises) performed within the original *Wiccan* tradition at the "*New Moon*"—although there are some *covens* that do observe a secondary "*Esbat*"[‡] observance on this eve and others that practice "banishing rites" (when one wishes to rid themselves of something).

And as the name suggests, the "*New Moon*" begins the month or lunar cycle—written as "day zero" on most lunar calendars. This means when a "spellbook" or "grimoire" recommends a rite be performed, for example, on the "sixth night of the moon," it refers to the sixth night after the "*New Moon.*"

‡ "Secondary" to the "*Full Moon*" as the primary monthly *Esbat*.

For "magical timing" purposes, *Witches* and *Wizards* have assigned additional titles for two other significant "*New Moons*" for their work. The "*sidhe moon*"[†] or "*faerie moon*" is named after the "elemental folk" that are acknowledged as more active during dark moons—whereas the Human Condition seems to find greater energetic charge during bright moons. In other *Wiccan* lore, these "*Dark Moons*" or "*Black Moons*" refer to the second time the "*New Moon*" phenomenon occurs in a single calender month.[*] It is treated as having all the properties and significance of a "*New Moon*" multiplied one-hundred times.

At the height of the "*waxing*" phase, the Moon is completely visible from the Earth as is considered "*Full.*" Traditionally, the "*Full Moon*" is the time of the month when a *Witch's* power soars. In fact, grimoires and spellbooks suggest most of their ritual performances for this eve—particularly if the "rite" is intended to *invoke* or draw something *toward* (such as in "attractive" magic for "wealth" and "love," &tc).

For purposes of "magical timing," *Witches* and *Wizards* have classified two other types of "*Full Moon*" in their lore. For example, a "*Blood Moon*" occurs when the Moon visibly appears "blood red." This typically occurs during the autumn season, or under the proper conditions of a "lunar eclipse" (which only take place during a "*Full Moon*"). The second type is called a "*Blue Moon,*" which unlike the former, is not named for its color. The "*Blue Moon*" is the second occurrence of the "*Full Moon*" phenomenon within a single "solar month," magnifying the significance of the "*Full Moon*" one-hundred fold.

When examining modern "moon lore," the lunar calendar used in the Western World is also referred to as the "Farmer's Moons"—hinting at the original agricultural significance of these observations. Each of the "*Full Moons*" are named, beginning with the full moon of December or that falls closest to the Winter Solstice.

> December (Winter Solstice): "Oak Moon"
> January: "Wolf Moon"
> February (Imbolc): "Storm Moon"
> March (Spring Equinox): "Hare Moon"
> April: "Seed Moon"
> May (Beltane): "Dryad Moon"
> June (Summer Solstice): "Mead Moon"
> July: "Herb Moon"
> August (Lughnassadh): "Barley Moon"

[†] "Sidhe" pronounced "*shee,*" referring to the Celtic Faerie Folk.

[*] Given that there are thirteen lunar cycles in a solar year, this is typical to occur once annually.

September (Autumn Equinox): "Harvest Moon"
October (Samhain): "Hunter's Moon"
November: "Snow Moon"

DRAWING DOWN THE MOON
(& THE FIVEFOLD KISS)

Aradian and *Gardnerian* traditions place supreme emphasis on the "High Priestess" as leader of a *coven*. In many respects, this custom is traced back to ancient pagan temples, when a "High Priestess" would *invoke* the "Goddess" and allow her own body to become a living vessel of the "Divine." In modern *Wicca*, this is referred to as "Drawing Down The Moon."[‡] The practice is commonly linked with another popular *coven* tradition known as the "Fivefold Kiss" or "Fivefold Blessing."

According to original drafts of the *Book of Shadows*, the High Priestess assumes the "Goddess Position" (arms crossed) while standing in front of the altar.[35] The High Priest,[∞] kneeling in front of her, then draws a "pentacle" on her body with the "phallus-headed wand" and speaks:

"I invoke and beseech Thee, O Mighty Mother of all Life and Fertility. By Seed and Root; by Stem and Bud; by Leaf and Flower and Fruit; by Life and Love, do I invoke Thee to descend into the body of thy servant and High Priestess [name]."

The "Fivefold Kiss" or "Fivefold Blessing" is then applied. Each member of the *coven*, in turn, comes before the High Priestess (now consecrated as a representative of the "Moon Goddess") and applies the following actions and incantations:

Kissing the feet: "Blessed be thy feet, that have carried thee in these ways."
Kissing the knees: "Blessed be thy knees, that shall kneel at the sacred altar."

---

‡ These practices are given in the original 1949 edition of *Book of Shadows* developed by Gerald Gardner with Aleister Crowley.
35 The High Priestess speaks (*from the north*): "As we breathe deeply in and out, it is not just air we take in; it is the soft silver light of the Moon, symbol of our Lady. With every pore of our bodies, we breathe in an out. And so does this Circle become a fitting place four our Lady's presence." (*raising arms*) "We are the Children of the Moon. We are born of shining light. When the Moon shoots forth a ray, we see within it the Goddess and ourselves."—*Outer Court Book of Shadows* (Ed Fitch).
∞ Referred to as a "Magus" in the original *Book of Shadows*.

Kissing the womb: "Blessed be thy womb, without which we would not be."

Kissing the breasts: "Blessed be thy breasts, formed in beauty and strength."

Kissing the lips: "Blessed be thy lips, which shall speak the sacred names."

ASTROLOGY AND THE MOON

Much as the Sun appears to be "backed" by the Celestial Sphere of "Zodiac Constellations" during the course of a year, so too does the Moon appear to travel through the "Twelve Houses" of astrology (from the perspective of Earth) in the period of a single month. This also means that the Moon only occupies each "sign" of the zodiac for a little more than two days.

The practice of treating a "lunar zodiac" with significance may be traced back to Astral Wizards of ancient Babylon—those that marked down the shifting of the starry skies with great precision. Thereafter, the Persian Magi, Arabs and the Orient all borrowed from this lore—each one applying their own mystical attributes and omens for consideration. For purposes of *Witchcraft* and keeping with its tradition of "following the moon," the significances of the "lunar zodiac" may be tracked and even incorporated into "practical magic" and "spellcraft."

Moon in Aries—optimism, outgoingness, opinions, impulsiveness, new beginnings, alchemy and fire magick.

Moon in Taurus—artistic, determined, overcautious, steadfast, habitat, solidity, physical/senses, new beginnings (with longevity in mind).

Moon in Gemini—versatility, wit, superficiality, manipulation, fluctuation/inconsistency, shortcuts, recreation, new beginnings (requiring external assistance).

Moon in Cancer—sympathy, protection, possessiveness, emotional, growth, family, relationships.

Moon in Leo—creativity, fun-loving, self-indulgent, overbearing, emotional healing, attraction, outer presentations, Hermetic magick.

Moon in Virgo—meticulousness, responsibility, stress, orthodox/standard, conformity, detailing, leadership, structure/hierarchies, schedules (cycles).

Moon in Libra—creativity, diplomacy, indecisiveness, frivolousness, introspection, meditation, enchantment, glamour.

Moon in Scorpio—ambition, emotion, secretiveness, dominance, increased awareness, karmic agreements, psychic/psionic, interconnectivity (entanglement).

Moon in Sagittarius—adventurous, open-mindedness, restlessness, irresponsibility, confidence, expansion, imagination, travel and growth.

Moon in Capricorn—responsibility, patience, materialistic, pessimism, foundations, regulations, structure (physical), tradition.

Moon in Aquarius—idealism, tolerance, tactlessness, fixedness, healing (physical), breaking habits, purification, personal transformation.

Moon in Pisces—sensitivity, vagueness, discontent, secrets/hidden, dreams, intuition, prayer, meditation, spiritual development.

MAGIC AND THE PLANETS

Ancient astronomical observers were also mystics and philosophers; they were the mathematicians and scientists of an age long past. These, soon to be known as, astrologers successfully followed the motions of the "visible planets" of the ancient world, which by their consideration, included the Moon and Sun. The others being: Mercury, Venus, Mars, Jupiter and Saturn—which are all apparent in the night sky, even without benefit of additional technological advancements and telescopes.

Each of the seven ancient planets correlates to not only seven notes of audible music and seven shades of a visible spectrum, but also the seven divisions observed between Earth and Infinity at ancient temples in Mesopotamia—and particularly Babylon—where the seven planets signified "Gates" that one would pass on the "Ladder of Ascension" (or "Ladder of Lights") as the Spirit makes its journey back to Source. Of course, this is not a guaranteed direction of travel; Ascension is not a reality for those that do not rise up above the trivialities of mundane existence and its gravity.

For the purpose of spellcraft, *Witches* observe that each day of the week is ruled by a planet—and when considering what some call "planetary hours," the first hour of daylight corresponds strongly to that ruling planet's influence. Many grimoires of ceremonial magic classify their pantheons or hierarchies of spirits based on their governing planets. These correlations are used by magical practitioners to determine the "most favorable time" to make contact with a particular spirit or current of energy. *Witches* commonly incorporate these correspondences to their "spellcraft."

Sunday (the Sun)—leadership, sacredness, solar observations, success magick, fire element.

Monday (the Moon)—faerie magick, psychic/psionic development, water element.

Tuesday (Mars)—courage, protection magick, military endeavors, victory/overcoming.

Wednesday (Mercury)—communication, divination, intellect, mental development, air element.

Thursday (Jupiter)—animals, business ventures, celebration, expansion, wealth acquisition.

Friday (Venus)—arts, beauty, enchantments, fertility, friendship, growth, love, earth element.

Saturday (Saturn)—banishing, binding, cursing, hidden influences, initiation, secrets.

THE COLOR OF MAGIC

Color plays a significant role in nearly all aspects of the Human experience, to which, mysticism and metaphysics are no exception. Everything from the ritual garments (robes, cloaks, &tc.) to the altar dressings; from the candle selection to the decoration of elemental tools—all objects employed in spellcraft and ritual magic (or even encountered in everyday life) carry a certain "tone" or "quality" that registers from their color. This becomes particularly important when a *Witch* is focusing their attentions on the magical work.

When the Forces of Nature are encountered in a *Witch's* energy practices, the various frequencies are likened to the spectrum of visible of light—likewise relayed as "Rays of Light." One sees this aspect come into play with various lore—such as the "*chakras*" and "*auras*"—which is often incorporated into modern *Witchcraft* traditions. But to be semantically clear and scientifically accurate: it is virtually impossible to consider facets of *color* symbolism without dealing with the subject of Light—for Light is the very medium that allows us to perceive the existence of color.

It is not difficult to demonstrate the simple truth that colors carry different energetic qualities, and in the "magical traditions," they are given a certain universal significance based on the way they can make us "feel"—or more preferably, how they assist us to focus on a specific type of energy. The most basic demonstration of this appears in the colors selected for "elemental candles" that a *Witch* sets out to distinguish the "Quarters." These facets of perception and understanding all combine to provide the magical experience for a *Witch* during ritualized spellcraft and other operations of magic.

White—akasha, blessings, consciousness, the entire visual electromagnetic spectrum, the full moon, the higher self, ice and snow, protection, purity, spiritual strength, truth and white magic.

Red—blood, chaos, courage, fire element, love magic, mars, passion, personal strength, red magic, reproductive energies, sexuality, vigor.

Orange (red+yellow)—attraction, business matters, charisma, courage, joy, legal matters, orange magic, personal magnetism, pleasure, pride, self-confidence, success, the sun.

Yellow—academics, air element, alertness, awareness, communication, confidence, logic, the mind, optimism, philosophy, spiritual development, the sun, yellow magic.

Green (yellow+blue)—balance, beauty, compassion, earth element, ecological (animals, plants, trees), envy, fertility magic, fortune, green magic, growth magic, healing magic, jealousy, physical appearance (glamour), renewal, venus.

Blue—awareness, blue magic, creativity, emotions, enchantment, glamour, illusion, imagination, jupiter, loneliness, peace, spiritual healing, spiritual protection, tranquility, water element.

Indigo (blue+red)—mercury, personal magnetism, psychic ability, reversal magic, spirits, storm magic, third eye (brow chakra), weather influence.

Violet (red+blue)—astral work, connectedness, healing magic, personal power, saturn, spiritual power, royalty, willpower and wisdom.

Brown—animals (protection and healing), business (prosperity), discrimination, earth element, energy clots (in auras), the home (protection), temperance, wealth magic, woodland spirits.

Gray—the astral, awakening, cancellation (magic), initiation, intuition, neutrality, the Otherworld, stalemate, threshold portals (dimensions/planes).

Silver—the astral, awareness, clarity, clearing, creativity, faerie folk, femininity, fertility magic (pregnancy), journeys, lunar cycles, mirrors, the moon, the Otherworld, wisdom.

Pink (red+white)—chastity, compassion, clearing, love magic, meditation, moderation, modesty, morality, purity, true love, truthfulness, virtue.

Black—black magic, clearing (purification), curses, death, hidden influences, invisibility (magic), loss, necromancy (spirits), resentment, the unknown.

CANDLE MAGIC & SPELLCRAFT*

"Beeswax" candles have a long-standing tradition of use in *Witchcraft*. Their application to rituals and spellcraft is based on color—which correlates to the

---

* Appearing here verbatim from the *"Sorcerer's Handbook."*

representative energy that a *Witch* is to focus on during the magical working. Prior to and during the operation—as with all tools of magic—the candles are *charged* with an intention or to be a sympathetic representation of a particular object or "target."

Candles—or some representation of Light—are employed in virtually all magical operations; but as a standalone nonspecific system, "candle magick" is also an effective form of spellcraft, placing particular emphasis on use of candles as an energetic catalyst and focal tool. Of course, incense, herbs and other tools may also be employed. Whatever each candle represents may be vocalized during the working. No other specific "jargon" or "incantation" need be memorized to cast spells: "candle magick" requires imagination and creativity to be effective.

Just as a *Witch* is best able to focus and concentrate their energies best by creating a microcosm of the universe when creating sacred space—or casting a circle—so too does "candle magick" operate best when performed at an altar. This all represents a "chessboard" for the Game of Reality to play out on. By manipulating the symbols on a representative playing field, the desired change is manifested first in consciousness and then projected outward like a beacon into the world-at-large.

If drawing something *to* you, use a candle to represent yourself and one (or more) for energies you want to attract. In the practice of spellcraft, candles are "symbols" representing "solids." For several successive nights—usually three or seven—the *Witch* is to perform the working, each time moving the candle (that represents the external energy) closer to yours. The opposite motion is employed for reversals and banishing spells.

The candle representing *you* should always be placed in the center of the working area or altar—since the *Witch* plays this Game out from the centralized perspective of *Self*. It remains fixed and unmoved in the center always—the other candles and energies are arranged and move around *it*. Words and names may also be written on the candles (and some *Witches* believe it is more powerful to do this in Runes, Ogham characters or some other obscure alphabet). Intentions and affirmations are made whenever lighting a candle and also before one is moved (if applicable).

The following are basic examples of applying "candle magick" to spellcraft. A *Witch* is encouraged to develop their own ritual texts—with incantations or affirmations—as needed.

> AFFAIRS—to break up a love affair: use two candles to represent the people involved; a black candle for the breakup; a brown for the dying love; and a light green to incite jealousy and discord.

BAD HABITS—to overcome a bad habit: place a black candle in the middle representing the habit itself; surround it with white candles symbolizing defeat of it.

DREAMS—to invoke prophetic dreams: surround your candle with a blue candle for peace and tranquility (required for restful sleep); use an orange to represent what you want to dream about; and a white for truth and sincerity of vision.

FEAR—to overcome emotions of fear: surround your candle with several orange candles representing personal strength and self-confidence; and a white for purity of thought.

JEALOUSY—to arouse jealousy in another: surround their candle with a few brown candles for hesitation and uncertainty; use light green candles to represent discord, illness, and of course, jealousy.

MEDITATION—to aid any acts of prayer or meditation: surround your candle with light blue candles for peace and tranquility.

POWER—to increase persuasion over people: take both your candle and the candle representing the subject and place them on the altar. Each day, move their candle closer to yours, symbolizing the magnetism. Also, surround your candle with purple for power and an orange candle demonstrating the attractive pull itself.

SPELLJAMMING—to remove a spell, hex or curse: surround your candle with red for strength and vigor; and white for purity and sincerity. Put a black and brown candle on either side. Black symbolizes the cursed spell and brown represents the uncertainty of its caster. Move the black candle towards the brown (and away from yours) each day of the working to deflect their spell.

HERBCRAFT—BY LEAF, STEM & BUD*

The practice of "herbalism" or "herbcraft" is an inherent part of both the ritual magic and folk customs found in *Witchcraft*. Use of flowers, leaves, plants, roots and tree-parts, as found in Nature (or reared in a personal garden) appears throughout ceremonial texts and rites of spellcraft—all based on a combination of physical traits and metaphysical properties or correspondences. This secret knowledge of Nature is studied by *Witches* and *Wizards*, preserving the lore once known exclusively to the Priests and Priestesses and eventually the *Gypsy-Witch* and rural-pagan apothecaries through the Middle Ages.

Today, pharmaceutical companies profit from synthesizing the same lore. All common medicines now used are synthesized compounds based on the prop-

---

* Section reprinted in "*The Great Magickal Arcanum.*"

erties of the same natural herbs and plants that have been in use for thousands of years. As opposed to commercializing the planet, *Witches* are known for executing greater "care" in their treatment of Nature when removing any parts of it; being careful to "use" but not "abuse" Nature—because obviously all herbal work requires harvesting or removing part of a plant or tree.

Respect and reverence is observed whenever a *Witch* takes anything from Nature. A knife used strictly for cutting herbs should be ritually consecrated for that purpose. Traditionally, a small white-handled (or bone-handled) *Dagger-knife* or *Sickle* is used—and sometimes called a *Boline*. Many *Witches* prefer to tend to (and harvest) herbs from their own gardens—and so it is not uncommon for a *Witch* to maintain a personal herb garden (or "*Witch's Garden*"); in fact, this is just one popular aspect of the type of "natural sustainable-living" observed even today among many pagans, rural or otherwise.

When necessary, most metaphysical and "New Age" retail outlets stock a supply of various herbs that are useful for "magical operations" and spellcraft. For any therapeutic or medicinal purposes, a *Witch* would want to acquire a fresher supply, such as may be stocked by herb-specific natural-type groceries and health stores. When treating living plants, care should be taken not to needlessly tear or damage the plant, particularly if only a part of it is removed and it is left to continue growing. The blade cut should be a single sure upward motion, removed silently, after first asking *permission* and uttering the statement (with intention): "*With this strike, may you grow stronger*"—and a "*Thank you*" afterward.

It should be noted here that practices and lore of "magical herbalism" differs from the type of "alchemical-apothecary" knowledge that is used to treat ailments. There is an obvious difference between the presence of an herb scattered about the altar, or rubbed on a candle, or sewn up in a square of colored fabric, or cast into a metal pot filled with alcohol to burn, or even as incense—versus the preparation of tinctures and extracts intended for personal consumption. For our present purposes within the scope of this book, we are most concerned with "magical herbalism."

The above being stated: a *Witch* could also boil potent tinctures or steep herbs in water (as a tea); or bottle herbs in alcohol;[‡] etc. etc. Most natural food outlets actually sell enhanced extracts in dropper bottles (typically in the vitamin section). These are excellent for experimenting in personal health and self-treatment because of their levels of potency. Yet sometimes, extreme potency is the opposite of what is sought.

In homeopathic practices, extracts are then reduced to a point where the molecular structure of the herb used is all but dissolved, leaving on a trace

---

‡   Never boil alcohol.

resonance. A practitioner will want to seek out additional information from multiple sources before proceeding in this area.

Within the *Witchcraft* tradition, practices of "magical herbalism" appear most often when applying *Incense*—or even anointing *Oils* and personal *Perfumes*—to rites and spellcraft. Additionally, various folklore concerning "charms" suggests a long-standing tradition of carrying various flowers, leaves and herb-filled sachet-pouches as *Amulets* to ward away particular types of misfortune and illness. For example, in the 1960's, the "lucky" four-leafed *Clover* (or the larger Irish *Shamrock*) was frequently carried by those wishing to "ward away" military service (or in this case, avoid the "draft").

Lunar Work (the Moon)—frankincense, sandalwood.

Love and Romance—cinnamon, rose, patchouli, sandalwood.

Peace and Serenity—bay (laurel), sandalwood.

Wealth and Business—cedar, cloves, nutmeg, poppy seed.

Studying—cinnamon, rosemary.

Success and Charisma—benzoin, cinnamon, dragon's blood.

Protection—frankincense, rosemary, sandalwood.

Examining a few other examples: *Nettles* is carried to protect against evil and overcome fear; a wreath of *Mistletoe* is present to ease pain during childbirth; *Vervain* is carried to escape one's enemies; *Acorns* are worn to remain youthful and vigorous; fishermen carried *Hawthorn* sprigs to ensure their success at sea; the list goes on and on... A close examination will reveal that each tradition—and even each regional culture—maintains some type of lore concerning use of local vegetation.

All-Spice—prosperity, relaxation.

Apple—love, happiness, relaxation.

Camphor—psychic power, clearing.

Cinnamon—protection, sexual vigor.

Eucalyptus—healing, purification.

Jasmine—love, sleep, relaxation.

Musk—courage, sexual prowess.

Myrrh—protection, purification, spelljamming.

Patchouli—peace of mind, sexual confidence.

Rose—love, peace, harmony, unity.

Sandalwood—healing, protection.

Some popular incense mixtures are known as "temple blends"—lore of which is retained in the classical grimoires of "*Medieval magic.*" For example: the

"Sacred Book of Magic of Abramelin the Mage" the formula calls for *Cedar* (or *Aloe*) balm mixed with *gum* and *storax*. The *"Key of Solomon"* suggests blending many sweet smelling *gums, Aloe, Nutmeg* and *Musk*. Another common multipurpose "temple blend" is made from equal parts *Frankincense, Myrrh* and *Sandalwood*—in fact, these essences appear quite frequently in operations of "ceremonial magic."

A *Witch* can also make their own small "blocks" or "cones" of *Incense* from a dough—even a thin stick could have dough worked around it. The charcoal-free recipe formula call for (6 parts) powdered cedar, pine or sandalwood; (2 parts) powdered frankincense, myrrh or benzoin; (1 part) ground orris root; (6 drops) of fragrant oil; and (4 parts) some other powdered incense blend. This is all mixed together with tragacanth gum-glue and worked like a baker's dough.[36]

Amulet-Bags—or *"Sachets"*—are made from pouches; or the *Witch* may fashion an appropriate bag using a four-inch square swatch of cloth (of an appropriate color); herbs and small items are placed in the center of the square and then the corners are brought together and tied up as a pouch. Alternatively, you could weave a drawstring around the outside of a cloth circle, add the items, and then pull it closed and cinch it up.

According to popular lore: three, seven or nine herbs (or items) are added to a single *Amulet-Bag* before it is *consecrated* and *charged* with a ritualized spell. [To achieve the desired effect, it may then be carried, slept on (under the pillow) or given away; whichever seems most appropriate.]

PROTECTION (white)—ash, basil, bay, dill, fennel, mistletoe, mugwort, periwinkle, rosemary, rowan, saint john's wort, trefoil, vervain.

HEALING (blue)—cinnamon, eucalyptus, garlic, lavender, myrrh, rosemary, saffron, sage, sandalwood.

LOVE (red)—apple, coriander, dragon's blood, jasmine, lavender, mandrake, marjoram, rose, rosemary, vervain, yarrow.

WEALTH/PROSPERITY (green)—basil, benzoin, cinnamon, clove, dill, nutmeg, patchouli, sage.

---

36 Scott Cunningham recommends the addition of *Saltpeter* (*potassium nitrate*) to the proportion of 10% of the total mixture (prior to the incorporation of the gum glue), which acts as a burn accelerator and keeps the finished product from repeatedly extinguishing once ignited.

RITES OF INITIATION
(Merlyn Stone, Spring '98)

Matters of *Initiation* widely separate various *Wiccan* traditions representing the modern *Witchcraft* movement. Significance behind *Initiation* is skewered in many portrayals—often reduced to exercises of egotism and/or authoritative control. Certain tenets set down in Gerald Gardner's original *Book of Shadows* (and other traditional beliefs concerning "How a *Witch* should operate") often restricted access to the *Wiccan* legacy exclusively to "*Covens*" and "*Groves*" throughout its development during the 20th Century. Of course, today, things are functionally different for newcomers and seasoned practitioners alike.

When Gardner originally set down standards for modern *Wicca*, the practice of *Witchcraft* was still very much practiced in complete secrecy.* By its own definitions for *Initiation*: only a *Witch* could *Initiate* another *Witch*. And what's more, by the original classification of *coven*-structure, only a female (Priestess) could initiate a male (Priest) and only a male (Priest) could initiate a female (Priestess), except in the case of a parent and child. Treatment of gender in this respect is obviously not present in "Dianic" traditions (which are exclusively female) and no longer appears to be a "typical" practice for "*New Age Wicca*."‡

Certainly, throughout history, there are many times when the existence of *Witchcraft* and other magical traditions is kept secret. In fact, under penalty of death, it was often necessary to do so. While membership of a *Coven* or *Grove* (or other "closed circles") is always to remain a privileged information, the basic knowledge of *Witchcraft* was also confined to personal apprenticeships and *Initiations* where a tradition could be passed on directly. Of course, until repeals of "Anti-witchcraft" laws—and even afterward—such a relationship required an outstanding measure of trust. Yet these days, widespread publishing of virtually *all* known materials has changed the game considerably.

INITIATION & THE WICCAN PATH

Many traditionalist still adhere to guidelines suggested in Gardner's *Book of Shadows*—but this standard is not directly applicable to solitary practitioners without modification; and we have seen a tremendous rise in "quiet solitaries" and even those *Witches* that do converse with others, but remain

---

*   Anti-witchcraft laws are repealed in England in 1951.

‡   This is not a typical practice within the occult. Modern *Wicca* places a greater emphasis on distinguishing gender duality and its energetic reunion than most other "magical traditions."

unattached to a specific *Coven*. Changing laws, mass publication and increased public acceptance has also paved the way for more and more solo-newcomers to form their own *Covens* and *Groves*. Yet, when starting upon (or even rededicating one's attentions) to the *Wiccan Path*, whether alone or in a group, the fundamental applications of *Dedication* and *Initiation* remain to be handled.

Although all ritual applications produce their own quality of psychological effect on a practitioner, the practice of an *Initiation* is unique in being both a "magical ceremony" *and* "rite of passage."[†] This differs greatly from, for example, a "*spell*"—that is typically treated as "magick"—and from a "*Sabbat*" or "handfasting" (wedding)—considered primarily as a "rite of passage." A true *Initiation* demonstrates elements of both.

However, to be semantically clear of the distinction: a *Dedication* is a personal intentional act and "rite of passage," whereby an individual makes a firm decision to enter upon the *Wiccan Path*. This is a personal decision conducted on Self-determination alone; there are no other qualifiers or permissions required for this to occur. An individual can *Dedicate* themselves to the pursuit of a particular tradition on their own accord—or to the pursuit of a particular path presented by a certain *Coven*, *Grove* or organization. This is often treated as the "first step" towards "*Initiation*."

Initiation differs from a *Dedication* in that it begins or "initiates" a *specific* cycle or period of work. In a *Coven* or group, the "rites of passage" are also intended to increase a close-knit relationship between membership of a similar knowledge base or degree/level of understanding. A structured methodology of *Initiation* is not unique only to *Witchcraft*; it may be found at the foundations of many other mystical orders and secret societies—from the "Freemasons" to the "Hermetic Order of the Golden Dawn."

Initiations represent a formal admittance into the group dynamic (or a certain "degree" or "level" of the group) when treated within a *Coven* or *Grove*. Such is intended to place attention or emphasis on the energetic harmony and security that follows with a sense of belonging and acceptance felt when participating in a group. The nature of the secrecy inherent in a *Coven*, and the freedom it provides the *Witch* in having a safe and open forum to communicate within, greatly resembles the qualities of a true "Socratic Society" referred to in the "*Pantheisticon*" of John Toland.[∞]

[†]   The term "Rite of Passage" is used in neopaganism to denote ceremonies observing a distinct "passage of time." Annually, this includes the eight seasonal "*Sabbats*" as the cycle-of-action reflected in Nature; for an individual during their lifetime, the traditional cycle-of-action is: birth/naming; coming-of-age; dedication; initiation; ordination; handfasting; birthing/"wiccaning"; and funerary.

[∞]   An annotated edition of John Toland's "*Pantheisticon*" (edited by Joshua Free) is available from the Systemology Society. It has since been reprinted in the Master

For longstanding organizations, there is also the matter of "Laying of Hands"—where an individual has had Power "passed" to them directly from a source; and they, in turn, dispense this further to others with physical contact. This manner of "anointing" may include ceremonial observance and oils, &tc., but it can just as effective be performed by placing the open palm on top of someone's head and "willing" a transference by "intention."‡

"Rites of Initiation" appear in Gerald Gardner's *Book of Shadows* for "Three Degrees" of traditional *Witchcraft*, but most *Covens* and *Groves* choose to write their own unique versions—and most will not readily publish or release their full "Three Degrees of Initiation" to the "outer court" (meaning also what is readily available in bookstores) in order to retain an air of mystery over performance of the rites themselves—and also what each degree entails. This is a fundamental attribute of a graded "Mystery School" or "Initiatory Tradition."

"Rites of Initiation" are only participated in by those members that have already attained the degree that the initiate is being installed to. In some *Witchcraft* traditions, an initiate must study and practice within the degree they are installed to for "a year and a day" (366 days).[37] This would mean that at minimum, to receive formal "Ordination" as a *Priestess* or *Priest*, a *Witch* must work with a coven for a little over three years (1098 days).

"Ordained" *Priests* and *Priestesses* and other Elders compose an "Inner Circle" or "Inner Court"* that is responsible for continuing success and survival of the *Coven*. These individuals are also charged with the task of determining a gradient criteria for the Three Degree qualifications, the installation of novitiates to those degrees of the "Outer Court" and dispensing (teaching) the material. [Really, there are so many details to "covencraft" alone—enough to dedicate an entire book to—but we have covered most of the necessary critical ground within the greater scope of *The Witch's Handbook*.]

THE POWER OF INITIATION‡

Since the inception of the Ancient Mystery School—stretching back on Earth's timeline into prehistory—every esoteric tradition, spiritual system,

---

    Edition of "*Merlyn's Complete Book of Druidism*" and in the Mardukite Master Course "*Instructor's Manual*" (and in "*The Complete Mardukite Master Course*").

‡ Or "prayer" by some semantic classifications.

37 "Except in unusual cases, at least three of the *Witches* [from the "Inner Court"] must both privately and to the coven have vouched for the candidate... at lest three full moons must have passed between [levels] of initiation."—Ed Fitch, *A Grimoire of Shadows*.

* Possibly even to include "Third Degree" initiates.

‡ Parts of this section reprinted in "*Crystal Clear*" by Joshua Free.

religious sect, mystical order and secret society has maintained one unique facet of "Self-Transformation" that has always proven quite effective when properly understood and executed: *Initiation.*

For many individuals, the concept of *Initiation* is reduced to antics of college fraternities (and sororities), which employ facets and ideals of *Initiation* to "imprint" the sense of "brotherhood" (or "sisterhood") and "fellowship" on their members. It is true that there is a "power" present when these formal group indoctrinations take place—but there is a deeper reason that they are effective, even if much of the original purpose and symbolism has since dissolved into obscurity.

When we examine *"Duncan's Monitor of Freemasonry"* and *"The Complete System of Golden Dawn Magic"*—or even the Gardnerian *"Book of Shadows,"* it is clear that "Rites of Initiation" are among the most colorful and widely published demonstrations of esoteric ceremony. They shine brightly in contrast to other more abstract philosophies and any underlying work that actually constitutes what a particular "degree" represents.

We can glance back into history; examining ancient Greek and Egyptian philosophical schools—now alluded to as Hermetic priesthoods and societies —not to mention the blatantly obvious demonstration of *"seven graded (tiered) initiation"* rituals observed in Mardukite Babylon; and everywhere else we find colorful depictions of "Rites of Initiation" prevalent in one or another form. For example: in ancient Europe, the Celtic Druids would lead initiates into caves—or blindfolded through elaborate labyrinths—to further demonstrate the "Journey of Self" successively reaching to higher and higher points on its Ascension.

The true purpose of *Initiation* is to "initiate" or "start" a new sequence or cycle-of-action. Mystical orders and secret societies maintain their own methods and terminology to *initiate* members; which is also why members are referred to as *"Initiates."* Each point marked by an *Initiation* is both the "end of" and "start of" a cycle, "degree" or "level"—which denotes that a changed state changed state or "transformation" has definitively occurred. If such a "shift" is not obvious to the *Witch*, then either the previous degree was not completed (or administered) properly, or the symbolism of the *Initiation* is not effectively relevant (or within the realm of present understanding and realizations).

Regardless of what type and flavor is evoked for an *Initiation*, the fundamental meaning behind such "Rites of Passage" remains the same: the death and reformation of the artificial; the shedding of old skin; and the rehabilitation of a clearer and greater, more widely encompassing, realization of *Self*—one step closer to its truest and highest state, sense of existence, or point-of-view. If the cycles of work and their dramatic representations in ceremony cannot accomplish this, the mode of play being taken in this Game is not truly effective as a "mysticism" or an "applied spiritual philosophy."

A true and effective "Rite of Initiation" requires more than a sequence of obscure actions and fancy words; it requires more than merely advancement to some new "title" or "rank" within a *coven* or social institution; requires far more than merely an ornately decorated setting, regalia and a lavish Temple. In fact, a truly effective "Rite of Initiation" requires none of these things mentioned. The most successfully employed "Rites of Initiation" must simply evoke effective symbolism and "presence" of the most important and powerful archetype of Self-transformation: death of the artificial self—the artificial personality.

THE PATH OF SELF-INITIATION[‡]

Originally, a practical revival of the *Witchcraft* tradition heavily depended on the *Coven*-unit and even its ability to network with other *Covens*. But regardless of whether or nor you formally decide to join (or develop) a "*Coven*," "*Circle*" or "*Grove*" of the *Wicca-Witchcraft* methodology—or by whatever name you choose to call such a close-knit "magical group"—a proper "Self-Dedication Rite" is really among the first true ritual operations performed by a modern *Witch.* This is a personal "solitary" occasion that is not dependent on any group—and in recent times, it has frequently substituted group-involvement altogether for those "flying solo."

Since the original customary traditions of *Wicca* all involved being "brought into the Craft" or "brought into the Circle" by a preexisting *Witch*, there is no emphasis on "Self-Dedication" in mid-20th Century *Gardnerian Wicca*. Within that same framework, the idea of "Self-Initiation" is unheard of. This attitude became increasingly more relaxed in the 1970's, when other variations (highly influenced by Gardner's *Book of Shadows*) began to increase in membership—such as *Alexandrian Wicca* (propagated by Alex Sanders).

During the same decade, many also began publishing their *ye olde* "family traditions" and allegedly "hereditary" *Books of Shadows*—all of which have been determined to be remnants of Gardner's *Book of Shadows* and/or other elements of the "Magical Revival" taking place in the late 19th and early 20th Century.

This all being said: when it comes to *Wicca*, there are no texts for "Self-Initiation Rites" from antiquity—however, for the past several decades, and

‡ Parts of this section appear in "*The Complete Elvenomicon*" by Joshua Free; reprinted in "*Merlyn's Complete Book of Druidism.*"

within other schools and paths, the idea of "Self-Dedication" and "Self-Initi-ation" is taken more seriously. Quite simply: independent practitioners have a greater access to resources—such as *this book*—than they did at the incep-tion of modern Wicca. Therefore, the appearance of such material in contemporary "New Age" literature is a relatively recent addition.

To provide at least one example for our present purposes, the following "Self-Dedication Ceremony" is included for use by the "*Elven Fellowship Circle of Ma-gick*" for official incorporation into the "*1998 Book of Shadows.*" The text is originally intended for this unique brand of "Celtic Faerie Tradition x Druid Witchcraft," but the language may be amended and adapted for specific ap-plications elsewhere. A variation of this rite appears in the original "*Elven-Faerie Grimoire.*" It may be performed without "elemental tools" and/or as a sentiment of solidification after these are made and consecrated.

Focused meditation and "Self-Dedication Rites" performed in Nature may aid in bridging the relationship with the "natural," "spiritual"—or otherwise "metaphysical"—side of Reality. All magical prowess and ability is accumu-lated over time as a result of the good health and consistent growth of this relationship.

Communication in this relationship assists to break down the artificial barri-ers of fragmented separation between the *Self* and the *Universe.* What is considered "magical authority" or "occult power" is really derived from the ability to operate as *Self* in perfect clarity.[*]

For the "Rite of Self-Dedication," *cast* a *Witch's Circle* in the manner you have been instructed previously—even if you have only envisioned doing so in your mind as you read *The Witch's Handbook* (because "imagination" is a form of magic itself, when the energy is properly directed). Have an "elemental candle" placed at each direction (if possible) before energetically tracing the boundary of the Magic Circle by hand (or by *Wand*).

Once the area is consecrated as "sacred space," go to the center of the Magic Circle—you do not necessarily need an *Altar* for this rite—and stand (or kneel), facing north, saying:

> "In my mortal form I am known as [*your given name*], but today [*tonight*] I come to you in my true[∞] form with the name [*chosen magical name*]. Spirits of the Universe, I approach you not as [*former name*] but as the Witch[†] [*new name*]."

---

[*] A concept referred to as "*Self-Honesty*" within the applied spiritual philosophies of "*Mardukite Systemology.*"

[∞] Originally given as "*Elven-Ffayrie.*"

[†] Originally given as "*Elf-Child*"; or "*Ffayrie-Child*" for females; or "*Elf-Friend*" for

Take a *Bowl of Salt* and remove a pinch, placing it on your tongue. Get the sense of the Earth elemental energy flowing through the body, then say:

"I am a Child of Earth; I am a Child of the Stars. I have studied the Way in preparation, but now I seek the Spirits of Nature to be my teacher— my instructor in the true mystic sciences of the Cosmos. O Great Spirits of the Universe, hidden in your fold likes the question and answer of Creation and Life, which is one and the same. We are One—and I am one with the entire Universe, seeking to share a communication with All."

Stand and move to the north and light the green "elemental candle," saying:

"Spirits of the Enchanted Forest, of plants and rocks and trees, awaken and know me as [*magical name*]. I come to this Magic Circle with peace within, in perfect love and perfect trust, and seek your aid in learning your mysteries. I vow this day [*night*] to ever uphold thy secrets, to ever walk the path of wisdom, and to ever share the illumination of enlightenment. Hear me, for I am a follower of the Wiccan Ways."√

Trace a symbol, "seal" or personal "sigil" representative of the Earth Element that you will use regularly in your rites to incite energetic activity *of* the Earth Element in the north. Traditionally examples include elemental "pentagrams" or other "signs of portal."[38] Envision this "Sign of Earth" as green in color, then speak:

"By this sign shall we know each other."

Move to the east and light the yellow "elemental candle," saying:

"Spirits of the Enchanted Breeze, of winds and sky and Air, awaken and know me as [*magical name*]. I come to this Magic Circle with peace within, in perfect love and perfect trust, and seek your aid in learning your mysteries. I vow this day [*night*] to ever uphold thy secrets, to ever walk the path of wisdom, and to ever share the illumination of enlightenment. Hear me, for I am a follower of the Wiccan Ways."

Trace your "sigil" representing the "Sign of Air" and see it yellow as you speak:

"By this sign shall we know each other."

---

mortal practitioners uncertain of their personal involvement with the Elven-Faerie legacy on Earth.

√ Originally given as "*Elven Way.*"

38 This line refers directly to illustrations and instructions given in "*The Sorcerer's Handbook*" (and also reprinted in *The Great Magickal Arcanum*).

Go to the south, lighting the red "elemental candle," and say:

> "Spirits of the Enchanted Mountain, of sun and star and flame, awaken and know me as [*magical name*]. I come to this Magic Circle with peace within, in perfect love and perfect trust, and seek your aid in learning your mysteries. I vow this day [*night*] to ever uphold thy secrets, to ever walk the path of wisdom, and to ever share the illumination of enlightenment. Hear me, for I am a follower of the Wiccan Ways."

Trace your "sigil" for the "Sign of Fire," seeing it red, and speaking:

> "By this sign shall we know each other."

Move to the west and light the blue "elemental candle," saying:

> "Spirits of the Enchanted Sea, of wave and lake and rain, awaken and know me as [*magical name*]. I come to this Magic Circle with peace within, in perfect love and perfect trust, and seek your aid in learning your mysteries. I vow this day [*night*] to ever uphold thy secrets, to ever walk the path of wisdom, and to ever share the illumination of enlightenment. Hear me, for I am a follower of the Wiccan Ways."

Trace your "sigil" representing the "Sign of Water," and see it blue as you speak:

> "By this sign shall we know each other."

Return to the center and take some anointing oil—a type of your own personal choosing.[39] The Magical Traditions teach to "anoint" with oil from the feet to the head (upward); and bless or wash from head to foot (downward). Therefore, begin by anointing your feet and say:

> "Blessed be the feet that bring me here this day [*night*] and enable me to touch the ground, to walk the Path of the Ancients, treading the Right Way always; never deviating from the ascending path of true enlightenment and wisdom."

Anoint your knees, saying:

---

39 The original edition eliminated any further suggestion here, although in the 1999 installment of "*Crystalline Awakening*" the author clarified that ancient pagans and *Witches* used a type of "Flying Ointment" during these rites, composed of substances and herbs that could be considered toxic, hallucinogenic or illegal in various areas. But, for academic purposes, most surviving recipes include: belladonna, betel, cannabis, datura, hemlock, henbane, opium and wolfbane.

360

"Blessed be the knees that bend to give reverence to the Higher Power of the Universe, to the Source of All Being in the Cosmos that gives me the strength to move forth on the ascending path of Light and the ability to make or break my stride at Will."

Anoint the palms of each hand and say:

"Blessed be the hands that lift in praise of the Universe and all Life. They are my commanding hands that I raise in power and I acknowledge their ability to direct my Will, as they are extensions of my creative mind."

Anoint the heart (left breast), saying:

"Blessed be the flame that burns strongly in my heart, that I may experience and know the True Love of the Universe, and in so doing, that I may recognize the Right Way by what is sensed deeply burning within my Spirit."

Anoint your lips and say:

"Blessed be the lips that speak the sacred words of incantation. May the words they speak only advance my evolution further on the ascending path, and never idle or in vain. From my mouth, I utter the Words of Power and share in the Breath of the All; yet I remain silent to those who do not know."

Finally, speak the following as you anoint your forehead:

"Blessed be the mind that seeks to understand its own nature and its connection to the True Self; the Mind that allows me the ability to communicate true knowledge and guidance from Self to this Body—which is connected by the Mind. Let my thoughts be pure and of only a nature that will move me forward on the pathway of my Ascension."

It is traditional to "dedicate" (and ritually "consecrate" if possible) an item—traditionally a *Pendant*—that signifies and solidifies the personal dedication and commitment to the Path expressed in this rite; and of course, is later worn as continuing representation of the same. It is very common for a *Witch* to select the "pentagram" or "pentacle" for this pendant, although this is not a strict criteria.* If you are skilled in "Rites of Consecration" then do so; otherwise, simply hold up your talisman and say:

---

* In the original "Elven-Faerie Druid" tradition this rite is derived from, it is more common to select a "septagram" or "seven-pointed star" (otherwise known as an "Elf Star" or "Faerie Star").

"May the Spirits of Nature, the Cosmos and Universal Ocean beyond, witness and bless this symbol of my dedication. Recognize this symbol and me, so that we may know each other in our future exchanges."

To complete the ceremony, thank and cordially dismiss all energies called to the rite and extinguish the Magic Circle.

THREE DEGREES OF INITIATION

The subject of qualifying requirements for defining a "First Degree Witch" (&tc.) from other degrees has been ambiguous since the inception of modern Witchcraft traditions—for while many may argue otherwise, there are essentially no "universal" designations set down in Gardner's Book of Shadows or anywhere else in antiquity for that matter, when pertaining specifically to "Witchcraft."

Given the background of its modern founder (or compiling publicist) and the relationship of "English Witchcraft" with other local esoteric movements, it is, of course, easy to draw obvious parallels between Wicca and degrees of "Druidism" (which are Ovate, Bardd and Derwydd); and even the most commonly observed master degrees of a "Masonic blue lodge" (of which there are three).

Initiation scripts from the Book of Shadows introduce (or indoctrinate) the Witch (initiate) to a standard of group dynamics coupled with "degrees" or gradients of experience, learning and practice—the extent of which has continued to grow more diverse in today's society, as increasingly more material and "personal traditions" are incorporated into the wide encompassing body of potential "Wiccan" and "spell" literature on the market today.

Prior to mass circulation of Gardner's original Book of Shadows, what many "founding authorities" would later present could only demonstrate just how far they had, themselves, reached in a preexisting group (that may or may not have been closer to a "source" for the tradition) before branching off to form their own covens.‡ The truth is: schisms of leadership and other issues are just as common in neopaganism as any other organizational system or institution—in spite of all the talk of "equality" and "acceptance" on the surface.

Traditionally, an initiate Witch is given official "charge" of their tools (or having tools they have made be ceremonially returned to them, once they are consecrated by the High Priestess, or an administrative leader of the group) at the "First Degree Initiation."

---

‡ This was once an issue with Alexandrian Wicca.

One common requirement for attaining "Second Degree" is to conduct an "original" *Esbat* ("Full Moon Rite") for the *Coven*; and an "original" *Sabbat* ("Seasonal Rite") for the "Third Degree."∞ A possible prerequisite for "Ordination"† might be performing and directing a group spellworking. Of course, this criteria is not set in stone; but the suggestion demonstrates an ascending gradient for practical understanding of *Witchcraft*.

We will treat the subject of *Gardnerian Initiations* later on in this notebook, but for present purposes, it is most important to illustrate "Rites of Initiation" as they are actually practiced by the *Elven Fellowship Circle of Magick* and its prospective developments into the *Order of the Crystal Dawn*.*

NEOPHYTE—FIRST DEGREE INITIATION§

To be considered for membership into *Coven*, and *Initiation* into each subsequent *Degree*, a candidate must be "sponsored" by a referral from a member in good standing, which is also responsible for securing a majority vote on this action from existing members. The "Sponsor" must also be present at the *Initiation* (or *Installation*) ceremony. Such group ceremonies or *coven* gatherings are only open to those members already initiated to the *Degree* (or above) that the Magic Circle is operated for.‡

∞ In 1998-1999, the first three degrees of the *Elven Fellowship Circle of Magick* were distinguished by: a demonstrable understanding of "pagan/Wiccan" religion and "seasonal" practices (*First Degree*); a demonstrable understanding of "ritual magick" and "spellcraft" (*Second Degree*); and a demonstrable understanding of "ceremonial magick" (*Third Degree*). [The modern *Mardukite Academy* observes the "Three Grades" entirely different for the *Mardukite Master Course*.]

† There are some traditionalist perspectives of *Witchcraft* that view *all* initiates as "Priests" or "Priestesses"—as in *every Wiccan* is considered "clergy." This extends back to the idea of *Witchcraft* as a rebellion to the Church, where parishioners are reliant on "intermediary clergy" for their connection with the "Divine." In more modern applications, a "*Third Degree Witch*" may opt to become "ordained" with full ministerial licensing to not only lead a *coven* but other *legal* sanctions (wedding services, &tc.) just as other "recognized clergy" when registered properly with applicable states, &tc.

* Original circulation of this "*Sorcerer's Notebook*" ("*Witch's Handbook*") in 1998-1999 was restricted to members of groups involved with or networking with Joshua Free (as "Merlyn Stone"). Portions of it later appeared in *The Great Magickal Arcanum* and *Elvenomicon.*

§ As modified from the "*1998 Book of Shadows*." Parts of this section appear in "*Elvenomicon*" by Joshua Free; reprinted in "*Merlyn's Complete Book of Druidism*." During the late 1990's, this rite was practiced publicly a dozen times in "Washington Park" (Denver, Colorado).

‡ With the exception of *Initiations* and certain levels of group "spellwork," a typical operating Circle for a *Coven* (group) is "cast" or "sealed" by the "First Degree"—such as for *Esbats* and *Sabbats* when participation by all members is encouraged.

The "Sponsor" leads a *blindfolded* "Initiate" to the northeast corner of the Magic Circle, where they are met by the "Guardian of the Grove" (which may also be the "Leader") standing at the boundary holding a sword. [In some versions, the hands of the "Initiate" are also bound behind their back; the ends of a cord are tied to each ankle, permitting the "Initiate" to walk freely without injury, but not necessarily "run."] Although a "Guardian" may always be "at arms" to protect the *Coven*, the later subsequent (standard) admissions into a "Circle of the First Degree" [also known as the *"Rite of the Blade"* or *"Passing the Kiss"*] are conducted with an *Athame*, or black-handled *Dagger*.

Guardian:	"Who is it there that you bring here to the very Gates of this Sphere most Sacred and Secret?"
Sponsor:	"I bring a Child of Earth and Star. They come seeking entrance; to be set on the Pathway of our Mysteries."
Guardian:	"Do you then present this person to the *Coven*,∞ vouching before us for their conduct and their dedication to our circle and the Wiccan Ways?"√
Sponsor:	"I do. I sponsor this Child of Earth and Star and take responsibility for them as they enter the Gates of this Sphere most Sacred and Secret. They remain outside the Circle now, in a state of darkness—blinded to the mysteries of our Sphere."
Guardian:	"Then as Guardian of this Gateway and Keeper of this Sphere, I open the Portal to our Magic Circle with this Sword. I permit you to enter this one time only by the Unspeakable Password."†

The "Sponsor" leads the "Initiate" to the center of the Magic Circle, where they stand before the "Leader" (or *High Priestess*) and encircled by the existing membership of the *Coven*.

Leader:	"I address the Initiate to answer—Do you come here seeking entrance to our *Coven?*
Initiate:	"I do."
Leader:	"Answer, Initiate—Do you come here of your own free will, free from the pressures of peers or others and free of ulterior motives or malevolent infiltration?"
Initiate:	"I do."

∞ Originally given as *"Grove."*
√ Originally given as *"Elven Ways."*
† The Magic Circle, being previously "Cast" by existing members, is energetically "cut open" in the shape of a "Doorway" with the *Blade* and then resealed with an opposite motion.

Leader:	"And one more, Initiate, answer—Are you willing to submit to an oath of secrecy sworn by the ancient covenant of Witches,* before the members of the Coven and the Spirits we have called to this Magic Circle?"
Initiate:	"I do."
Leader:	"Then kneel and submit yourself to this Assembly."

The "Sponsor" may assist the "Initiate" to kneel and then joins the outer circle of members. These encircling members begin to "murmur and whisper" softly as they rotate their position clockwise around the boundary of the Magic Circle. The "Leader" (or *High Priestess*) speaks the following passage while circling closely around the "Initiate" counter-clockwise.

Leader:	"You have entered a place that is not a place; a time that is not a time; and still you are here. You have entered the Deep Woods and found yourself in the Enchanted Forest of the Elves and Faerie unsolicited. You step foot on ground held most sacred to the Keepers of the Earth; those that maintain and celebrate the Ancient Ways. Under penalty of death, no mortal shall step foot in our Kingdom unbidden, and thus you not render yourself to the mercy of this Court. Fear has no place here in the Otherworld—and it is the will of this court that you be sentenced to death if you now enter this place without the passwords. If you bring mortal fear in your heart to our world, you will surely summon your demises. So, I ask you again, Initiate— how do you seek to enter our world?"[40]

The final line is asked with the "Leader" (or *High Priestess*) standing in front of the "Initiate," at which time the surrounding motions and murmuring ceases. The "Sponsor" also returns to the side of the "Initiate."

Initiate:	"With the passwords—*perfect love* and *perfect trust*."
Leader:	"I address the Sponsor to answer—has the Initiate been properly prepared? Have they completed their Self-Dedication to our ways? Are they recognized by the Elemental Watchtowers?"
Sponsor:	"The Initiate is prepared. They are properly dedicated.

---

* Originally given as "*by the ancient covenant of the Mystic Wizards of the Earth and this Council.*"

40 This passage is based heavily on records from Rev. Robert Kirk; see "*Elvenomicon*" by Joshua Free, also reprinted in "*Merlyn's Complete Book of Druidism.*"

	They are recognized by the Elemental Realms."
Leader:	"We shall find out... May the the Source of All Being and Creation grant us protection; and in protection, strength; and in strength, peace; and in peace, understanding; and in understanding, knowledge; and in knowledge, wisdom; and in wisdom, love; and in love, the love of all things; and in the love of all things, the love of all the Universe and Creation...‡ The Initiate may rise."

The "Sponsor" summons the "Initiate" up from their knees, then guides them on a cross-quarter journey to the various "elemental directions" in the Magic Circle before returning them to the center again. In ancient times, this would have been conducted in a cave or labyrinth.

The following ritual text[41] is read by the "Leader" (or *High Priestess*) on one side of the "Initiate," while movement around the Circle is led by the "Sponsor" from the other side.

South:	"In the Beginning was the Infinite Void of Nothingness—a canvas with no form, a screen without picture. But then came Light; the Dragon; the Cosmic Law—that which gave all existence its form; waves of potentiality sprawling across the matrix-fabric of the Universe as the Fires of Life."
East:	"And when the Fires of Life burned down to glowing embers, they breathed existence into the Air—they breathed the knowledge and Life into the Air; and was born the Spirits˷ of the Breeze."
West:	"Then more and more tangible did the formless Spirit of Light become. When the Waters emerged, its ripples were sent out to every corner of existence as an All-Encompassing Sea. But the waves and currents of energy chased one another and became even more solid."
North:	"So, the Formless Fire gave birth to Air; the gaseous Air gave way to Water—the Sea would yield finally to the Land, the Element of Earth; a powerfully strong and

---

‡ This passage is known as the *"Druid's (Gorsedd) Prayer."*

41 The ritual text is based heavily on the "Chaldean Oracles of Zoroaster" (as given in the *"Anunnaki Bible"*), which were also used as inspiration by the Hermetic Order of the Golden Dawn for their "Watchtower Ceremony."

∞ Originally given as *"Elves, Ffayrie and Sylphs."*

stable foundation to solidly hold up the less tangible manifestations. The Earth is home to the planetary Spirit of G'ea.^√ She has had 'Keepers' and 'Guardians' at all times, and in all places, to maintain the balance of the Elemental World and thwart all that would cause disharmony to Life on Earth and in the Cosmos."

Center: "As you have come to us in the darkness of ignorance, know that we are the 'Keepers of the Earth', the 'Guardians of the Green World' and 'Scions of the Secret Knowledge' kept since the times of the Ancient Mystery School. [*Removes blindfold from "Initiate."*] As you emerge, reborn into a Realm of Light and our world of enchantment, your given name is no longer appropriate and is retired at the boundary of the Magic Circle.^† By what name shall this *Coven* know you as?

Initiate: [*Answers.*]

Leader: "Then, Lords and Ladies of this *Coven*, I present to you our new Initiate, [*name*]. We welcome them into our Magic Circle as a Free Person."^*

APPRENTICE—SECOND DEGREE INITIATION^§

The "Second Degree Initiation" used by the *Elven Fellowship Circle of Magick* is otherwise known as the "*Rite of the Law*"—part of which is standard for sealing a "Circle of the Second Degree" (coupled with the "*Rite of the Blade*" and "*Passing the Kiss*"). The *Rite of Initiation* is, itself, only one part of achieving the actualized state of "Awakened Apprentice."

In some versions, the "Initiate" is placed in a wooden *Coffin* or alone in a *Crypt* for a period of time prior to any ceremonial performance or interaction. Such "introspection" is meant for an "Initiate" to overcome "reactivity" to personal "programming" and any "mental imagery" that is conjured to mind as a result—all of which must be "worked out," until the "Initiate" is sufficiently

---

√ Also "*Gaia*" or "*Gaea*."

† Originally given as "*Sacred Grove*."

* Each of the members, starting with the Leader, formally greets the Initiate by name "as a Free Person." In some "Gardnerian" inspired versions, the Leader (or *High Priestess*) would also entrust the "Third Password" to the Initiate, which is "*a kiss*." [The first two passwords are "*perfect love*" and "*perfect trust*."]

§ As given in the "*1998 Book of Shadows*." Parts of this section appear in the "Appendix" to the 21st Anniversary Collector's Edition "*Sorcerer's Handbook*" by Joshua Free (writing as Merlyn Stone).

"emptied."‡

Historically, this has also left things open for abuses and other mishandling, because an individual may also need to resolve "panic responses" to feeling that the "body" is trapped; when the realization intended here is for *Self* as *Spirit* to realize they are not restricted to the *Body*, and in essence, become free of these considerations. It is not uncommon to experience *Self* apart from the *Body* during this exercise.

When practiced alone, an "Initiate" may simply choose to isolate away reclusive for a time; making sure to have minimal stimuli in the environment—clearing out a special room or covering up shelving and furniture around the house. During deep periods of this work, no electronic devices or artificial lighting is permitted; and a dietary fasting on breads and water is encouraged. While many elements discussed in this section of *The Witch's Handbook* may seem extreme, I would invite readers to also consider the preparatory purification work suggested in the text: *Sacred Magic of Abramelin the Mage.*∞

Ancient records and accounts of *True Initiation Rites* do not give the type of detailed descriptions of ritual instruction and ceremonial verbiage is taken for granted today in the "New Age"—since the magical revival of the late 1800's or even the reconstruction of *Freemasonry* in 1717. In an archaic account by W. Winwood Reade—"*The Veil of Isis -or- Mysteries of the Druids*"—we are given at least one amazing perspective on the awesome symbolism and power of imagination in connection to *Initiations* of the Ancient Mystery School:—

> *"During a period of probation, the Ovate was closely watched; eyes, to him, invisible, were ever upon him, noting his actions and his very looks, searching into his heart for its motive, and into his soul for its abilities. He was then subjected to a trial so painful to the body, so terrible to the mind, that any lost their senses for ever, and others crawled back to the daylight pale and emaciated, as men who had grown old in prison.*

> *"These initiations took place in caves, one of which still exists in Denbighshire. We have also some reason to believe that the catacombs of Egypt and those artificial excavations which are to be found in many parts of Persia and Hindostan were constructed for the same purpose.*

> *"The Ovate received several wounds from a man who opposed his entrance with a drawn sword. He was then led blindfolded through the winding alleys of the cave which was also a labyrinth. This was meant to represent the toilsome wanderings of the soul in the mazes of ignorance and vice. Presently the ground would begin to rock beneath his feet; strange sounds disturbed the*

---

‡   For additional information on this type of energy work, refer to "*The Tablets of Destiny*" and "*Crystal Clear*" by Joshua Free.

∞   For details, refer to "*The Great Magickal Arcanum*" by Joshua Free.

midnight silence. Thunder crashed upon him like the fall of an avalanche, flashes of green lightning flickered through the cave displaying to his view hideous spectres arrayed against the walls.

"Then lighted only by these fearful fires, a strange procession marched past him, and a hymn in honor of the Eternal Truth was solemnly chanted by unseen tongues. Here the profounder mysteries commenced. He was admitted through the North Gate or that of Cancer, where he was forced to pass through a Wall of Fire. Thence he hurried to the Southern Gate or that of Capricorn, where he was plunged into a flood, and from which he was only released when life was at its last gasp. Then he was scourged and buried up to his neck in snow. This was the baptism by fire, of water and of blood.

"Now arrived on the verge of death, an icy chill seizes his limbs; a cold dew bathes his brow, his faculties fail him; his eyes close; he is about to faint, to expire, when a strain of music, sweet as the distant murmur of the holy brooks, consoling as an angel's voice, bids him to rise and to live for the honor of his God. Two doors with a sound like the fluttering of wings are thrown open before him. A divine light bursts upon him, he sees plains shining with flowers open around him.

"Then a golden serpent is placed in his bosom as a sign of his regeneration, and he is adorned with a mystic zone upon which are engraved twelve mysterious signs; a tiara is placed on his head; his form naked and shivering is clothed in a purple tunic studded with innumerable stars; a crozier is placed in his hand... He is a king; for he is initiated; for he is a Druid."

Returning to our practical application: if some method of "solitary confinement" has been applied, then the "Leader" (or *High Priestess*) is responsible for opening the door or coffin-cover for the "initiate" and welcoming them into the Magic Circle (or lodge, as this *Rite* was originally conducted indoors). However, it is not always possible for the formerly described *"Awakening Rite"* to precede the ceremony; in which case, the "Initiate" is blindfolded with their hands bound behind them—as is customary for all *Rites of Initiation*.

Second-Degree and Third-Degree members wait within the Magic Circle, properly prepared according to the Grade of *Installation* (and the "Sponsor" begins among them). The "Leader" (the "Master of the Craft" or *High Priestess*) stands in the center; the "Guardian" waits at the door (or northeast threshold) with drawn sword; the "Initiate" is left waiting outside the door to the lodge (or some distance away from the Circle or Grove).

Guardian: "Master of the Craft, I come with news of an Initiate awaiting entrance into the *Second Degree* of our *Coven*."[√]

[√] Originally given as *"our Sacred Order,"* in preparation for continued use by the *Order of the Crystal Dawn*.

Leader:	"Who accounts for this candidate?"
Sponsor:	"I do. They stand outside the Magic Circle seeking entrance to the *Second Degree*."
Leader:	"Is the candidate properly prepared for the *Second Degree?*"
Sponsor:	"They are."
Leader:	"Then I permit you to break circle and accompany the Guard to see that the candidate is properly prepared for this installation ceremony."

The "Sponsor" and "Guard" go and prepare the "Initiate" for the ceremony, bringing them to the door of the lodge or northeast boundary of the Magic Circle. The password for admittance to the *Second Degree* is a "knock" sequence: 1-2-3 or /-//-///. This is traditionally done on the door to a ceremonial chamber, though when conducted outdoors, an artificial "knocker" or "clacker"[†] is used, or even a bell.

The "Guard" then opens the door (and "cuts the doorway" for the Circle as previously described) and announces to the *Coven*.

Guardian:	"I return with the Initiate and their Sponsor."
Leader:	"Is the Initiate properly prepared?"
Sponsor:	"They are."
Leader:	"Then bring them forward and let the installation ceremony commence. Guard, seal the Doorway to this Magic Circle and let no one interfere with these operations."
Guardian:	"The Magic Circle is sealed."
Leader:	"Then we may proceed. Sponsor—you may present your candidate for initiation."
Sponsor:	"Master of the Craft, it is my honor to present this candidate for initiation to the *Second Degree* of our *Coven*. I petition this assembly to allow this candidate installation to the *Second Degree* of this *Coven*, and mark its occasion."
Leader:	"Let the candidate speak for themselves, now. Initiate—

---

† A wooden "Clacker" (a hammer-like piece strikes a board) or "Clapper" (thin boards slap against a center board) is still used in some churches today in place of bells during lent—particularly the Easter Triduum of Holy Week. The correct term within the Roman Catholic Church is "*crotalus*" (Latin) from the Greek "*krotalon*" ("rattle").

	what do you come here seeking from us?"
Initiate:	[*Answers.*]
Leader:	"Initiate—is there any reason why you would be unable to submit yourself to the confidence and commitment of this Assembly at this time?"
Initiate:	[*Answers.*]
Leader:	"Fine. Thank you. Then, I address the Assembly—is there any member of this *Coven* that does not believe this candidate is worthy of the *Second Degree*?"
Respondents:	[*Answer, if applicable.*]
Leader:	"Then if there will be no objections, it is with great pleasure and esteem that we elevate and install you [*name of candidate*] to the *Second Degree* of the [*name of Coven or group*]. By the reputation of your Sponsor and on the recommendation of this Assembly, we are assured that you are befitting of the *Second Degree* among *Witches*,* and that you fully understand the sacred trust bestowed on you by this fellowship. Those who come to this fellowship in Self-Honesty seek to be Self-Masters; assisting themselves and assisting others to assist themselves on the Pathway to Ascension. Initiate—do you understand all of what I have said?"
Initiate:	[*Answers.*]
Leader:	"To be an integral part of this *Coven*‡ is to seek Self-Honesty, Universal Truth, and the power laden in both. We seek to understand the true nature and potential of the Human Condition, now waiting to be unlocked within you. You are here this day to reconfirm your place on the Pathway to Ascension, the quest for ultimate potential and the promise of its loftiest uses, affirming that the Spark of the Divine is within you— and that Humans are not Animals. Initiate—are you able to solidify this commitment here before your *Coven*?"
Initiate:	[*Answers.*]
Leader:	"The Sponsor may remove the bindings from this Initiate; in doing so, know that you are now unbound to the potential of the *Second Degree*, free to pursue its teachings and receive its instruction from this *Coven*."

---

* Originally given as "*Brothers and Sisters of this lodge.*"
‡ Originally given as "*Sacred Order.*"

The Sponsor removes the bindings from the Initiate.

Leader: "The Sponsor may remove the blindfold from this Initiate; in doing so, know that you are now seeing the light of this *Coven's Second Degree* for the first time. With new eyes you are free to see and realize its teachings and the actualized potential within yourself in Self-Honesty. One cannot seek what they cannot see."

The Sponsor removes the blindfold from the Initiate and greets them as a "Free Person of the *Second Degree*"; after which each members of the *Coven* also comes up to do the same before returning to the Assembly.

Leader: "We officially declare [*name*] a Free Person initiated to the *Second Degree*. Initiate—you may now join the greater Assembly of this *Coven*, gathered together to affirm the Law given to those that Ascend the Pathway."

The Initiate joins the Assembly for the remainder of the ceremony, which is the "*Rite of the Law.*"[42]

Leader: "Some want to watch the things that move. Some want to tear with teeth and claws. Some go out in the world, fighting. Some go out biting. Punishment is sharp and sure for those who act against the Law. You have heard of the Law of the Jungle; but we follow the Law of the Highest! A Human is not an Animal. Man is not an Animal. Today, I am the Sayer of the Law. Speak the words and learn the Law! Not to go on all fours; this is the Law."

Respondents: "Not to go on all fours; that is the Law."

Leader: "Not to tear at plants and trees; this is the Law."

Respondents: "Not to tear at plants and trees; that is the Law."

Leader: "Not to snarl and roar; this is the Law."

Respondents: "Not to snarl and roar; that is the Law."

Leader: "Not to show teeth or fangs; this is the Law."

Respondents: "Not to show teeth or fangs; that is the Law."

Leader: "Not to destroy our possessions or habitats; this is

---

42 Versions of this rite were popularized as "*TierDrama*" in the 1960's-70's by those employing "*Satanic Rituals*" of Anton LaVey, where it is presented under the premise of a 1776 Bavarian Illuminati ritual. The text is more likely derived from its earlier appearance in the 1896 novel by H.G. Wells, titled: "*The Island of Dr. Moreau.*"

	the Law."
Respondents:	"Not to destroy our possessions or habitats; that is the Law."
Leader:	"Not to kill without thought; this is the Law."
Respondents:	"Not to kill without thought; that is the Law."
Leader:	"Humans are God."
Respondents:	"Humans are God."
Leader:	"We are Human."
Respondents:	"We are Human."
Leader:	"We are Gods."
Respondents:	"We are Gods."
Leader:	"Ours is the hand that creates; this is the Law."
Respondents:	"Ours is the hand that creates; that is the Law."
Leader:	"Ours is the hand that wounds; this is the Law."
Respondents:	"Ours is the hand that wounds; that is the Law."
Leader:	"Ours is the hand that heals; this is the Law."
Respondents:	"Ours is the hand that heals; that is the Law."
Leader:	"Ours is the lightning flash; this is the Law."
Respondents:	"Ours is the lightning flash; that is the Law."
Leader:	"Ours is the deep salty sea; this is the Law."
Respondents:	"Ours is the deep salty sea; that is the Law."
Leader:	"Ours is the stars in the sky; this is the Law."
Respondents:	"Ours is the stars in the sky; that is the Law."
Leader:	"Ours is the rulers of the land; this is the Law."
Respondents:	"Ours is the rulers of the land; that is the Law."
Leader:	"This is what is ours to have; this is what we are."
Respondents:	"This is what is ours to have; this is what we are."
Leader:	"The Rite of the Law is ended, but its truth ever remains. Blessed Be."∞
Respondents:	"Blessed Be All."

For "Outer Court" purposes, this "*Rite of Initiation*" may also be amended for installation to a *Third Degree*.√

∞ Originally given as "*So Mote it Be.*"

√ Additional suggestions may be found in the Appendix of the 21st Anniversary Col-

THE GARDNERIAN INITIATIONS

Many versions of *Initiation* are presented by Gerald Gardner during his lifetime, with later modifications provided by Doreen Valiente. Original "Gardnerian Initiations" are a staple of *Wiccan* foundations for not only Gardnerian traditions, but much of the popular *Witchcraft* that came afterward—new traditions frequently based on "word-of-mouth" versions of the same *Book of Shadows*, by those who had actually participated in Gardnerian *Covens*. In modern times, given how widespread the *Book of Shadows* has reached, any "Mystery" surrounding *Initiation* through "three degrees of *Witchcraft*" has been all but threshed out. Most *Covens* have since opted to write completely different *Rites of Initiation*, such as seen above.[*]

In descriptions for *"First Degree Initiation,"* the "Initiate" (referred to as the "Postulant") is cable-towed to the edge of the Magic Circle. There hands are bound with a red cord that is also around the neck—a practice that would be perhaps ill-advised today. The "Initiator" commands that the "feet be neither bound nor free," which is a strange instruction, worked out as described in a previous section above. In another version, a short cord is attached to the right ankle, and another just below the right knee.

One interesting characteristic of early *Gardnerian Wicca* is the inclusion of the "Kabbalistic Cross" during the Opening Rites, commonly used in Jewish mysticism and by the Golden Dawn magicians—and given in the text of *The Sorcerer's Handbook*. However, during the *"Rite of Initiation,"* the Magic Circle is left "open" at the northeast threshold, where the "Postulant" stands just outside of it in wait; their "Sponsor" standing behind them. Otherwise, the Magic Circle is "cast" in the usual manner.

Another significant facet is the *"Rite of the Blade,"* where the "Initiator" approaches the "Postulant" standing outside the Magic Circle and says: *"You who stands on the threshold between the pleasant world of men and the dread dom-*

---

lector's Edition of *"The Sorcerer's Handbook"* by Joshua Free writing as Merlyn Stone. Note the details for "Installation of a Master," which is dependent on knowledge and experience with ceremonial arts described in that volume. The *"1998 Book of Shadows"* (now *"The Witch's Handbook"*) was intended primarily for "Outer Court" (training coven) use; and secondly, for incorporation with the original *"Sorcerer's Handbook"*—along with *"Draconomicon"* and its follow up *"Druid's Handbook"*—which, when combined together, represent the complete "Third Degree" ("Master") library established during the "Merlyn Stone" period from 1995 until 2000. This collection of materials later constituted the core of *The Great Magickal Arcanum*, first released in 2008.

[*] This section regarding *Gardnerian Initiation* contains some material never officially practiced by the *Elven Fellowship Circle of Magick;* it is included here only for academic purposes and posterity.

ains of the Lords of the Outer Spaces, do you have the courage to attempt to enter this Circle?"

The "Initiator" then places the point of the *Blade* against the Postulant's chest, continuing: "*For I say verily, it were better to rush upon my blade and perish, then make the attempt with fear in your heart.*" And the "Postulant" responds: "*I have two passwords: Perfect Love and Perfect Trust.*"

When the "Initiate/Postulant" is finally brought into the Magic Circle, the "Leader/Initiator" (or *High Priestess*) entrusts the "Third Password" (a *"kiss"*), then comes around to behind the "Postulant" with their embrace as they nudge/thrust them into the Circle.

The purpose of this is described in Gerald Gardner's novel "*High Magic's Aid*," where an *Witch* is questioned by outsiders with: "Who led you into the Circle?"—and the appropriate answer, being: "They led me from behind." Once inside the Circle, the Postulant is escorted to (and announced before) each ritual station of the Elemental directions—"Take heed, Lords of the Watchtower of the East, that [*so-and-so*] is properly prepared to be initiated a *Witch* and *Priestess* [*or Priest*], &tc."

Once brought to the center of the Magic Circle, existing *Coven* members begin to circle around *deosil* (sun-wise, clock-wise), chanting: "*Eko, Eko, Azarak; Eko, Eko, Zomelak; Eko, Eko, Kernunnos; Eko, Eko, Aradia*" over and over. In one version, *Coven* members make efforts to disorient the Postulant by pushing them back and forth and sometimes turning them toward a new direction.

A bell is rung three times and the "Leader/Initiator" calls for the actions to cease—at which point the Postulant is turned toward the Leader (or *High Priestess*). The Leader (or *High Priestess*) kneels before the "Initiate" saying: "*In other religions, the postulant kneels, while the priest towers above him. But in the Arts Magical, we are taught to be humble, and we kneel to welcome them as we say...*"—and she continues speaking and administering the "*Rite of Fivefold Blessing/ Kiss*" (feet, knees, and so on).

Next, the "measure" is taken—a facet seldom observed in modern traditions. It is theorized that a body measure recorded and maintained by the *Coven*—along with personal nail clipping and hair—could be used for future magical purposes to either help or harm a member.

It is not generally considered wise to enforce continuing membership against their will; but what if the *Witch* were to betray her *Coven*? Today it is considered a "symbolic rite," although those experienced in practical magick will undoubtedly observe all the significance held between the lines.

So, the "Sponsor" hands the *High Priestess* an eight-foot length of string, who then announces that she *"will now take your measure."* With the assistance of another *Priestess*, she takes a "measure" of the Initiate's height; stretching the string from the feet (where it is held by the assistant) to the head. The measured spot is pinched off and another assistant uses the *Boline* (or white-handled knife) to cut the string. Additional measures are taken with the string: around the head; around the chest; around the hips—and each time a knot is tied to mark it.[†] Finally, it is wound up and placed on the *Altar*.

The final portion[‡] of the original *Gardnerian* "First Degree Initiation," is a formal introduction to the "Elemental Tools." It is sometimes unclear whether or not an *Initiate* would have constructed all of their own tools at this juncture of development, or if this is simply a demonstration by the *High Priestess* using *Coven* materials. We do, however, know that by the "Second Degree Initiation," a *Witch* must have found, made or been gifted with components for a complete set of personal tools—which are consecrated by the *High Priestess* and then returned to the *Initiate* for them to demonstrate their use at the Quarters during that *Rite of Initiation*.

The "Second Degree Initiation," in *Gardnerian Wicca*, is essentially identical to the steps of the first (and those illustrated within the "Outer Court" degrees of the *Elven Fellowship Circle of Magick*)—but this time, as stated above, the *Initiate* demonstrates use of their "Elemental Tools." In Gardner's version, it is also during the "Second Degree Initiation" that a *Witch* takes on, and is introduced to the *Coven* as, their "magical name." The *Initiate* is then taken to each Quarter and announced to the *"Lords of the Watchtowers"* by their new name as a *"Consecrated Witch"* and *Priestess* (or *Priest*).

The Oath taken for this *Rite* goes: *"Repeat thy new name after me, saying: 'I, [name], swear upon my mother's womb, and by my honor among men and my Brothers and Sisters of the Art, that I will never reveal, to any at all, any of the secrets of the Art, except it be to a worthy person, properly prepared, in the center of a Magic Circle such as I am now in. This I swear by my hopes of salvation, my past lives, and my hopes of future ones to come; and I dedicate myself and my measure to utter destruction if I break my solemn Oath.'"*

A final distinct point of Gardner's "Second Degree Initiation" is unique in contrast to the traditional "Italio-Celtic" flavor his *Book of Shadows* usually demonstrates: *"The Descent of the Goddess Inanna-Ishtar,"* which is dramatically

---

[†] A note from personal experience: each of the three measures are made starting with the same end of the string. If you were to start from each new measure knot, it would typically require a greater length of string.

[‡] Editor's Note: It is an interesting point of fact that the present author has refrained from any instructions regarding "ritual scourging," which is actually quite paramount to *Gardner's Book of Shadows*.

reenacted—and quite blatantly Mesopotamian (Sumerian/Babylonian) in origin. This winks loudly to a little-known legend regarding true origins of the "Witch-Cult" among the "Priestesses of Inanna," even extending back to pre-Babylonian "Uruk Sumerians" (*c. 4th millennium BC*).[∞]

It is at this point that we see a distinction in the developing literature for *Witchcraft* through the 20th century, because in many instances, a reader may discover the *"Descent of the Goddess to the Underworld"* used in substitution for Gardner's own "Third Degree Initiation."[43] One reason this commonly occurred is because *Initiates* often opted to prematurely break away from early *Covens* before being released with a "Third Degree Initiation" to officially go an start their own. Many other *Covens* and *Books of Shadows* released in the 20th Century have also been based, in part, by second-hand knowledge from diverse sources that were simply incorporated into contemporary presentations of *Wicca* and *Witchcraft* today.[*]

At the start of the "Third Degree Initiation," according to the original *Gardnerian Book of Shadows*, the High Priestess ties the "Magus" (High Priest) to the Altar for a scourging, then he is released and does the same to her. This is apparently quite common in the old "traditionalist" flavor of *Wicca*. The Quarters are addressed announcing the *Initiation* of the new *Priest* or *Priestess* and then the "Magus" says something to the effect of *"Assist me to erect the Ancient Altar,"* at which point the *Priestess* lies down in the center of the Magic Circle and arranges the appendages of their body in the styling of a pentagram.[44] After which, a series of "kisses" and "blessings" are exchanged, saying *"Make open the path of intelligence between us. For these truly are the five points of fellowship..."* and so on—as with "The Great Rite."

∞ For additional details regarding Mesopotamia, refer to the Mardukite library titles dedicated to such topics, including: *"The Complete Anunnaki Bible"* and *"The Sumerian Legacy,"* both of which are contained in the Master Edition hardcover anthology: *"Necronomicon: The Complete Anunnaki Legacy"* by Joshua Free.

43 As seen, for example, in *Lady Sheba's Book of Shadows*, published by Jessie Wicker Bell ("Lady Sheba") in 1972.

* This became increasingly common starting in the early 1970's with the work of Alex and Maxine Sanders—and increased dissemination of *"Alexandrian Wicca."*

44 The actual instructions read: "Priestess lies down in such a way that her vagina is approximately at the center of the Circle."—*Gardnerian Book of Shadows*.

NANCY'S BOOK OF SHADOWS
-or-
Everything I Need to Know About The Craft, I Learned From
"THE CRAFT"
(Merlyn Stone, Summer-Autumn '98)

It may seem strange how much time and attention has been taken on *Notebooks* for *The Witch's Handbook* this year,[*] and yet unlike the original treatment of *The Sorcerer's Handbook*, very little has been directed here toward the subject of "*magick*" directly. This is not an oversight. For one, it is basically assumed that those receiving this material will have immediate access to *The Sorcerer's Handbook* first edition. Secondly, it is already expected that material from the former will be combined with this one to compose a more accessible third edition of the *Handbook*.[‡]

More importantly, when one considers the subject of true *Witchcraft*—especially as it is demonstrated in the 20th century—we are really concerned with a "pagan" (or "neopagan") "*religious tradition*" far more than we are dealing with a particular brand, flavor or style of "magick." As we have seen from various installments distributed for our "*1998 Book of Shadows*" this year, the development of "modern" *Witchcraft* is really a combination of reviving customs and traditions from the "Ancient Ways" (or what many now consider "*Ye Olde Tyme Religion*") coupled with several centuries of ongoing reinvestigation into archaic "occult philosophies" and the *Arts of Magic*. In today's society, the proliferation and propagation of these efforts takes on many forms...

◊ ◊ ◊ ◊ ◊ ◊ ◊

---

[*] Each main section of *The Witch's Handbook* was originally prepared as a separate installment (during the course of a year) for inclusion into the greater body of work known as "*1998 Book of Shadows*" for the *Elven Fellowship Circle of Magick*.

[‡] Facets of the first edition "*Sorcerer's Handbook*" (Spring 1998) and the second edition (as the "*Witch's Handbook*" or "*1998 Book of Shadows*") were combined for the *Sorcerer's Notebook*, released publicly in Autumn 1998 as the third edition of *Sorcerer's Handbook*, distributed globally as this format through all of 1999.

There are some in the pagan community that remain upset over the 1996 Columbia Pictures release of "*The Craft*." It does, however, arrive in the mainstream during a critical turning point in the widespread development of "New Age" practices and the modern *Witchcraft* movement in general. Although the movie does illustrate several rites inspired by Ceremonial Magic (including some facets described as such within our "*1998 Book of Shadows*"), semantically speaking, very little actual "*Wiccan*" tradition is expressed—perhaps, most notably, the blatant absence of emphasis on a "goddess"-centric magical system or ever popular "*grrrrl power*"-type we might otherwise expect.[45]

The movie follows events taking place after "Sarah" (*played by Robin Tunney, later to star in "End of Days"*) moves to Los Angeles with her parents and transfers to a new Catholic School. There, she finds herself initiated into a small *coven* led by "Nancy Downs" (*the amazing goddess, Fairuza Balk, who starred in "The Worst Witch" as a child*), with her two friends "Rochelle" (*Rachel True*) and "Bonnie" (*Neve Campbell, known from "Scream" and "Wild Things"*). Needless to say for those who have already seen the film: things take a bit of a turn when Sarah's incorporation seems to advance the power of the group beyond the temperance and wisdom of its members to properly use it.

The Craft debuted in theaters just after Beltane 1996 based on a script treatment developed by *Peter Filardi* (best known for writing "*Flatliners*")—although the final screenplay was amended by joint-writer and film-director *Andrew Fleming*, with some assistance by a technical consultant, *Pat Devin*, a member of a *Wiccan* organization known as "*Covenant of the Goddess*" (*CoG*).

Pat Devin is not only a "*Dianic Wiccan*" herself, she serves for the public-relations office at *CoG*. She was interviewed by Llewellyns New Worlds magazine-catalog regarding her participation on the set of *The Craft* shortly after its release. It was also noted in interviews and production commentary notes that *Robin Tunney* had at least some independent interest and knowledge in the subject of *Wicca* prior to the movie and *Fairuza Balk* was certainly no stranger to the *Craft*, having a family background in many of its facets and going on to purchase *Panpipes Magickal Marketplace*—the oldest occult shop in Los Angeles, established in 1971—mainly to save it from going out of business at the time.

There are, of course, many "Hollywood-ized" elements found in *The Craft*, which are unique to its own take on magic and are included purely to "put on a good show." That being said, there is a considerable amount of effective data that may be drawn from the film and of which has served, in some ways, as an elementary introduction for young girls and boys of this generation

---

45 Portions of this paragraph are rewritten as the entree for "*The Craft*" found in "*The Great Magickal Arcanum*" by Joshua Free.

that are interested in *"magic"* and *"witchcraft"* and see this work as a type of "Rite of Passage" in itself—a means for an individual to come into their own power. Those traditions that deal heavily in "Self-empowerment" are predicted to be on the "rise" well into the 21st Century as more of the "up and coming" population begins to direct its attentions away from the religious institutions that have set up authoritarian intermediaries to the truth.

◊ ◊ ◊ ◊ ◊ ◊ ◊

NANCY'S BOOK OF SHADOWS: AN APPENDIX
(Practical Notes from "THE CRAFT")

[0:45]*   OPENNING CHANT
> *Now is the time; this is the hour.*
> *Ours is the magic; ours is the power.*

Chanted by each individual of the coven simultaneously to attune the members. [The girls are seen seated around a small circular table/Altar on an outdoor patio space that is decorated with magical tools, stones and many candles.]

[6:30]   A FOUR-MEMBER ELEMENTAL COVEN-STRUCTURE
> *A new wholeness and with it a new balance;*
> *Earth, Air, Fire and Water.*

The "Quarters"† or directions are treated by their "Elemental" properties in ritual magic. A "Circle" is correlated to symbolism of four "Elemental directions"—and each station may be effectively represented by a member of the coven. Although magic can be practiced by any number of individuals, there is a certain symmetrical balance in a four-member coven-structure. [Bonnie is reading to the other girls from *The Witches' Almanac* and predicting they might finally meet a "fourth" member.]

[14:45]   PERSONAL BOOK OF SHADOWS
> *You put spells and power thoughts in it.*

A personal notebook or "Book of Shadows" is kept to record one's own magical journey (like a diary) and also to include any rites one has written—and to copy the group rituals and liturgy practiced within one's coven. [Bonnie attempts to convince Sarah to steal a blank "Book of Shadows" from an occult shop.]

[18:15]   PATRON DEITIES FOR THE COVEN TRADITION
> *Maybe he'll really listen now...*

---

*   Approximate time-stamp from the film, starting with Universal logo.
†   Referred to as *corners* in the film.

Witchcraft, as a religion, holds a certain concept of "Divinity," however unique or individual that may be. [The group gathers in a park to educate Sarah about "*Manon*"—a specific persona of Divinity that the coven is dedicated to. The name chosen for the movie was intentionally fictitious.]

[*29:15*] ELEMENTAL CHANT
Earth. Air. Fire. Water.

Chanted by each of the four members of the coven, while seated in a circle, holding hands. All four simultaneously chant "*Earth. Air. Fire. Water.*" in total four times, then each speaks only their own respective element four times (or eight times). [The four girls take their first major outing together, traveling by bus to a rural grove set in a meadow.]

[*29:30*] RITE OF THE BLADE
—It is better that you should rush upon this blade
than enter the circle with fear in your heart.
How do you enter?
—With perfect love and perfect trust.

Similar to the original *Gardnerian Initiations*,* before entering the working area, each member of the coven stands in line waiting to be admitted into the Circle. The dagger/*Athame* is held up to their chest, the challenge is said, passwords are given, and finally the passing a kiss (the third password). [On film, Rochelle initiates Bonnie; Bonnie initiates Nancy; and Nancy initiates Sarah. Nancy then takes the dagger/*Athame* and raises it up, pointed to the sky, speaks "*As above,*" and then plunges it into the ground with everyone saying "*So below.*"]

[*30:30*] COMMUNION OF WINE
I drink of my sisters
and I take into myself (stated intention).

Group magic or Circle magic may be a combination of coven energy, collected from all members and then channeled toward individual intentions. [Wine is poured into a communal *Chalice*. Each of the girls pricks their finger with a pin (or needle) and pinches a drop of blood into the Wine.† Rochelle begins the rotation, stating: "*I drink of my sisters and ask for the ability to not hate those who hate me...*" and then she takes a drink. The *Chalice* is passed to each in turn to do similar. Nancy completes the cycle and says, "*Blessed Be,*" which is then echoed by the others.]

THE LOVE SPELL
This spell is to be practiced for seven days in succession,
preferably during the waxing cycle of the Moon

---

* Refer to "*Rites of Initiation*" (*Spring 1998*) section of the *BoS*.
† Included in this review, but not necessarily recommended for practice.

and beginning on a Friday.
Each day, the two candles are moved closer to each other.

The Circle is cast and the witch petitions their patron deity and says, "*Hear my plea to you; my plea of love for ___ and their desire.*" A talisman may be employed here, and the words spoken: "*Sator, Arepo, Tenet, Opera, Rotas. Iah. Iah. Iah. I summon to me what all I desire.*" Light the candle representing you (on the right-side or projective side of the *Altar*) and say: "*This flame burns as does my spirit. The love I have for ___ is great and burns deep within my being.*" Light the candle representing the target of the spell (on the left-side or receptive side of the *Altar*), saying: "*This is the heart and soul of ___, whom I see and conjure a picture of before me.*"

In your Mind's Eye, see an image of the other person smiling and coming toward you with an open embrace. Push that image into your body and say, "*The love ___ has for me grows as does this flame. It burns as does this candle and is forever drawn to me. Great is the love I have for ___ and great is the love ___ has for me.*" Light a third (red) candle and say: "*I draw ___ to me; the one toward the other; and the thought of me shall be constant.*"

Release the energy and direct it toward the target, saying: "*My spell is upon you ___, and my desire for you is great. May love blossom and sweeten between us. My spell is upon you ___, I have directed the powers of the Universe to coax you into my arms.*" [Sarah uses magic to cause her high school crush, Chris (*played by Skeet Ulrich*), to fall helplessly "in love" with her.]

[48:30] THROWING A GLAMOUR

Glamour—to throw an illusion so real
as to fool an onlooker
is one of the oldest forms of magic.

As its name implies, a "glamour" is an illusion—but this is not unique, because the "persona" or "façade" you display outward in the Physical Universe is already an illusion of sorts. Furthermore, what you project as Self on a physical level also has its influence from the emotional, psychological and spiritual systems of beingness.

This spell should be practiced at night, or at dusk or twilight, preferably on a Friday or Saturday (evoking influences of Venus and Saturn) during the waxing phase or on a Full Moon. Some versions specify the New Moon.

You will require a red candle (charisma) and a green candle (Venus and beauty), a mirror (preferably black, or some other skrying speculum, like a crystal ball) and a stone amulet to "charge" and "program" the changes, which is worn afterward.

Set yourself comfortably in front of the mirror with the candles on either side of you, consecrated and lit. This is the only source of illumination that should affect the Magic Circle, but the actual flames should not be reflected visible in the mirror. Gaze into this speculum and allow the Mind to clear, then Will and see the desired changes. Magically burn, impress or charge this image into the amulet with a verbal affirmation, such as: "*What I will is the face I wear.*"[46]

[On film, Sarah is seated before a piece of white paper marked with a pentagram in black marker. It is sprinkled with herbs and pink flowers and encircled with feathers. A single pink candle is lit in the center of the star. She places her open palm hand face down above the candle and says: "*This is to feel.*" She moves her hand to the left side of the candle, saying: "*This is to be*"—and then covers her face with both hands, "*Shape and form it for all to see. By the power of three time three, as I will it, so shall it be.*"][47]

[*52:30*] THE LAW OF THREEFOLD RETURN

> *Life keeps a balance on its own.*
> *Whatever you send out*
> *you get back times three.*

Wicca acknowledges energetic repercussions of personal actions in a way similar to the "*karma*" of Eastern traditions, evolving to a popularized statement about "threefold returns." Prior to this, Gardnerian Wicca emphasized "As you harm none, do what thou will," amending Crowley's own sentiment of simply "Do what thou will." [Occult shop owner, Lirio (*played by Assumpta Serna*), attempts to educate the girls on the ethics of magic and energy handling. Meanwhile, Nancy is enamored by an animate illustrations in a book, titled "*Invocation of the* Spirit"—which is really a copy of A.E. Waite's "*Book of (Black) Ceremonial Magic.*"]

[*53:30*] MAY'S EVE (BELTANE) RITE—"INVOKING THE SPIRIT"

> *EXT. BEACH - NIGHT*
> *Bonnie finishes laying a ring of stones in the sand.*
> *Nancy starts a fire in the middle.*
> *Sarah finishes lighting a circle of black candles.*
> *She looks at the snake in the jar.**

The ritual practiced on the beach contains many elements of ceremonial ma-

---

46 In "*Great Magickal Arcanum,*" this is followed by conjuring the spiritual hierarchy commanded by the entity "*Magoth,*" of which a roll-call of names—*Nacheron, Natolico, Mesaf, Masadul, Sappipas, Faturab, Ubarim, Rotor* and *Arabim*—are also summoned. The amulet is then held in the left hand and run down the face, top to bottom.

47 Author's Note: I found a modern "three-times-three banishing" spell buried in the back of Timothy Roderick's "*Dark Moon Mysteries,*" but it applies to a later scene far better than this one.

* Excerpting a draft of the screenplay. The scene was shot in Malibu, at Leo Carrillo Beach. According to rumors, when Fairuza Balk (Nancy) began speaking the incantations, the film crew lost power (from their generators).

gic (that are referenced within *The Witch's Handbook* sections), particularly the "elemental" attributes and "calls" to the "Corners" (Watchtowers). [Rochelle carries a "goldfish" in a bag; Bonnie carries a "butterfly" in a jar; Sarah carries a "bird" in a small cage; Nancy carries a larger jar containing a "snake."]

On screen, the ritual script begins with Nancy: "*Hail to the Guardians of the Watchtower of the East; The powers of Air and Invention; Hear (us).*" Then, Bonnie: "*Hail to the Guardians of the Watchtower of the South; The powers of Fire and Feeling; Hear (us).*" Rochelle: "*Hail to the Guardians of the Watchtower of the West; The Powers of Water and Intuition; Hear (us).*" Finally, Sarah: "*Hail to the Guardians of the Watchtower of the North; By the powers of Mother and Earth; Hear (us).*"

Nancy continues the incantation: "*Aid us in our magical working on this May's Eve. Serpent of old, ruler of the deep, guardian of the bitter sea—show us your glory, show us your power. We pray of thee. We invoke thee. O serpent one, hear our calls; hear our prayers. Ancient wise one, teach us thy ways. We summon and stir thee. Lend us your powers. Show us your glory. We invoke thee! We invoke thee!*"

[72:15] BINDING SPELL

> *I bind you, ___, from doing harm;*
> *Harm against other people*
> *And harm against yourself.*

A lot of nonsense is written about "white witchcraft" versus "black magic" and so forth. Magic is magic. But, needless to say, there are *Witches* that would use these abilities to cause harm.

Binding spells are treated as ethical means for defending against "malevolent magic" or "baneful intentions" These rites sidestep negative kickback because it simply "returns" or "deflects" the originally directed energy back to its sender, adding to it no ill-Will. [Sarah cuts an image of Nancy out of a group photo and proceeds to wrap a white ribbon around it as she makes her incantation.]

[86:30] THREE-TIMES-THREE

> *By the powers of three times three;*
> *Make them see, make them see.*

Using the dagger/*Athame*, inscribe an appropriate representative word or name near the bottom of a black candle. Charge it with residual negative energies that have been attached to you from the target. Tie a length of white cotton twine securely at the bottom and then proceed to wrap it around the candle, moving upwards counter-clockwise, while visualizing a deflective mirrored sphere encircling your body.

The incantation suggested by Timothy Roderick in "*Dark Moon Mysteries*" (published the same year "*The Craft*" was released) is: "*Three times three, as ye have sown; Is thine to reap, thy harvest grown. For best, for worst, for praise or chide;*

The Gods alone your fate decide." Continue wrapping the candle until the twine reaches the top, then saturate it with lamp oil. Place it in a cauldron that has its bottom lined with sand (to hold the candle in place and also for fire protection) and burn the candle until it has completely melted away. Bury any of the remainder.

[Sarah defends herself against further attacks by Rochelle and Bonnie by projecting a glamour to show them the threefold repercussions of their actions. She combines this with a binding incantation to battle Nancy later.]

FINIS

WOULD

YOU

LIKE

TO

KNOW

MORE

? ? ?

MARDUKITE
MASTER COURSE
The Key to Gates of Higher Understanding

*Now you can experience the Legendary "Master Course" from
anywhere in the Universe, exactly as given in person by Joshua Free
to the "Mardukite Academy of Systemology" in September 2020.*

800+ pages of materials collected in this volume provide Seekers with
full transcripts to all *48 Academy Lectures* of the legendary "*Mardukite
Master Course*" combined with all course outlines, supplements and
critical handouts from the original "*Instructor's Manual*"—making this
the most complete definitive single-source delivery of New Age
understanding and spiritual technology.

This book references 25 years of research, development and publishing,
including the textbooks "*Necronomicon: The Complete Anunnaki Legacy,*"
"*The Great Magickal Arcanum,*" "*The Systemology Handbook*"
and "*Merlyn's Complete Book of Druidism.*"

IN A WORLD FULL OF "TENS" BE AN
ELEVEN

THE METAPHYSICS OF STRANGER THINGS

TELEKINESIS, TELEPATHY SYSTEMOLOGY

by Joshua Free

Mardukite
Systemology
Liber-011

Experimental
exploratory
edition

Discover the metaphysical truth about the Universe—and maybe even yourself—as we explore what lies beneath the
epic saga, *Stranger Things.* You're invited to a world where fantasy, science fiction and horror unite, and games like
Dungeons and Dragons become reality.

Uncover a world of secret "mind control" projects, just like those at *Hawkins National Laboratory.* Decades of psychedelic
experiments among other developmental programs for
psychic powers, remote viewing, telekinesis (psychokinesis, PK-power) and more are revealed. Get an inside look at the
operations of a real-life underground organization pursuing the truth about rehabilitating spiritual abilities for an actual "metahuman" evolution on planet Earth.

Premiere edition available in paperback and hardcover!

Commemorating the Mardukite 15th Anniversary!
Deluxe Oversized Revised Hardcover Edition!

NECRONOMICON
THE COMPLETE ANUNNAKI BIBLE

collected works by Joshua Free

The ultimate masterpiece of Mesopotamian magic, spirituality and history, providing a complete collection—a grand symphony—of the most ancient writings on the planet.

The oldest Sumerian and Babylonian records reveal detailed accounts of cosmic history in the Universe and on Earth, the development of human civilization and descriptions of world order.

All of this information has been used, since ancient times, to maintain spiritual and physical control of humanity and its systems. It has proved to be the predecessor and foundation of all global scripture-based religious and mystical traditions thereafter.

These are the raw materials, unearthed from the underground, which have shaped humanity's beliefs, traditions and existence for thousands of years —right from the heart of the Ancient Near East: Sumer, Babylon and even Egypt...

The dark world of the occult on planet Earth revealed!

NOVEM PORTIS (DELUXE EDITION)
NECRONOMICON REVELATIONS,
NINE GATES OF THE KINGDOM OF SHADOWS
& CROSSING TO THE ABYSS
10th Anniversary—Deluxe Hardcover (*Liber-R, 9+555*)
Collected Works by Joshua Free

Commemorating completion of the "Necronomicon Shadows" cycle of
research and development by the Mardukite Chamberlains (2009–2012).

Originally intended as a research-companion to
"*Necronomicon: The Anunnaki Bible*" and the remaining 'Core',
a Mardukite anthology of this cycle of work
—known as "*Nine Gates*" or "*Novem Portis*"—
eventually developed into an underground bestseller by itself.

In addition to other bonus articles and supplements,
a complete collection of material from *Liber-9*, *Liber-R* and *Liber-555* are
together in a deluxe hardcover anthology edition for the first time ever!

New Deluxe Oversized Hardcover Edition for 2023!

Commemorating the 20th Anniversary!

THE COMPLETE ELVENOMICON
A TREASURY OF ELVEN MAGICK,
FAERIE SPELLS & DRUID LORE

(Deluxe Edition Hardcover Anthology)
collected works by Joshua Free

An underground classic for two decades—now expanded!

This tome collects the original material ("*Secret Book of Elven-Faerie,*"
"*The Elven-Faerie Grimoire,*" and "*The Enchanted Forest*") along with three
recently released never-before-published companion texts ("*A Secret
Legacy of Elves and Fairies,*" "*Elven-Faerie Spellbook,*" and "*The Book of
Ogham*")—providing six-books-in-one volume.

"*The Complete Elvenomicon*" by Joshua Free offers an entire exploration
into the Elven Way, Celtic Faerie Tradition and Danubian Druidism as
never seen before. Drawing from hundreds of sources and underground groups, the "Elven-Faerie" tradition and system of magic is
presented in its candid entirety, as applicable and alive today as it was
thousands of years ago—and critically needed for our times, and in our
current environmental conditions.

The Pathway to Self-Honesty

THE ORIGINAL UNDERGROUND INTRODUCTIONS
REVISED AND REISSUED IN HARDCOVER

SYSTEMOLOGY

The Original Thesis of Mardukite New Thuoght

by Joshua Free

(Mardukite Systemology Liber-S-1X)

The very first underground discourses released to the "New Thought" division of the Mardukite Research Organization privately over a decade ago and providing the inspiration for rapid futurist spiritual technology called "Mardukite Systemology."

THE POWER OF ZU

Applying Mardukite Zuism & Systemology to Everyday Life

by Joshua Free
Foreword by Reed Penn

(Mardukite Systemology Liber-S-1Z)

A unique introductory course on Mardukite Zuism & Systemology, including transcripts from a 3-day lecture series given by Joshua Free in December 2019 to launch the Mardukite Academy of Systemology & Founding Church of Mardukite Zuism just in time for the 2020's.

SYSTEMOLOGY

FUNDAMENTALS OF SYSTEMOLOGY

A New Thought for the 21st Century

The Official
Systemology Society
Basic Course

ALL *Six Lessons* in one
*Collector's Edition Hardcover
or Paperback Workbook*

All *six* lesson-booklets of the first official
Basic Course on Mardukite Systemology
are combined together in *one volume* as
"Fundamentals of Systemology."

Also available individually.

"Being More Than Human"

"Realities in Agreement"

"Windows To Experience"

"Ancient Systemology"

"A History of Systemology"

"Systemology Processing"

SYSTEMOLOGY

THE PATHWAY TO ASCENSION

A New Thought for the 21st Century

New Standard Systemology
Professional Course
Level 0 to 6

ALL *Sixteen Lessons* in *two*
Hardcover Volumes or
one Paperback Workbook

All *sixteen* lesson-booklets of the newest
Professional Course on Mardukite Systemology
are combined together in *two volumes* as
"The Pathway to Ascension."

Also available individually.

"Increasing Awareness"

"Thought & Emotion"

"Clear Communication"

"Handling Humanity"

"Free Your Spirit"

"Escaping Spirit-Traps"

...and many more!

∞

JOSHUA FREE

A mystic philosopher, world renowned underground occult expert and prolific writer of over 100 books on systemology, ancient history, magic and "esoteric archaeology" since 1995. He founded Mardukite Ministries (Mardukite Zuism) in 2008, is director of Mardukite Research Organization (Mardukite Academy) and its New Thought division "The Systemology Society."

PUBLISHED BY THE **JOSHUA FREE** IMPRINT REPRESENTING

The Mardukite Academy of Systemology & Founding Church of Mardukite Zuism

mardukite.com

www.ingramcontent.com/pod-product-compliance
Lightning Source LLC
Chambersburg PA
CBHW081527120626
46550CB00009B/2644